Help My Unbelief

Related titles available from Continuum

Joyce: A Guide for the Perplexed
Peter Mahon

Joyce and Company
David Pierce

Joyce's Ulysses
Sean Sheehan

The Reception of James Joyce in Europe
Edited by Geert Lernout and Wim Van Mierlo

Help My Unbelief
James Joyce and Religion

Geert Lernout

continuum

Continuum International Publishing Group
The Tower Building   80 Maiden Lane
11 York Road   Suite 704
London SE1 7NX   New York, NY 10038

www.continuumbooks.com

British Library Cataloguing-in-Publication Data
A catalogue record for this book is available from the British Library.

ISBN: 978-1-4411-3108-9 (hardback)
         978-1-4411-9474-9 (paperback)

Library of Congress Cataloging-in-Publication Data
A catalog record for this book is available from the Library of Congress.

Typeset by Newgen Imaging Systems Pvt Ltd, Chennai, India
Printed and bound in Great Britain by CPI Antony Rowe Ltd, Chippenham, Wiltshire

Contents

Acknowledgements   vi

List of Abbreviations   vii

Introduction   1

Chapter 1   Joyce and the Church According to the Critics   13

Chapter 2   The Holy Roman Apostolic Church   28

Chapter 3   Heresy, Schisma and Dissent   52

Chapter 4   Joyce's Own Crisis of Belief   94

Chapter 5   Loss of Religion in Retrospect: From *Epiphanies* to *Exiles*   111

Chapter 6   'You behold in me a horrible example of freethought'   140

Chapter 7   Free Lay Church in a Free Lay State   157

Chapter 8   After *Ulysses*   191

Conclusion   206

Notes   218

References   222

Index   231

Acknowledgements

This book has had a fairly long history. The first ideas developed as part of my work with Vincent Deane and Daniel Ferrer on the edition of the *Finnegans Wake* Notebooks at Buffalo, but only in early 2004 did I begin the writing in earnest when I took up a Mellon Fellowship to do research at the Harry Ransom Humanities Research Center of the University of Texas. I am particularly grateful for the help received from Tom Staley and his expert staff on that and many other visits to Austin. I also thank the staff at the University of Antwerp library for their valuable help. At a fairly late stage, Steven Morrison gave me a chance to consult his doctoral dissertation, which helped me a great deal to get back on track. This is also the place to thank Fritz Senn, Ursula Zeller, Ruth Frehner and of the James Joyce Stiftung in Zürich and John McCourt and Laura Pelaschiar of the James Joyce School in Trieste, Luca Crispi and Stacey Herbert of the Dublin James Joyce Centre who gave me the chance to present some of this material in an early form. The Joyce world is a very friendly place and this book has benefited greatly from real-life and digital discussions with a large number of people, both Joyceans and goyim: Fritz Senn, Luca Crispi, Stacey Herbert, Ron Ewart, Daniel Ferrer, Maria Wells, Andrew Gibson, John McCourt, Christopher Whalen, Marysa De Moor, Vincent Deane, Terence Killeen, Joe Schork, Sam Slote, Ron Ewart, Chrissie Lees, David Berman, Judith and Richard Harrington, Vincent Neyt, Scarlett Baron, Peter Shillingsburg, Ronan Crowley, Michael Groden, Wim Van Mierlo, Warwick Gould, Peter de Voogd, Ron Bush, Tom Staley, Vincent and Christine O'Neill, Martha Campbell, Peter Robinson and many others. In particular I feel privileged to have in Dirk Van Hulle a very knowledgeable and extremely generous colleague at the University of Antwerp: every day he reminds me of what a university is supposed to be like.

Joe Schork, David Pierce, John Smurthwaite and Dirk Van Hulle read early versions of the book or parts of the book and without their critical comments and generous help it would never have been published. I am also grateful for the anonymous comments from a number of readers which forced me to tighten the argument and which resulted in a better book, I hope.

List of Abbreviations

Joyce's Works

D   James Joyce, *Dubliners: Text, Criticism, and Notes*, Robert Scholes and A. Walton Litz, eds. New York: Viking, 1979.

FDV   Hayman, David, *A First-Draft Version of 'Finnegans Wake'*. Austin, TX: University of Texas Press, 1963.

FW   James Joyce, *Finnegans Wake*. London: Faber and Faber, 1964. The page number is followed by the line number.

JJ   Richard Ellmann. *James Joyce*. New York: Oxford University Press, 1982.

Letters I, II, III James Joyce, *Letters of James Joyce*. Vol. I. Stuart Gilbert, ed. New York: Viking, 1957, reissued with corrections 1966. Vols II and III. Richard Ellmann, ed. New York: Viking, 1966.

P   James Joyce, *A Portrait of the Artist as a Young Man: Text, Criticism, and Notes*. Chester Anderson, ed. New York: Viking, 1968.

SH   James Joyce, *Stephen Hero*. John J. Slocum and Herbert Cahoon, eds. New York: New Directions, 1963.

U   James Joyce, *Ulysses: The Corrected Text*. Hans Walter Gabler with Wolfhard Steppe and Claus Melchior, eds. London: The Bodley Head, 1986. The chapter number is followed by the line number.

Introduction

In the library chapter of *Ulysses* Stephen Dedalus admits that he does not believe the theory on Shakespeare that he has just been expounding at great length. John Eglinton replies that there is a Herr Bleibtreu in Berlin who has his own theory but at least this German Shakespearean has the benefit of actually believing what he preaches. This comment leads Stephen to a brief bit of interior monologue that gave me the title of this book: 'I believe, O Lord, help my unbelief. That is, help me to believe or help me to unbelieve?' (*U* 9:1078–9). In the privacy of his own mind, Stephen Dedalus simply reacts to Eglinton's comment, but his thoughts have much wider significance. The first sentence is a quotation from the bible, more specifically from the second half of Mk 9:24, part of the story of the healing of an epileptic boy. The verse runs: 'And straightway the father of the child cried out, and said with tears, Lord, I believe; help thou mine unbelief.'[1] The phrase is important for all kinds of reasons; first it demonstrates what Jesus has said in the preceding verse: 'Jesus said unto him, If thou canst believe, all things are possible to him that believeth,' a truth that is then demonstrated in this particular healing. Earlier the disciples had failed to heal the boy and when they asked their master for the reason of their failure to cure him, Jesus replied: 'This kind can come forth by nothing, but by prayer and fasting.'

But there is a completely different and much less pious message too. The disciples' inability to heal the boy reminds the bible reader of their master's failure to perform miracles in his hometown just three chapters earlier in the same gospel. As only bible specialists and militant unbelievers know, this is one of the places where two evangelists clearly contradict each other and it is no coincidence that it involves the issue of unbelief. In Mk 6.1–3, Jesus returns to Nazareth where he preaches at the synagogue, but the local people reject him, precisely because they know him, his brothers and his sisters:

4. But Jesus, said unto them, A prophet is not without honour, but in his own country, and among his own kin, and in his own house. 5. And he could there do no mighty work, save that he laid his hands upon a few sick folk, and healed them. 6. And he marvelled because of their unbelief.

Matthew, whose account is based on that of Mark, has a significantly different version of the same event at the end of his chapter 13:

> But Jesus said unto them, A prophet is not without honour, save in his own country, and in his own house. 58. And he did not many mighty works there because of their unbelief.

By the time Matthew wrote his version of the events of the life of the Messiah, it seems to have become problematic that the Son of God had been unable to do 'mighty work.' In the revised version, Jesus at least does 'not many mighty works.' Only now the reason for this renewed effort of miracle doing is given: it is the unbelief of the inhabitants of Nazareth; Mark's Jesus had simply marvelled at the unbelief in his native town. Equally troubling to Matthew seems to have been the suggestion that Jesus had brothers and sisters, because they too have disappeared, even in the direct quote of what bible scholars call the *ipsissima verba*, Jesus' very own words.

Apart from the fact that both James Joyce and his autobiographical hero saw themselves as prophets without honour in their native land, in this brief passage (to which we shall return later in the book, in Chapter 7) Stephen is clearly making fun of the bible passage and of religious belief in general. How can you ask the deity to help your unbelief? Does that mean that God should help you get rid of your unbelief, as is clearly meant by Mark? But in that case, why should you pray to a deity to take away doubts about that deity's very existence? Or can we mischievously read this bible verse as a plea addressed to the deity to help and strengthen our unbelief, another paradox?

Religious belief and unbelief, and the tensions between them, are the central concerns of this book and in religion it is always best to put your cards on the table from the start. First of all I believe, and I intend to demonstrate in this book, that James Joyce was an unbeliever from the start of his life as a writer, that he never returned to the faith of his fathers and that his work can only be read properly if that important fact is taken into account.

Secondly, I am an unbeliever myself: like so many young catholics of my generation I lost whatever faith I had as a boy as soon as I began to think for myself and I have remained an atheist, despite occasional moments of doubt when it is tempting to revert childishly to a belief in the existence of an evil deity who can then be blamed for everything that goes wrong in our lives (in the same library chapter Joyce calls this malignant deity by its Italian name: *dio boia*, the hangman god).

Thirdly, and most importantly, I strongly believe that my own lack of religious feelings has had little or no impact on the reading of the works of James Joyce that is presented in this book. As will be explained more thoroughly later, the religious or anti-religious beliefs of mine or of any other reader of Joyce should by no means affect the claims made in this book: these claims are historical (and not theological or philosophical). *Help My Unbelief* is a book about the religious beliefs of a historical figure, James Joyce, who was born in Dublin in 1882 and who died in Zürich in 1941. What is investigated in this book is Joyce's convictions about religion and the effect that his unbelief had on the writings that made him famous. My own beliefs or lack of belief do not affect Joyce's religious position and I hope that the same is true for my reader's beliefs. I honestly believe that nothing in this book would need to be changed, not if I suddenly accepted Christ in my heart, not if I became a follower of Monseigneur Lefebvre, nor – the lord help me – of Benedict XVI.

For close to a century, both Joyce's works and his person have fascinated and inspired readers of different cultures and from different backgrounds. His work is remarkably provincial and firmly rooted in the catholic middle-class Dublin culture of the turn of the previous century, but paradoxically it appealed first and foremost to readers outside of his native city. It is only during the last three decades that Ireland has adopted its most famous writer-in-exile: it took over half a century for Joyce to become a prophet in his own country. Despite their apparent parochialism (with the exception of a few poems and the otherwise exceptional *Giacomo Joyce*, all of his works have a Dublin setting), Joyce's novels manage to appeal to readers all over the Western world and beyond. A couple of years ago the young writer Pascal Khoo Thwe described how after growing up as a member of an ethnic minority in a small village in Burma, he became fascinated by *A Portrait of the Artist as a Young Man*, which led to a meeting with an Oxford don, his involvement in civil rights action, and ultimately his escape and exile.

There is another implication of the strange cultural universalism of Joyce's work, which has everything to do with religion. It cannot be an accident that it was *A Portrait of the Artist as a Young Man* that had such an appeal for the young Pascal Khoo Thwe, who had been educated by Italian priests and who had briefly planned to attend a seminary. Joyce's first novel seems to have a great attraction for young catholics who struggle or have struggled with the same questions of sex and guilt that form the core of that novel.[2] Despite the fact naturally, that the appeal of Joyce's work goes beyond catholicism, it is the religious dimension of his work that I would like to focus on in this book. We all know that religion and the loss of religion is a major theme in *A Portrait of the Artist as a Young Man* and we find the same or similar concerns in *Dubliners* and in *Stephen Hero* and, in a different vein, in *Ulysses* and *Finnegans Wake*. While Joyce's own attitudes to the faith of his family and his nation were probably just as negative as those of the protagonist of his autobiographical novels, some catholic critics have tried to rescue the writer for the faith. This is usually attempted by showing how until the end of his life Joyce continued to be fascinated by the detail of catholic ritual and doctrine and by quoting the more ambiguous pronouncements that Joyce himself made about his attitude to the church. This has enabled some scholars to claim that the writer's work should be read in a catholic context and that he himself may never have left the Church of Rome.

As one of the academic organisers of the 2002 International James Joyce Symposium, I was struck by the number of paper proposals we received that offered to discuss Joyce's relationship to religion. Not only the traditional role of Joyce's catholic education and background seemed to fascinate, but also the role of judaism, protestantism and even buddhism and islam. Part of this turn to theology may have had something to do with the search for certainty in the world after September 11 (this being a literature conference, there were also papers on 'Joyce and the Twin Towers'), but in a way these scholars were rediscovering a theme that has haunted Joyce criticism since its very beginning.

Of course Joyce's early fiction was critical of the church, with *Dubliners* meticulously documenting the stunted lives under the iron fist of the church of the catholic inhabitants of the 'seventh city of Christendom,' and *A Portrait of the Artist as a Young Man* equally scrupulously charting the way to apostasy of the autobiographical hero. The catholic reactions against this kind of writing and the more extreme rejection of his even more extreme *Ulysses*, clearly marked the field of engagement. Contemporary reactions to Joyce's work on the one hand are marked either by aesthetic and cosmopolitan celebration, or by a reactionary rejection. With hindsight we can see that these reactions were part of the writer's master plan: Joyce eagerly excerpted the most salient passages in the most dismissive reviews and used them for publicity (and later even incorporated some of them in *Finnegans Wake* in his portrait of the autobiographical Shem the Penman). This is the view of Joyce's negative relationship with the catholic church that was established in the 1920s and for which the author himself seems to have been responsible. It is also the official academic reading of Joyce's relationship with religion, first developed independently by J. Mitchell Morse in the late 1950s and then consecrated in Richard Ellmann's biography.[3]

According to Ellmann, Joyce had to conquer his catholicism in order to become a writer; if he did retain something of his religious background, it was only in the form of an essentially non-religious respect for the Jesuits who had given him an excellent education:

> If Joyce retained anything from his education; it was a conviction of the skill of his Jesuit masters, the more remarkable because he rejected their teaching. 'I don't think you will easily find anyone to equal them,' he said long afterwards to the composer Philipp Jarnach, and he corrected his friend Frank Budgen's book on him by remarking, 'You allude to me as a Catholic. Now for the sake of precision and to get the correct contour on me, you ought to allude to me as a Jesuit.' (*JJ* 27)

Ellmann's biography describes the religious zeal of the young boy in two schools run by the Jesuits, Clongowes and Belvedere College, and he focuses on the boy's choice of Aloysius as his saint's name, his duties as altar boy and as a member and later prefect of the Sodality of the Blessed Virgin Mary. This religious zeal was interrupted at age 14 by his first sexual experiences, which resulted in a loss of religion and an indulgence in sin, followed by a brief period of remorse ('some months') after a retreat and then the slower and less dramatic process that led to his final loss of faith. Although ten pages later Ellmann writes that Joyce's public confession of unbelief came only later, it is clear that for the biographer this is the moment that, unlike his brother, James Joyce decided for a tactic that Ellmann calls 'transmutation' and that differs from Stanislaus's more open atheist denial that is such a prominent theme in the latter's Dublin diary. James Joyce 'preferred disdain to combat' and Ellmann continues in appropriately christological language:

> He was no longer a Christian himself; but he converted the temple to new uses instead of trying to knock it down, regarding it as a superior kind of human folly and one which, interpreted by a secular artist, contained obscured bits of truth. (*JJ* 66)

This sentence represents Ellmann's ultimate judgement on Joyce's religion: in the index to the biography this is marked as the final mention under the heading of the writer's 'religious attitudes.' Joyce lost his youthful faith as a result of his sexual appetites, and in contrast to his brother, he did not simply deny his faith but instead transformed its structures into the basis of his artistic creed. The process was not a sudden conversion, but rather a gradual realization after the retreat's brief regression into faith, which is described by Ellmann in these terms:

> What had seemed piety now seemed only the last spasm of religious terror. This point of view, which he gives Stephen in *A Portrait*, was growing in his own mind, as later letters and remarks confirm. It was also true, as he declared flatly some time afterwards to a friend, that sexual continence was impossible for him. He felt he must choose between continual guilt and some heretical exoneration of the senses. By conviction Joyce could not abase himself before Catholic doctrine; by temperament he could not abase himself before other men. (*JJ* 49–50)

As is especially clear in this characteristically elegant passage, Ellmann's description of Joyce's religious attitude is typical of his overall portrait of the artist as a young man: it is on the one hand based on the picture in Joyce's autobiographical novel and on the other on information provided by Stanislaus, thus relying heavily on the younger brother's later view of his famous sibling.

In his biography of the young Joyce, Peter Costello has painted a picture with a slightly different chronology. Joyce here is still a catholic when he enters university and his first sin with a prostitute happens much later, when he is seventeen. But possibly because he was unable to locate the precise time of Joyce's final apostasy, Costello neglects to discuss it at all and in this version Joyce

begins his study at UCD as a catholic and then without a radical break in his first
year he begins to behave like a freethinker.

In the current revisionist climate one might be tempted to dismiss Ellmann's
view of the post-catholic writer as this particular biographer's quirk, but it is
simply impossible to ignore the overwhelming evidence for this interpretation.
That for most of his life as a writer Joyce was not a friend of the catholic church
is obvious if we read his letters and if we look at what he told the one person
who shared most of that life with him about his attitude towards religion. This
evidence begins with the letter to Nora Barnacle that dates from the early weeks
of their acquaintance and in which the young writer pompously declares to his
catholic girl friend:

> Six years ago I left the Catholic Church, hating it most fervently. I found it
> impossible for me to remain in it on account of the impulses of my nature.
> I made secret war upon it when I was a student and declined to accept the
> positions it offered me. By doing this I made myself a beggar but I retained
> my pride. Now I make open war upon it by what I write and say and do.
> (*Letters II* 48)

The openness about his antagonistic relationship with the church seems to
have lasted until Joyce's death, when Nora, approached by a catholic priest,
refused a religious service for her husband with the words: 'I couldn't do that
to him' (*JJ* 742).

Yet in the last 50 years this Ellmannian consensus about Joyce's religion has
not gone unchallenged. In fact we already find examples of this attitude during
Joyce's lifetime and in circumstances that suggest at least Joyce's knowledge and
possibly even connivance. In one of the articles that the writer himself commis-
sioned for a 1929 volume of studies on his new book, 1 of the 12 'apostles' studied what he called 'the Catholic element' in 'Work in Progress.' In the article
Thomas MacGreevy, a Dublin catholic, librarian and friend of Samuel Beckett,
claimed that Mr Joyce's new work is, like *Ulysses*, marked by a 'deep-rooted
Catholicism,' which has to be distinguished from the 'pastiche Catholicism' of
some of the book's critics in England. Since he goes on to mention the cardinals Manning and Newman as 'over enthusiastic converts,' the target seems to
be the 'temporary Romanizers' in English Catholicism who cannot fail to be
shocked by 'the more profound "regular" Catholicism of Ireland' (MacGreevy
1929: 121).

In an interpretation of *Ulysses* with a great future in religiously inspired interpretations of the novel, MacGreevy sees the book simply as Joyce's *Inferno*
'of modern subjectivity,' which cannot fail to address the ugly side of life. But
MacGreevy is not quite honest in his reading of Joyce: he points out, against the
'inquisitorially minded' that in 'Circe' the Voice of all the Blessed call out 'Alleluia,
for the Lord God Omnipotent reigneth' after Stephen has 'put out the light
on the scene that revolted him.' (MacGreevy 1929: 123). Rather disingenuously

MacGreevy fails to mention either the full irony in this call, or the real target of Stephen's anger. The rest of the essay does not tell us much about Joyce or catholicism, but in this vague way, MacGreevy's article is the first in a long series of claims made for a peculiarly Irish catholicism, closer to the medieval religion of Dante and Aquinas than to contemporary Roman or English forms of christianity.

It is clear that since that moment, Joyce's catholicism has indeed been discussed by catholic critics, some of them priests and Jesuits. One fairly typical example is Michael Paul Gallagher, an Irish Jesuit and popular catholic author, a former teacher of literature at University College Dublin who is currently dean of theology at the Gregorian University in Rome. In 1982, on the occasion of Joyce's centenary, he published a small article on Joyce's atheism in *Doctrine and Life*, the journal of the Irish Dominicans. There is a double irony here: not only is a Jesuit invited to write on 'the Society's famous past-pupil' in a Dominican magazine, but one of the most famous of the catholic critics, Shane Leslie, wrote his most critical review of *Ulysses* under the pseudonym *Domini Canis*, dog of the Lord.

The author opens his essay with the statement that in Joyce's centenary year there is 'a new level of Irish acceptance' of Joyce's work and this is a finding I can confirm from my own experience. When I left the city in 1979 after finishing my Master's degree at University College, Dublin, the only visible presence of Joyce in the city was the museum in the Martello tower in Sandycove and a little bronze plaque on the birth house in Rathgar, which made it clear that this small token of appreciation had been paid for entirely by Americans. This was still the old Ireland that was in turmoil because the Dail was considering a bill that would lift the ban on contraceptives. Dublin after 1982 has become a completely different city: if anything, the city now is chock-full of Joyce mementoes. Michael Gallagher wonders about this change and he remembers Bloomsday 1964 when he asked an Oxford librarian in the Bodleian for a copy of *Ulysses*, to be told that this book could be borrowed only with special permission from the curator of forbidden books. 'I remember thinking,' he concludes, 'that Joyce would be tickled by the thought of an Irish Jesuit caught in such a trap of Oxonian prudery' (555).

Gallagher then addresses the issue of Joyce's relationship with his teachers and he begins by observing that while the Dublin writer in his letters called Jesuits 'black lice,' his treatment of the Jesuits in his work was much more nuanced. This is part of a more general phenomenon: it is possible to see a clear difference between the biographical reality and Joyce's portrayal of that reality in his fiction. As central in Joyce's psychology, Gallagher sees the 'cold mood of bitterness' from which Joyce suffered and which in the fiction is relieved only 'at rare moments' by its opposite: the final pages of *Dubliners* are offered as such an instance, as is the final 'yes' at the end of *Ulysses*. A similar moment can also be found, Gallagher writes, at the end of *A Portrait of the Artist as a Young Man* and in this case the reference is 'to the Jesuits of all people!' The conversation of Stephen Dedalus with the Jesuit dean of studies ends with an 'influx of understanding' for 'this faithful serving-man of the knightly Loyola.' According to the critic, and he admits that he is echoing Father Noon S.J. here, it is 'against the recognition of his "easily embittered heart" and his occasional emergence into freedom from it that Joyce's rejection of faith can be more deeply understood' (557).

Joyce's atheism, Gallagher continues, was 'more of the anti-church variety than denial of God's existence' and this means that his negative reaction towards religion was 'mostly a matter of negative reaction to his experience of church-forms of faith.' As a result of some experience (probably not unrelated to his 'easily embittered heart') he fell out with the official mediation of God and then he found himself in an 'eclipse of God' situation, to use Martin Buber's term.

The origins of such an experience of loss can be described in sociological or psychological terms. The latter seems to be relevant in a statement in the same letter to Nora that I quoted earlier: Joyce claims that he left the catholic church because he found it 'impossible for me to remain in it on account of the impulses of my nature.' But the decision clearly has equally a sociological or political background as well: in 1905 Joyce described himself as a socialist and the open war with the church that he claims he had been waging since his graduation, should also be seen in this particular context. For most young intellectuals after the turn of the century, the church was an objective ally of the oppressive forces in Irish, British and European politics. To continue in Gallagher's terminology, the first period of *alienation* was followed by one of *anger*, and in its turn it was replaced, two years later, by the writer's disillusion with socialism and with a new period of 'detached and lasting *apathy* over both religion and nationalism' (558). These 'three A's,' alienation, anger and apathy, provide a structure that is not just typical of Joyce's attitudes, but that according to Gallagher constitutes 'a quite classic progression' of the withdrawal from religion.

The three phases neatly divide Joyce's early work, but in the end they do not seem to be all that helpful: with the exception of 'The Dead,' all the stories in *Dubliners* were written during the second phase, and thus all of Joyce's work, with the exception of the early poetry, miscellaneous prose and *Stephen Hero*, belongs to the final 'apathy' phase, in which Father Gallagher thinks he can observe a progressive softening towards the church and the Jesuits. He quotes a letter from the end of Joyce's life, in 1939, in which the Irish author writes to C.P. Curran about the death of their old dean of studies and in which Gallagher detects 'a note of affection' which leads him to the conclusion that in a way 'Joyce the man' was catching up with 'Joyce the creator' (559). In the final paragraph of the essay Father Gallagher writes that in Joyce there are clear signs of what T.S. Eliot called a 'religious sensibility,' which is all that is left after belief itself, has gone. Although Gallagher admits that in Joyce we do not have an 'instance of frustrated religiousness' like the one we find in Yeats, the years of silence on the topic after 1907 leave room, he feels, for supposing that in Joyce's case there was a sensibility that is related to the 'larger and deeper issues of religious feeling, the hungers beyond apathy, and most of all the struggle – indeed the fundamental option – between bitterness and compassion' (560). The essay ends with this challenging *argumentum ex silentio*. It will be the brief of this book to argue against the implicit and explicit arguments in Gallagher's article, although it might be appropriate to point out already that Gallagher's line of reasoning is impossible to contradict, since it implicitly does not seem to have room for a position outside of christianity.

What we should first realize is that the passing of time, even of a just a single century, can obscure the historical reality in which a writer lived. This is a process of transformation that we can observe to have done most of its work by the time Joyce was a student. English romanticism as a radical movement had been domesticated in the course of the nineteenth century, first because over the years some of the poets distanced themselves from their radical youth, second because the times themselves changed and, most importantly, because the canonization process of an author or a movement often creates the impression that these writers or movements were in some deep sense representative of their age. In his study of romantic atheism Martin Priestman observes that the later nineteenth century was careful to actively forget the radical thinking of writers such as Wordsworth, Shelley, Byron and Keats, not only by accepting the older authors' self-censorship of their youthful radicalism, but also by cataloguing these views as no more than 'mildly idiosyncractic' forms of Christianity (1999: 2). What we need to do in order to put Joyce back into his own historical context is what Priestman attempted to do in his study of the romantic poets: 'What makes many excellent studies of Romantic literature "suppressive" on the religious front is the lack of a sense of shock, that these people said these things at this time. It is partly to restore that sense of shock that this book foregrounds the issue of "atheism" as central to the age; though to restore the sense of context, it positions it in relation to as many as possible of the softer variants of unorthodoxy which are also essential to fill out the picture' (1999: 2–3).

My study of James Joyce's attitudes to religion will be contextual and historical, so we must first define exactly what we mean by the word 'catholic' and then explore the religious ideas of James Joyce (1882–1941) within the religious context, particularly that of catholicism, as it existed in his own time. There is a crucial difference here with some of the existing criticism of Joyce's work in which it is sometimes difficult to know whether we are discussing the critic's views on religion or those of James Joyce.

First we must distinguish between Roman catholicism as it exists today and the catholicism that Joyce knew. We will see in Chapter 2 of this book why such a distinction is necessary, but in this particular case there is more. What post-Vatican Council II catholics tend to forget is that before 1963 their church forcefully rejected the very idea of doctrinal development and thus, in a way, of historical knowledge itself and this despite the fact that in the discussion with protestants the Church of Rome had always insisted on tradition and thus on history, an irony that Joyce does not fail to explore in the *Dubliners* story 'Grace.'

Liberal catholics today are usually aware that in 1963 church policies did change, but they do not always understand the magnitude of the change, and neither do they realize how much today's church differs from the church that Joyce knew in the first half of the twentieth century. The attitudes of this new church are strictly speaking not relevant to my study: Gallagher may well be correct in saying that the contemporary Church of Rome would be willing and able to accept Joyce's work. But this is an issue that is not only outside the scope of this book, it is a question that can and should be answered by the church and its representatives, and not by this particular Joyce critic.

This is not to say that such a posthumous reconversion (or de apostasy) could be no more than the baptism for the dead practised by the Church of Jesus Christ of Latter-day Saints or in other words, it would tell us more about the church willing to do this than about the poor soul who is the victim of such practices. In any case theological discussions under the past two popes have taught us that the Church of Rome is certain or united about very little and I am sure that accepting the likes of James Augustine Joyce back into its fold would be an issue that could divide a parish, let alone a diocese or an entire church. Maybe we should allow the church time to figure out first in which direction it wants to go, now that the roads opened by Vatican Council II are being closed again. In the last half century the catholic church has become, like so many mainstream protestant churches, much more diversified in terms of doctrine and ritual practice than it has ever been before: it is not even clear if we can still speak of a single Church of Rome.

We will begin this book with a survey of the earlier attempts to define Joyce's relationship with religion in general and with catholicism in particular in the period after the war. In this first chapter we will see that in the last few years there has been a revival of the view of Joyce as a fundamentally catholic writer. On the one hand there are the political Joyce critics who want to see Joyce's work as part of the postcolonial and anti-imperialist struggle that in the Irish context is almost by definition catholic, and on the other hand the heirs of post-structuralism who read Joyce's works in terms of a neo-orthodox catholic philosophy. Still other critics manage to find, without the benefit of postcolonial or post-structuralist theory, different ways of reconciling Joyce and his work with catholicism or with other forms of religion. My claim in this book will not be that catholics or religious people in general cannot or should not read Joyce. Instead I will argue that these and other attempts to recuperate Joyce for the faith of his fathers' fail to do justice to the historical circumstances of Joyce's loss of faith and the important role of his profoundly anti-religious attitudes in an understanding of his literary works.

In order to place Joyce's works in their exact historical context, in Chapter 2 we will describe in detail the particular state of the church that Joyce felt he had to leave and in Chapter 3 we will look closely at the alternatives to the catholic faith that were available to a Dublin unbeliever at the turn of the century. In Chapter 4 we will carefully study all the available evidence about Joyce's personal relation with religion, in order to come to the conclusion that from the beginning and throughout his writing career he saw himself as outside the fold. It is only at this point, when we have defined the historical context and Joyce's own place in it, that will we move on to a chronological study of the religious theme in Joyce's work. The reader should not expect exhaustive interpretations of these individual works and we do not plan to offer surveys of the enormous secondary literature that has accumulated about Joyce's work. What can be found here are discussions of the relevance of religion in the early fiction (Chapter 5), *Ulysses* (Chapters 6 and 7) and *Finnegans Wake* (Chapter 8). In the final chapter we will then return to the basic question of James Joyce's attitude to religion in general and to catholicism in particular.

Terminology

But first we must deal with a touchy point of terminology. In English, most words that have to do with religion are written with capital letters (Jews, Islam, Koran, Bible, Catholics, Christian churches), presumably out of respect for the deity and for the adherents of the respective religions. In fact my MS Word spell checker insists on correcting me every time I commit this particular sin. Those who do not have a religion such as atheists or followers of more exotic religions, like pagans and wiccans, seem to be exempted from this rule: their collective names are written with lower case initials. For reasons of his own, Joyce wrote all of the words referring to the adherents of different religions with a lower case letter, a decision he could only act on because for his later books he was able to define his own house style. A few years ago this habit earned him the charge of anti-semitism from an overeager Joycean (a word, incidentally, that like 'Jesuit' we do write with a capital), who had not noticed the general rule to which Joyce's spelling conformed. In English and in most other European languages the word denoting the deity, except the word deity itself, is capitalized, except when the word is used in the plural, as if polytheistic religions do not deserve similar levels of respect. In this book I have adopted Joyce's spelling conventions, although, needless to say, in quotations I will use the original author's spelling.

And finally, before we move on, we must exclude some references to the deity from the discussion. Like his brother Stanislaus and other non-religious Irishmen,[4] Joyce's distance from the church and from God did not prevent him from referring to the godhead in everyday speech. Like many other atheists he continued to use expressions like 'God knows,' 'God forbid' and 'thank God.'

In letters to Frank Budgen in 1921, for example, he frequently looks forward to the time when, 'thank God,' he will finally finish *Ulysses*, and in the 1920s and 1930s he used similar expressions in letters to Harriet Weaver, who was, incidentally, an unbeliever too. As should be obvious, these references to the divinity have nothing to do with religion in the way it will be discussed in this book.

Chapter 1

Joyce and the Church According to the Critics

In the early history of Joyce's criticism, the study of the author's religious attitudes was often marred by sweeping generalizations and unnecessary misunderstandings. In 1967 Virginia Moseley wrote of Joyce's 'extensive theological training' (1967: v), whereas only two years later William Noon claimed that Joyce 'had received no formal training in philosophy, scholastic, Catholic, or any other at all' (1969: 12). Moseley also claimed that because 'the Jesuits focused on the Christian religion, the Bible was probably the one literary work that Joyce knew best by the time he received his university degree' (1967: ix), which shows a rather limited understanding of the role of the bible in catholicism: later in life Joyce told his father that catholics should not read the bible at all.

Stanley Sultan's influential *The Argument of 'Ulysses'* represents a different misunderstanding: all through his general reading of *Ulysses* book he stresses the links between Bloom and Jesus and he sees Stephen's day as a deliverance, with the young poet going from mock-mass to communion with Bloom, 'from near breakdown to salvation' (1964: 393). In his conclusion Sultan sees in the novel's coincidences and dreams examples of divine intervention: 'God announces, almost simultaneously, to each character the circumstances that shall attend his rescue and those circumstances promptly, almost simultaneously, occur' (455). Two pages later Sultan explicitly associates Joyce with what Jacques Maritain called a 'theocentric humanism' which is directly opposed to an age that is secular and that has no room for God at all. Sultan deftly avoids the issue of Joyce's own lack of religious beliefs and he attributes the religious relevance to the novel, an option that is available, as is Maritain's original distinction, only to those people who really do believe there is a God.

As we see from the very beginning of the reception of his work, Joyce has been read both by critics who are religious or not religious. Although I do not know if it has ever been tested, I will assume that more than a few Joyceans are either atheist or agnostic and that most of them consider their own religious convictions (or lack thereof) to be irrelevant to the way they read literature or write literary criticism. But there have always been catholic Joyceans too: in fact the first Belgian to defend a doctorate on Joyce's works was father Jean Schoonbroodt, who is today one of only the two Joyceans who has attended all the Symposiums of the International James Joyce Foundation. Inevitably, perhaps, some of these catholic Joyceans were Jesuits and the most important scholars that are relevant for this study were certainly William T. Noon and Robert Boyle.

Given the openly anti-catholic nature of his work, the catholic interest in Joyce is surprising, especially in the period before Vatican Council II. Under the old catholic way of thinking, which tended to hold on to the political principles from before the French revolution, most of the early catholic critics who did not completely reject Joyce had to argue with their peers that deep down the Irish writer was not really an atheist or a pornographer. A fairly typical example is Curt Hohoff's 1951 essay on Joyce in *Wort und Wahrheit*, an Austrian catholic monthly with an explicitly modernist agenda. Like many of the earliest catholic critics of Joyce's work, Hohoff identifies the writer with Stephen, and he calls his essay 'James Joyce and loneliness.' Not without the occasional mistake (inevitable, perhaps, in the pre-Ellmann era), Hohoff provides his readers with basic information about Joyce's work, but he also warns them that the theme of *Portrait* is the transformation of someone who is cradled by the belief in authority, into somebody who only recognizes his own authority and thus falls into a form of 'human, artistic and civil loneliness' (1951: 507). Ironically, this corresponds exactly to Stephen's view of his mission at the end of *A Portrait*, but what Joyce describes as a call to arms, becomes a curse in Hohoff's version. In 1961, in the journal of the ecumenical Council of the Churches of Christ in the United States, another critic, Edward J. Ahearn makes a similar point in reading Joyce in the same way that Georg Lukács had tried to salvage the work of a bourgeois writer like Thomas Mann for communism: as an accurate representation of a deeper truth that the writer himself need not have been aware of. About *Ulysses* Ahearn writes:

> The novel has a definite religious dimension – even a religious purpose – in displaying the unhappiness of our world as a product of our loss of religion. Bloom's voyage fails, because to encounter woman and reality fruitfully, man must be equipped with an ennobled conception of human nature. Further, the novel suggests in its emphasis on Mary, man must return to the concepts of the supernatural and of grace if he is to penetrate reality meaningfully and be renewed by his voyage. (1961: 144)

To today's readers this may seem like a perverse misinterpretation of *Ulysses*, but we should not forget that before Vatican Council II catholics in many ways did live in a different world in which the certainties of the faith were simply unassailable and other faiths or beliefs were not just wrong but simply impossible.

Ahearn was an exception (perhaps it is significant that he went on to write about literature and Karl Marx) and in this period most catholic critics seem to have preferred not to write on Joyce at all. Those few catholic Joyceans whose work is still read today, such as Marshall McLuhan and Hugh Kenner, were liberal exceptions and it may not be entirely coincidental that both were converts. Although they could be considered as politically conservative, their own co-religionists correctly suspected them of subscribing to a modernist aesthetics that was not acceptable to orthodox catholics. Jeffrey Segall (1993) has shown how Kenner's early view of Joyce was shaped by T.S. Eliot's interpretation of *Ulysses* as a modern materialist hell. Kenner, famously against Ellmann, rejected sentimental readings of the novel that sympathize with Stephen, Bloom or Molly and he warned against the belief that the views they express are necessarily those of their creator. Segall sums up: 'What links Eliot's essays and Kenner's first book on Joyce to Catholic exegeses is the assumption that beneath the impressive technical apparatus of Joyce's fiction lies a deep-seated and profoundly religious sensibility' (156). This view was shared by other catholic readers of Joyce, such as Kevin Sullivan, who claimed that if Joyce ever really left the church, it was only for a brief period. Especially his later work can only be understood from within a catholic context:

> So it is that in *Ulysses*, and even in *Finnegans Wake*, the shadow-structure is the Catholic Mass in which the priest, performing the specific sacrifice for which he was ordained, celebrates the communion of God and man. But the artist secularizes this function of the priest, and his sacrament is a celebration of the communion of humanity. (quoted in Segall 1993: 162)

Ironically, Sullivan finds communion in exactly the same place where Hohoff and other traditional catholic critics had only seen pride and loneliness.

Sullivan, Father Noon and Father Boyle adopted the idea that even if Joyce was not a catholic, then at least his Jesuit training had given his mind a catholic structure, whatever that may be. The extent of the catholic education of the Irish writer was not always clear and we have seen that Virginia Moseley and William Noon stand at completely opposite ends on the issue of the depth of Joyce's knowledge of catholic theology.

In his book on Joyce and Aquinas, Father Noon had shown the relevance of the medieval philosopher for Joyce's thinking and thus for a study of his work, but as Thomas Staley (1991) has pointed out in a thorough essay on his criticism, Noon is much better at interpreting the theological relevance of some of the religious references in the book, than in offering new insights about Joyce's work as a whole. In *Ulysses* Noon finds 'a pathological protest against the human condition itself' that is 'not all Aquinian or even Christian. One could hardly construct a fair picture of the Thomist synthesis or of the Irish Christian fact if he had nothing else to work with but the Joycean catharsis' (quoted in Staley 1991: 162). In a 1969 essay Noon attempted to define Joyce's religious position with more precision. He begins by pointing out, correctly as we will confirm in the next chapter, that the church Joyce was rebelling against bears very little resemblance to the church after Vatican Council II. Noon adds that as an artistic attitude, Joyce's way of thinking is much too complex to be described in

terms of a single religious position. Noon concludes: 'Has the description of
Joyce's various religious positions that I have ventured, tentatively, to offer here
amounted to my saying that I believe Joyce was a humanist? Possibly, but, then,
not a humanist pure and simple' (1969: 18). In fact Joyce turns out to be a
peculiarly catholic kind of humanist: 'In order to be perfectly a human being,
or perfectly a humanist, Joyce is saying, so anyway to me, that every man and
every nation need some supernatural, otherworldly, transcendent image, an
image not of nature but of grace' (18–19). Rather mischievously, Noon answers
the question whether *Ulysses* rests on a 'religious posture' by referring to Loyola's
comment that we should find God in all things (19) and he asks if the great
variety of opinions among Joyceans which, again mischievously, he calls their
'catholicism,' may be related to Joyce's Catholicism, 'with a large C, howsoever
we may define it' (20). Robert Boyle went one step further by reading Joyce's
decision to become a priest of the imagination as a mystical journey towards
what the poet Gerald Manley Hopkins had discovered before him: religious
(or Jesuit) love. Noon's book *James Joyce's Pauline Vision* is correctly subtitled
'A Catholic Exposition' because that is exactly what it is. The book is a contribution to theology, not to literary criticism.

   In the theoretical 1970s and 1980s, Joyce's religious views retreated in the
background of Joyce criticism; older scholars such as Hugh Kenner adopted a
more ambiguous attitude in which deconstruction and the instability of final
meanings replaced the earlier moralist certainties. As I have tried to show in
The French Joyce, it was paradoxically within the heart of French post-structuralist
thinking that a new catholic orthodoxy was first spelled out.

   In 1977 Philippe Sollers, one of the earliest and most radical of the French
architects of the political post-structuralist interpretation of Joyce (he claimed
at the 1975 Joyce Symposium that *Finnegans Wake* was 'une révolution'), was also
the first to formulate a politically conservative return to religion, and more specifically, a return to the catholic form of christianity, as a basis for all serious
critical thought. At the time Sollers only managed to shock French left-wing
critics and his influence on Joyce criticism outside of France is close to negligi-
ble, but a number of Julia Kristeva's works in this vein were translated into
English and had some impact on other critics. The only more substantial influence outside of France of this brief outbreak of neo-catholicism was a thesis by
one of Kristeva's students, Beryl Schlossman, who opens her book with the
statement that the sacred 'is at the heart of Joyce's writing experience' and that
for the writer the 'Passion of the Word' is 'fully Catholic only when it is outside
the boundaries of the Church' (1985: ix).

   Joyce's Catholic Comedy of Language does not do much more than compare
the evolution of Joyce's work to the Celtic illumination practices displayed in
the *Book of Kells* and in general it can be claimed that Schlossman merely gives
a catholic or mystic slant to the language of post-structuralism, much in the way
that Sollers and Kristeva had been doing in the late seventies and early eighties.
Not surprisingly Joyce's work is shown to be leading to the Paschal and the

Pentecostal comedy in which language reveals itself in the very process of its deconstruction. Schlossman's book stays very close to what was, at the time, a new orthodoxy in France, but as far as I can tell, the book failed to have much direct impact on Joyce criticism in the rest of the world.

Seemingly independent of this French development, a few British, Irish and North-American writers attempted to formulate a new approach to the issue of Joyce and religion. One of them is the Irish scholar Eamonn Hughes, who offered one of the more ambitious recent attempts to claim Joyce for catholicism in an essay in a 1992 book edited by Robert Welch under the title *Irish Writers and Religion*. Hughes takes two statements by Stephen Dedalus as his starting point: on the one hand Stephen's famous pronouncement at the end of *A Portrait of the Artist as a Young Man* that he will not serve that in which he no longer believes 'whether it call itself my home, my fatherland or my church' (*P* 146–7) and on the other hand the same character's claim to Haines in the opening chapter of *Ulysses* that he is 'a servant of two masters, [. . .] an English and an Italian . . . and a third [. . .] who wants me for odd jobs' (*U* 1:638–41). Ignoring the differences between the two triads, Hughes concentrates on the one thing they have in common, namely Stephen's Italian master, 'the holy Roman catholic and apostolic church' of which the young poet in *A Portrait* says that he refuses to serve her and, somewhat later in *Ulysses*, that he is her servant.

Hughes argues against what he condemns as a new critical and anti-historical reading of Joyce and of his role in modernism by critics who have failed to deal with the 'totality of Joyce's work,' especially as it relates to the 'totality that is Catholicism' (1992: 117). As a result, a 'rampant relativism' of criticism has turned Joyce's works into:

> [a] mirror to the various vanities of a secular criticism which elevates his works to the level of sacred texts to endorse those vanities. That Stephen also says 'I am a servant' is a contradiction with which most critics choose not to cope preferring to ignore Stephen and Joyce's testament to the power of Catholicism. (1992: 120)

Hughes fails to see that the contradiction between the two statements disappears if we take the word 'servant' in its biblical meaning of 'slave.' Instead he decides to concentrate on the idea that while Joyce's denial of catholicism is fairly clear, it is his assent that needs to be demonstrated and he proposes to do that in three movements. The first is economical: we know Joyce was very good at working with the materials he had at his disposal. If we apply this knowledge to our problem, 'he and his work (including his denials) can best be understood in Catholic terms and by means of Catholic concepts' (Hughes 1992: 123). The second movement is based on Thomas MacGreevy's comment in his essay for *Our Exagmination . . .* that *Ulysses* displays a 'deep-rooted Catholicism.' Although Hughes does acknowledge that these comments are 'chauvinistic and

almost bigoted,' he believes that Joyce's nihil obstat for the publication of the
essay in the collection shows that Joyce himself is 'pointing his critics to the specific reality of Irish Catholicism as a means of understanding his work' (123).

The third movement focuses on the context of Stephen's discussion with
Haines and Hughes quotes Stephen's description of himself as a 'horrible
example of free thought.' First he decides to ignore the usual meaning of the
last two words as referring to 'secular rationalism':

> It can equally mean free will and would then suggest that Stephen, having
> freed his thought, has yet remained in service by choice. (Since free thought
> is associated with his conversation with Haines about his belief in God we
> need not concern ourselves here with the consequences of that freedom for
> Stephen's remarks on the British Empire and Ireland.)

Hughes adds that these ambiguities 'reveal a mode of thought that the
Englishman Haines is unable to understand' (1992: 124), but surely you do
not have to be English to fail to understand such an interpretation of what the
fictional character is trying to say. When Stephen at the end of *A Portrait* is ready
to fly by the nets of 'nationality, language, religion' (*P* 203), Hughes claims that
this phrase 'is ambivalent referring to both denial (escape) and assent ("flying
by" = "flying with," i.e., using the nets as wings),' which seems to make as much
sense in semantics as it does in aerodynamics.

Similarly Hughes deals with the 'I will not serve' passage in *A Portrait* by
stressing that the famous statement is qualified by the phrase 'that in which I no
longer believe':

> So even when Stephen is making what received wisdom claims as his credo
> he cannot escape ambivalence. His refusal to serve is conditional on not
> believing but he appears to be unable to make a plain statement of disbelief.
> When Cranly [in *A Portrait*] challenges him: 'if you feel sure our religion is
> false,' Stephen immediately responds: 'I am not at all sure of it.' (Hughes
> 1992: 124)

But surely there is an enormous difference between no longer believing
something and being certain that it is false. As one of the characters of Salman
Rushdie's *The Satanic Verses* has pointed out, ceasing to believe may well be the
same as passing the stage of being capable of certainty: if that is correct, not
being certain loses the negative value that doubt has in religious thought.[1]

Hughes then proceeds to paint a picture of the Irish that differs from the
'received view' of George Moore and Simon Dedalus as a 'priestridden God-
forsaken race' by using the church's own doctrinal definition as 'One – she is
Holy – she is Catholic – she is Apostolic' (1992: 125; Hughes is quoting from
the Maynooth cathechism). On its own definition, the church is by definition a
decentred totality, combining universality *and* the uniqueness of each individual.

In addition, Hughes believes, the specifically Irish form of catholicism was able to stifle both modernism and socialism in a way that he calls ironic but that leads to a fundamental ambiguity, which the critic, with some help from contemporary Irish intellectuals like Seamus Deane and Richard Kearney, describes as liberating because it replaces 'the orthodox dualist logic of either/or' with 'a more dialectical one of *both/and*' (Kearney's terms): 'Irish Catholicism is, it seems to me, one of the most important forms by which this dialectical tendency is both expressed and reinforced. The works of Joyce are another' (Hughes 1992: 129).

What Hughes has so adroitly done here, is to reclaim Joyce for catholicism by turning the Irish form of the Church of Rome into a force of deconstruction. In the rest of the article, Hughes uses the same radical reading methods to find more instances in Joyce's work where he displays signs of assent. When M.P. Hederman and W.J. McCormack attempt to situate Joyce's work in a context that is wider than a purely Irish catholic one, Hughes reminds these two Irish critics (in the present context it is probably not irrelevant to point out that the former is a Benedictine monk and the latter a Dublin methodist):

> That the human condition is, in Catholic terms, one of exile (we are all 'the poor *banished* children of Eve'). Given this perspective, the Joycean exile is not just a separation but also an experience shared with humanity. Even in exile Joyce is not self-sufficient. (Hughes 1992: 130)

Perversely, Hughes then goes on to claim that Joyce's thoughts on property and on paternity came from Aquinas (through pope Leo XIII's championing of the philosopher) and in consequence 'the roots of Joyce's concept of freedom are in Catholicism' (131). Hughes then correctly assumes an implied discussion on the part of Joyce with George Moore, not as I will argue later in this book, as rival champions of an un-Irish secularism, but with Joyce refuting Moore 'by assenting to Catholic doctrine in a way that reveals Joyce's faith in Catholicism as a mode of consciousness and as an epistemology of human (and especially Irish) experience' (132).

The Christmas dinner is also exposed to the 'amphibiguous' reading practice that enables Hughes to come to the conclusion that Dante's negative answer to Simon Dedalus's question 'You didn't stir out at all, Mrs Riordan' (*P* 28) can only mean that the poor woman did not go to mass on Christmas Day! In fact he cleanly reverses the positions in the famous row, turning Mr Casey and Stephen's father into upstanding and church-going catholics and Mrs Riordan into a person who has just committed a mortal sin, conveniently forgetting that Mrs Riordan may have attended the Midnight Mass. As a result, 'Stephen is not, therefore, faced with a simple choice between politics and religion, but has [. . .] to confront their symbiosis in Irish experience' (1992: 134). In conclusion Hughes reinterprets the paralysis in *Dubliners* and the partly female Trinity of Stephen, Bloom and Molly in *Ulysses* as Joyce's way of being ahead of Catholic doctrine by at least a century, which is a strange enough conclusion, because if catholicism really is all that Hughes claims it is, how could catholic doctrine possibly have changed?

Both T.S. Eliot and Edward Said are criticized for overlooking the fact of catholicism in their analysis of Joyce's works and Hughes stresses that for Joyce the church represented an order that had not failed:

> Rather it was an order which answered to the affective and experiential needs for integration and community and which did so both in the form of a Church possessing a universal grandeur and in the form of a local Church which had moulded itself to the shape of Irish experience. (1992: 137)

In conclusion Hughes writes that this newly analysed relationship of Joyce with catholicism has nothing to do with Joyce's own personal beliefs (which he claims 'have *not* been under discussion'), but that henceforth it will be necessary to adopt a new way of looking at Joyce as a literary modernist and even a new way of looking at the nature of modernism itself.

If this essay is not a hoax, it must be listed among the more perverse readings of Joyce. In almost every instant it manages to misrepresent what Joyce actually thought and what he made his characters say and do. Instead of putting Joyce in his proper context, Hughes wilfully distorts the evidence and he confronts a real writer with a view of the catholic church that very few people in the church of Rome would recognize.

Hughes's work should be seen in the light of the post-colonial reading of Joyce's work which has managed, in the last two decades, to turn on its head Richard Ellmann's portrait of Joyce as an essentially non-political writer with a liberal distaste for nationalism. Critics such as Vincent Cheng believe that in some suitably subtle way Joyce was an Irish nationalist. Andrew Gibson (2002) claims that the introduction of theory marked the beginning of a new interpretation of the role of Stephen in *Ulysses*. First he discusses the view of older critics, which he describes as 'humanist' and, surprisingly, in the almost exclusively American context of Joyce criticism, as a 'Leavisite consensus' (2002: 22). The critics targeted here, Richard Ellmann, Hugh Kenner and Bernard Benstock, see Joyce as being critical of Stephen, but in the 1980s a new generation of critics has managed to create an entirely different Stephen. In the wake of the efforts by post-colonial critics like Seamus Deane, Vincent Cheng and Lenn Platt, the image of Stephen has become politicized. The new Stephen is aware of his own subject status and that of his people, with whom ('albeit with reservations') he identifies. Gibson believes that the stakes are high. If you hold on to the old humanist view of Stephen, what you are doing in fact is 'to collude in Stephen's dispossession' (23).

In a similar vein, but taking the argument one step further, Stephen Sicari in *Joyce's Modernist Allegory* (2001) argues explicitly against the 'dogmatic scepticism' propagated by most post-strucuralist critics. He believes that Joyce uses the post-strucuralist understanding of how language works in order to achieve something that according to post-structuralism cannot exist. As a 'secret and subtle idealist,' Joyce 'works with extraordinary care and ingenuity to bring readers to an apperception of something ideal.' Joyce is shown to be sceptical of his own scepticism and 'in this movement beyond scepticism he finds a way to cling to a belief in something outside language that can serve as the ground on which we can erect meaning for our lives' (Sicari 2001: 2). The representation of what Sicari calls 'an event outside the web of language that can ground our idealism' can only be effected by a return 'to the central mystery of Christianity, the Incarnation, and the model of reading that was able to comprehend that mystery, the allegory of theologians. [. . .] Outside of language is the Christ event: outside of words is the Word' (9).

Joyce's modernist allegory is therefore nothing but the theological form of allegory that was first developed by Saint Paul in the letter to the Galatians where he 'reads' the two wives of Abraham as representing the two covenants: 'One is from Mount Sinai, bearing children for slavery; she is Hagar. Now Hagar is Mount Sinai in Arabia; she corresponds to the resent [sic] Jerusalem, for she is in slavery with her children. But the Jerusalem above is free, and she is our mother' (Gal. 4.24–6, quoted by Sicari 2001: 10). This christian form of allegory becomes the model for Joyce's alleged attempt to replace the genre of the novel by that of the allegory. In Sicari's reading of *Ulysses*, it is Bloom who becomes the new incarnation of Christ, although it is only at the end of 'Ithaca' that he is formally recognized as such by Stephen. Nearly everything in the book is grist to Sicari's interpretative mill: if Joyce spends much energy on descriptions of the bodies of his two male heroes, we find the reason here: 'Bloom's elevation to an ideal height, his ascension if you will, is with body intact, like Christ's Ascension' (2001: 15). The whole book is read from the perspective of the penultimate chapter in the same way that the entire bible really only deals with Christ's incarnation and sacrifice:

> So we must learn to see how 'Ithaca' contains an analogous 'Christ event' and so functions as the fixed perspective from which the rest of the novel may be read and understood, in the same way that the Christ event organizes and gives meaning to Dante's itinerary and as the Incarnation functions as the fixed point from which to review the Hebrew scriptures. *Ulysses* is 'reread' from the privileged vantage point of 'Ithaca.' (2001: 16)

Somewhat later Sicari repeats his central thesis: 'only the reader who has followed Stephen through to "Ithaca" will be able to provide a full rendering of the opening scenes, just as only the person who has experienced the Christ event can read the Old Testament properly' (47). If reading Christ into the books of the jewish bible constitutes a 'proper' reading, it is hard to imagine what Sicari would regard as an illegitimate interpretation.

The conclusion, for this critic, is that in *Ulysses* Joyce has tried to represent a truth that is timeless by definition:

> That love and mercy are the value that exist outside of space and time and outside of language itself, and that they can be the basis of a permanent order, or of a Church at 7 Eccles street to which the few of us who care to do so may belong. If Molly is still unfaithful on the literal level, and even if Stephen never crosses paths with Bloom on the novelistic level, and even if the new epic family proves to be just another culturally relative configuration becoming fascistic, the love and mercy of Christ as seen in Bloom – first by Stephen, then by the reader, and then by Molly – are eternal. (2001: 192)

But the relevance of the 'Christ event' is not restricted to Joyce, and in his conclusion Sicari briefly reads poems by Eliot, Stevens and Pound to show that his type of reading offers a new way of interpreting both modernism and postmodernism. With William Lynch, a contemporary Jesuit philosopher, Sicari argues that one does not even have to believe in Christ to 'appropriate this principle as the cornerstone of the artistic project' and thus he comes to a conclusion that also functions as a project for further study:

> Christ becomes the model of the genuine artistic project as he has been the center of a theology, and in the work of these four high modernists we see the Christian imagination establishing a model for our lives in time. In the model for reading that I have suggested may lie a hope that we can read for the ideal and the permanently valuable in the texts we have come to cherish as part of our cultural heritage. (2001: 221)

Gian Balsamo is another neo-catholic reader of Joyce who finds his inspiration in Dante and Saint Paul, but he comes from the more philosophical side of the post-strucuralist field that is allied in all kinds of ways with the radical orthodoxy movement in theology. I will limit myself to his latest book, *Joyce's Messianism* because in a way it brings the arguments of his previous books and articles together. Although in the beginning of his book Balsamo claims that he will offer a non-metaphysical answer to 'the current debate about mystical and (negative) apophantic experience' (4), it is clear from the sources that he quotes that he places himself in a particular corner of the critical field, consisting partly of the catholic readings of Joyce such as those of Robert Boyle, and in more structural fashion, that of the theological form of deconstruction practised by philosophers and literary scholars like René Girard, Jean-Luc Marion and of John D. Caputo, who in the 1970s and 1980s created a catholic version of post-structuralism. This is clearly the frame of reference in Balsamo's first chapters on Saint Augustine and Dante: the religious branch of French Heideggerianism ,which uses literary studies to stage their interpretation of the essentially theological nature of language and which is not unrelated to the 'radical orthodoxy' movement in theology.

Balsamo opens the book with John Freccero's deconstructive interpretation of the central dilemma in Dante's endeavour to represent the unrepresentable. In theological terms: 'Apophantic experience [the mystical union with either god or death] is such that it cannot be phenomenally experienced, and yet, it provides the Euclidean axes, the α and ω, of finite existence' (10). With the help of Heidegger, Marion, Derrida and Caputo, Balsamo then proceeds to posit this transcendental experience of impossibility as the very foundation of all existence. For him the two distinct experiences, death and the mystical union with god, come together in what he calls the 'messianic self' or, more precisely, though not necessarily more clear, 'one may envisage an Augustinian order of presence bridging the cleft between these two distinct orders of absence' (14). Linking this with two different views of the relationship between the Eucharist and the crucifixion, Balsamo claims that Jesus's death:

> Affects the worshiper as an existential rather than virtual repetition, as the incorporation of a factical blood-shedding, intimacy with the divine is lived through in all its repulsive and irresistible concreteness, as an individual feat of organic theophagy. (15)

These 'individual instantiations of negative existence' are disseminated all over Joyce's writings, although one has 'to wait for Joyce's messianic protagonists [. . .] before the existential negativity and the messianic self may become fully and unmediatedly recognizable in its linguistic expression' (23). In the rest of his book, Balsamo reads all references to death or burial in this rather harsh light, to finally reach the ultimate sacrifice, which turns out to be Shem writing on his own body with his own excrement. This latter passage (*FW* 185.14–26) represents no less than the closing of a 'bimillennial cycle of opposition between Word and Flesh that had been inaugurated for the consciousness of the West by Pauline and Augustinian writings' (118). *Finnegans Wake* is then, ultimately, the result of the process of:

> Reverse filiation whereby the Incarnate Word, whose messianic coming is typologically announced in Scripture, undertakes to beget – under the guise of a character from *Finnegans Wake* – a novel inscription of the divine *Verbum*, ultimately a novel origination of the original act of Creation itself. A reverse filiation of Scripture: but how does filiation reverse itself into an original generation of its own origin? The answer found in Shem's transaccidentation is that such a reverse filiation occurs via an act of revisionary writing that reconceives and restipulates the entirety of Scripture, down to the materiality itself of its inscription – a novel inscription of the divine *Verbum*, in other words, as though upon a virtually inverted Veronica, or *vera icona*, as though

upon the decomposing skin [. . .] of the divine *Verbum*'s own sacrificial corpse. (116)

But this is not the end, because this drama includes all of us as readers:

It is not recommendable to any and everybody, therefore to engage in a Joycean liturgy of transaccidentation; to do so, one must don Shem's Veronica – his corpus, his body's *vera icona* – and face (or be-toward) one's ineluctable fate in death and decomposition. Far from being the superfluous ballast that [. . .] one must be 'decontaminated' from, one's own flesh becomes the protagonist of an autobiography of sacrificial *anamnesis*. (119)

The internal logic of Joyce's work leads straight to *Finnegans Wake* in which Joyce 'embarks upon a full-scale deconstruction of the tyranny of ordinary and common experience,' which turns Joyce's last book into 'the Bible of negative existence' by dismantling 'the ordinary notions of identity and temporality by means respectively of character amalgamation and chronological destabilization' (125). There are all kinds of links between this particular way of reading literature and the radical orthodox tendency in contemporary protestant and catholic theology, which claims that the fate of modernism and atheism are so much intertwined that a postmodern world can only be post-atheist (another popular term is 'post-secular'), either returning to a premodern religious sensibility or creating an entirely new postmodern religion. Like most of the contributions to this theology, interpretations of Joyce's work such as Balsamo's seem to be addressed only to those of us who already share these particular christian beliefs.

Next to these neo-orthodox interpretations of Joyce's work, there have also been more neutral studies on Joyce and religion, which refuse to assign Joyce either to the Ellmannian anti-catholic or to the unwittingly catholic camp. In his dissertation Steven John Morrison argues for a third way, between the Scylla and Charybdis of Joyce as 'the guilt-free apostate' on the one hand and 'the Catholic *malgré lui*' on the other. Morrison claims that both of these portraits fail to do justice to Joyce's work:

To assign to Joyce a single and easily categorised stance regarding Catholicism in the interest of interpreting his work is actually not to interpret at all, but to impoverish and drastically to oversimplify both Joyce's art and the place of Catholicism within it. (1999: 12)

While it is true that in the second half of his life Joyce remained silent on the subject of religion, this does not necessarily tell us that he belonged to one or the other camp: it represents 'a way of refuting absolutely any neat religious identification, of himself certainly, but, more importantly, of the religious element of his writings.' In that context catholicism retained its privileged position as the religion of his youth and as 'the only form of religion to which he *might* assent' (12), but it was heresy and its history that offered him the chance to challenge catholicism instead of merely rejecting it.

Morrison follows this reasoning in great textual detail in Joyce's work and he identifies the exact relationship between religious and theological deviance, as in the case of 'The Sisters':

> The indeterminacy of 'The Sisters,' far from being some undirected narrative experiment, is the demonstration of the anti-dogmatic principle in opposition to the demonstration of the dogmatic principle in 'Grace.' The question of whether Father Flynn is himself a heretic, formal or otherwise, is ultimately irrelevant, because the story which centres around him is itself an elaboration of the anti-dogmatic principle of heresy; and the reader or the critic's inability to specify Flynn's error, far from being an unachieved objective, is itself precisely the point. (44)

In a similar vein Morrison looks at the important role in Joyce's later works of heresy and dissent, but in order to stress the heroic nature of Stephen's revolt, he remains blind to the reality of the Dublin that Joyce grew up, which was hardly the uniformly catholic milieu that Morrison makes of it. As we will see in Chapter 3, there were quite a number of other religious and ideological options available to Joyce and Stephen.

Via a different route than the one I will take here, Morrison comes to a conclusion that I will be able to corroborate:

> In Stephen Dedalus, the servant who will not serve, Joyce represents the struggle which is necessary for one determined by dogmatic thought – one to whom his mental organs 'dictate' – to contest the hold that thought has on him without simply falling back into the same dogmatic pattern, a struggle which is necessarily without end. In Leopold Bloom, the truly 'impossible person' (*U*.1.222) of *Ulysses,* Joyce represents what the end product of such a struggle might actually look like, were it possible to conclude it. (140)

In the most recent contribution to the debate Roy Gottfried tackles the same problem, but he comes to slightly different conclusions. He adopts the word 'misbeliever' that he finds in a letter to Lady Gregory with which the young Joyce had described his own position: Gottfried believes the term misbelief describes best Joyce's ambiguous position towards the certainties of the catholic faith:

> A misbeliever is one who engages the issues and tenets, the figures and forms of dogma, from a distance, a place that is off, separated. Misbelief shares with belief the same terms, the same facts of history, the same forms of worship, but want to handle them differently, wrongly, of course, by slightly misapplying

or misdirecting them. [. . .] To be a misbeliever is to set oneself away from
faith, alien from it, but always aware of its place, its shape and topology. [. . .]
Misbelief, looking always at unitary belief from afar and defining itself by that
distance, is a sort of chosen exile. In that space of distance, of exile, is an
openness crucial to Joyce's misbelief: he wants to challenge the 'narrow' view
of religion, the only definition of the believer, with an openness to possibilities of redirection. [. . .] Religion is for Joyce an intellectual problem, a challenge to all orders of epistemology, history, and culture. (2007: 4–5)

Joyce is therefore a special kind of heretic, who respects the strict and coherent
philosophy, but still rejects it:

[T]o be a misbeliever rather than a believer or an unbeliever was, for Joyce,
to be always mindful of orthodoxy while attempting to break its hold of unitary meaning, its narrow sense, and to open up personal possibilities that
led to artistic ones of rebellious challenge and freedom. (Gottfried 2007: 8)

Gottfried emphasizes Joyce's interest in dissent, in schism, in all the possible
alternatives to the orthodoxy of the Church of Rome: not just the heresies, but
also the protestant faith – for example when Joyce seems to favour the protestant King James translation of the bible – or the Greek orthodox church of
which Joyce borrowed the terminology (*epicleti*) to describe what he had been
trying to do in *Dubliners*. But we know that the reading 'epicleti' should be abandoned: as Wolfhard Steppe pointed out a long time ago, Joyce only claimed that
his stories were 'epiclets' and it really is not relevant, as Gottfried points out,
that this word is just as bad English as 'epiclesis' is bad Greek: 'epiclets' is the
word that Joyce wrote down, *not* 'epicleti' which Ellmann and Gottfried seem to
prefer only because it allows for more elaborate and more interesting interpretations. Similarly, Joyce's preference for the King James translation does not
necessarily indicate any stance towards catholic or protestant interpretations or
religion in general. In English literature the King James version is the standard
translation for most important bible verses: the catholic versions have had much
less influence on literature. Gottfried therefore seems to be much more interested in the aesthetic possibilities of Joyce's texts than in the historical context
in which they were written and in which, I believe, they make sense.

   This is an aspect of what was described above as 'proper' readings: aesthetic
value judgements should never precede editorial or historical decisions, because
interpretations must be based on facts, not the other way around. Literary
works, like all works of art and like all texts, have a meaning in their own context that is informed both by the author and by the immediate audience of his
contemporaries. A literary text may acquire other meanings at a later point, in
the same way that the bible did, and these later meanings can be studied by
reception studies, as long as we realize that there is a difference between these

meanings and what Umberto Eco has called the *intentio operis,* the original context in which the text first made sense to the writer and his audience.

For the earliest readers of Joyce's work, the religious dimension of his fiction was an important issue. We will see later in this book that it clearly made more sense for contemporary religious readers like Shane Leslie to reject Joyce's work, than for others to 'save' him for catholicism, although Joyce's catholic friends and acquaintances like Mary Colum and Thomas MacGreevy led the way by insisting on the catholic structure of his mind and thus of his work. Before we can look in more detail at what the biographical materials have to tell us about Joyce's attitudes towards religion, we must first devote the next chapter to a necessarily sketchy survey of the ideological context in which Joyce lived, if only because it differs greatly from the world that we live in today. In addition I will also describe the different alternatives that a young man of James Joyce's talents and temperament might have turned to in the context of his planned war against the church. During his writing career Joyce lived in four different countries and it is relevant to devote some time to a discussion of the particular relations between the church and its alternatives, not just in Great Britain and Ireland, but also in Italy, France and other European countries where the same or similar battles were fought. In each of these countries the situation was different and it would be a mistake to think that the role of the church was the same.

Chapter 2

The Holy Roman Apostolic Church

Church of Rome

In order to fully understand Joyce's problems with the Church of Rome, we must first historically ground the discussion by describing exactly what he was rebelling against and that is impossible without a look at the history of christianity in the nineteenth and early twentieth century. Writing a non-partisan history of the different forms of christianity and catholicism in Europe is difficult: there are at least two kinds of church history. There is a liberal or whig view of that history, in which the forces of Darkness, usually represented by the Church of Rome and other conservative religious and political powers, defend themselves forcefully but ultimately in vain against the forces of Light, which consist either of the increasingly more enlightened churches or of the secular democratic movements that succeeded them. If it is true that history is always written by the victors, then it is not surprising that most of the writers of the history of the catholic church, and especially of the period between 1830 and the 1960s have not always been on the side of Rome. Yet there have also been historians who have tried to present (or better, to defend) the church's own view of its history.

In itself this development is fairly recent. Michael Novak writes that since the Council of Trent in the sixteenth century, catholic theology 'might fairly be described as "non-historical" or even "anti-historical." It favors speculation which is not called to the bar of historical fact, past or present: [indeed] it often seems to fear principles which could make it face such a bar' (quoted in Cochrane 1977: 456). It was only in 1883 that Leo XIII published a pastoral letter on historical studies (*Saepenumero considerantes*), which opened the Vatican archives and at the same time announced a new interest in the history of the church for which the pontiff quoted Cicero's exhortation to historians not to lie and not to be afraid to speak the truth. At the same time, he made it clear that the truth could only belong to the church in a formulation that may have been echoed by Stephen Dedalus in his conversation about history with Mr Deasy: 'All history in a way shouts out that it is God whose Providence governs the varied and continual changes of mortal affairs and adapts them, even in spite of human opposition, to the growth of his Church' (quoted in Weber 1962: 350).

The result was that both in Europe and America, catholic universities and seminaries began to develop the serious study of history and for that purpose catholic historical associations were founded. But at the same time, and especially after the condemnation of modernism, catholic historiography was carefully controlled by the hierarchy and greatly restricted in what it was allowed to say about the history of the church. Good examples of this apologetic attitude can be found among the contributors to the *Catholic Encyclopedia* or in the work of E.E.Y. Hales, who was working before Vatican Council II. In 1957 he published *The Catholic Church in the Modern World* with a nihil obstat and an imprimatur from the American Cardinal Spellman. Similar overt or covert restrictions on the work of catholic historians lasted at least until the 1970s.

In a 1974 address Eric Cochrane as president of the American Catholic Historical Association attempted to formulate a new kind of catholic historiography, claiming that the old type of pre-Vatican Council historiography had lost credibility, not just with non-catholics, but even within the fold. With many examples Cochrane shows how the old theological form of history had acquired an unassailable logic and 'a fairly original scheme of historical development' on the basis of a limited number of presuppositions. The first was that the papacy and most religious orders were exempt from 'the normal effects of human fallibility and temporal change' (Cochrane 1977: 446). In addition some historical events were thought to be wholly good (scholasticism and neo-Thomism), others were wholly bad (nominalism, the spiritual Franciscans, renaissance humanism). The end result was a view of history that was 'almost as satisfying for ordinary Catholics as the metaphysics and moral frame of reference provided by neo-Thomism' (447). The president of the American Catholic Historical Association then goes on to describe how in the 1960s and 1970s this consensus became not just discredited among historians, but equally unacceptable to post-Council theologians. If Cochrane is correct, the work of this older type of catholic history should be used preferably as a series of symptoms of the problem of the history of the catholic church, not as genuine attempts at historical study.

For the history of the catholic church, my sources will therefore be limited first to the collaborative efforts of the writers of the most authoritative recent history of the christian churches, the relevant volumes of *Histoire du christianisme des origines à nos jours*, second the recent and scrupulously unpartisan general history of European catholicism from 1750 by Nicholas Atkin and Frank Tallett and finally to the slightly older work of Owen Chadwick who has covered this period in two books in a manner that cannot be accused of subscribing to the whig view of history.

As the historian Jonathan Israel (2002) has shown, the roots of the modern form of liberal democracy and of religious tolerance lie in the enlightenment philosophies of the seventeenth and eighteenth centuries, first in Holland and England, later in the United States, Germany and France. In the early nine-teenth century these ideas were codified in the *code Napoléon* that revolutionized the legal systems in most of Europe and that was responsible for the introduc-tion of liberal and democratic ideals in most countries and, sometimes after a lengthy process, the establishment of the modern and secular nation states that we know today.

Established religion had been an integral part of the *ancien régime* and in the period after the French revolution it was inevitable that in most parts of Europe the established churches became an important target of dissidents and liberals. The catholic church in particular came under attack and this had everything to do with the particular situation of the Church of Rome in the wake of the successive revolutions of 1789, 1830 and 1848 and with the difficult birth of the modern state of Italy, built on the ruins of the Papal States. But in order to understand the various strands of the opposition against the Church of Rome in the period when Joyce was growing up, it is necessary first to describe the peculiar history of how in the course of the nineteenth century the Roman catholic church managed to transform itself radically and how it paradoxically managed to do so in the name of tradition.

The hierarchy in Rome had been shocked by the anti-religious excesses of the French revolution and it had only reluctantly found a way of dealing with the more enlightened form of the nouveau régime that developed under Napoleon. The French revolution and the ensuing terror had strengthened the alliance between the church and conservative governments all over Europe, especially after the final defeat of Napoleon in Waterloo. In this generally post-revolutionary period the church enjoyed what Atkin and Tallett call 'something of a honeymoon' (2003: 84). Rome's reaction to the revolution accordingly consisted of centralizing its power and strengthening its anti-liberal stance.

In the camp of the enemies of the catholic church, of christianity and of religion in general, the social and political revolutions of 1830 and 1848 radicalized philosophical ideas, with now for the first time – and in most of these revolutionary movements – a complete rejection of organized religion. Especially in Germany and France, where the political revolutions had been brutally oppressed, intellectuals formulated anticlerical principles. The first unambiguously atheist manifestos were published and the struggle between conservative catholics and progressive liberals would begin to mark European politics and culture for the next 100 years.

This antagonism was the direct result not only of specific conditions in a country like France that had a strong royalist and anti-liberal tradition, but also of the extremely conservative response from Rome. In reaction to the revo-lution, but mostly as a condemnation of catholics such as the French priest Félicité Robert de Lamennais who had argued for a more liberal form of cathol-icism, the encyclical *Mirari vos* of 1832 unequivocally condemned the liberal ideas of freedom of conscience, freedom of the press, the separation of church and state, religious tolerance and even the very idea of democracy itself. French liberal catholics such as Lamennais and the count of Montalembert were forced to submit and they did so reluctantly; the latter wrote that *Mirari vos* placed the church 'in direct hostility to science and freedom' and that this signalled the end of the catholic party in France: 'We will be silent again, although we realize that it is not up to us to save what the pope and the bishops insist on losing' (Gadille, 1995a: 23). In his survey of this period of French history, Jacques Gadille writes that the immediate result of the incident was the total alienation from catholicism of the romantic writers, the generation of Sainte-Beuve, Michelet and Victor Hugo, whereas an older generation of authors such as Chateaubriand had still managed to create a new and romantic form of catholicism that had been quite influential, even outside of France.

In Italy the problem was that the new nation state could only establish itself at the cost of the temporal powers of the Papal States. The 1830 revolutionaries in Italy claimed mischievously that since Jesus himself had said that his kingdom was not of this world, there was no doctrinal basis for the pope's temporal powers. In the world of revolutionary Italy, papal power could only be forcefully maintained by a French and Austrian military occupation. A similar crisis occurred in 1848: under pressure of democratic clubs in Rome and inspired by the revolutions in Paris, pope Pius IX, whom Chadwick calls 'the liberal pope,' at first granted a limited number of civil liberties to the inhabitants of the Papal States. The *Risorgimento*, the movement for a united Italy under the leadership of the kingdom of Piedmont, was widely supported by liberals from the north and from Sicily in the south, and in the summer these groups united in an unsuccessful attempt to rid the Italian peninsula of the occupying Austrian troops. Frustrated by their defeat, the liberals in the Papal States demanded more civil rights, mobs besieged the pope's residence in the Quirinal palace and in November 1848 the pope was forced, with some help of the French and Bavarian ambassadors, to flee Rome disguised as a priest. Immediately the insurgents elected a new Roman assembly that summoned the two leaders of the *Risorgimento*, Giuseppe Mazzini and Giuseppe Garibaldi: the former became the First Triumvir, taking the Quirinal palace as his residence. Pius IX appealed once more to the catholic nations for help and France responded by sending troops that reconquered Rome in July of the following year. But as a result of the continuing unrest, the pope had to wait until the spring of 1850 to return to a Rome where once more civil liberties had been abolished. The pope was no longer a liberal: the conservative Jesuits were restored to power and henceforth the papacy would be even less patient with liberal and democratic catholics and would cling to a strategy of defending the pope's temporal powers that the pontiff apparently had received during nightly visitations from the early martyr saint Philomena (Norman 1985: 237).[1] In fact the *débâcle* of 1848 had a profound effect on how the papacy would view its political role well into the next century: when Pio Nono came back to Rome, he did not return to the Quirinal palace, but went to the Vatican instead. This move was symbolical for a fundamental change of policy: henceforth the papacy would slowly and with great reluctance give up most of its political power, but instead increase its hold over the local churches and over catholic doctrine. The pope's intransigence in spiritual matters was certainly due to the loss of his temporal powers, but it was also in the field of doctrine that he believed a solution could be found for the grave dangers that the church was facing. At the end of 1851 he began a large-scale consultation of the bishops about what Pius thought of as the two most important themes of the day, the errors of the modern age and the Immaculate Conception of Mary. Jacques Gadille writes that for Pius IX (as, incidentally, for today's neo-orthodox theologians) the reference to original sin and to a better understanding of the Incarnation represented the best antidote against the pretentions of rationalism and materialism (1995a: 28). This was accompanied by a new and growing tendency among ordinary believers towards popular devotions such as those of the Sacred Heart, the Eucharist and the Blessed Virgin, seemingly supported by miraculous appearances of the Mother of God. By these appearances the Blessed Virgin herself announced (or 'seemed to authenticate,' as Jacques Gadille puts it) the new dogma (1995b: 125).

In 1854 the Immaculate Conception was officially proclaimed and two years later followed the allocution *Singulari quadam*, a tract against rationalism and indifferentism (the doctrine that all religions, and not just roman catholicism, can lead to salvation). This papal text contained the polemical political statement that the church was 'a perfect society, a supreme law-giver and guarantee of all human legislation' (quoted in Gadille, 1995a: 28).

Piedmont under Victor Emmanuel II, the most powerful of the Italian states, adopted liberal and increasingly anticlerical policies with which the government under Prime Minister Camillio Cavour tried to challenge the church's monopoly in the fields of education, justice and censorship. Cavour believed that the world needed a 'libera Chiesa in libero Stato,' a free church in a free state, a sentiment adopted and elaborated on by Leopold Bloom, when in the 'Circe' chapter, as Lord Mayor of Dublin, he calls for 'Free money, free rent, free love and a free lay church in a free lay state,' to which O'Maddan Burke comments: 'Free fox in a free henroost' (*U* 15.1693–5).

In 1854, as part of this power struggle between church and state, convents and monasteries were abolished in Piedmont. When it became clear that Pius IX could no longer count on the French and Austrian armies to defend his authority, an international army was raised; among them an 'Irish Brigade of Saint Patrick.' In the summer of 1860 an international catholic legion failed to defend the Holy City against the invading Piedmontese army and the Irish brigade had to be repatriated at the expense of the British government (Norman 1985: 238).

Earlier in the year the pope had published *Syllabus errorum in Europa vigentium*, a collection of all the theological errors that were condemned in the strongest words: these errors could only be interpreted as part of a demonic attack against the church of Christ. The doctrinal statements and the political reactions followed each other rapidly, and it must have appeared to the faithful that the end times had really begun. Although the greatest part of the Papal States was in the hands of the insurgents, the pope himself was protected by the French army and it was only in 1870, when France needed its troops to defend *la patrie* against Prussia, that the Piedmontese were finally able to enter the Holy City. This was the end, according to the catholic historian Hales, of 'the oldest temporal sovereignty in Europe' (1960: 122).

Just a few years before Pius IX had appended the Syllabus of Errors to his encyclical *Quanta cura*. This remarkable document of 1864 ended with a condemnation of the claim that the pope 'can and ought to reconcile himself with progress, with liberalism, and with modern civilization' (quoted in Chadwick 1975: 111). Ten years later the pope could still congratulate French visitors on their efforts on behalf of the struggle against the 'horrible plague that has afflicted human society.' He was referring to universal suffrage.

In his history of the papacy in the nineteenth century, Owen Chadwick claims that for the next 50 years the Syllabus had an enormous political impact in most European countries, and that the general feeling at the time was that the pope, in taking sides against freedom of conscience, tolerance and equality before the law, was 'morally wrong.' And this was not just the opinion of protestants, Chadwick quotes the prominent catholic intellectual Lord Acton who in the course of a conversation in Rome in 1867 said 'I pray to God that I may live to see the whole of this Fabric destroyed and the Tiber flow with the blood of the massacred Priests' (2003: 112). Although this was an extreme reaction by one of the most respected liberal catholics of his time, Hales quotes a 1952 catholic study that came to the conclusion that at the time of the publication of the Syllabus, 'the majority of Catholics were stupefied' (1960: 125).

The opposition against the Syllabus within the church was strong: a third of the bishops who had been consulted rejected its theses (90 had not bothered to reply) and most important national churches had large groups who openly opposed it, with centres of resistance strongest in the more advanced democracies France, Germany and Belgium. In England the group led by Lord Acton had the support of the prominent convert from anglicanism, the later cardinal Newman. In 1863 the Belgian archbishop organized a conference where Montalembert spoke and a month later at another conference in Munich, the German scholars and theologians demanded the necessary intellectual freedom to study the early history of christianity without interference from the hierarchy.

Trying to contain the damage done by the publication of the *Syllabus errorum*, the French liberal bishop Félix Dupanloup developed a tortuous argument (originally invented by the Jesuit journal *Civiltà cattolica*) according to which the meaning of the pope's words was the opposite of what he had in fact written: it was not because the pope condemned absolute freedom that he had also denied the value of relative liberties. This free interpretation may have saved a number of liberal catholics a certain measure of embarrassment, but it was already too late. The damage had been done and for most of the next 100 years, the catholic hierarchy would stick to the literal meaning of the text; in consequence the church remained one of the most important conservative forces in the world.

Lord Acton had not been alone in his opposition to the *Syllabus of Errors*. One of the most influential liberal catholics in Germany was Johann Joseph Ignaz Döllinger who publicly defended the right of catholics to study the church's writings and its history in the same independent spirit as protestant scholars. The pope countered with Error 57 of the *Syllabus*, according to which it is was wrong to claim that 'the science of philosophy and morals can and should be independent of divine and ecclesiastical authority.'

Pio Nono's *Syllabus* may have dismayed liberal catholics, but the pope's intervention in the debate was applauded by conservatives everywhere. Hales specifically names Louis Veuillot, the French conservative journalist, W.G. Ward of the *Dublin Review*, Queen Isabella of Spain and the archbishop of Westminster, cardinal Henry Edward Manning. It was this group of political conservatives that was instrumental in the organization of the First Vatican Council of 1870 where they planned to consolidate the conservative victory over liberals and moderates. A constitution was drafted to counter all so-called materialist philosophies and the resulting text, *Dei filius*, duly rejected the ideas of rationalism (reason is sufficient without faith), pantheism and naturalism (the denial of what cannot be apprehended by the senses). The constitution was unanimously approved by the delegates and ratified by the pope. This first step had not been too difficult, because it largely represented what most bishops and cardinals could agree on, but they also wanted to redefine the nature of the church, its authority and its relationship with the temporal powers. About these matters there was much difference of opinion between the *ultramontanes*, the conservative followers of the pope, and those cardinals who were either more liberal or more attached to their own local authority and thus opposed to all attempts to create a stronger central authority in Rome.

The leader of the *ultramontanes*, the British cardinal Manning, intended to solve the issue of the pope's damaged authority by a solemn proclamation of papal infallibility, an amazing novelty for a church that prided itself on being conservative. Before 1870, doctrinal pronouncements were the prerogative of a general council of bishops, not of the pope. Liberals like Acton, Dupanloup and the German priest and theology professor Döllinger fought the conservatives all the way. Although the motion was at first defeated, Manning persevered and won. When this became clear, the liberals avoided the vote by leaving Rome; in the end only 533 of the more than 700 who had attended the opening ceremonies were present during the final vote on 18 July 1870 when the motion was carried, with only two delegates voting against it, one Italian and one American. While a *Te Deum* was sung to celebrate the new dogma, a thunderstorm broke out which, Chadwick writes, 'was variously interpreted' (2003: 214). In any case, this was the end of the council, with only 2 of the 51 documents finalized: Germany invaded France, the French troops were withdrawn from Rome and the pope was left defenceless.

Among those who had been absent at the final vote was John MacHale, the archbishop of Tuam who had supported Daniel O'Connell's movement in the fight against anti-catholic legislation in London. At the council he argued and spoke against the declaration; he also voted against it in the first ballot and left Rome with the other moderates before the second vote. But he immediately submitted to the decision; according to the *Catholic Encyclopedia*:

> In his own cathedral he declared the dogma of infallibility 'to be true Catholic doctrine, which he believed as he believed the Apostles' Creed,' a public profession that further raised John of Tuam in the estimation of all who admired his great genius and virtue.

A deliberately garbled version of what happened appears in Joyce's *Dubliners* story 'Grace.'

As had happened before with the Syllabus, the Pope's extremely anti-liberal declaration was 'translated' into more liberal terms to make it palatable to those catholics who preferred to live in the nineteenth century and in fact, as Atkin and Tallett write: 'successive popes have been chary of explicitly invoking the doctrine of infallibility, only doing so on one occasion, in 1950, on the question of the Assumption' (2003: 139). Immediately after the council, Döllinger protested openly and in 1871 he was duly excommunicated, despite international protests. Some of the other liberals, most of them intellectuals from the German speaking countries, felt that they had had enough; they joined the Old Catholic church, a church that never attracted a large audience, but in the 1930s [Joyce could still visit the *Altkatholische Kirche* in Zürich.

The council did not mark the end of the liberal opposition against the increasingly centralist ultramontane church, which with the doctrine of infallibility had created the perception of catholicism, in the words of Atkin and Tallett 'as a transnational faith whose adherents owed primary allegiance to the Bishop of Rome rather than to the nation or the nation-state' (2003: 144). At the end of the century, the new pope Pius X had another set of liberals and a new heresy to contend with: modernism. The most prominent members of this movement (which, despite what the church itself claimed, never were part of a group) were the Frenchman Alfred Loisy and the Irish Jesuit George Tyrrell. Like their German predecessors they were scholars who wanted only what their protestant colleagues had: the freedom to study the bible and the early church without theological interference or ecclesiastical censure. The more liberal way of thinking was also increasingly popular among catholic intellectuals and it is described by Hales as the 'potentially most powerful of all heresies' (1960: 178).

With its rejection of secular science and of democratic politics, the church had not made things easy for its intellectuals: by 1860 the University of Louvain in liberal Belgium was the only catholic university outside of Rome (cardinal Newman's brief experiment in Dublin in the mid-1850s had not been a success). In half a century the church had almost succeeded in making the expression 'catholic intellectual' an oxymoron. Ironically it was especially in the most liberal and democratic countries with strong alternatives to the church of Rome, such as Belgium, Germany and France, that the church's censure put catholic apologists at a decided disadvantage.

The major conservative measures were preceded by a few hesitant steps on the part of the hierarchy towards more liberal attitudes. Initially Leo XIII seems to have been intent on making the church move closer to the realities of the age. This is evident in a number of his decisions, such as the opening of the Vatican archives, but the most important of these steps was the encyclical *Providentissimus Deus* of 1893 that addressed the thorny issue of biblical criticism. In this field the situation of catholic scholarship could not have been more difficult: a century earlier the great monastic centres of catholic scholarship in Europe had been destroyed in the French revolution and they had not reopened. Under influence of university reforms originating in Germany, all intellectual life would henceforth be concentrated at the new universities, which for the most part catholics were not allowed to attend. Only at a few of the modern German universities was there a lively competition between protestant and catholic theologians that forced the latter to keep up academic standards. But as late as 1906 Albert Schweitzer could write that catholic exegetes did not 'take account of and explain the great historical problem' of the bible (quoted in Ratté 1967: 12). This was of course part of the general rejection of rationalism and historicism. For the most part catholics rejected and ignored the historical and critical study of the bible by protestants such as David Strauss or ex-catholics like Ernest Renan. Much like religious fundamentalists today, they believed that this kind of study could only lead to scepticism and loss of faith. And of course in the case of Strauss, Renan, and many of their nineteenth-century readers, these fears had been shown to be not without foundation.

In contrast, towards the end of the nineteenth century, most of the mainstream protestant churches in Germany, Great Britain and the United States found a way of coping with a critical reading of the bible and of other early christian texts. Most protestant scholars now agreed that Moses did not write the Pentateuch, that the different gospel accounts could not be easily reconciled and that the early church was less united in its doctrine than had been assumed; mainstream protestant churches reluctantly began to accept these historical facts. Theologically, the acknowledgement of the findings of historical criticism entailed a new view of christianity and especially of the role of Jesus. By treating the bible as a book written in a specific period of history by human authors and for a specific audience, Jesus had been turned from a God into a man who had tried to build an essentially ethical kingdom of God, but who had resolved to sacrifice himself when his followers began to desert him:

'Coming as it did when moral optimism was a keynote of Western society and culture,' this assumption of theology into morality, typified by the teachings of Albert Ritschl, 'appealed to man's conviction that he could save himself by sanctifying himself.' Christianity had become an ethical religion, and Jesus the archetype of the enlightened man. (Schweitzer quoted in Ratté 1967: 71)

This shift can also be observed in the evolution of the classic Lives of Christ that had been such bestsellers in Victorian Britain from the publication of F.W. Farrar's *Life* in 1875 until the end of the century. Daniel Pals has explored these Victorian Lives and he finds that in Britain it was only at the end of the nineteenth century that the pious accounts were beginning to be replaced by more liberal versions in which the findings of the higher criticism were finally acknowledged. In this evolution the liberal protestants had been anticipated by rationalists such as Renan and the German critics, but also by a small group of English rationalists such as Edward Clodd, whose works Joyce still read in the 1920s and 1930s. In 1880 Clodd published a rationalist *Jesus of Nazareth*, which is characterized by what Pals calls the familiar formula that would become standard by the beginning of the new century: 'the moralist-teacher-humanitarian Jesus, opponent of the fossilized religious establishment of his day' (1982: 111).

The Church of England had ordered a revision of the biblical text and of the King James translation in accordance with the findings of biblical criticism, which resulted in the Revised Version of the bible that began to be published in 1881. And it was the kind of moral and liberal interpretation of christianity represented by such German bible scholars as the great Adolf von Harnack that had become central in protestantism by the end of the nineteenth century and that as a loyal catholic the modernist scholar Alfred Loisy was trying to counter.

Providentissimus Deus is often interpreted as a sign that the liberal Leo XIII was finally giving catholic scholars a chance to engage in the serious study of the bible, if only to answer their protestant critics. But if we read the text, we can only conclude that these scholars were only granted the right to study the bible on condition that they focused on the Vulgate, the Latin translation that the Council of Trente had chosen as the only version of the bible that catholics were allowed to use. The problem was not only that this was obviously a translation of the Hebrew and Greek, but also that both protestant and catholic critics knew that it had at best a tenuous relation with the original texts of the Old and New Testament: no serious criticism of the bible was possible without recourse to the originals.[2]

In their newly tolerated study of the bible, catholic scholars were also expected to accept all the anti-modernist and anti-rationalist premises that had guided the papacy in the previous decades and that effectively made the church of

Rome side with conservative protestants such as the English Dean Burgon who continued to defend the fundamental inerrancy of scripture against more liberal protestants willing to accept some of the findings of the Higher Criticism. Leo XIII also upheld biblical inerrancy, not just regarding the purely religious statements, as the bible critics had hoped and as cardinal Newman had cautiously suggested in 1884, but for the bible's every word. The real author of the sacred texts was the Holy Ghost:

> It follows that those who maintain that an error is possible in any genuine passage of the sacred writings, either pervert the Catholic notion of inspiration, or make God the author of such error. And so emphatically were all the Fathers and Doctors agreed that the divine writings, as left by the hagiographers, are free from all error, that they labored earnestly, with no less skill than reverence, to reconcile with each other those numerous passages which seem at variance – the very passages which in great measure have been taken up by the 'higher criticism;' for they were unanimous in laying it down, that those writings, in their entirety and in all their parts were equally from the afflatus of Almighty God, and that God, speaking by the sacred writers, could not set down anything but what was true. (Papal Encyclicals Online)

Providentissimus Deus suffered the fate of most encyclicals in the last two centuries: it was and continues to be interpreted in totally opposite ways, as both supporting and prohibiting the serious study of the bible. Although the pope officially seemed to allow and even support the study of the sacred scriptures, in effect he made it impossible to do so in any other than a carefully circumscribed apologetic manner. It is no surprise that at the time many catholic bible specialists interpreted the encyclical as an attack on catholic bible critics whom the hierarchy was beginning to brand as 'modernists.' In 1902 a Biblical Commission was set up in Rome with the aim, as the *Catholic Encyclopedia* puts it, 'to secure the observance of the prescriptions contained in the Encyclical "Providentissimus Deus" for the proper interpretation and defence of Sacred Scripture' ('Biblical Commission'). A few years earlier the pope had strongly condemned what he called 'Americanism' and what we would now call the acceptance of human rights: freedom of religion, freedom of speech, liberal democracy, the separation of church and state, public schools.

In this particular debate it seems history is to blame. What the dreaded modernists did have in common was, apart from the fact that all of them were in reality somewhat isolated intellectuals, a willingness to accept the usefulness of history in the realm of religion, which was at least one step beyond what the hierarchy in Rome was willing to tolerate. Adolf von Harnack had demonstrated historically that the catholic church had changed the original biblical doctrines. In his 1902 reply *L'Évangile et l'Église* Loisy showed how the church, guided by the Holy Ghost, had done nothing else than *develop* the truth that was already contained in the gospel. This seems to be simply a statement of fact and it must have been especially clear for catholics in the late nineteenth century, when such doctrines as papal infallibility and the Immaculate Conception had only recently been turned into dogma. In fact the idea that doctrine could have a history had been most forcefully expressed by cardinal Newman in his *Essay on the Development of Christian Doctrine*. Loisy took an additional step in applying this insight to the gospel by placing Jesus and his message in history, but, in doing so ever more sceptically, he came to the same conclusion as his protestant colleagues: there is very little about the life and teachings of Jesus of Nazareth that we can really be certain of.

Another modernist scholar was George Tyrrell, a Dublin protestant who had converted to catholicism and joined the Jesuits. A strong internal religious life led him to attempt the historicization of catholic dogma that he had begun to see as the necessarily incomplete rationalization of the essence of christianity, an essence that one needed to keep in touch with the ever changing reality of the world. In 1906, when he published these thoughts, Tyrrell was expelled from the Society of Jesus and suspended from the priesthood. Tyrrell hoped that he could remain in the church while writing his defence under the title *Through Scylla and Charybdis*.

Around the same time an Italian novelist was also caught up in the debate about modernism: in 1905 Antonio Fogazzaro's novel *Il Santo* was placed on the index of forbidden books. The author was an Italian senator who accepted the theory of evolution and the higher criticism of the bible, in addition to believing that the church, like any other human institution, had a long history of adapting to the times and that it would continue to do so. In fact by this time his attitude did not differ from that of most anglicans or other moderate protestants, but it meant, in effect, that he advocated a reform of catholicism along modernist lines.

Joyce knew Fogazzaro as a writer: still in Dublin he had read the author's earlier novel *Il piccolo mondo antico* in 1901 and he may have first encountered the Italian author's name as one of the main catholic antagonists of the decadent and naturalist writer Gabriele d'Annunzio. William Roscoe Thayer, author of an introduction to the 1906 English translation of *Il Santo*, writes that the novel's hero is 'a mingling of St. Francis and Dr. Döllinger, a man of to-day in intelligence, a medieval in faith' (Fogazzaro 1906: xiii–xiv). The novel itself tells the story of a modern saint (a rationalist mystic) who tries in vain to bring back a simple form of active christian faith and who even pleads with the pope himself to heal the four wounds of the church: the spirit of falsehood, of clerical domination, of avarice and of immobility. Piero Maironi has had a religious experience and as a lay brother he devotes his life to God and to helping the poor.

In the introduction to the translation Thayer emphasizes that the novel has been adopted by the Christian Democrats in Italy, who 'yearn to put into practice the concrete exhortations of the Evangelists' (Fogazzaro 1906: xx) and who thus get involved in what Thayer calls 'slumming,' in an effort to improve the

material and moral condition of the poor, not by charity, but by better
legislation. Because the Vatican had forbidden catholics to participate in the
Italian elections, the road to legislative reform was unavailable, until finally
in 1905 the new pope Pius X silently gave up his resistance to the democratic
process. The same pope's condemnation of the novel should be seen in the
light of the anti-modernist struggle: Fogazzaro's novel is a severe but ultimately
loyal critique of the church that must have been intolerable to the hierarchy
precisely because it came from within catholicism.

There seems to have been some confusion about the exact relationship of the
novelist to the church. The *Catholic Encyclopedia* article on 'Italian literature'
concludes on a positive reference to his work, after summarily dismissing his
great literary rival, the decadent Gabriele d'Annunzio: 'Antonio Fogazzaro
(born 1842), a Catholic and an idealist, whose romances tower above the rest of
modern Italian fiction, and of which the keynote is found in the author's conviction that the one mission of art is to strengthen the Divine element in man.'
This article was probably finished before the author's novel was put on the
index, because it is clear elsewhere that the church did consider Fogazzaro
as a dangerous modernist: his name appears in the *Encyclopedia*'s article on
'Modernism' which quotes *Il Santo* as one of the 'modernist sources.'

A few months before his 1907 encyclical *Pascendi Gregis*, Pius X published
a decree against modernism, which in fact constituted a new *Syllabus errorum*,
listing in all 65 errors, with a strong emphasis on the study of the bible and on
the nature of dogma. Whereas the decree was simply a list of erroneous ideas
(most of them later accepted by the church), the encyclical seemed to define a
coherent set of beliefs that were called modernist and that were based on the
liberal ideas introduced in Europe and America during the previous century:
democracy, freedom of conscience and of expression, the central role of history
and science. The language of Pius X was very strong, indicating that the pontiff
was aware that the greatest danger to the church was coming from within: the
modernist position was called a 'delirium,' an 'insanity' and a 'monstrosity'
(quoted in Hales 1960: 188). As a defence against these aberrations the pope
recommended the study of scholastic philosophy (and of Thomas Aquinas in
particular) and he suggested a complete control over all seminaries, bishops
and priests, the censorship of all catholic writings and the setting up of secret
vigilance committees to collect evidence of modernist leanings among clergy
and laymen. As a result the attacks on historical scholarship increased: studies
on the bible by prominent modernists were put on the index of forbidden
works. Two of the most visible victims of what the church historian Alec Vidler
called 'an ecclesiastical reign of terror' (quoted in Smith 1967: 231) were Loisy
and Tyrrell. Both were excommunicated and as late as 1930 Rome also excommunicated Joseph Turmel, a French priest who had published rationalist critiques of the church under 14 different pseudonyms: we know that Joyce read
at least 1 of these books. Tyrrell died in England in circumstances fictionalized
by Shane Leslie in his novel *The Anglo-Catholic*: Rome refused to allow a catholic

burial and the local bishop even punished a priest who had made the sign of the cross at the funeral.

As part of the reaction against compromised catholic biblical studies, the Jesuits opened the Pontifical Bible Institute in direct competition with the existing Biblical School which was considered too liberal. It was not until the 1943 encyclical *Divino Afflante Spiritu* that catholic historical–critical scholarship on the bible was finally accepted (though without much enthusiasm). It is difficult to believe that Joyce remained unaware of biblical criticism and of these liberal critiques within the church: the modernist debate was raging while he was a student at University College and when he first resided in Pola and Trieste. He was sufficiently aware of bible study to know (or to care) that J.S. Bach had mistakenly added part of a verse from the gospel of Saint Matthew to the libretto of his Saint John Passion. We will see in the next chapters that Joyce's interest in biblical scholarship can be documented and that it had an impact on his writing as well. Joyce was well aware of the fact that the catholic church of his day had problems and most of his sources on the study of the bible or of early christian history were either liberal protestant or militant atheist.

The Church in Ireland

In order to understand the role of the Irish church in Joyce's life, we must not only look at the political situation at the turn of the century, but also try to establish what kind of church it was that James Joyce and Stephen Dedalus rebelled against. In order to see clearly the particular form the Irish catholic church had taken at the end of the nineteenth century, it is essential to know that its peculiar nature does not only derive from the now traditional equation of being Irish with being catholic. Of course Joyce's attitudes to the catholic church should be seen first and foremost in the context of the history of the Irish church that he knew and that history is bound up with the political Irish struggle. Like most intellectual young Irishmen of his generation, Joyce was aware of the anticlerical criticism from within the nationalist movement. Especially in the generation of his father John Stanislaus Joyce, there had been great disappointment with the role of the church in the struggle for home rule. This political situation, in no way peculiar to Ireland, was fairly common in those European countries where disenfranchised groups of catholics rebelled against non-catholic states. Ironically they often did so in name of the same civil liberties that the catholic hierarchy officially condemned in the rest of the world. As the French royalist Louis Veuillot had formulated this paradox: 'When I am the weaker, I ask you for my freedom, because that is your principle; but when I am the stronger, I take away your freedom, because that is my principle.'

The same irony was present in the movement for catholic emancipation under Daniel O'Connell. Calls for an end to the discrimination of catholics in England and Ireland began immediately after the Vatican had finally accepted the legitimacy of the Hanoverian dynasty in 1766 and it became a central issue in the debate over the Act of Union. But it was only in the context of the liberal democracy that had developed in the meantime, that the electoral success of O'Connell's 'Catholic Association' in 1828 and 1829 (and the support of the popular archbishop of Tuam) forced the British government to introduce the Catholic Relief Act of 1829. In the following years and under continuing pressure of catholic politicians, the remaining forms of discrimination were removed. As a result the political influence of the catholic bishops in Ireland also increased. In an impressively detailed account of the political role of the hierarchy in the Irish struggle for independence, the American historian Emmet Larkin has shown that to a large extent the major battles were fought not only in Ireland or in London, but also in Rome where the Irish hierarchy was facing British diplomats and in some cases even English bishops.

At the same time the catholic church in Ireland was going through one of its most drastic transformations. Larkin has demonstrated that around the middle of the nineteenth century the devotional practices that would characterize the Irish church for the next century, were not a continuation of centuries of Irish catholic life, but an entirely new development that was designed to channel and eradicate older and specifically Irish devotions, precisely those semi-pagan devotions that somewhat later Celtic twilighters like W.B. Yeats would unsuccessfully try to connect with (Larkin 1972). In his own detailed study of Irish catholic practice in South-West Donegal, Lawrence J. Taylor (1997) has shown that already under Cardinal Cullen (1803–1878), the Irish church had begun to reform itself into an ultramontane Roman church with the introduction of unprecedented practices such as the rosary and devotions to the Sacred Heart and the Immaculate Conception. Following similar developments in Italy and France this changed the new devotional practices created what Atkin and Tallett call 'the commodification of Catholicism' in the nineteenth century (2003: 186).

But the main battlefield was political. Bishop John MacHale of Tuam was particularly adroit at playing Rome: on the one hand he claimed that those of his colleagues who resented his nationalist efforts were Gallicans who would rather support the protestant British, whereas he and his nationalist supporters were ultramontanists loyal to Rome, but on the other hand the genuinely ultramontane Cardinal Cullen would discover soon enough that MacHale chose to be a peculiar kind of ultramontane, the kind that on occasion refused to obey either the pope or his archbishop.

With the death of the conservative cardinal Cullen in 1878, a new phase in the relationship between the catholic hierarchy and the Irish movement for home rule began. Emmet Larkin has described the process in a series of detailed studies of the relevant correspondence between all the different parties: the government in London, the nationalists in Ireland and the hierarchy in Ireland, England and Rome. After the cardinal's death, a new generation of Irish bishops and archbishops began a slow process of rapprochement with the Irish nationalist party that was led by the protestant Charles Stewart Parnell. By October 1884 these contacts had developed into what Larkin calls an 'informal concordat' between the bishops and Parnell's Parliamentary Party. The bishops were given the initiative and control over all educational issues, in return for the acknowledgement that Parnell's party was 'the bona fide medium for decisions on an acceptable solution to the land and Home Rule questions.' In tandem with this agreement at home, Parnell in London created an alliance between his party and Gladstone's Liberals. The result for Ireland, Larkin writes, 'was fundamental to making the Parnellite de facto state as legal as it was real' (Larkin 1979: xvii).

When the Conservatives succeeded in government after Gladstone's failure to pass the Home Rule bill in 1886, the Prime Minister Lord Salisbury and his chief secretary for Ireland (and nephew) Arthur Balfour did everything in their power to attack the alliance. The target of most of their efforts was the so-called Plan of Campaign that had been devised to deal with the issue of high rents by John Dillon and William O'Brien, two members of Parnell's party. Tenants were told not to negotiate with their landlords on their own but to combine their efforts and to use boycotting as a weapon. Shortly after the launching of the Plan in October 1886, the leader of the Irish bishops, William J. Walsh, publicly declared that this strategy was morally acceptable. The British government disagreed and it began to apply a strict Coercion Act. Lord Salisbury then decided to take the issue to Rome, where he was greatly helped by the fact that Pope Leo XIII, for internal Italian political reasons, desperately needed an official embassy in London and recognition from the British government of the papacy as a temporal power. With the aid of the most important English catholic peer and a conservative Irish catholic landlord, the British government managed to convince the pope to send Monsignor Ignatius Persico to find out what was going on in Ireland and to report directly to Cardinal Rampolla, the pope's secretary of state. Persico found that both the Plan of Campaign and the tactic of boycotting were evil and in April 1888 the pope officially condemned both. The bishops, in an unprecedented letter that was signed by 28 of a total of 30 Irish bishops, replied to the pope that since they knew more about the local situation, they were going to ignore his Decree. If they did not, it would mean the loss in the catholic faith for millions of Irishmen at home and abroad. As Larkin puts it: 'By refusing to enforce the Roman Decree, the Bishops, in effect, had chosen allegiance to the Clerical-Nationalist alliance rather than to Rome' (1979: xx). The result in any case was that despite the disobedience of the Irish hierarchy, Rome in the end decided not to enforce its own Decree.

This was not the last of the British government's attempts to drive a wedge between the bishops and the Parliamentary Party on the one hand and between that party and the British Liberals on the other. In secret talks with Rome, the government next tried to play a role in the election of Irish bishops (which until the end of the nineteenth century had been a general practice) and it even suggested that it might be willing to fund a catholic university in Ireland (the Irish catholics refused to attend non-catholic Trinity College), but arch-bishop Walsh did not take the bait. In the end it was Parnell's naming in the O'Shea divorce trial in 1889 that was the real, but only temporary problem for the alliance between the Irish catholic hierarchy and the nationalists.

Most astonishing in the quotations from the letters of government officials and of the Irish bishops that are presented by Larkin is how candid all partici-pants were in expressing their views. When archbishop Walsh heard from Rome that the hierarchy was not impressed by the Irish bishops' reactions to the prov-ocations of the Italian government, he wrote back that the Irish people had their own problems and did not care much about the pope's present *temporal* difficulties: 'It is perfectly plain to us all here that the [se difficulties] were origi-nally brought on by downright mismanagement. It is equally plain that by the exercise of the most ordinary tact, they could have put an end to long ago' (quoted in Larkin, 1979: 9). It is clear that the archbishop of Dublin was not afraid of telling his pontiff how to conduct his *temporal* business, despite the fact that at least two of the Irish bishops had not signed the joint letter about the Decree and that they regularly wrote to Rome complaining of his and some of his other colleagues' disobedience. In fact both archbishop Walsh and his equally nationalist colleague Croke, the archbishop of Cashel, showed them-selves quite as adept as the British politicians in using all the means at their disposal for getting what they wanted.

When in 1889 Rome suggested that the Irish bishops might write a joint pro-test against the scandalous decision of the Italian state to erect a statue of the freethought martyr Giordano Bruno in the Campo Dei Fiori in Rome, where Bruno had been 'terribly burned,' archbishop Croke drily replied:

> If there is anything to be written about Bruno, of whom nobody in Ireland ever heard a tittle until the Pope's letter was read for them in the Churches, the Primate is, I should think, the person who should initiate the matter, and have the Bishops collectively take it up. Such publications do not suit us here at all. Our people are in blissful ignorance of Continental depravity and mischief making, and the less said about fellows like the Apostate Bruno the better. (Larkin 1979: 80)

The next month Logue, the archbishop of Armagh, dryly wrote to Rome that it was 'far from prudent to familiarize our simple people with the character of Giordano Bruno or the doings of his followers' (81).

This may seem a mere detail in the correspondence between Rome and the Irish bishops, but anticlericalism was a constant threat to the delicate position of the bishops in the Nationalist–Clerical alliance. The lay politicians of the Irish Parliamentary Party had already made it clear that they did not appreciate what they saw as the interference of Rome in Irish politics by the censure of the Plan of Campaign and especially archbishop Walsh stressed in his letters to

Rome that the result of more papal inference would be the rise of the kind of anticlericalism that was prevalent all over the European continent. This was by no means a vain threat. The conservative bishop of Limerick Edward Thomas O'Dwyer told his clergy not to attend a Nationalist meeting where the Plan of Campaign was going to be discussed and as a result the bishop was attacked in the most vicious terms by John Dillon and William O'Brien. It took all Walsh's diplomacy to defuse this new problem for the alliance, but it had become clear that Irish loyalty to Rome was an asset that if necessary, the bishops could use against Rome.

The fall of Parnell was not quite, as Joyceans sometimes assume, as simple as it is made out to be in the Christmas scene in *A Portrait of the Artist as a Young Man*. The bishops initially needed Parnell just as much as he needed them, because both were weary of letting the Land War take over the entire movement. they saw it only as a means to an end. When Parnell's affair with Mrs O'Shea became known, it was first the alliance between Nationalists and Liberals that came under pressure: Gladstone made it clear that his party would no longer accept Parnell as leader of the Irish Party. Larkin quotes letters from Walsh in the early days of the affair in which it is clear that the archbishop is happy that in these circumstances he and the bishops can stand by and blame the British Liberal Party without having to declare for or against Parnell. The English cardinal Manning, on the other hand, in almost continuous contact with Walsh, pointed out to his Irish colleague that the Parnell affair offered a fine opportunity for taking the initiative in the alliance away from the lay politicians whom he felt had become too dominant. It was only when Gladstone openly declared his problems with the election of Parnell and when the Irish Parliamentary Party still elected him as their leader, that Walsh came under attack from some of his fellow bishops who felt that the initiative had been taken from them, so that the protestant Gladstone got the chance to teach the Irish bishops and archbishops christian morality. Via an intermediary the pope told the Irish bishops to condemn Parnell and this time they obeyed. When Walsh finally did speak out against Parnell, Manning wrote triumphantly to Rome that this represented 'the subordination of politics to faith and morality' (quoted in Larkin 1979: 226).

Parnell's refusal to accept defeat began the well-known struggle between the two factions of the Irish Parliamentary Party. Since Parnell's group had control of most of the party's funds and infrastructure, his opponents depended for their organization on the bishops and this ensured the bishops' power over the party in the next decades. The church's support for the anti-Parnellites was unequivocal: in 1892 bishop Nulty of Meath made the following observation:

No man can remain a Catholic as long as he elects to cling to Parnellism. The dying Parnellite himself will hardly dare to face the justice of his Maker till he has been prepared and anointed by us for the last awful struggle and the terrible judgment that will immediately follow it. (Miller 1973: 50)

As is well known, the battle between the parties became very ugly: in the country anticlerical attacks were common: priests were verbally and physically attacked in the street. The *Freeman's Journal*, which supported the Parnellites, reported clerical interference in the polling booths. Bishop Croke was now able to write to Rome about Parnell:

> The lower stratum of society in Ireland is almost entirely for him. Corner boys, blackguards of every hue, discontented labourers, lazy and drunken artisans, aspiring politicians, Fenians, and in a word, all the irreligious and anticlerical scoundrels in the country are at his back. (Larkin 1979: 249)

What the bishops had warned Rome about had in fact happened: Ireland now had its own European-style anticlerical underclass. With hindsight it was claimed that Parnell had always been anticlerical. Walsh wrote to cardinal Manning that in fact the crisis was a great opportunity for the church: 'For ten years [Parnell] has raised a spirit which would have ended as it has in France by shutting up religion in the Sacristy. Nothing but a great moral scandal could have deposed him: and even this had hardly done its work a day too soon' (Larkin 1979: 261).

These words were nothing if not prophetic: in the end the bishops won the battle, Parnell's party was crushed and the church had won. The Irish Nationalist members of parliament now knew the price of trying to go around the bishops: it was a mistake that for a very long time few politicians would be prepared to make. From now on the Irish catholic church would be actively involved in the running of the country on all issues that the bishops considered crucial (such as education and social affairs) and no mere politician could afford to challenge their authority. Given that Larkin also writes that 'the reality of British power in Ireland had been rendered marginal by 1890' and that this power would continue to decrease gradually until its final dissolution in 1921 (1979: 297), the result was that by the time that James Joyce went to Belvedere College, the Irish bishops had acquired a de facto political monopoly that was unique in Europe and that would last for almost a century.

The bishops did not even have to pay a price for their victory: the nationalist movement would continue to have an anticlerical fringe, but it would be limited to the larger cities such as Dublin and Cork and consist mostly of the politically inconsequential people that archbishop Croke had described. The advantage of the new position was worth the price of having some people in Dublin and Cork who knew who Giordano Bruno was. An additional bonus was certainly that the bishops had convinced Rome of their continued loyalty. James Joyce grew up with a father who was part of what Larkin at the end of his book calls the 'very sizable, hard-core, anti-clerical minority, which would continue to exist whether it could find adequate expression in Parliament or not' (1979: 288).

As a young man in Dublin, Joyce cannot have avoided seeing the enormous influence of the church on the politics of his day. The hierarchy of the church did not hesitate to demonstrate its power in the field of education, especially in its hostility to all non-sectarian organizations. In 1898 the Irish National Teachers' Organization (which represented both protestant and catholic teachers) wrote in a memorial to the National Board that a recent court case was 'only an illustration' of the power that local school boards had in dismissing teachers (quoted in Miller 1979: 33). This is what had happened to a Leixlip teacher of 25 years who had been summarily dismissed by a local curate. In court the teacher won three months' salary and £200 damages, but after a letter from the archbishop of Dublin, the union was forced to back down. But that was not enough:

> At its 1899 Annual Congress the Organisation solidly voted out the President (a Protestant) and the Vice-President and the proposer and seconder of the original memorial. The election changed the religious composition of the executive committee from five Protestants and eight Catholics to three Protestants and ten Catholics. (Miller 1973: 33)

This was still not enough: in two provinces catholic clerical managers refused to hire teachers who were members of the Organization. It is clear that the church felt that in the field of education it could not afford to relinquish the least bit of control over what it saw as purely its own business.

The Gaelic Athletic Association (GAA) and the Gaelic League, with their respective agendas of promoting Irish sports and the Irish language, were potentially an even greater threat to the church, despite the fact that the former was created to stop catholics from 'playing Protestant sports' (Atkin and Tallet 2003: 177). The GAA had been founded in 1884 with support of Parnell, Michael Davitt and of bishop Croke, who in a letter deplored the fact that Irishmen were importing from England, 'not only her manufactured goods . . . but . . . her fashions, her accents, her vicious literature, her music, her dances [. . .]' (quoted in Collins 2002: 113). Kevin Collins claims that this letter is echoed by the protestant Douglas Hyde when ten years later he founded the Gaelic League, an initiative that was initially non-sectarian and thus frowned upon by the church, in a context where any infringement on the local power of the parish priest was perceived as a threat. When one of the young members of the organization who had gone to the Aran islands to practise the language told islanders that they should walk out of the church if the priest preached in English, the latter's reply was clear: 'I would have banded the men of the island together and we would have got him into a boat & packed him off from the island' (Miller 1973: 35). Soon enough Hyde learned to work with the church, not against it. This is the situation described by Joyce in *Stephen Hero* and referred to more obliquely in some of his other works: young idealist priests taught the young male and female Irish intellectuals the Irish language, but with that language also an anti-British and at the same time anti-modernist ethic.

The Gaelic League was all too aware that although the younger clergy being trained in Maynooth were on their side, on the local level the older more conservative generation of priests could make their work impossible. Before new branches of the League were established, attempts were always made to get the approval of the local clergy. Archbishop Walsh became an early supporter and by 1899 it was clear, as Miller writes, that 'unlike the effete little language societies which had preceded it, the League was a force to be reckoned with in Irish society' (1973: 36). The other bishops followed Walsh's lead and in 1900 the hierarchy even approved the teaching of Irish in primary schools. But tensions were still possible on the local level, if over-enthusiastic Leaguers too eagerly put pressure to introduce Irish in the curriculum of schools (and thus on the local priests who controlled the schools). This could be avoided by having almost all the school managers in Irish districts (under pressure from the episcopate) sign an agreement that they would force the National Board to enable the introduction of bilingual curricula. But in the case of conflicting loyalties, the hierarchy always knew where its priorities were. In 1907 Irish was dropped as a compulsory course at Maynooth and when at a meeting Douglas Hyde read a strongly worded address condemning the decision written by Father Michael O'Hickey, the chair of Irish at Maynooth, the latter was dismissed.

Although the League was clever enough to tread softly in all controversial domains, by September 1900 a weekly *The Leader* had been established by D.P. Moran to fight under a catholic banner against what it called 'West Britonism' wherever it found it, mostly in the form of 'gutter literature' and the 'imported amusements' of the theatres and music halls (Miller 1973: 41). In the first years of the new century Moran's new militantly catholic weekly (in which he claimed that 'Irish Ireland is Catholic Ireland. Catholic Ireland is Irish Ireland') succeeded in alienating both protestants and secularists. In this way the Irish Ireland movement became a vocal partner in the close alliance between nationalists and the church.

Kevin Collins has described how in the second half of the nineteenth century the catholic hierarchy had been instrumental in establishing the equation of Irishness and catholicism that had first been formulated in the seventeenth century by clerical figures such as Geoffrey Keating and the Four Masters and that would have a crucial influence on the formation of the new Irish state in 1922. By the time James Joyce came of age, church and state in Ireland had become entwined and it was this particularly militant church that he would turn against, a church that had become considerably more powerful than it had been at mid-century.

Anticlericalism

Cardinal Cullen had been one of the most outspoken supporters of the Pope and at the end of Vatican Council I, he was the one given the task of formulating the dogma of papal infallibility, which the *Catholic Encyclopedia* calls the church's 'great article of faith.' In the half-century after the Famine and in the specific political situation we have just described, Ireland had indeed become 'priest-ridden': the number of priests, nuns and other religious rose from 5,000 to 14,000, while in the same period the number of inhabitants in Ireland dropped by a third (McCarthy 1908: 625). As Adrian Frazier points out in his biography of George Moore, these changes were clearly visible to that cosmopolitan writer when at the beginning of the century, after an absence of 15 years, he returned to Dublin. And it was the shock of seeing the changes, combined with his analysis of the detrimental role that the church was playing in the Irish cultural revival of which he wanted to be a part that led to the explicitly anticlerical stories in Moore's *The Untilled Field.*

These radical changes had also not gone unnoticed by critical catholics. In 1902 a provocatively titled book was published in which Michael J.F. McCarthy warned his fellow-catholics against the enormous increase in power of the Irish church, which he considered a disaster for the economic and political future of Ireland. Although *Priests and People in Ireland* was welcomed by protestants in Ireland and England, it would be a mistake not to read it also in the light of an anticlerical movement *within* catholicism, a movement that was closely allied to modernism. In fact, the book is an explicit plea for the separation of church and state, and it carries as its motto a statement from a speech in February 1902 in which the King of Italy announced such a separation of the temporal and the spiritual powers. In his introduction McCarthy explains that in the last decades of the nineteenth century, Ireland has seen the rise of a new power ('or rather, an old power in a new environment'). The catholic clergy now possesses 'an effective organisation in Ireland which outnumbers the services of the imperial and local governments combined' and it is claimed that they work single-mindedly for the consolidation and increase of that power (xii–xiii). While other catholic nations have achieved economic wealth and political independence, Ireland lags behind and the only reason for this state of affairs is the bad influence of what McCarthy calls 'priestcraft,' the all pervasive influence of the clergy on the lay population. The priestly power is based on simple economics. All over Ireland priests and bishops are made the beneficiaries of wills and they use the accumulated wealth, which could have been invested in the Irish economy, to build churches and new houses for the religious orders. At the same time the catholic charities seem to be unable to do anything about the extreme poverty and the open prostitution in the same 'Mecklenburgh street area' that is part of Archbishop Walsh's parish. McCarthy can only conclude that the opulence of the life of the priests and the clergy in the religious houses stands in stark contrast to the dereliction of the Dublin slums: the priests seem to be more interested in making money than in assisting the catholic poor.

McCarthy not only describes an enormous increase in clerical activity and influence, he also warns against a development that had almost become a reality in his own time and that would stay in place for almost a century: the practical establishment of the catholic church in Ireland, not yet 40 years after

Gladstone's disestablishment of the Church of Ireland in 1869. This was not so much a matter of politics as of culture and economics. By the beginning of the twentieth century, the Irish catholic clergy not only controlled education, health care and poor relief, they did this with lavish government subsidies, which were not administered by local authorities, but by catholic agencies that in their turn were controlled by the clergy. The trouble with the influence of the church was therefore not just the hold of powerful parish priests over their flock, but the monopoly acquired by an increasingly efficient organization that used government funds made available for the people of Ireland, for the upkeep of its own agencies over which lay catholics, let alone non-catholics, had no say at all.

The monopoly on education and health care also created a political power base that made it impossible for the Irish members of parliament to do any-thing that opposed or hindered the hierarchy's agenda. McCarthy's book describes Ireland as the sole exception to the process of secularization in Europe; he stresses that the poor Irish catholics sent an annual sum of £30,000 to Rome as the so-called Peter's Pence, while not a penny of those funds ever came back to Ireland. In the half-century after the Famine and in the specific political situation we have described, Joyce's Ireland had indeed become a 'priest-ridden country.'

McCarthy's book was published in a polarized atmosphere in which the hier-archy controlled most, but not all of the Irish press: the *Catholic Encyclopedia* article on the history of Ireland writes that the catholic church in Ireland does not have an official mouthpiece:

> There are, however, in most of the provincial towns weekly newspapers, often owned by Catholics, and always ready to voice Catholic opinion. In Cork and Belfast there are daily papers animated with the same spirit, and in Dublin the 'Freeman's Journal' and the 'Daily Independent.' In Dublin also is the 'Irish Catholic,' which is a powerful champion of Catholicity; and there is the 'Leader', not professedly Catholic, but with a vigorous and manly Catholic tone.

In the catholic press McCarthy's book could be ignored, precisely because it was sanctioned by the protestant press (it was also read with interest by British and American nativists) and it is only recently that the book has been taken seriously.[3]

Despite the fact that the European catholic church entered the twentieth century claiming to cling to the old traditions by attacking everybody within its ranks whom it suspected of holding 'modern' ideas, it is clear that in the last decades of the nineteenth century the church had been changed, changed utterly. Its philosophy and theology had become Thomistic and its structure much more centralized and hierarchical than it had ever been before. Accord-ing to the encyclical of 1879 the philosophy of Aquinas was adopted as an antidote against the modern spirit, because Saint Thomas 'still supplies an armoury of weapons which brings us certain victory in the conflict with false-hoods ever springing up in the course of years' (quoted in Atkin et al., 2003: 161).

Instead of slowly modernizing and adapting to the realities of an increasingly liberal and democratic age, as most of the protestant churches in Europe were in the process of doing, the pope had lost his temporal powers but in the field of church doctrine and discipline, he acquired all the trappings of an absolutist monarch. In terms of the church's own history, the fight against the modernists was based on a principled denial of history in general and of the church's own history in particular that helped to hide the awkward fact that in the nine-teenth century the Church of Rome had undergone a remarkable and radical make-over.

Of course the catholic church had transformed itself many times before and in fact the forcible introduction of Thomism as the new philosophy of the church was ironic because the philosophy of Thomas Aquinas had played a similar role in the unprecedented adoption of Aristotle's thinking in christian theology in the late Middle Ages. In his work Joyce shows a remarkable knowl-edge of the historical backgrounds to the history of the Church of Rome and thus to the many historical challenges to its claim to be One, Holy, Roman, Catholic and Apostolic.

McCarthy may have been a catholic himself, but he had been educated at Trinity College (where catholics were not allowed to study) and his book is clearly addressed to protestants and liberal catholics. This position was not uncommon. Owen Chadwick writes about the difficulty for liberals at the end of the nineteenth century in countries with a sizable catholic population: on the one hand liberals supported universal suffrage, but they also realized that in the prevailing circumstances, the clergy's hold on the poor would certainly ensure a landslide victory for the conservative catholic party (1975: 45). This is a paradox that democracy still has to deal with. W.E.H. Lecky, the Irish historian of the spirit of rationalism in Europe, believed that the power of the catholic church over its flock was so great that confronted with it, no nation could afford universal suffrage: 'When a large proportion of the electors submit to such dictation, that nation is very unfit for representative institutions' (quoted in Chadwick 1975: 45). In fact McCarthy's book *Priests and People* belonged to a not exclusively protestant tradition of 'rationalist' or liberal support for disestab-lishment that had Irish precursors in writers such as Lecky who belonged to one of the counter-traditions to catholicism that we will turn to in the next chapter.

Chapter 3

Heresy, Schisma and Dissent

Grecian mythology tells us of a marine deity, whose distinguishing characteristic was the faculty of assuming different shapes. Proteus was the very symbol of infidelity. Its history is but a history of changes.

Rev. Thomas Pearson

Many critics have addressed Joyce's interest in heretical and schismatic thought, but sometimes we forget that accounts of religious dissent are always told from the perspective of the orthodox church. As critical historians of the church have known at least since Edward Gibbon and as Joyce himself certainly knew, the history of the church, like all histories, should not be told from the perspective of the victorious party alone. We often evaluate and account for heresies and other challenges to orthodox thinking by silently assuming that the latter is a constant, as if orthodoxy miraculously manages to escape the forces of history. If we do this we accept, *a priori*, the church's unhistorical view of its own history, as if there really is an eternal doctrine that was given by Jesus to his disciples and that does not essentially differ from what Benedict XVI teaches today.

The reality is different. If like Joyce we take Arianism as the proto-typical christian heresy and we study its rise and fall, we can only come to the same conclusion as with any other so-called heresy. Detailed studies such as the four volumes of Jaroslav Pelikan's *The Christian Tradition* show that in every instance these conflicts start with at least two doctrines or interpretations fighting for supremacy. For reasons that have little to do with doctrine and more with ecclesiastical and/or real-world politics, at a certain point one of these competing ideas becomes the orthodoxy while the other, by necessity, turns into heresy. All who refuse to submit to the new orthodoxy become heretics, they are persecuted and, if necessary, burned.

But sometimes, especially early in the history of the church, conflicts between opposing views were not directly addressed. It was only the first christian emperor Constantine the Great who forced the bishops to decide between the two camps and this for reasons that had nothing to do with religion. The victim in this case was Arius, who was only narrowly defeated by his opponents, but whose influence continued for centuries after his death. Constantine clearly valued civil peace over doctrinal purity, because it seems that personally he did not even agree with the bishops' final decision. When at the end of his life Constantine decided to let himself be baptized, he received the sacrament from an Arian bishop.

Even after the adoption of christianity as the religion of the Roman Empire, there was no coherent doctrine and catholics had to wait for Saint Augustine to create a genuine catholic philosophy. In the early centuries the number of books accepted as part of the canon, their textual form and their order in the bible had not yet been decided. Despite the insistence of the Roman emperors and their successors on doctrinal unity, such concord was only achieved on rare occasions and then only for a limited time. In the early centuries of the medieval period, after the adoption of the Roman form of belief by the last Gothic rulers in Italy and Spain (most of the Goths had been Arians), a coherent set of doctrines may have seemed to exist in the European church, but that was only because there was so little contact between the local centres that for most of the time it was not even possible to find out whether one's ideas were heretical or not.

Thus the most serious division of the christian churches was the division between the western and the eastern churches. For centuries it was only in the eastern empire that a surviving political structure necessitated and enabled the maintenance of a single doctrine. And it was only during those moments when there was a strong political power in the west, such as during the reign of Charlemagne, that the doctrinal differences between the eastern and western churches became relevant. The slow decline in the relations between the church of Rome and Byzantium that according to some accounts culminated in the actions of the writer and patriarch Photius, is another example of the relativity of the term orthodoxy (apart from the irony that in this particular case it is the schismatic eastern church that catholics now call 'orthodox').

Like most of the doctrinal discussions, the long struggle in which Photius was involved, was a political fight that had little to do with theological doctrine. The Byzantine patriarch saw the difference of opinion with the western church as an opportunity to strengthen his position at home. And it should be stressed that in terms of history Photius was right and Rome was wrong. The creed or *symbolum*, the summary of catholic doctrine that Constantine had forced the Council of Nicea of the year 325 to formulate, ended with the statement that the faithful were also expected to believe 'in the Holy Ghost.' Because of continuing controversy about the precise definition of the Trinity, these words were expanded at the Council of Constantinople in 381:

And in the Holy Ghost, the Lord and Giver of life, who proceeds from the Father, who together with the Father and the Son is to be adored and glorified, who spoke by the Prophets. And one holy, catholic, and apostolic Church. We confess one baptism for the remission of sins. And we look for the resurrection of the dead and the life of the world to come.[1]

To the Latin version of the first sentence, in the middle of the fifth century, the Spanish church (Spain was ruled at the time by Arian Goths) added the phrase 'filioque' or 'and the son' to turn it into: 'And in the Holy Ghost, the Lord and Giver of life, who proceedeth from the Father *and the Son*.' Although the addition was rejected by several councils and even formally condemned by Leo III in 809 (against Charlemagne), it became generally accepted in the next centuries. The *Catholic Encyclopedia* coyly describes what happened next:

> While outside the Church doubt as to the double Procession of the Holy Ghost grew into open denial, inside the Church the doctrine of the Filioque was declared to be a dogma of faith in the Fourth Lateran Council (1215), the Second Council of Lyons (1274), and the Council of Florence (1438–1445). Thus the Church proposed in a clear and authoritative form the teaching of Sacred Scripture and tradition on the Procession of the Third Person of the Holy Trinity (under 'Filioque').

Photius saw this particular addition as proof that the church in Rome had embraced heresy and most scholars agree that his protest marked an important break in the church. But this certainly does not mean, as the *Catholic Encyclopedia* writes in the same article, that Photius was 'throwing off all dependence on Rome.'

The idea of a schism between East and West had been prepared long before Photius and it would become effective long after him, but this does not mean that there was such a thing as the kind of centralized church hierarchy that we have today. In reality, until the nineteenth century, the original form of doctrinal authority in the church was the council, not the pope. Local ecclesiastical power was in the hands of originally three and later five patriarchs, the heads of the churches of Jerusalem, Rome, Constantinople, Antioch and Alexandria. Matters of doctrine involving the whole church could only be decided by general councils, not by a patriarch or a pope. There were practical problems too: as a result of the extreme difficulty of travel and of communication, strong central leadership was a practical impossibility.

It is no coincidence that the rise of cities and the economical boom during what we now call the 'high middle ages' created a new atmosphere in which the church began to make claims for temporal power. This latter story has been told recently by Richard E. Rubenstein in *Aristotle's Children* where he shows that economic changes led to an intellectual revolution that in its turn and with the help of the rediscovery of the major writings of Aristotle gave rise to a rationalist grounding of christian doctrines under the great scholastic philosophers Peter Abelard, William of Occam and Thomas Aquinas.

During the same period we also see the rise of what R.I. Moore (1977) calls 'dissent,' unorthodox groups challenging the monopoly of the church as the sole purveyor of spiritual goods. It is important to stress that doctrine and beliefs were generally less important in these movements than we tend to think; in most cases the difference between heretics and infidels was one of practice and not of beliefs. Differences of doctrine were usually no more than an excuse for persecuting dissidents. From the high middle ages onwards, the church was constantly challenged by dissident groups, all considered as threats to its monopoly. Some of these radical movements, such as the beguines or the Franciscans, turned out to be flexible enough to be accommodated within the church, others were less lucky.

We will see in the chapters to come how Joyce remained fascinated by all kinds of religious dissent, just as in his reading about Irish or other forms of historical catholicism he would always focus on its more extravagant practices and ideas. In his work he would identify his autobiographical characters with schismatics such as Photius, with heretics of all kinds, such as Sabellus and Arius, and with movements that threatened the hegemony of the church such as the Franciscan movement and its apocalyptic teachings as in Joachim of Abbas. Although, as Stephen says in *A Portrait of the Artist as a Young Man*, converting to protestantism was never an option, it is clear that Joyce also read quite a bit in the blatantly anti-catholic literature of militant and nativist protestant groups.

Militant Protestantism

As we will see in the following chapters, Joyce seems to have had a lifelong interest in the chequered history of the catholic church, especially in those aspects of history that contradicted the way the church in the early part of the twentieth century insisted on seeing itself. A second major source of criticism of the catholic church predictably came from protestants, more specifically in the form of the wave of anti-catholic propaganda that started in the mid-nineteenth century and that must have been particularly widely available in Dublin. Needless to say, the propaganda war between catholics and their diverse protestant opponents had its own history and it effectively started on 31 October 1517 when Martin Luther nailed his 95 theses to the door of the church of Wittenberg Castle. Luther himself expressed his surprise at how the printing press enabled the rapid spread of his revolutionary ideas throughout Europe and the success of the new invention in its turn may well have been partly as a result of the explosive need for the transmission of partisan religious pamphlets and books during the early years of reformation and counter-reformation.

From the early sixteenth century onwards, the Church of Rome would remain engaged in a propaganda war with various protestant groups that only ended at the time of the Vatican Council II when under pope John XXIII the church adopted a somewhat more relaxed attitude towards other christianities, by at least accepting the possibility that some pockets of truth could be found outside the limits of its own doctrine. It is thus only in the 1960s that the church of

Rome officially began to communicate, and to some extent even to cooperate, with other christian churches. Ironically it is this openness that continues to be the main reason for conservative catholics to reject the Vatican Council II.

During the early period of the reformation in the sixteenth and seventeenth centuries the propaganda war between catholics and protestants was fought on two fronts: there were scholarly debates between theologians of the two main groups of believers, but more importantly there was also a seemingly endless series of pamphlets for a general public. The discussion among theologians was fierce and the major theologians on both sides were talented polemicists. But this theological combat was not just rhetorical: intrinsically the quality of the religious debate benefited from this form of free market competition, something that is especially clear in the case of the scholarly study of the bible. Paradoxically, some of the writers who first anticipated the findings of the textual bible scholars of the nineteenth century were catholics. Catholic polemicists quickly realized that it was important to a defence of the catholic doctrine to demonstrate that the bible alone was not reliable as a source for doctrine (as protestants thought), which could therefore only be guaranteed by the traditions of the catholic church.

Protestant apologetic writings were translated into a more easily readable form, to be distributed among the general public, presumably both to educate and strengthen the faith of the believers and to attempt to convert catholics and dissidents. In England, this had been the province of the Society for the Propagation of Christian Knowledge (SPCK) of the Church of England, established in 1699.

When by the middle of the nineteenth century literacy levels among the British population began to rise and under the pressure of the political emancipation of catholicism and Irish immigration the efforts of the protestant propaganda were increasing, cardinal Newman wrote about the need for a catholic laity that was no longer docile and uneducated. In 1884 another convert to catholicism, James Britten, convinced the later cardinal Herbert Vaughan to counter the stream of protestant propaganda by issuing a series of pamphlets under the name of the Catholic Truth Society (CTS), offering reliable guidance to readers who were catholic, as well as reliable information about catholic doctrine to those who were not, despite the fact that as late as 1890 a catholic publisher complained that catholics did not read books (quoted in Pals 1982: 123). And increasingly this became true of protestants as well, or at least they stopped reading religious books: while in 1859 more than 30 per cent of all books printed were religious, by the end of the century that figure had dropped to less than 10 per cent (Pals 1982: 189).

While both the SPCK and the CTS used their publications to put their respective views before a wider audience, their main purpose was to argue against their religious opponents. Readers who had finished their copies were invited to leave the cheap pamphlets in the bus, tram or train so that their beneficent influence could be passed on to other readers. The religious competitors were the main targets; it was only in the 1930s that the CTS began to consider communists as serious opponents. In the last two decades of his life, Joyce made active use of the CTS and SPCK pamphlets, but he seems to have been most interested in a third group of publications: mass market books and pamphlets distributed by the smaller and usually more extreme forms of evangelical protestantism.

These had a history that goes back to the beginning of the reformation when anabaptists and all sorts of other radical groups tried to bring their case before the public in the form of an underground literature that had its own channels of distribution. In the nineteenth century the more radical protestant groups slowly acquired the evangelical and sometimes apocalyptic form that they still have today, with access to the mass media of the time and an influence that swept through the United States in the early part of the nineteenth century in a wave of spiritual enthusiasm that is called the Second Great Awakening. This popular religious movement not only led to the christian forms of evangelical christianity but it also saw the rise of mormonism and of other forms of non-christian spirituality and apocalypticism. On the basis of his documented reading we can see that Joyce had periods in which he seems to have been interested in the Church of Jesus Christ of Latter-Day Saints and its colourful leaders, and in other forms of sometimes wildly heterodox belief, such as the Church of Zion of John Alexander Dowie.

We can also document Joyce's interest in publications of another kind of religious group that was to some extent an heir to the more extreme forms of protestantism in England and America but that in addition had an explicitly political agenda. Because of the economic conditions in most of Europe in the middle of the nineteenth century, the industrial and prosperous England and America saw an influx of immigrants from predominantly catholic countries. In England these immigrants were mostly Irishmen fleeing the conditions in Ireland for work in the new industrial centres, while at the same time the success of movements in Ireland such as those of Daniel O'Connell necessitated a change in the legislation against catholics, with the Catholic Emancipation Act of 1829 as a first result. Initially catholics were given the same rights as so-called dissenters or nonconformists, protestant groups that refused to accept one or more of the central tenets of the Church of England or the established churches in Scotland and Ireland. It was mostly from within the ranks of these radical groups that a counteroffensive was launched against what was perceived as the threat of a catholic takeover in both religion and in politics. Combined with the Fenian agitation in the United Kingdom, this led to occasional street violence and caricatures of the primitive Irish.

Around the same time a similar movement arose in the United States, where anti-catholicism had deep roots in both the rhetoric of early protestantism and in the writings of the Glorious Revolution that had defended the protestant kingdom against popish plots. In 1835 Samuel F.B. Morse and Lyman Beecher formulated the theory that the wave of mostly catholic immigrants represented an attempt by the Vatican to establish its dominion in the United States. This theory of a 'papal conspiracy' led to a flood of nativist publications that either elaborated on this threat to American values or that attacked the Church of Rome for perceived offences against the values of the republic. Predictably some of these publications took the form of sensationalist pamphlets that described the political manoeuvring of the Jesuits and the debauches of priests, nuns and monks. One of the most influential writers in this vein was the abbé Chiniquy whose book *Why I Left the Church of Rome* is mentioned in *Ulysses*, when Bloom notices a copy in the reverend Thomas Collennan's bookstore (9.1070–1).

Charles Paschal Télesphore Chiniquy (1809–1899) was a Quebecois priest who was very active in the catholic temperance movement, a popular and charismatic speaker who was also useful in forcefully attacking protestants who were trying to convert catholic French Canadians. But he had problems with authority and with celibacy, so that in 1851 his bishop was happy to see him move to Illinois, where he ran a successful mission among French-Canadian immigrants. In 1856 he got into trouble when he asked for more Canadian priests, because he did not trust the Irish priests in the American church. After much scheming on both sides, the Irish bishop in Chicago first suspended and then excommunicated him. Chiniquy refused to budge and kept the loyalty of his parishioners, until in August 1858 when the excommunication was reconfirmed and he left the church, joining the presbyterian church in 1860, first in Illinois and then, after another quarrel, back in Canada. From 1873 he devoted most of his enormous energy to trying to convert French-Canadians to protestantism, sometimes making outrageous claims, as when he said that the Jesuits were responsible for the murder of Abraham Lincoln. He also organized spectacular and well-publicized performances: during one of these Chiniquy first consecrated wafers and then trampled them to demonstrate that they were indeed nothing but biscuits. His work was quite successful in French Canada and by the last decade of the century, especially after his memoirs had been translated into English, his influence reached further afield:

> In 1892 translations of the French version into nine languages were circulating. By 1898 it had reached 70 editions. All over the world bishops were seeking information from their colleagues in Quebec so that they could counter the influence of Chiniquy's memoirs.[2]

Chiniquy's most influential book was *The Priest, the Woman and the Confessional,* cited later in *Ulysses* by Virag (*U* 15.2548) along with *Sex Secrets of Monks and Maidens.* The latter tract has yet to be identified, but the juxtaposition seems appropriate: Chiniquy's bestseller denounces the practice of 'auricular confession,' which was one of the major themes in his anti-catholic campaign. Carefully combining condemnation of this vile practice with well documented but sensationally written case studies, Chiniquy shows how confession corrupts both women and priests. Women are forced to discuss sexual practices, which by themselves they would never know and they were enticed into this by a male who was not even a relative: like so many of his contemporaries, Chiniquy does not seem to consider women as independent agents. The Gothic style contributes to the lurid interest the book still manages to have: when in 1965 Scholes and Kain annotated *The Workshop of Dedalus*, they described a similar anti-catholic production *The Escaped Nun* (referred to in Epiphany 18) as a 'pornographic title' (1965: 28).[3] Books like these, which must have been widely available in partly protestant Dublin, were doubly forbidden for the young catholic readers that are described in the epiphany.

This genre of anti-catholic writing, which has recently been revived on the internet (most of Chiniquy's oeuvre is available on-line), was only the particularly virulent incarnation of the more general protestant polemic that marked the second half of the nineteenth century, both in England and in the United States. In England emigration and the general drift of the rural poor to the cities had created an underclass that was generally thought to be either catholic or irreligious. On the other hand the higher levels of literacy in the middle classes had created a very competitive market for religious tracts of all kinds. The emancipation of catholics in England and the tensions within the anglican church between High, Low and Broad churches (different in their attitude towards catholics) resulted in lively polemics between catholics and protestants. The most dramatic event in the relations between the two churches was the Oxford Movement, a group of High Church intellectuals who stressed the continuity with the Church of Rome by claiming that the catholic, orthodox and anglican churches were three branches of the one catholic (general) church. These ideas were published in tracts, which explain why the people involved are sometimes called 'Tractarians'. In Tract No. 90 John Henry Newman made the claim that the doctrines of the Church of Rome as defined at the Council of Trent, were compatible with the 39 Articles, the founding principles of the Church of England. In 1845 Newman took this logic to its ultimate conclusion by converting to catholicism, followed by many other High Church intellectuals over the rest of the century.

As the most prominent of these catholic converts, Newman remained a controversial figure in Victorian England, not only in the eyes of his fellow catholics (he was involved in a long feud with the much more conservative cardinal Manning, another convert), but even more as the bête noir of English protestants. Repeatedly Newman was attacked by protestant polemicists, most notoriously by Charles Kingsley in a controversy that is referred to in the discussion in *Stephen Hero* between Stephen and the President of the College, who calls him 'Poor Kingsley' (Scholes and Kain 1965: 79). In the second half of the nineteenth century Kingsley was not just one of the few protestant clergymen to accept Darwin's theory of evolution, he was also a champion of the anti-catholic movement within the anglican church and with D.F. Maurice a supporter of social action, which they themselves called 'christian socialism.' Both in his novels and in his historical writings he had a very negative view of the role of the church in history. His novel *Hypatia: Or, New Foes with an Old Face* tells the story of the fifth-century Alexandrian mathematician and philosopher, whose tragic death had become a symbol of the bigotry of the christians. As Maria Dzielska has shown in her study of the reception of the story of Hypatia, by the middle of the nineteenth century the figure of the female philosopher had become a common place of anti-catholic and anti-christian freethinking. Kingsley himself was considered a freethinker, he is one of the nineteenth-century figures discussed in a 1920 study by the feminist Janet E. Courtney (together with F.D. Maurice, Matthew Arnold, Charles Bradlaugh, T.H. Huxley, Leslie Stephen and Harriet Martineau).

At the other end of the spectrum, Kingsley's novel and its attack on fanaticism and asceticism earned its author a place in the Index of forbidden works of the Vatican, even with his popular children's book, *The Water Babies.* Perhaps wisely, the church of Rome does not seem to have distinguished much between the rationalist freethinkers and its older protestant enemies. In fact, radical protestants and freethinkers used very similar arguments against the catholic church and other established religions.

Freethought

After the history of dissent within the church and the protestant propaganda against the Church of Rome in the second half of the nineteenth century, the most powerful source of anti-catholic and anti-religious information for the post-catholic Joyce were the writings of the freethinkers. As we will document with biographical information in the next chapter, Joyce lost his faith while still very young, at least partly in a spirit of rebellion against his parents and his superiors, with some level of support from his equally sceptic brother Stanislaus. Despite the fact that James felt isolated among his fellow students, there seems to have been a small group of companions, among them at least Cosgrave and Gogarty, who indulged in blasphemy and with whom he could share his sceptic opinions.

In the Dublin social circles that he frequented, James Joyce was thus not quite as isolated as his fictional self-portraits would suggest. And neither was his rebellion as exceptional as it is made out to be. In fact both Dublin and the rest of Europe offered a young man numerous examples of people with similar dissenting and radical opinions. From the middle of the nineteenth century and all over Europe, young men of all classes consciously rejected established religion and sometimes, even religion itself. It is in this context that Joyce's work and opinions should be seen.

But before we can begin to discuss the intellectual climate that gave rise to this radical critique of religion, we must briefly discuss a question of terminology. What name do we have for people who are not religious? It is easy to refer to religious people or to describe their allegiance to a particular group or sect and we have already seen that these names are automatically capitalized by our spellchecker, but this is definitely not the case for words describing the non-religious or irreligious. The problem is visible in the way we have been describing these people: it seems to be impossible to find a word that is not at least implicitly negative: atheist, unbeliever and infidel. People who simply do not believe in a deity often object to the fact that all the words referring to their opinions imply something inherently negative, as if a perfectly natural belief in one or more gods is a virtue that is sadly not granted to some of us. This is certainly related to an old problem in religious and anti-religious debates regarding the burden of proof: is it up to the atheists to prove that there is no deity or do the believers have to demonstrate that he does exist (Dennett 2000)? The lack of religious belief (another negative expression) is an exceptional position: in most cultures religion seems to be the rule. Whatever word we use for them and their condition, atheists have always been a small minority and true atheism (the positive claim that there is no god) is a relatively late invention (or discovery, depending on your point of view).

This does not mean that the word itself is recent: in pagan Rome and Greece the word 'atheist' was first used to refer to the christians, because they were the ones who did not believe in the gods. It is was only when the Emperor Constantine initiated the project that would lead to the christianization of the Roman empire, that the word was adopted as an insult for almost anybody who objected to christianity. Most christian churches still list atheists, with heretics, apostates and schismatics, as their enemies. This is not the only reason why unbelievers (yet another negative expression) do not like the label: it implies that atheists are opposed to one or more divine beings. In reality they know that there are no gods. This constitutes a logical fallacy that christian and other apologists do not tire to point out. In fact the word simply means that a person is without a god, but this implies a kind of certainty that has led some unbelievers to prefer T.H. Huxley's term 'agnostic' which at least avoids the problem of denying the existence of something of which one claims not to have any knowledge. But agnosticism carries a connotation of doubt and this leaves the kind of opening that creationists or adherents of intelligent design make use of when they claim that Darwin has only produced 'a theory' that is not fundamentally different in nature from other theories. Many unbelievers, like the nineteenth century British freethinker Charles Bradlaugh, point out that agnosticism is nothing but 'a mere society form of Atheism' (quoted in Arnstein, 1965: 11; the capital is Bradlaugh's).

In the eighteenth and nineteenth centuries, deists and atheists were anticlerical, united in their opposition to the political impact of the churches in general and of the catholic church in particular. As an anticlerical movement, the free-thinkers and humanists opposed neither religious belief in itself nor the people who held these beliefs: instead they fought the established churches because these energetically opposed freedom of expression and freedom of religion, non-religious or neutral schools, civil liberties, and the separation of church and state. Politically freethought was an heir to the American revolution of 1776, to the French revolution of 1789 and to the European liberal revolutions of 1830 and 1848. By the end of the century and in its more radical forms, it would become an important item on the socialist and anarchist agenda. The established churches, and especially the Church of Rome, fought the atheists and secularists the whole way, but we can only conclude that they lost this particular war in most parts of the world. In the 1960s even the Church of Rome accepted the basic democratic principles that it had so long and so strongly opposed.

The most neutral label to describe the beliefs of a freethinker is probably that of secularism, the idea that religion and politics should not be mixed, that church and state ought to function entirely as separate entities. At least this is a philosophy or ideology in which the belief in god or gods plays no part: John Mill even wrote that to claim that the word secular means irreligious is equivalent to 'saying that all professions except that of the law are illegal' (quoted in Wilson 2000: 44). It seems, therefore, fair to say that in Europe at least, the vast majority of contemporary christians are secularists in that sense of the word. Other terms that have been used for varieties of this position include heretic, infidel, sceptic, disbeliever, misbeliever, unbeliever, agnostic, rationalist, atheist, sceptic, freethinker and doubter. No wonder that Daniel Dennett has attempted to introduce the more neutral or positive label 'bright' as an alternative.

History of freethought

In its heydays between 1870 and 1914 the ideologues and historians of freethought claimed a long tradition of unbelief that stretched back beyond christianity and judaism into prehistory. For the most part, the history of freethought has been written by the freethinkers themselves and it is not surprising that for polemical purposes the emerging doctrine had to be provided with solid historical roots. The most important of these were found in Greek philosophy and in the Enlightenment. Joyce might have read such early histories of rationalism, freethinking and atheism as the books by the Irish historians W.E.H. Lecky and J.B. Bury, the Englishman J.M. Robinson or the German Fritz Mauthner. All these writers begin their survey in prehistory and in their earliest chapters they concentrate on the critique of religion in Greek and Roman philosophy.

Greek philosophy began as a critique of mythology and thus of the gods; as a result most Greek philosophers were accused of atheism. Mauthner found Greek and Roman examples of explicit unbelief or at least criticism of religion in authors such as Xenophanes, Anaxagoras, Diagoras of Melos, Democritos, Socrates, Lucretius and Cicero (Mauthner 1920). This does not mean that the idea itself is relatively recent: the possibility of atheism may well be as old as religion itself and it is certainly already present in the Jewish bible, where the fourteenth psalm begins with the words 'The fool says in his heart, there is no god.' We already saw that the Greek word *atheist* was first used to refer to christians and later adopted as an insult for non-christians. This use of the word lasted until the Reformation when the Church of Rome no longer had a monopoly on belief: now both catholics and protestants accused each other of being atheists. Francis Bacon wrote: 'All that impugn a received religion or superstition are by the adverse part branded with the name of atheists' (quoted in Turner 1986: 26).

In the first chapter of his history of atheism in England, David Berman points out that in the eighteenth century there were serious doubts about the existence of genuine atheists: how could an intelligent man deny the existence of the deity? In a famous anecdote the extremely sceptical David Hume told the baron d'Holbach at a salon in Paris that he wondered whether atheists really existed: he himself had never met one. The baron replied: 'You cannot have been very lucky then, because for the first time in your life you see around this table fifteen of them' (Berman 1990: 101). But the baron and his friends were exceptions. In fact, most of the people who had been condemned and sometimes executed for the crime of atheism were actually theists or deists, as were the great majority of the critics of religion in the Enlightenment of the eighteenth century, and quite a few of the members of the freethought movements in the nineteenth. Theists and deists share with most religions a belief in a god who created the universe, but they deny the fact that the deity has ever revealed itself to mankind or that it actively interferes in the world. The deist god is not even a personal god but at most a philosophical principle, just like the Aristotelian prime mover or the god of Spinoza (and Einstein) who is identical with nature.

More positive terms for what it is that unbelievers believe in is materialism, a term that was popular in the last part of the nineteenth century, especially among political radicals such as socialists and anarchists, who saw it with Karl Marx and Friedrich Engels as turning Hegelian idealism on its head. But the word also had obvious negative connotations and some unbelievers therefore preferred the term monism, which was offered as an alternative to the traditional dualism of body and soul of the established and newer religions. The most neutral label for the beliefs of a freethinker is thus, as we have seen, secularism. In a recent book on what in Italian is called *laicità*, Geminello Preterossi has defined modern secularism. Secularists are:

> Those who – whether they are agnostics, atheists or believers – refuse to base politics, institutions and civil society on theological or faith-based foundations; those who use a public discourse that has an ethical and cultural horizon that is not 'absolute,' that is based on a plurality of arguments and on critical openness; all those who are not willing to give up the freedom and neutrality of the state for a religious belief (which does not mean hostility towards religion, just respect for the religious freedom of all). (2006: 3)

According to this definition, the real history of freethought begins in the eighteenth century, although some of the roots of the enlightenment can already be found in the reformation and to some extent even further back in scholastic philosophy. It was only when the intellectual monopoly of the Church of Rome was challenged, as happened in the thirteenth century, and later in the sixteenth century during the debates between reformation and counter-reformation scholars, that a true religious debate could develop. These religious differences were not only talked about but also acted upon, with grave and sometimes violent consequences, especially during the religious wars in the sixteenth and seventeenth centuries. In this period, most critiques of religion, such as those of Spinoza, began as a reaction against the horrors of the religious wars.

The polemics between protestants and catholics needed a common basis that was necessarily historical: protestants claimed that they differed from the church of Rome because they dared to go back to the original meaning of the foundational texts, whereas catholics appealed to the weight of tradition represented by the church fathers and the present hierarchy. In order to demonstrate the inadequacy of the bible as a basis for doctrine, it was strangely enough the catholic scholars who developed the most stringent historical criticism of the bible text. Protestant critics applied the same principles to the study of the texts by the church fathers and of the early church documents. By the nineteenth century both of these paths would lead to the same end. The historical reconstruction of the religion of Israel and of the thinking of Jesus Christ and his immediate circle of followers on the one hand and of the first three or four centuries of church history on the other hand would reveal a form of religion that was much more alien to contemporary concerns than either protestants or catholics were willing to accept. Some of this bible criticism remained within the churches, but especially by the middle of the nineteenth century, the historical basis of christianity was attacked and mocked by agnostics and atheists.

Freethinking had a history that would have been impossible without the relatively liberal climate in protestant nations such as England and Holland. Because at least for some periods in their history, these countries allowed the coexistence of different religious groups, they had to guarantee a certain degree of freedom of religion and of expression. It was this freedom that made freethinking possible and that eventually made even atheism acceptable, although it should be pointed out that the first forms of freedom of expression were limited: Spinoza's critical work on the bible was immediately censured in Holland and in 1697 the Scottish student Thomas Aikenhead was hanged for claiming that the bible was full of 'madness, nonsense and contradictions.'

These early radical critics of religion were exceptions, but by the late eighteenth century the rise of militant deism caused much concern in all christian churches. Philosophical deists or freethinkers were often accused of being atheists but in reality only few of them denied the existence of god. Most freethinkers argued strongly against the traditional christian god who transcended the laws of nature, who had been revealed in history and who actively interfered in the world. Deist freethinkers believed in a distant and non-interventionist god who had only created the world to leave it alone. A stance that is not dissimilar to my grandfather's when he was asked by a hospital official about his religious affiliations: 'Catholic, but without the miracles.'

Baruch Spinoza is generally considered to have been the first to formulate the modern rationalist and sceptical view of the bible with his *Tractatus Logico-Philosophicus*. In a book that is basically an extended argument for freedom of speech in an enlightened society, Spinoza studied the bible closely to come to the conclusion that it is impossible to base a politics or a philosophy on that book, a conclusion that was at least as relevant to the recent history of religious wars in the rest of Europe as to the concrete political situation in Holland. But it is not sure whether he can be seen as an atheist: Spinoza seems to have been a pantheist who believed in the spiritual reality of the totality of life.

The period between the publication of *Tractatus Logico-Philosophicus* and the French revolution was the heyday of philosophical freethinking: with few exceptions most of the major philosophers were deists who rejected revealed religion and who argued for different means of limiting the powers of the church and its influence on the state. Two entirely different traditions of freethinking took their cue from Spinoza. His most direct heirs were the representatives of what Jonathan Israel has called the 'radical enlightenment,' the left wing of the political and philosophical movement that formulated the basis of the democratic and secular political system that is in force in most of the world today. Initially this way of thinking was liberal protestant and it had its most important base in Holland and England with writers such as Hugo Grotius and Daniel Heinsius, Anthony Collins, John Toland, David Hume and John Locke. Even before Spinoza, Hugo Grotius had been disturbed by the bloodshed of the religious wars abroad and by the local Dutch unrest as a result of the intra-calvinist quarrels about predestination. He unsuccessfully attempted to find a common basis for a kind of christianity that would be acceptable to all parties. The increasing scepticism of Dutch critics towards the christian texts led the English king Charles II to joke that the philologist Isaac Vossius was willing to believe anything, as long as it was not in the bible.

Anthony Collins popularized the term freethinking in 1713 when he published *A Discourse of Freethinking*, a book that was so controversial that he was forced to leave the country for a while. By the middle of the eighteenth century the centre of this deist philosophy moved to catholic France with radical enlightenment writers as Diderot, d'Alembert, Voltaire, the baron d'Holbach and Rousseau. And by the end of the century Immanuel Kant brought all these ideas together in a synthesis that would guarantee that in the beginning of the twentieth century the catholic church still felt that the name 'Kant' stood for all the evils of modernism.[4]

Freedom of expression and freedom of religion were a central concern for enlightenment political theorists from Thomas Hobbes to Thomas Paine and negatively these ideas led to the anti-religious excesses of the French revolution that convinced conservative believers to think that the end times had arrived.

Positively they resulted in the liberal constitution of the United States (and, sooner or later, to those of most of the modern nation states). The American Constitution was a remarkable document: it explicitly placed the origin of political power not with god but with the people: 'We the people.' Just as some European states have recently tried to introduce the Christian God in the European constitution, the absence of the divinity in the American constitution was deplored from the very beginning and it still is, although typically present-day religious conservatives claim that what they want is to put God *back* into the constitution (Jacoby 2004: 105).

The other strand of Spinoza's influence in Germany and England became a topos in romanticism, with writers like Shelley and his early essay 'The Necessity of Atheism,' and the strong tradition of spinozism in German literature and philosophy that starts with Goethe and Schiller. The pantheist school also led to the idealist philosophies of Hegel and Schelling: idealism attempted to replace religion by a rational belief in the world soul and it led in its turn (dialectically, Marx would claim) to the explicitly anti-religious materialism of Ludwig Feuerbach and Marx, to the socialist and communist rejection of religion, to the romantico-historical study of the bible by Strauss and Renan and to the various non-christian and heterodox spiritualist reactions to what was seen as the materialism of the late nineteenth century. In one way or another, all these movements will be relevant for our study of Joyce's critique of religion.

In addition to this political dimension, central in the history of freethought in Europe is the increasing role of science and technology in the debate about religion in the second half of the nineteenth century. Although religion had been under attack for almost two centuries, it was only in the more liberal conditions of the nineteenth century that the debate really could become relevant to more than the intellectual elite. Darwin's findings played an important role here, not just for what the theory of evolution and scientific developments could contribute to the discussions about the origin of man and of civilization, but mostly because the descent of man became the rallying point for all kinds of liberals and secular thinkers. Secular individuals and organizations used the prestige of the new science in the fight against what they saw as the unholy alliance between conservative churches and the existing states to thwart the forces of progress and freedom. As we will see in the discussion of the situation in the different European countries that are relevant to Joyce, in all these cases secular organizations directly pitted science against religion.

English freethought

England had not only invented the word 'freethinking,' its history of relative tolerance of religious minorities made it one of the places where freethought almost became an alternative to religion. In his study of secularization, Owen Chadwick described the changes in the nineteenth century:

The forties was the time of doubts, in the plural and with a small d; turmoils of Arthur Hugh Clough or John Stirling or young James Anthony Froude. In the sixties Britain and France and Germany entered the age of Doubt, in the singular and with a capital D. (1975: 184)

In Europe the process of secularization took place in the last third of the nineteenth century: the very word only acquired its present meaning around 1870 and the process created such a radical change that the French catholic poet Charles Péguy concluded that the world had changed more in the last three decades of the nineteenth century than in the preceding 1,500 years (quoted in Atkin and Tallet 2003. 193).

The British freethought movement attained the peak of its political influence between 1880 and 1886, during Gladstone's second term as prime minister. The elections of 1880 had produced a landslide victory for the liberal party: the British elected 347 Liberals, 240 Conservatives and 65 Irish Home Rulers. Since the latter often voted with the Liberals, the government's majority was in fact even more comfortable: no wonder that the deeply religious Gladstone discerned the hand of God in this electoral success. But despite the great promise, the liberals failed to capitalize on their majority to implement their agenda: part of this lack of success was certainly due to the difficulties in Ireland, but equally crippling was the peculiar fate of one man: Charles Bradlaugh, 'atheist, republican, advocate of birth control, and Member of Parliament' (Arnstein 1965: 1).

Bradlaugh was a radical liberal, who had become the president of the London Secular Society in 1859. Seven years later he founded the National Secular Society which had, by the time of the elections, 6,000 members all over Britain. Through his weekly journal, *The National Reformer*, which the largest newspaper distributor in the country W.H. Smith & Son refused to distribute, Bradlaugh made his opinions known throughout Britain. Atheism was for him not an aim in itself but only a means to promote political and social justice, at home and abroad: like most of the secularists at the time he was a radical and a republican. Abroad he not only supported Garibaldi's struggle in Italy for independence, but also the nationalist movements in Poland and Ireland.

In 1880 Bradlaugh was elected as an MP for Northampton but since he had publicly come out as an atheist, he could not take the parliamentary oath. By careful manoeuvring the conservatives had made it impossible for him to either take it or not take it. A few decades earlier and in similar circumstances Lionel Rothschild, who had been elected in 1847, also could not swear the christian oath; he had to wait 11 years before he could officially take up his seat as a jew. In the next years the House of Parliament repeatedly rejected Bradlaugh (with the Irish members voting against him), despite the fact that Bradlaugh had been re-elected twice: he was physically thrown out of the House, arrested and locked up. The christian churches in England shared a rejection of atheism, but not sufficiently united to organize a single petition: Newman even refused to sign cardinal Manning's catholic petition. The conservative christian prime minister Gladstone (who at the time was still convinced that Moses had written the Pentateuch) stood by Bradlaugh as a matter of principle and in 1888 the member for Northampton finally won the right to 'affirm' instead of swearing an oath.[5] The Bradlaugh case was indicative of a new mood in the country and this period is generally considered as the high point of the secular movement, even by the highly critical Owen Chadwick (1975: 91).

The success of freethought in general had been worrying enough for the churches. As everywhere else in industrializing Europe, workers who had moved to the city lost interest in religion. This was exacerbated by the defection of the church's intellectuals and even its clergy. In 1870 a *Clerical Disabilities Act* had to be passed so that anglican priests who had left the church would be able to retrieve their civil rights. Openly heretical or non-religious writers and intellectuals such as George Eliot (who translated David Friedrich Strauss's *Life of Jesus* into English), Francis Newman (the Cardinal's brother), Algernon Swinburne and Leslie Stephen tried to dissociate religion and morality. Socialist and freethought organizations held meetings and created magazines and book clubs to publicize their views. It was in this atmosphere, in 1888 that Mrs Humphry Ward published *Robert Elsmere*, one of the bestsellers of the nineteenth century and a novel in which the central theme was religious doubt. The novel's hero loses his faith in discussions with the cynical landowner Squire Wendover, but replaces it by social action, moving to the London slums and teaching the poor courses in botany, zoology and New Testament criticism.

By the 1880s and 1890s freethought had become respectable in England: there were different organizations, with their own journals, such as the *Free-thinker* and the *Secular Review* and their own publishing ventures: the Pioneer Press, the Rationalist Press, the Clarion Press. In his history of the London heretics, Warren Sylvester Smith lists more than 20 of these periodicals in the period between 1845 and 1914. Most important for Joyce was the Rationalist Press Association, founded in 1899 with its headquarters in Johnson's Court in London which came to be called 'The Blasphemy Depot' (Smith 1967: 69). The subscription club started with one hundred members and by 1906 had more than one thousand subscribers: 'One of the earliest works to be published by the R.P.A., Joseph McCabe's translation of Ernst Haeckel's *Welträthsel – The Riddle of the Universe* – was the kind of success of which publishers dream. Within a year the first 2,000 were nearly sold out. [. . .] and the cheap reprint of *The Riddle* had sold 100,000 copies by 1905' (Royle 1980: 166). If we can believe *Ulysses*, Buck Mulligan seems to have been one of these readers.

The militant freethinkers of this period often took the bible as a point of attack: the editor of the *Freethinker*, G.W. Foote wrote:

Searching the Scriptures is the best cure for believing in the Scriptures. Many a man has been made a Freethinker by having his attention drawn to texts he never suspected. . . . There is 'rot' enough in the Bible to damn a thousand volumes. Some of it is unscientific, some of it is silly, and some of it is down-right beastly. Anybody who put together such stuff nowadays, and called it God's Word, would be regarded as a lunatic or a criminal, and sent to the asylum or the gaol. (quoted in Royle 1980: 168)

One of these attacks from a socialist freethinker was *God and My Neighbour* by Robert Blatchford, a militant labour leader who was inspired by William Morris and who founded the newspaper *The Clarion.* In November 1903 his Clarion Press (located in London's Worship Street) published *God and My Neighbour,* a strong anti-religious tract, dedicated to Blatchford's son. These are the first words of the preface:

INFIDEL!
I put the word in capitals, because it is my new name, and I want to get used to it.

INFIDEL!
The name has been bestowed on me by several Christian gentlemen as a reproach, but to my ears it has a quaint and not unpleasing sound. (v)

In his 'Forewords' Blatchford recommends a whole list of books as further read-ing, which contains the reprints of the Rationalist Press Association, as well as other books by freethinkers, some of which were in Joyce's library in Trieste. *God and My Neighbour* is a good example of the popularization of unbelief at the turn of the century: Blatchford states his case against theism and in favour of a critical attitude to all dogmas: 'The history of civilization is the history of successions of brave "Heretics" and "Infidels," who have denied false dogmas or brought new truths to light' (1911: 4). Among these heretics we find Copernicus, Bruno and Galileo. This is followed by an inverse creed in which Blatchford lists all those things that he cannot believe: that the christian reli-gion is true, that the Bible is the word of God and so on. He examines the Old and the New Testament, looks at christian apologies and then denies that christian ethics are either unique or special.

By the end of the nineteenth and the beginning of the twentieth century freethought had been all but accepted in England, but the churches were still resisting, especially the catholic church. In a recent book Andrew Gibson has explained the importance of the Jesuit Father Bernard Vaughan as one of the prime targets of Joyce's ire in terms of the British Jesuit's imperialism in an October 1906 letter that we will return to in the next chapter. In reality, the context of Joyce's comments make it clear that Joyce's critique of the Jesuit has little to do with nationalism or imperialism but is directed instead at Vaughan as the representative of a worldly and conservative purveyor of apologetics for the catholic church that Joyce particularly loathed.

Father Bernard Vaughan, younger brother of the Cardinal and Archbishop of Westminster Herbert Vaughan, was the closest equivalent within the English catholic church for the kind of larger-than-life preachers that had become prominent in the American evangelical churches. He first made his name at the turn of the century when in 1898 he preached in the presence of the future king Edward. Naturally, the sermon that had so impressed the Prince of Wales was transcribed and published and the relationship of a Jesuit with the future head of the Church of England generated its own publicity in the special climate of anglican conversions to catholicism. But Bernard Vaughan really made a name for himself when he became involved in a big anti-Jesuit trial in London and when he gave a series of lectures in Mayfair about *The Sins of Society* in which his main target was what he called 'the "vulgar rich," who haunt the neighbourhood of Mayfair' (1907a: xv). In his diagnosis of what was wrong with Society he attacked everything about what was called the 'Smart Set' but also the climate that had produced it, especially the 'materialistic evolutionist' philosophy of Kant, but also the gutter press and 'the sewage literature in which only too many of the present generation disport themselves and wallow swinelike' (1907a: xviii). In conclusion he prayed for a return to a national belief in Christ. It is probably the many reactions to the series of sermons in the British press that were the reason for father Vaughan's prominence (clips of the reactions were included in the back of the book) and these may have been the occasion of Joyce's outburst, not British imperialism.

After 1906 father Vaughan continued in the same vein and the popular press loved to quote his more outrageous statements. Despite his charitable work, he was a Tory and an anti-modernist in any definition of the word: he spoke against women's suffrage, against socialism and against contraception, which he called 'race suicide.' When in 1910 he travelled to the United States, he created a stir even before his arrival by criticizing the right of women to vote (he spoke of 'women marching to the polls when they ought to be at home minding their babies') and by claiming that catholicism was the only hope for America. We know from the correspondence that Joyce followed Vaughan's adventures in the press. But the reference to Vaughan's use of cockney in his sermons, which Father Conmee comments on in 'Wandering Rocks' is an anachronism: according to his biographer C.C. Martindale, s.j., the sermons in which he used London dialect date from April and May 1911 (140–1).[6] We can be sure that Joyce continued to be fascinated by Vaughan: when the most famous British Jesuit died in 1922, Joyce noted from an obituary in the *Irish Times* that in 1916 the pope had granted Father Bernard Vaughan 'the privilege of a portable altar.'[7]

France and Germany

After the United Kingdom and Italy, France was one of the European countries with a most active organization of freethinkers. This had everything to do with the tradition of French anticlericalism and atheism in the eighteenth century and with the role that the ideals of the French revolution continued to play in French politics, especially during the revolutions of 1830 and 1848. In France there was not just a conservative catholic tradition that fought the centralizing powers of the papacy (the so-called 'gallican' opposition to ultramontanism, which demanded an unconditional support for the pope and his centralizing ambitions) but also a strong liberal catholic tradition that attempted to combine the best of liberalism and catholicism. In the course of the century both liberal catholics and anti-catholics became increasingly frustrated by the church and especially in the wake of the later revolutionary periods in 1848 and 1870, the anti-catholic party fought ever more bitterly against the perceived power of the church to interfere in the social and political life of the country. As a result, an organization of freethought was first attempted in the late forties in France and later in Belgium where quite a few of the prominent French *libre penseurs* had found asylum during the Second Empire. Under the Third Republic the freethinkers were allowed to return to France and to create their own organizations. Some of the activities of these organizations did not differ much from their British counterparts, but the fact that in French politics the two parties were engaged in a struggle for political power gave their activities a stridency that was lacking in Great Britain. One of the symptoms of the higher stakes was the organization of deliberately shocking festive meals on Good Friday (when in commemoration of Christ's death catholics were supposed to fast). The first of these banquets was held in 1868 and was attended by major freethinkers such as Hyppolite Taine, Gustave Flaubert, Renan and Sainte-Beuve. On the website of the 'Union rationaliste' we can read that this tradition is still alive today.

Leo Taxil was a fairly typical French freethinker. He was born as Gabriel-Antoine Jogand-Pagès in 1854 and educated by the Jesuits, but he lost his faith and became one of the foremost propagandists of freethinking, publishing a number of anticlerical periodicals that in 1876 forced him into exile in Switzerland. On his return in 1881 he founded first a freethought 'groupe Garibaldi' and a few months later an Anticlerical League that described itself as 'essentially socialist' (Lalouette 2001: 57). Taxil began to publish anti-catholic books with titles like *Les Maîtresses du Pape, Les Amours Secrètes de Pie IX*, and *Le Manuel du Confesseur*. In 1882 his League had 4,000 members and 27 local organizations all over Europe. After a brief adventure with Freemasonry, his many business ventures failed and in 1884 his 'Librairie Anti-Cléricale' was forced to close down.

After a very public reconversion to catholicism, Taxil next began a vicious battle against his former anticlerical and masonic brethren. In an atmosphere of strong conservative anti-masonic feeling, Taxil even claimed to have evidence that the masons worshiped the devil. In the beginning Taxil's contributions were welcomed by conservative catholics who had already blamed a conspiracy of jews, masons and socialists for everything that went wrong in France since the war with Prussia. This group was delighted that somebody finally supplied proof for their suspicions about a vast anti-catholic and diabolical conspiracy.

At the end of 1896 his work earned Taxil an audience with the pope, but doubts surfaced about some of his statements and at a meeting in April of the following year Taxil announced that all his anti-masonic writings had been part of an elaborate anticlerical hoax. Despite this public admission, his stories about the masons' devil-worship can still be found on christian websites where the claim is made that it was Taxil's retraction that had in fact been fraudulent: in the end, the devil worshiping masons had managed to pressure him into silence. In *Ulysses* a similar boisterous and mischievous anticlericalism is present in the person of Buck Mulligan who opens the novel with a blasphemous parody of the mass and who repeatedly plays the role of the freethought provocateur.

Some of the anti-catholic propaganda in France and Belgium was playful, like Taxil's *La Vie de Jésus* that Stephen Dedalus seems to have read in Paris. The book is part of a campaign to make fun of all the important sources of religious doctrine. Taxil also wrote *La bible amusante*, which had 400 'dessins comiques' accompanied by literal translations from the bible and refutations by such 'wise philosophers' as Voltaire, Lord Bolingbroke and Toland. Taxil also brought out a collection of quotations from the secret books in use at seminaries, which prove 'the horrible immorality of the confessional,' an attack on the catholic sacrament that the freethinkers shared with some protestant groups. Books like *La Vie de Jésus* had something else in common with the more salubrious anti-catholic protestant propaganda and that is the thin line between denunciation of the clergy's immorality and sexual titillation. The edition of *La Vie de Jésus* that I own includes a catalogue of books of which Taxil's are the most serious, others have as their subjects the adventures of incestuous monks and the sexual exploits of nuns and cardinals. Among the novels that are advertised we find titles such as *Au Harem, Marriage Forcé, Paris-Gomorrhe*.

La vie de Jésus, originally printed in Paris at the Rue des écoles, close to the library of St Geneviève where Stephen Dedalus did his research,[8] does not belong in the same category as the homonymous books by Strauss or Renan: this is a 'roman comique' of the kind that seems to have been common at the time. Taxil opens his introduction with the statement that there are three possible views on Jesus: he may be a god who spent time on earth in the skin of a man; he could be a jewish revolutionary who after his death was turned into a god by the supporters of his kind of social reform; or else neither he nor his apostles ever existed, but they were invented by those who exploit human stupidity. After careful consideration Taxil has come to the conclusion that the third option is correct and thus the book should not be seen as an attempt to belittle Jesus as a god in order to exalt Jesus as a man. What he really wants to do is to tell the story of the gospels in such a way as 'to demonstrate that the history of Jesus Christ, from the beginning to its end, and from whatever perspective one might choose, is nothing but a web of immoral and stupid fables' (Taxil n.d.: 5).

The structure of Taxil's book does not differ from the pious biographies of Jesus, but the titles of the chapters do: 'Christ's Infancy; The Word's Beginnings; Jesus At Work; The Disagreeable Week; Miracles Behind Closed Doors.' The opening paragraphs are flippant and blasphemous:

> In those days, the Word – i.e. Monsieur Jesus (aka: Alphonse) – had not yet been born; but there was, among the priests of Jerusalem, a levite whose name was Zechariah. This Zechariah lived in the countryside; his summer cottage stood at Juttah, in the middle of the mountains of Judah. He had a wife (jewish priests did marry) who responded – when one called her – to the name of Elizabeth. (Taxil: 9)

Although in the next paragraph Taxil quotes from Luke's gospel, this cannot have been his sole source, because he claims that the parents of John the Baptist lived in Juttah and that is a detail that does not occur in the bible at all, but that was first suggested by the Dutch orientalist scholar Adriaan Reland in 1714 who claimed that the city of Juttah must be referred to in Lk. 1.39 and that the text of that verse should be emended to read that Mary travelled to the 'city of Juttah' instead of to a 'city in Judah.' This detail goes to show that the jocular tone of the book should not fool us into believing that Taxil did not do his homework.

Starting on its third page the book contains a number of illustrations that are just as blasphemous as the text: the first shows a rather dishevelled Mary (with loose hair and décolletée) held in the arms by a winged man about town who looks a bit like a healthier brother of Marcel Proust: the caption says 'The angel Gabriel greets the young Mary, in his own way.' The second picture is the one that illustrates the scene Stephen quotes from in *Ulysses*: in the background a suspicious and much older Joseph berates an obviously pregnant young Mary while the caption reads 'Joseph being suspicious, Mary said "It is the pigeon"' (Taxil: 17). The scene in Chapter V opens with Joseph arriving at the house of his fiancée to bring her the accustomed bouquet of flowers (explicitly said to contain the appropriate lilies). When he is confronted with her belly that had taken on 'disquieting proportions,' Joseph tells her parents that if they think that under the circumstances he will marry their daughter, they might just as well wait until the apricot tree grows feathers. Mary tries to convince her future husband of her innocence:

> – Joseph, my big bunny, I give you my word of honour that I have always been true to you. . . No man can boast that he has kissed the tips of my fingers. . .
> – Tsk, tsk, don't try to pull the wool over my eyes. . . Who then, if it was not a man, has placed you in this bloody position?
> – It is the pigeon, Joseph!
> Immediately the carpenter turned all red.

– The bitch! She makes fun of me all over the city . . . Bloody hell, it is a good thing that she has started her games before we passed by the mayor . . . If the vows had already been said, yours truly would really be up shitcreek. (Taxil: 20)

Joseph leaves and Taxil writes that it is a real pity that the evangelist Matthew has neglected to give us the exact words of the conversation. The words that Taxil has put into Joseph's mouth can only be a shadow of those that must have been used by the angry carpenter.

Taxil continues in this vein until Christ's Assumption: the final illustration sees the son of God ascending into heaven holding an umbrella, with the caption saying: 'From earth into the heavens by direct train.' But the book closes with a rather more serious 11 page conclusion in which Taxil shows that he has thoroughly researched his subject: he refers to the theories about the mythical origins of christianity, shows how the christians misappropriated jewish thought and customs and how there is no independent evidence in pagan Roman or Greek literature that Jesus ever existed. The book itself closes with the statement that both judaism and christianity are mistaken when they think that they represent the present and the future: 'since Voltaire's laughter, freethinking has successfully beaten all low and ridiculous superstitions: the future belongs to liberating, conquering freethought.' At the very end of my edition there is a note that this corrected version was finished on the three-hundredth anniversary of the sacrifice of Giordano Bruno:

Who was not a mythical figure, the sublime martyr of freethought, held eight years in the dungeons of the Holy Office, tortured by the Inquisition and burned alive in Rome, on February 17, 1600, by the Pope and the Cardinals, the princes of the priests. (Taxil 371)

Taxil was a most outspoken and very visible exponent of the French anticlerical tradition and Joyce refers explicitly to his Jesus biography in *Ulysses*, but he was certainly not a lone figure.[9]

In 1911 Edouard Daanson published a Rabelaisian *Le livre du bien et du mal*, an anticlerical bible and an alternative history of the world in which the Eternal One blows into the void and creates 'un ange superbe et flamboyant' (1911: 11.). Lucifer, as he is called, is destined to bring light and justice to the world and he promises God that, for His greater glory, he will fight against His mistakes. And he is immediately sent away. In the rest of the book we see the spirit of denial in his growing opposition to the party of God. Daanson's mischievous version of the bible quotes liberally from the book but concentrates on those parts that are most open to critics: passages in which YHWH reveals himself as all too human or where judaism is unfavourably compared to Babylonian and other rival religions. Some of these stories read like *midrashim*, narrative commentaries that explain problems or anomalies in the bible text, as when the existence of infirmities in the world is explained as one of Lucifer's bad ideas. At other times troubling quotations from Old and New Testament are quoted liberally. The story reaches the time of the book's publication: God elects an ass for pope who promptly proclaims the encyclicals *Vehementer Nos* (condemning the French law of the separation of church and state, 1906) and *Pascendi dominici gregis* (against modernism, 1907); the book ends with Lucifer's own version of the sermon on the mount. Quoting Nietzsche and Epicurus he calls on mankind to enjoy the world (including sex), to forget religion and replace it by science. There is no evidence that Joyce ever read this book but it is an indication how freethought often attempted to turn christian mythology against itself.

Freethinking and religion have both survived the jokes, hoaxes and provocations of Taxil and his like. Because of the peculiar history of France, with its successive waves of revolutions and of conservative governments, freethought had become a central issue in French politics and around the end of the century the French had become increasingly less religious. The Dreyfus affaire made the split between progressives and conservatives even wider and in 1902 the French elections had been fought mainly on the issue of the relation between religion and the state. The left-wing parties defeated a coalition of catholics and nationalists and the resulting government under Emile Combes began a concerted anticlerical campaign.

By closing down congregational schools, the French state attempted to protect secular education by making life difficult if not impossible for the catholic schools. On 4 September 1904 Combes claimed to have closed down almost 14,000 schools. Although Pius X made some attempt to minimize the damage, the relations between the Vatican and the French government deteriorated quickly and in December of 1905 the separation of church and state was officially declared. In February 1906 the pope protested against the fact that the organization of the cult was no longer in the hands of a hierarchy 'divinely appointed by the Saviour.' There was great agitation when catholics defended their churches against the *gendarmes* when, according to the new law, inventories of church property had to be made. As a result of the civic unrest, the government fell and after a while a less strict way of dealing with the church was found.

When we turn to literature, we can only observe that most of the French writers that Joyce admired were not just anticlerical but even atheist. Authors like Victor Hugo, Gustave Flaubert and Emile Zola made the issue an important theme in their work, the latter most famously and most explicitly in novels like *La faute de l'Abbé Mouret* (1875), *Lourdes* (1894) and *Vérité* (1903). It is not really surprising that for the teachers and fellow-students of both James Joyce and Stephen Dedalus, Zola was the prototypical atheist writer. But also Flaubert's novels and his correspondence are marked by his anticlericalism; in *Madame Bovary* he created a negative character, the apothecary Homais, who is a caricature of the French freethinker. Most of the anticlerical writers of this period depicted priests as ruthless libertines: for freethinkers like Octave Mirbeau and Zola the catholic church had reached its final decadence.

With its temporal power and authority seriously challenged, the language of
the Church suffered a fall from a transcendent symbolism to something more
like the symbolism of Maeterlinck and Mallarmé –uncertain, atmospheric,
sensual, a bit neurotic. (Hanson 1997: 7)

Octave Mirbeau's 1890 novel *Sébastien Roch*, which Joyce read in Rome in
December 1906, describes the psychological and actual rape of the protagonist
by a particularly nasty spiritual advisor in a Jesuit boarding school. As in Joyce's
own first novel, the third person narrative in *Sébastien Roch* is interrupted by
extracts from the hero's diary.

By the end of the century, the pendulum began to swing the other way and
anticlerical realism and naturalism began to be attacked from within. The erstwhile decadent writers created a movement that in the opening chapter of one
of its key works, the novel *Là-bas* Joris-Karl Huysmans called 'spiritual naturalism.' As Ellis Hanson has shown, a new generation of writers began to adopt the
image of a catholic church that was at once 'endangered and dangerous' (1997:
10). Other French writers such as Villiers de l'Isle Adam or English and Irish
counterparts like Oscar Wilde and Walter Pater offered a romantic answer to
what they saw as the nihilism of an all too materialist age. The catholic literary
revival in France was led by converts such as Paul Bourget, Maurice Barrès and
Paul Claudel, who chose the most conservative elements in catholicism in such
a manner that Richard Griffiths speaks of a 'reactionary revolution' (Griffiths
1966: 353). Gadille also describes how the later representatives of this revival
found in the philosophy of Thomas Aquinas a perversely adequate answer to
the requirements of a godless age (365). This may not have been a concerted
effort to resacralize the world, but it certainly was perceived as such by opponents of the movement such as Max Nordau. His book *Entartung* (the title
was translated into English as *Degeneration*) 'condemned virtually all the great
writers of his time as neo-Catholic hysterics – including Wagner, Baudelaire,
Verlaine, and Huysmans' (Hanson 1997: 8).

Next to this aesthetic catholicism, the Dreyfus affaire also created a right-wing
catholicism in the form of Charles Maurras's *Action française*, which was royalist,
anti-semitic and ultra-catholic or integralist, a dangerous combination that was
actively supported by such conservative journals as the *Civiltà Cattolica*, which
helped spread the rumour that jews were responsible for both liberal democracy
and the killing of children (Atkin and Tallet 2003: 166). More surprisingly, anti-
semitism can also be found among those catholics who had adopted the Social
Question, basing themselves on an interpretation of Leo XIII's encyclical *Rerum
novarum* in trying to save the working-classes from socialism and atheism.

As a result of another set of political developments, the religious situation in
Germany was completely different. In the new Germany, catholicism was an
important minority religion that became the focus of a so-called *Kulturkampf*:
like most other new nation states Otto von Bismarck's new Germany attempted
to define a separation between church and state, but the Kanzler was strongly

opposed by both the catholic hierarchy and a catholic Centre Party that was thought in Germany to represent a 'black international' led by Rome. In 1871 the government under the influence of the liberal party began to take away catholic privileges and to limit the influence of the church in education and elsewhere. The following year the Reichstag passed a law against the Jesuits and the government sent as its representative to the Vatican a cardinal who did not accept papal infallibility and who in his turn was unacceptable to the Vatican. But all these measures failed and in the end the Bismarck government only managed to make both the church and the catholic Centre Party stronger; these political realities forced Bismarck to change his policies. Under the new pope Leo XIII the old anti-catholic measures were withdrawn and in return Bismarck was given the highest papal honour: the Supreme Order of Christ, the first protestant to receive this reward, a fact that the *Catholic Encyclopedia* does not see fit to mention. Wits claimed that in the conflict with Rome, Bismarck had burned himself badly on Holy Water.

The *Kulturkampf* did not have a clear winner, despite the fact that the *Catholic Encyclopedia* identified a coalition of liberals and protestants as the main enemy and these had been joined in the meantime by the social democrats, who were feared by both Bismarck and the church as a 'red international,' as opposed to the black international of the Church of Rome. Freethought had been a philosophical option in Germany at least since the time of Immanuel Kant and there had been publications against the power of the churches in the period leading up to the revolution of March 1848. But it was only in the 1880s that an organization of atheists was founded by Ludwig Büchner, one of the first scientific materialists. Next to Friedrich Nietzsche, who famously proclaimed the death of God, Ernst von Haeckel was the most influential German freethinker: like Büchner he was a pioneer in Germany of Darwin's evolution theory and in 1899 his book *Das Welträtsel* or *Riddle of the Universe* sold 100,000 copies in a year. According to Owen Chadwick the book represented 'the apogee of the scientific materialism of the nineteenth century' (1975: 177).

Italy

With the particular history of the new Italian state and the papacy, it cannot be a surprise that their relationship had never been cordial: there was a time that the only thing catholic and nationalist Italians could agree on was that it was impossible to be both catholic and a patriot. Apart from the real political and military conflicts, in the middle of the nineteenth century the church was waging a cultural war against the emerging nation of Italy that was supported by a coalition of liberals and freethinkers all over the world, who would look up to Garibaldi as one of their heroes. In June 1858 the papal military police abducted the six-year-old Edgardo Mortara from the house of his jewish parents. While seriously ill, the boy had been baptized by his catholic nurse and since the Holy

Inquisition believed that catholic boys had the right to be educated in their own religion, it was felt that this could only be done outside his jewish home, despite protests from the parents and from more enlightened catholics. For liberals all over the world, the Mortara affair was just another symptom of the church's defiant rejection of civil liberties and it hardened the positions on both sides, resulting in an anticlerical tradition in Italy that was at least as strong as that in France. The irony of the affair was that Mortara later became a priest (Kertzer 1979).

In 1865 Giosué Carducci, whose work Joyce tried to read while he lived in Rome (the Italian poet had won the 1906 Nobel Prize), composed a hymn to Satan that celebrated the Enemy of God as a life force, as rebellious Reason. The 'Inno a Satana' that would become an anthem for the Italian freethought movement ends with these words:

> Hail, Oh Satan
> Oh rebellion,
> Oh you avenging power
> Of human reasoning!
>
> Let holy incense
> And prayers rise to you!
> You have utterly vanquished
> The Jehova of priests! (Carducci 1964)[10]

In his turn Pius IX forbade the Italian catholics to get involved in the elections (*né eletti, né elettori:* neither as candidates nor as voters) and this policy of *Non expedit* would continue into the twentieth century. In addition, in 1870 he also excommunicated all who had taken part in the attack on the Roman papal states. In its war on modernity, the church became ever more militant, and it even adopted a military form of organization: Jean-Dominique Durand writes that in these decades the pope began to see himself as the general in an army where the faithful were the soldiers and the parish priests their captains. Needless to say, the church's enemy was the democratic form of government, anticlericalism and even those moderate catholics who looked for reconciliation with the state (1995: 625).

Attempts by liberal Italian catholics to follow the example of their Belgian, German and French co-religionists in finding a compromise between their religious beliefs and political democracy were short-lived: those who did not submit to the authority of Rome had no other choice than to leave the church. When in 1876 the anticlerical parties inevitably won the elections in which the catholics had been forbidden to participate by their own church, the Italian state began to adopt measures that were designed to limit the powers of the church in education and elsewhere. All over Italy popular anticlericalism became a political reality until it reached the point that when the corpse of Pius IX was transported from the Vatican it had to be defended against an angry mob. Anticlericalism became one of the binding forces in Italy between radical liberals and socialists. It was only in 1905 when Pius X felt that the danger of socialism had reached a crucial threshold, that the new pope reluctantly allowed catholics to become part of the democratic process (albeit on an individual basis) and it took another eight years to formally reverse Pius IX's decision. In the meantime the already existing Christian Democratic party, led by the modernist Romolo Murri, was left out in the cold. Officially the pope continued to reject all liberal virtues and even the catholic historian Hales is forced to admit that catholics in protestant states such as Prussia and the United States were freer in terms of religious rights than those who lived in the catholic kingdoms of Spain and Portugal. Although the pope embarked on the building of a truly christian society on the basis of the ideas of Thomas Aquinas and at least in theory the total rejection of modernity continued, in practice from 1904 there was a 'silent reconciliation.' The pope allowed Italian catholics to participate in the elections as candidates, but only on the (somewhat anti-democratic) condition that they would be representative catholics and not catholic representatives (Durand 1995: 629).

While in Pola and Trieste, Joyce lived close enough to Italy to be in almost immediate contact with the ideological debates there, and between August 1906 and March 1907 he lived in the nation's capital. Domenic Manganiello (1980) in *Joyce's Politics* has traced the author's interest in contemporary Italian culture and radical politics, especially in the writing of Guglielmo Ferrero, so there is not much point in going over this material again, but I will concentrate not so much on the socialist politics as on the anticlerical issues that were topical in this particular period.

In 1906–1907 the political situation in Italy was similar to the one in France and the presence of the pope in the capital and the crucial role of the church in education and in other aspects of public life made the city one of the major battlefields of the ideological war between catholicism and freethought. As in France, most Italian freethinkers in the second half of the nineteenth century had been radical liberals or socialists, and the ideologues of both these groups had become openly and virulently anticlerical. Arturo Labriola, leader of the syndicalist faction of the Socialist party and editor of *Avanguardia socialista* whom Joyce commented on in letters to Stanislaus, was also a prominent free-thinker. In addition, between 1901 and 1914 the *Partito radicale* considered the fight against the catholic church as one of its central platforms. The historical heroes of freethought in Italy were martyrs of the struggle such as Lucilio Vanini (executed for atheism in 1619) and Galileo Galilei, but most important of them all was Giordano Bruno, a victim of the obscurantist forces in the church, a martyr of Italian and International freethought. On 9 June 1899 during a mass demonstration with six thousand atheists from all over Europe, a statue of Bruno was unveiled in the Campo dei Fiori. One of the speakers at that occasion, Giovanni Bovio, claimed that the celebration of that day must hurt the Pope more than the loss of the Papal States and that was most probably

the whole idea of the exercise (quoted in Chadwick 1975: 178–9). Bruno had
been chosen as a hero of the freethinkers precisely because he was, in the words
of Stephen's teacher of Italian, a 'terrible heretic' and this particular square
was chosen because it was there that, in the words of Stephen, the freethought
martyr had been 'terribly burned.' It was 307 years after that date that Joyce
witnessed a procession to commemorate the martyr's death, but Joyce's interest
in the heretic already dates from the Dublin years: there is a reference to him
in 'Days of the Rabblement.' It is not clear how Joyce learned about Bruno,
although the three-hundredth anniversary of his martyrdom in 1900 may not
have gone unnoticed, even in Dublin. In 1903 the Italian national association
of freethinkers, which still exists today, named itself after Bruno.

   During his stay in Trieste and Rome, Joyce also seems to have become interested in anarchism: his library contained books by Kropotkin and Bakunin.
These and other anarchists, like the American Benjamin Tucker, considered
church and state as the two-headed monster that enslaved the people. Although
Richard Ellmann in the second edition of his biography (*JJ* 142) claims that
Joyce read these anarchists while still in Dublin, this is not likely. More probable
is that he read them in Trieste, where copies of most of these books were left
after the family moved to Paris.

   Interesting also is Joyce's mention in letters to Stanislaus from Rome that he
is reading the anticlerical weekly magazine *L'Asino*. Like the works of Leo Taxil,
L'Asino is usually dismissed as a particularly vulgar type of anticlerical propaganda (Candeloro 1970: vii), but in reality this publication's long history is
much more varied. *L'Asino* was founded in 1892, in the same year as the Italian
socialist party; the journal's title was from a saying of Francesco Domenico
Guerrazzi, a Tuscan writer who in 1849 with Giuseppe Mazzoni and Giuseppe
Montanelli had been part of the triumvirate that assumed power in the new
Tuscan state. Guerrazzi had said that 'the donkey is like the people: useful,
patient and stubborn' and it was this motto that the editors adopted as the title
of a satirical magazine that began in black and white, but that began to print in
colour a year later. According to Candeloro, anticlericalism only became a central issue in the magazine in 1901, a phase that lasted until the beginning of the
First World War. Before that time the necessary secularization of life in the new
Italy had been part of the agenda of the bourgeois liberal movements, which
also counted liberal catholics among their members. The more radical anticlerical turn of *L'Asino* in 1901 was due partly to the fact that at that time the Italian
socialists were much closer to achieving real power than ever before and partly
in reaction to the growing conservatism within the church, culminating in 1903
when the extremely conservative cardinal Giuseppe Sarto became Pius X and
the attack on modernism began in earnest. It is in these circumstances, when
the church began to give up its policy of *Non expedit* and ordered the faithful to
vote against socialist candidates, that *L'Asino* became increasingly more anticlerical. And it is also just a few years after the first general elections in which
the Italian catholics had participated and around the time that the socialist

party held an important conference that Joyce read *L'Asino*, in the middle of the magazine's open war with the church. Whereas the hierarchy and the clergy wanted people to believe that the socialists were violent anarchists and enemies of morality and the family, *L'Asino* described the priests as

[R]ich, jealous, greedy, corrupted and corrupting, always ready to take advantage of the ignorance and the superstition of the poor and at the same time of the fear and bad conscience of the rich to satisfy their libidinous yearnings, to accumulate wealth and to increase the material powers of the Church. (quoted in Candeloro 1970: xiii)

The Italian anti-clericals had the same enemy as the French and British freethinkers and it is only natural that they fought with the same weapons. Their immediate targets were the sacraments of confession and celibacy, beyond that the dark history of the church and the catholic reverence for relics. In a well-publicized case, on 24 December 1906, while Joyce was in the Holy City, one of the editors of *L'Asino* at the Casa del Populo in Rome had a chemist duplicate the miracle of San Gennaro or Saint Januarius, in which a hardened quantity of the Neapolitan saint's blood was shown to become liquid during public displays at the Duomo in Napels (see the *Catholic Encyclopedia*, under 'Saint Januarius'). Twice a year the miracle is repeated until this day.

While still in Dublin, Joyce was exposed to European freethought ideas by reading French anticlerical novelists like Flaubert and Zola and heretical thinkers such as Giordano Bruno; when he lived in the Austrian–Hungarian empire and in Rome he immersed himself in Italian freethought and he read atheist, communist, anarchist, anti-catholic and anti-religious literature for most of his writing career. The context of his freethinking is therefore much wider than that of the British history of freethought, and it even includes an important American component.

United States

Although in recent years a substantial part of the country seems intent on transforming the nation into a theocracy, the United States was the first truly secular state in the world and as Susan Jacoby (2004) has shown, the American tradition of religious tolerance has always been a formidable presence, one that was especially clear in the period between 1875 and 1914, which in her history she calls 'the Golden Age of Freethought.' Central in that presence was not so much atheism but secularism, the idea that church and state needed to be kept separate in order to vouchsafe the right of individual Americans to choose their own form of religion (even if that choice involved the rejection of all religion). This feeling was especially strong in a country that had been founded by people who had been forced out of Europe for religious reasons: unlike Great Britain, the nation's Founders decided, the United States would never have an estab-lished church.

Organized freethinking in North America developed in much the same way as it did in England and it seems to have had a comparable political agenda. Robert Ingersoll, whom Jacoby calls 'the great agnostic' and who is ironically referred to in *Ulysses*, had the same enemies as his British counterpart Charles Bradlaugh. These included those who wanted to limit religious or ideological freedom, but like their European counterparts, American freethinkers were involved in all the social and political issues of the nineteenth century, includ-ing anti-slavery actions, feminism and socialism. Just as anywhere else, American freethinkers rebelled against the increased activity of the churches (which was, needless to say, itself a reaction against what was seen as the general loss of faith, especially among the working people). Not only was there an explosion of evan-gelical revivalism in the first half of the century and of alternative christianities and religions such as the Church of Jesus Christ of the Latter-Day Saints, from the middle of the century organized religion became more central in the life of individual Americans: whereas in 1790 only 5 per cent had formal ties with a church or a synagogue, by 1910 more than 43 per cent of Americans did (Jacoby 2004: 151). Some of this increase may well have been due to the growth of the catholic church, as a result of mass immigration from Ireland, Poland and southern Europe, but the same wave of immigration also brought large groups of freethinkers, especially German refugees who left their country after the failed 1848 revolution and non-religious jews from Germany and eastern Europe. In that period the most important point on the political agenda of the secularist–religious debate was education and then, as now, this meant that secularists fought against attempts to introduce religion into public education.

Freethinking was an issue that was local (the town of Comfort in the Texas Hill Country was founded as a freethinking stronghold) as well as national. The magazine *Truth Seeker*, which began publication in 1873, was the chief journal that united American freethinkers from the most remote regions, but as Jacoby points out, the important platform for freethinking ideas was the lecture cir-cuit, which ran alongside the evangelical and other christian revivals. She calls Ingersoll one 'of the two most important figures in the history of American secularist dissent' (the other is Thomas Paine); he became such a central figure by bridging 'the gap between the theoretical deism of the Enlightenment and the practical freethought, focusing on specific social problems, that defined the late-nineteenth-century movement' (157–8).

A brilliant speaker, Ingersoll was the most important propagandist for secularism from the big cities to the smallest towns and he became, in the words of one of his many enemies who in 1925 deplored the fact that he had not yet been forgotten, 'the nearest approach we Americans have had to Voltaire' (quoted in Jacoby 2004: 184). In one of his most popular lectures he expressed his views on the secularist intentions of the framers of the American constitution:

They knew that to put God in the Constitution was to put man out. They
knew that the recognition of the Deity would be seized upon by fanatics and
zealots as a pretext for destroying the liberty of thought. They knew the terrible history of the church too well to place in her keeping, or in the keeping
of her God, the sacred rights of man. They intended that all should have the
right to worship, or not to worship; that our laws should make no distinction
on account of creed. They intended to found and frame a government for
man, and for man alone. They wished to preserve the individuality of all; to
prevent the few from governing the man, and the many from persecuting
and destroying the few. (quoted in Jacoby, 184–5)

Ingersoll was certainly not alone and Jacoby points out that, as in Great Britain
and France, quite a few of the major American writers of this period were freethinkers. Walt Whitman was a self-confessed follower of Thomas Paine; his
Leaves of Grass and especially the attempts in 1881 to publish an unexpurgated
version of this poem became a central issue in the fight between American
freethinkers and their christian opponents. Other authors who supported
freethinking and who wrote against religion included Mark Twain (Schwartz
1976).

America was not only important to Joyce because it offered prominent
examples of alternatives to catholicism, one catholic American initiative would
become an important source for his work. The *Catholic Encyclopedia* in 15 volumes was first published in 1907 by the Robert Appleton Company (which had
been specially created for this project) and it carried a 'nihil obstat' by the censor and an 'imprimatur' from John Farley, archbishop of New York. Work on
the project began in January 1905 with the specific purpose of giving catholic
readers an encyclopaedia that could be trusted on all matter of doctrine. As the
preface explains:

> THE CATHOLIC ENCYCLOPEDIA, as its name implies, proposes to give its read-
> ers full and authoritative information on the entire cycle of Catholic inter-
> ests, action and doctrine. What the Church teaches and has taught; what she
> has done and is still doing for the highest welfare of mankind; her methods,
> past and present; her struggles, her triumphs, and the achievements of her
> members, not only for her own immediate benefit, but for the broadening
> and deepening of all true science, literature and art – all come within the
> scope of THE CATHOLIC ENCYCLOPEDIA.

Although most of the contributors were American, the encyclopaedia also carried articles by English scholars and catholics from all over the world. In 1912
the company's title was changed to The Encyclopedia Press.

These dates and a quick look at some of the more problematic articles
such as 'Science and the church' make it clear that the *Catholic Encyclopedia* was
(or became) an explicit attempt to defend the church against all the modern

heresies that Pius X had summed up with the word 'modernism.' This is one of the reasons why according to the *Encyclopedia* catholics are better scientists than their colleagues outside of the flock:

> It is true, the believer is less free in his knowledge than the unbeliever, but only because he knows more. The unbeliever has one source of knowledge, the believer has two. Instead of barring his mind against the supernatural stream of knowledge by arbitrary postulates, man ought to be grateful to his Creator for every bit of knowledge, and, panting for truth, drink from both streams that pour down from heaven. Hence it is, that a well-instructed Christian child knows more of the important truths than did Kant, Herbert Spencer, or Huxley. Believing scientists do not wish to be free-thinkers just as respectable people do not want to be vagabonds. ('Science and the Church')

The *Catholic Encyclopedia* is not only important to this study because James Joyce made frequent use of it during his most productive years, it has already helped us to determine the church's position on a number of issues that are of special interest when we want to understand the catholic church as it saw itself and the world at that particular point in its history.

Ireland

Because of its peculiar religious development, Ireland was almost entirely free of militant atheism as a serious intellectual presence. In his history of popular freethought in Great Britain between 1865 and 1915, Edward Royle points to the particular problems of the radical movement in Ireland. Whereas in the rest of Europe people who were not catholic could be freethinkers, in Ireland things were different: if you were not a catholic, you had to be a protestant:

> Often of the fiercest, most aggressive and most unreasoning kind. There was no room for freethought in Ireland. As the *Freethinker* commented in 1882. 'Father Fennelly is proud that no "infidel societies" have been established in Ireland. Quite so. They go in for "assassination societies" over there. Murder isn't half as bad as infidelity. Better beat out your neighbour's brains than believe that Jonah was not swallowed by a whale.' (1980: 71)

In the 1862 census, no more than 21 atheists were counted in Ireland, 20 'secularists' and 19 'deists.' Secular societies were established in both Belfast and Dublin in 1875, but they disappeared quickly. The American freethinker Samuel Putnam wrote in 1894: 'In Europe the terms Socialist, Republican, and Freethinker are, by the government papers and orators, employed to denote any person who expresses radical political and religious views, and hence it has come to pass that the public at large cannot conceive of a Republican or Socialist who is not at the same time a Freethinker, and vice versa' (quoted in Royle 1980: 77). Things were very different in Ireland: Catherine Candy quotes Paul Dubois who noted in 1908 that the anticlerical movement there was confined 'to a small group of intellectuals who "naively admired the worst anti-clericals of France," some politicians who had occasional quarrels with the clergy, and the Fenian hard core' (Candy 1995: 19). In Ireland freethinkers were always only a tiny minority and they had no political influence.[11]

However, this certainly does not mean that there was no strong criticism of the church and its political power in Ireland. James Joyce did not have to look far if he wanted to criticize the church. As is the case in other predominantly catholic countries, anticlerical attitudes ran in his family, and his father's bio-graphers John Wyse Jackson and Peter Costello trace it back at least to his father's grandfather. In Ireland anticlericalism was partly social and partly polit-ical. As Wyse Jackson and Costello show, the immediate ancestors of James Joyce were mostly critical of the priests because the latter belonged to a superior social class and they represented the kind of power that the Joyce family did not have. Although he began life as a fervent catholic, John Stanislaus Joyce was anticlerical most of his life and these attitudes were considerably strengthened during the Parnell years; he would remain anticlerical until the end of his life. Typically, in the biography of John Stanislaus we find that in the index under 'character' the item 'anticlericalism' is, with 'sociability' and 'wit,' by far the longest entry. But Joyce's father was at times more than just anticlerical: in a story he probably heard from the elder son, Padraic Colum tells a story about John Stanislaus who was reproved by a friend for his cursing when it had begun to rain: 'Don't you know that God could drown the world, John?' Joyce père pithily replied: 'He could if he wanted to make a bloody fool of himself' (Colum 1958: 21–2).

His eldest son must have been aware that there was a small group of free-thinkers in Dublin, as is clear from the words that in 1903 he uses to describe his perceived enemies in Dublin: he called them among other things 'damn editors, damn free-thinkers' (*Letters II* 28). Ireland may have been a priest-ridden country, but at the turn of the century there was quite a bit of anticleri-cal opposition too, especially in literary circles. The focal point of much of the anti-catholic feeling within the Irish revival was George Moore; he had joined the movement in its earliest stages but had serious misgivings about the all-pervasive influence of what he called the 'Roman' church.

Moore had been raised as a member of a catholic landowning family, but even before he went to Paris to study art and thus before he discovered Flaubert and Zola, he had informed his mother that he no longer believed. This particular path to unbelief seems to have passed by way of Kant and Shelley: the young Moore carried a copy of the former's *Critique of Pure Reason* with him and seems to have discovered atheism via the romantic poet's work, a reading that then led him to the works of Spinoza, Godwin and Darwin. Despite his own well-publicized claims in 1903 that he had converted to protestantism, Moore was and remained an unbeliever in the European vein. From the first play he wrote on Martin Luther, he attacked the Church of Rome. But much like Joyce and like some of the French writers, he continued to remain interested in the history of christianity. His earliest heroes read the Latin christian writers and in the last part of his career he even wrote novels and plays about early christianity.

As we know from his own account in the autobiographical trilogy *Hail and Farewell* Moore's Dublin years were virulently anticlerical. Not only was he fighting censorship and church influence in the cultural movement, his most important works of the revival, the stories in *The Untilled Field* and the novel *The Lake*, have priests as their central characters. In the former book the stories describe the detrimental influence of the church in rural Ireland where priests rule supreme: creative or inquisitive people are driven out of the country. On 24 September 1902 he wrote to a friend that the story collection had exhausted him: 'Fourteen stories in ten months is too much. Fourteen priests in ten months is too much' (Moore 1929: 44). This particular letter was addressed to the dedicatee of *The Lake*, his good friend Edouard Dujardin, who shared his interest in the origins of religion and who had written a book on *Les sources du fleuve chrétien* (a work Moore attributes to one of his novel's characters). *The Lake* began as a short story about a priest in the west of Ireland leaving his parish and his calling, but Moore quickly developed the tale into an ambitious novel that Joyce, despite what he claimed in letters to his brother, must have read with more than a little jealousy (Lernout 1980). It was because of the dedication of the book to Dujardin that Joyce discovered the French author's novel *Les lauriers sont coupés* and thus, he later claimed, the technique of the interior monologue. But there was more: both *The Untilled Field* and *The Lake* are thoroughly European books, part of an anti-religious aesthetic and literary tradition that included Flaubert and Ibsen and that Joyce yearned to introduce in Ireland. But Moore had been there before him.

In addition Moore was, or believed that he was, engaged in the same kind of battle with Irish catholicism that Joyce wrote to Nora about. And Moore clearly saw that the fight was part of a more general European conflict: on Saint Patrick's day in 1904 the older writer wrote to Dujardin: 'One of my friends has started a tiny review in Dublin, somewhat on the lines of the *Revue des Idées*, that is, it has an anticlerical bias.' Moore refers to *Dana: An Irish Magazine of Independent Thought*; not only did he financially support the magazine, he contributed articles regularly 'to give it a lift' (Moore 1929: 49), and he also translated an article by his friend Dujardin on the Abbé Loisy, one of the modernist catholics under attack from the hierarchy in Rome. In the 'Introductory' that opens the first issue of *Dana*, the editors claim that 'the elemental freedom of the human mind' has been absent from the Irish literary movement. Instead of avoiding divisive but fundamental issues, the editors will provide an 'outlet for honest opinion on all such matters' (Moore 1929: 2). Yet the editors also admit that they would rather not be 'suspected of any disposition to be truculent or nasty in the cause of what is called Free Thought':

> In truth, the more distinctively religious press in this country does not pres-
> ent a standard impossible to emulate in the furtherance of the gospel of
> peace and good-will to men. We would simply assume that people are sincere
> when they advocate tolerance, understanding by tolerance not a conspiracy
> of silence in regard to fundamental and essential matters, but a willingness to
> allow the freest expression of thought in regard to these. (Moore 1929: 3)

Also in the first issue of *Dana* was an essay by John Eglinton in which he does not pull punches in his attack on the kind of pietist literature written by the only worthy catholic writer that Ireland had produced, Canon Sheehan: 'A fig for that belief in God which implies for its obverse a disbelief in man!' (1904: 16). Dujardin's article stresses the importance of Loisy's writings on the history of the church and he identifies the reasons why the church is unwilling to accept Loisy's groundbreaking work on the history of catholic doctrine:

> One readily understands that the Catholic Church does not recognise the
> existence of doctrinal development through which she has passed; the truth
> is, says M. Loisy, that she has not taken cognizance of it, and that she has
> no official theory regarding the philosophy of her own history. (Dujardin
> 1904: 19)

Prophetically Dujardin concludes: 'For this, the Catholic Church has now solemnly condemned him. It is, probably, the beginning of a great misfortune for the Catholic Church' (1904: 21). A similar note appears in the final article by the socialist Fred Ryan in which the author claimed that the Irish have to stop dreaming of their eternal reward and start working for a better world here on earth: 'We need in Ireland a spirit of intellectual freedom, and a recognition of the supremacy of humanity' (1904a: 31). The second issue of *Dana* opened with an article by John M. Robertson, a prominent British freethinker who had collaborated with Charles Bradlaugh's daughter on a biography of her father and who published a history of freethinking and many critical studies on the historicity of the bible. In his contribution 'Catholicism and Civilisation' Robertson explains that the future in Ireland does not depend on the country becoming protestant (and thus free of conservative catholicism). Like other originally catholic and now progressive nations in Europe (France, Belgium, Spain and Italy), Ireland will not become protestant, it will simply become 'more secular.' What we need now is not Saint Augustine's City of God, but a simpler and more hopeful 'City of Man.' *Dana* stopped publication after just 12 issues.

When the encyclical against modernism was published in 1907, Moore responded to a question from Dujardin, that unfortunately the Irish catholics had not reacted at all to the attack on catholic intellectuals ('Ireland is the cemetery of Catholicism'), but at least Moore himself was still writing his 'Messianic book *Hail and Farewell*' (Moore 1929: 66). Moore became so fanatical in his fight against the church that he even argued publicly that catholicism had never produced any genuinely great art. When in an obituary for his younger brother the *Irish Times* had claimed that he came from an 'old Roman Catholic family,' Moore fired back a protest that his family had been protestant until his great grandfather had been forced to convert for purely pragmatic reasons. In the same letter Moore's grandfather is claimed as a man of letters, 'a disciple of Gibbon, and many passages in his published writings show him to be an agnostic' (Gray 1996: 271).

Some of Moore's biographers have not been comfortable with his anticlericalism and atheism. Joseph Hone called his opinions on religion dangerous, and Tony Gray does not even seem to be aware that Shelley was an atheist: he writes that it was 'what [Moore] calls "Shelley's atheism"' that led him to other sceptical writers (Gray 1996: 56). Moore remained uncompromising in his anticlericalism until the very end: when his mother was buried he began to make arrangements for his own funeral in a most unchristian fashion, but in the end an Anglican clergyman officiated who did offer prayers for his soul, 'but out of respect for Moore's views [he] omitted all references to specifically Christian dogmas such as "the sure and certain hope of immortality"' (Gray 1996: 329).

In 1904 Dublin had at least one journal that was explicitly anticlerical, but articles critical of religion had appeared even earlier: in 1901 John Eglinton had published an essay called 'The New Age' in Standish O'Grady's *All Ireland Review* in which he expounds a kind of commonsense scepticism about all forms of religion. In a recent study of Joyce's relationship with the two Irelands (protestant and catholic), Eglinton is identified as the only writer of the revival who in this early phase addressed the religious question (Potts 2000: 2).

Precisely because the catholic church played such a central role in Ireland, political movements could not afford to alienate the church and this led to resentment, even within the 'Irish Ireland' movement that would be instrumental in equating being Irish with being catholic. In the first decade of the twentieth century, there was a growing resentment among catholic laymen against what they saw as the disproportionate power of the clergy. We have already seen the role of McCarthy, but there were other catholic laymen who advocated freedom of thinking and who were openly critical of clerical dominance in Ireland. Two editors of the journal *Irish Peasant*, Patrick D. Kenny and W.P. Ryan, supported freedom of expression and attacked the clerical control over Irish organizations, part of what Kenny called 'parochial terrorism.' Almost as if the church wanted to confirm their analysis both journalists were removed after pressure from the clergy, first from local priests and in the case of Ryan, after a letter from cardinal Logue that forced the suppression of the paper in December 1906 (Biletz 2000).

Joyce only rarely paid his ideological debts, and while he must have had sympathy for the ideas of these local freethinkers, he never acknowledged them as precursors. On the contrary, in *Ulysses* he seems to go out of his way to put Moore, Eglinton and Ryan in a bad daylight, giving his intellectual creditors much the same treatment that his father had given his financial backers. In the library chapter Eglinton is an intellectual sparring partner, but Moore is only present in spirit, when Stephen is all too keenly aware that unlike everybody else, he has not been invited to an evening chez Moore. When the future of national writing is discussed it is assumed that it is Moore who will write the national epic. The case of Frederick Ryan is even stranger: when Stephen mentions briefly first that he owes money to him and then when Eglinton says that he may not get Stephen's work published because of an article on economics that Ryan is going to write, we have the queer pun *Fraidrine* on the latter's name. Although Ryan contributed to almost every issue of *Dana*, he never wrote on economics. In fact, in the August 1904 issue that contained 'Song' by James A. Joyce, there is a long article on 'Empire and Liberty' by Frederick Ryan and in the September issue an article on 'Criticism and Courage' in which Ryan defends the cause of independent thinking in Ireland. He deplores the fact that religious matters apparently cannot be discussed anymore, that the two churches in Ireland seem to have agreed on a truce and that they have stopped trying to convert the other party, because the catholic press considers it a 'heinous offence.' There will also be no more discussions between protestants and catholics at the Rotunda: 'Doubtless it was realized that such performances were more likely to make Freethinkers than converts to either Catholicism or Protestantism' (1904c: 147). Ryan protests at this lack of courage and he mentions Canon Sheehan who at a meeting of the Catholic Truth Society advocated 'the cultivation of "passionless" literature and the bowdlerising of poets like Burns and Byron, and in addition referred to the large numbers of cheap rationalist publications which were now openly sold in a "Catholic city" like Dublin' (1904c: 148). Ryan attacks what he calls 'the pride of ignorance' of the catholic church whose representatives can say that they have never heard of the Abbé Loisy whose work *Dana* published and he mentions:

> a well-known Jesuit preacher, within a few months of the publication of the *Encyclopedia Biblica* (which was itself a redaction of current continental scholarship) tell a rather high-class congregation that modern criticism had left the Bible untouched. [. . .] it is this mental and moral cowardice, for which orthodoxy is primarily responsible, that helps to keep us as a people intellectually inferior. (1904c: 149)

It is hard to believe that Joyce did not share these feelings, especially because the well-known Jesuit may well have been Bernard Vaughan. David Pierce (2005) has shown what an interesting political figure Fred Ryan was in the context of the Ireland before the Easter rising. Stephen's distance from all these Irish freethinkers certainly contributes, both in *A Portrait of the Artist as a Young Man* and in *Ulysses* to that character's fierce independence of anything that was on offer in the Dublin of the turn of the century. But it does not paint an accurate picture of the ideological climate in the Dublin in which his creator grew up. Something very similar can be observed when Joyce writes about theosophy.

Theosophy

Stanislaus Joyce wrote that his brother's relationship with religion in his Dublin years was marked by one major disappointment, which he cynically described as his brother's 'interim religion' (1958: 140). From our perspective, educated in part by Joyce's later views, it might seem strange that the young writer would fall for the blatant charlatanry of theosophy. But we should not forget that in this respect too, young James Joyce was part of the artistic and intellectual avant-garde. All over Europe writers and artists were turning away from scientific materialism towards a new spiritualism that meant either, as in the case of a number of French decadent writers, rediscovering the old orthodoxies of catholicism, or trying to move beyond materialism towards a new spiritual synthesis, which could take the form of theosophy, anthroposophy, occultism, rosicrucianism, and even the supposed scientific study of spiritualism. All over Europe writers such as Maurice Maeterlinck in Belgium, Villiers de l'Isle-Adam and René Guénon in France, Stefan George and Ludwig Klages in Germany were discovering the occult.

In England and in the rest of Europe, philosophy and theology were moving in the same direction. The idealism of Hegel and Schelling had made inroads into departments of philosophy and were thought to be supremely capable of countering what was seen as the dangers of a materialist irreligion. In a way, whereas freethought was generally liberal and later socialist, spiritualism tended to be 'a heresy of the right' as a student of London heretics has written:

> Theosophy [. . .] in spite of protestations to the contrary, rested on revelation. It became, as it developed, mystical, other-worldly, ritualistic, select. It was a rival religion that failed to develop an adequate theology. (Smith 1967: 142)

Theosophy was the religious wing of a movement that also included a scientific faction in the Society for Psychical Research. The former was founded by Madame Blavatsky and attempted to formulate an alternative to both christianity and materialism. The Russian medium claimed that she communicated with the Mahatmas or Masters who really ran the world and that she was the sole vessel through which they would communicate with mankind, most importantly through her books *The Secret Doctrine* and *Isis Unveiled*. Although she was unmasked relatively quickly as a charlatan, she acquired a following among intellectuals and artists, among them William Butler Yeats and George Russell

(AE): the latter called *The Secret Doctrine* 'the most exciting book in a century' (Smith 1967: 156).

Although in a competitive market of unorthodox ideas, theosophy and similar movements were intensely critical of each other; they had in common that they saw themselves as opposing both the new materialism and orthodox christianity. They stressed the continuity of pagan and heretical ideas, found support in gnostic religion, mysticism, Indian and Egyptian religion and formulated a syncretic creed that combined what they considered to be the best of all religions and myths. Self-made scholars such as Gerald Massey (1829–1907) discovered that the central beliefs of christianity had been borrowed from Egyptian myths.

Quite a few of the new spiritualists, like Annie Besant, who came to think that she had been Giordano Bruno in an earlier incarnation, originally came out of the freethought movement; just before and after the first world war, the freethought movement had to redefine its strategies in fighting ever new forms of irrationalism (Cooke 2004: 78–82). In an earlier life Gerald Massey had been a Christian Socialist and he was widely supposed to have been the original of George Eliot's Felix Holt, the Radical. He opposed what he called 'Historical' or 'Anthropomorphic' christianity not only for its failure to face its own history and for not accepting the reality of spiritualist phenomena, but for the same moral and ideological reasons that were put forward by the freethinkers: christianity's central dogmas of original sin, hell, salvation, the discrimination of women and the rejection of the body. 'The doom of Historic Christianity is sealed, because it was based upon Dogmas against which the highest instincts of the race will forever rise in insurrection, and Doctrines that are certain to be rejected by the growing moral sense of enfranchised humanity' (1900: 268). In fact, Massey saw himself as an heir to freethought and he celebrated a religion of life as supposed to one that celebrated death:

> The religion of the future has got to include not only Spiritualism, but the salvation of humanity for this life – any other may be left to follow hereafter. It has to be a sincerity of life, in place of pretended belief. A religion of science, in place of superstition. Of joy, instead of sorrow. Of man's Ascent, instead of his Fall. A religion of fact in the present, and not of mere faith for the future. A religion in which the temple reared to God will be in human form, instead of being built of brick or stone. A religion of work, rather than worship; and, in place of the deathly creeds, with all their hungry parasites of prey, a religion of life – life actual, life here, life now, as well as the promise of life everlasting! (Massey 1900: 286–7)

The sentiments expressed here, apart from the spiritualism, do not differ from the creed of freethinkers such as Ingersoll. This is different in Blavatsky's thought, although she used Massey's critique of christianity in her own work: in a letter to Massey that she published in *The Agnostic Journal* she writes:

Never mind that you differ from us and our views. What matters it that your conclusions are opposed to ours, when all your fundamental premises are identical and the same; and when, moreover, they (these conclusions) are only with regard to the aspect, or the version, of the archaic Esoteric Wisdom of one nation, the Egyptian, now radiating in so-called Christianity in a thousand broken rays. Let us, then, work in peace, harmony, and alliance against our common foe – the modern enemy and curse of humanity – Exoteric Christianity – though we may (in appearance only) be working on two different lines. (1891: 214)

In orthodox christianity ('exoteric' as opposed to its genuine 'esoteric' form) Blavatsky not only found the same enemy as the freethinkers, she also used the same imagery of bringing light to the benighted. Her theosophical journal, founded in 1887 (predating the publication of *The Secret Doctrine*), was called *Lucifer*, and was designed to 'bring to light the hidden things of darkness.' Two years later the freethinker Annie Besant, after reviewing *The Secret Doctrine*, converted to theosophy. She broke with her freethinking friends and became co-editor of *Lucifer* and after the death of Blavatsky, the erstwhile materialist became president of the Theosophical Society.

In Ireland Joyce had the example of Yeats (whose father was a freethinker) and AE, members of various theosophical groups in Dublin, who both wrote poems and stories in which the occult played an important part. These stories were Joyce's favourites and it was probably there that he discovered such heterodox writers as Joachim di Fiore and William Blake. In the late twenties, Joyce himself must have thought that the spiritualist movement had been important enough to the writing of *Ulysses* because he told Stuart Gilbert to read a number of strange books in preparation for Gilbert's study of the novel: there are references in this book to Blake, Blavatsky, A.P. Sinnett's *Esoteric Buddhism*. In the *Finnegans Wake* notebooks we find occasional references to all kinds of esoteric doctrines and as late as 1937 he was making notes from Yeats's *A Vision*. In his work Joyce treated the theosophists and the followers of other esoteric doctrines in much the same way as he did the Dublin freethinkers. And it is not at all clear why Joyce at times seems to have retained a measure of interest in what is now no longer taken seriously, not even as an alternative to religion. It is an issue that deserves more contextual study.

Conclusion

Both in the enlightenment and during the nineteenth century, theists, atheists and followers of esoteric and other unorthodox and dissenting groups were united in their opposition to the established churches in general and to the catholic church in particular. As a powerful movement against the church, the freethought or humanist movements opposed neither religious belief nor the people who held those beliefs, they demanded from the established church freedom of expression and of religion, civil liberties for the individual, and the separation of church and state. Freethought was an heir to the American revolution of 1776, to the French revolution of 1789 and to the European revolutions of 1830 and 1848. Its more radical forms would lead to the socialist and anarchist struggles of the turn of the century, which especially in France and Italy became increasingly radical and anticlerical. The established churches, and especially the catholic church, fought these revolutionaries and the modernist tendencies all the way, but it seems that in most parts of the western world they lost that war. In the 1960s even the Church of Rome finally accepted the basic democratic principles that it had resisted for so long.

In the last 40 years or so and in most of the western world, with the exception of the United States, organized freethinking has been the victim of its own success. Freedom of thought and of religion, and freedom of expression in general, have been accepted as basic human rights and only very few democratic governments can get away with giving priority to a single religion. There are modern states that officially still have an established church: in the case of roman catholicism in Europe we have the four very small nations Monaco, Liechtenstein, Malta, Vatican City and four Swiss cantons (while three other cantons in Switzerland are officially 'old catholic'), but none of them would dream of discriminating against religious minorities or limiting the freedom of religion. Whereas the philosophy of freethought has been silently adopted everywhere, there are still groups of people who advocate its ideas. Most countries in the west have 'freethinking' or 'humanist' or 'secular' organizations that function as alternatives to religions and that are even officially recognized as such in some states. Over the last century, the freethought and secular movements have lost membership and most of their political influence, but this development should not make us forget the importance of these movements, both in the history of modern democracy and in the life of one Irish writer. In the next chapters we will see how Joyce's personal crisis of belief can be seen in a historical context in which religion played a completely different role than it does.

Chapter 4

Joyce's Own Crisis of Belief

I couldn't do that to him.
Nora Barnacle

We have already noted that the most influential view of Joyce's attitude to religion is Richard Ellmann's. To some extent his view of the crucial moment early in Joyce's life when he transformed a religious calling into an aesthetic mission provided a structure for his biography and it was a topic that Ellmann returned to on several occasions. Some critics have even claimed that this simple view of Joyce's artistic mission distinguished Ellmann's approach from that of his major competitor as the most influential Joycean of the first generation, the catholic and more complex critic Hugh Kenner.

Although Stephen's rejection of religion is such a central theme in the autobiographical writings, the non-fictional reports of his attitudes are less certain than Ellmann would have us believe, despite the fact that in the biography this problem is not prominently visible due to the biographer's habit of not always clearly distinguishing between the two. If we are careful to keep the two realms apart, as I think we should and as I will try to do in what follows, we may discover a slightly different Joyce, less a portrait of the artist by an older man, but something closer to the reality in which Joyce himself lived his life. The most relevant period to study Joyce's religious attitudes might be the final years in Dublin, from his first apostasy to his continental exile. There are two privileged witnesses for Joyce's life in these years, Stanislaus Joyce and Oliver St John Gogarty; we will look at the latter first, because we have direct evidence for his opinions in the relevant period.

Oliver St John Gogarty

Unfortunately we have no contemporary materials that document Joyce's loss of faith itself, just echoes after the fact and testimonies by family and friends. The latter do not constitute objective facts that can be usefully opposed to Joyce's fiction. Stanislaus Joyce's diary has been edited and the many reminiscences of the writer's early acquaintances were written long afterwards.

The only genuinely contemporary witnesses of this period seem to be Joyce's own letters and those of early acquaintances such as Oliver St John Gogarty, whose letters to his Oxford friend G.K.A. Bell of the relevant period were published by James F. Carens. These letters act as genuinely independent witnesses to Joyce's life because they were of course never available to Joyce, his family or his friends, or to Gogarty himself, who in his many reminiscences of Joyce tends to embellish his memories.

What is clear from this correspondence is that the portrait of Mulligan in *Ulysses* is quite close to the bone. Gogarty was the closest friend that Joyce had at the time and their later alienation explains the violence and the venom in the novel's characterization. As he kept repeating after 1922, St John Gogarty was much more than a character in Joyce's novel. He grew up in the same catholic upper middle class that Joyce's had dropped out of, with an education at Clongowes and Stonyhurst, before going to Trinity. The portrait in the novel may be a bitter one, but as his letters to his English friend Bell show, it is very close.

Gogarty's letters of the period show that like Buck Mulligan in the novel, he was besotted by the Greek and Roman writers and by English romantic and decadent poets like Shelley, Keats, Arnold and especially Swinburne (whom he does call Algy in the letters). Of these four poets who are quoted or parodied again and again, three are associated with heterodox views and even atheism, most explicitly Shelley, who was expelled from Oxford for publishing the pamphlet *The Necessity of Atheism*. His early philosophical poem *Queen Mab* carried Voltaire's motto 'ECRASEZ L'INFAME.' Half a century later, while a student at Oxford, Swinburne narrowly avoided being sent down for the same sin and as a result the English poet has been described as the Poet Laureate of atheism. In *My Brother's Keeper*, Stanislaus Joyce writes that when the Dean of Studies at University College read Joyce's poems in manuscript he 'no doubt expected to find turbulent dithyrambic atheism after the manner of Swinburne' (1958: 176).

Even the parody of religion seems to play a part in Gogarty's thinking, just as it figures so prominently in that of his fictional counterpart. In February 1905, a retreat at a monastery which his mother had insisted on forced Gogarty to reflect on the difference between christianity and pagan Rome. When he hears the monks sing the *Requiem* he quotes the first two lines and in an Edward Gibbon-like mood he compares its language to classic Latin: 'I remember thinking with indignation to what a pitch the language that chanted *Aeneadum genetrix* had come' (1971: 80). The Latin represents the first words of *De rerum natura* by the Roman philosopher Lucretius, not to be chanted, to be sure, but nevertheless the introduction to this work is one of the greatest anticlerical statements in classic literature with a powerful indictment of religion that ends in the line, 'tantum religio potuit suadere malorum' (l. 101: *So readily religion leads to evil*), a quotation of which Voltaire hoped that it 'would last as long as the world.'[1]

admirable mixture of simplicity and roguery and very typical of the Catholic
Church. (1962: 44)

At times Stannie makes a point of distinguishing his own ideas from those of his
brother, but on the subject of religion they seem to be generally in sympathy in
their acceptance of a scientific way of life as a substitute for worship. Stannie
calls himself a 'scientific humanist' (1962: 47) but is also capable of joking
about his opinions: 'Matter is indestructible, scientists tell us, so here is an epi-
taph for us mortalists: "Here lie the immortal remains"' (1962: 111). The main
difference between the brothers seems to be the reasoning behind their respective rejection of religion: in distinction to his own Nietzschean attitude, Stannie
sees in his brother a move towards libertinism:

> Jim boasts – for he often boasts now – of being modern. He calls himself a
> socialist but attaches himself to no school of socialism. He marks the uproot-
> ing of feudal principles. Besides this, and that subtle egoism which he calls
> the modern mind, he proclaims all kinds of anti-Christian ideals – selfishness,
> licentiousness, pitilessness. (1962: 48)

In fact, the elder brother's licentious ways are described as an attempt to
deepen the break with the church; in a marginal note Stannie adds that his
brother is trying to commit the sin against the Holy Ghost purely 'for the purpose of getting outside the utmost rim of Catholicism' (1962: 49). This is a
reference to a passage in the New Testament that has troubled philosophers
and theologians because it sets a limit to God's grace: saint Augustine even
called it one of the most difficult ideas in scripture: 'And whosoever shall speak
a word against the Son of Man, it shall be forgiven him, but unto him that blas-
phemeth against the Holy Ghost it shall not be forgiven' (Lk. 12.10). Even our
most trustworthy source on doctrine, the *Catholic Encyclopedia*, is not quite sure
whether to follow the interpretation of Saint Augustine or that of Saint Thomas.
For the former, only final impenitence qualifies as the vilest of sins that could
be truly unpardonable, whereas Saint Thomas remains closer to the text of the
gospel by claiming that the sin against the Holy Ghost is blasphemy. Pope Pius X
had less difficulty in identifying this sin: in his catechism, he answers the
question on how many sins against the Holy Ghost there are: 'The sins against
the Holy Ghost are six: (1) Despairing of being saved; (2) Presuming on being
saved without merit; (3) Opposing the known truth; (4) Envying another's
graces; (5) Obstinately remaining in sin; (6) Final impenitence.'[3] It is not clear
whether Joyce ever read this catechism and it seems more likely that for him, as
for Saint Thomas, blasphemy was the sin he was aiming for. If that is the case,
he was in good company: Gustave Flaubert had achieved something similar in
'Un Cœur Simple' when he had his pious heroine in her final moments take
her stuffed parrot for the Holy Ghost.

It is clear from his diary that Stanislaus Joyce's early ideas are part of a fundamentally anti-bourgeois attitude. Like his older brother he despises priests and

especially the Jesuits who had trained him; in his beliefs (which he claims he only rarely communicates to others) he distinguishes himself from his peers, but he does so at a considerable price, which in a passage that echoes Pascal's wager he seems eager to pay:

> I have no certitude in me. If they are right, then I lose all. If I am right, they certainly suffer nothing. I quite envisage the fact that my policy is bad policy, but I could not change with them if I would. I can answer them no questions, but I do not believe their blessed fable of Jesus Christ nor in the Church they have built out of it, and though I am quite without principles and accuse myself of inconsistency, a personal honour will not let me try to believe for policy's sake. This enlivening of my faith in unbelief seems to me not unworthy. (1962: 97)

This self-portrait of the Nietzschean heroic and male unbeliever is one that is not untypical for the period between the 1860s and 1914.

In the two accounts of the relationship with his brother that were published in 1950 and 1958, Stanislaus Joyce confirmed what he had written in his early diaries, which of course he relied on heavily in the preparation of both *Recollections of James Joyce* and *My Brother's Keeper*. But it is clear from his strong language that his feelings about Ireland and the church had not changed in the almost half-century that separated his older from his younger self. The new account simply has more details about the power of the church over education and over the lives of ordinary Irish men and women and it is clear from the diary that it was especially the sentimentalism of Irish politics and religion that Stanislaus objected to.

In *Recollections*, a translation of two essays that had appeared in Italian just after his brother's death in 1941, Stanislaus was at pains to correct misapprehensions about his brother such as the fact that unlike Stephen Dedalus, James did not refuse to pray at his mother's death bed. This correction itself leads to the observation that Joyce's relationship with his catholic mother remained problematic until the end of his life, as when the last time the two brothers met in Zürich in the spring of 1937 he was trying to convince another composer to work on a libretto he was going to write about Byron's *Cain*: 'He did not succeed; but I knew that the idea of conflict between the mother, who lives in fear of God, and the outcast son, wandering cursed upon the hostile earth, was still milling about in his mind, and it saddened me' (1950: 11).[4] In the same context Stanislaus also claims that theosophy briefly served James 'as a religion of transition: He read Swedenborg, Blake, Madame Blavatsky, Col. Olcott, Leadbeater, and Annie Besant' (11–12). Although James later considered this enthusiasm to be the only one that had been a total waste of time, it was itself replaced by something else and here we find an affirmation of the idea of Joyce's secular priesthood: 'In truth, it was not to theosophy but to art that Joyce transferred the ardor of his temperament and quite a bit of his intransigence' (12).

In *My Brother's Keeper*, published posthumously in 1958, Stanislaus writes
that he cannot recall Joyce's religious crisis (as it is described in Chapter 3 of
A Portrait of the Artist as a Young Man), although there were signs of his brother's
return to the church, which Stanislaus observed with some disdain, despite the
fact that as the younger brother he himself reluctantly went to mass and had
not yet made the final step into unbelief. Useful as a corrective to some critics'
faith in Joyce's native knowledge of the bible are Stanislaus's comments:

> In Catholic homes and in Catholic schools the Bible is never read. In all the
> years from the time when I was at a nuns' school at Blackrock to the time
> when I left Belvedere, never once was the English Bible, or Douay version,
> or Latin Vulgate opened or read or discussed in or out of class. [. . .] The
> Catholic Church has its own shrewd reasons for preferring to keep the Bible
> a sealed book in a dead language. Religions thrive on the ignorance of
> religion. (1958: 114)[5]

It is the reading of an English edition of the gospels that had been left by the
previous occupiers of the new house and which the Joyce children discovered
in the back of the garden that leads Stanislaus to his break with religion, which
is here described in greater detail, but, of course, retrospectively. He mentions
reading Renan's *La vie de Jésus* 'in the cheap translation published by the
Rationalist Press Association' (which cannot have been before 1904, when this
edition was first published), although he was not really impressed by what he
calls the ex-priest's 'picnic Christianity.' He also read Luther's conversations
with Melanchton and Carlyle's essay on Luther, but thought that the first
reformer suffered 'the mental attitude of some sturdy Irish parish priest' (1958:
115). All this reading and thinking led to what he calls the 'attitude of benevo-
lent agnosticism' (146) that would be his philosophy for the rest of his life and,
more urgently at the time, the refusal to do his Easter duty that led in its turn
to the problems with his father and for which his mother held his older brother
responsible. In his book Stanislaus takes pride in claiming that he refused to do
his Easter duty before his brother had made that decision and that in *Stephen
Hero* James borrowed sceptical ideas from his diary, one that Jesus could have
strengthened the human part of his nature by having been born ugly and
misshapen and the other that the saviour's relations with women suggest that
he certainly was not a eunuch.

After describing his own growing sense of unbelief, Stanislaus claims that his
brother's attitude towards religion was different:

> He felt it was imperative that he should save his real spiritual life from
> being overlaid and crushed by a false one that he had outgrown. He felt that
> poets in the measure of their gifts and personalities were the repositories
> of the genuine spiritual life of their race, and that priests were usurpers.
> (1958: 120)

Later in the book Stanislaus claims that his brother was an 'unwilling unbeliever like Renan' (1958: 227), but here he writes that James's continuing interest in the church was based on 'the fact that he considered Catholic philosophy
to be the most coherent attempt' to establish the stability in life that enables
ordinary people to survive, by inoculating them against the realities of the
world. In the future, literature would replace religion and therefore it had to
present the world as it is, not as it ought to be. Anybody who compromised with
that aim committed the literary equivalent of simony: 'Falsity of purpose was
the literary sin against the Holy Ghost, and he was vigilant to detect it. In his
fashion not unlike Carlyle's ideal of the poet as priest, he watched, though he
did not pray' (121). Stanislaus rejects attempts such as those of Italo Svevo 'to
represent him as a man pining for the ancient Church he had abandoned, and
at a loss for moral support without the religion in which he was bred.' Stanislaus
also disagrees with his brother's ideas about the role of the church:

> He found its theologians ruthlessly logical, granting their premises, and sug-
> gestive of thought even when he did not agree with them, and something of
> the pomp and ceremony with which the legend of Jesus is told impressed him
> profoundly, but on almost all the points of first importance, his attitude
> towards Catholicism was more like that of the gargoyles outside the Church
> than of the saints within it. (1958: 139)

In the same spirit Stanislaus rejects the notion that his brother's mind was
structured by the Jesuits: 'Their aim is to enslave the mind completely, and
make it work for their ends. In my brother's case, they failed signally' (139).
Stanislaus repeats that through Yeats and Russell his brother found in theosophy 'a kind of interim religion' but the enthusiasm was brief and James came to
regard the episode as the only one that had been a complete waste of time,
although it did lead to his reading of mystical writers about a 'real spiritual
experience,' an interest that Stanislaus had no sympathy for. Stanislaus Joyce
was a perfect example of a nineteenth-century freethinker and it is only natural
that at the end of his introduction to Stanislaus's book, Ellmann concludes:

> His Triestine friends thought of Professor Joyce as like Cato, and there is
> something of Cato's almost monumental integrity in his life. Incapable of
> anything less than honesty, he antagonized imperial and fascist authorities
> alike. In his liberal and anti-clerical views, he was a democrat of the school of
> 1848. (1958: 25)

Joyce's Letters

The most reliable guide to Joyce's thoughts on religion may be found, not in his
work, in the Stanislaus diaries or in the memories of his friends written decades

after the fact, but in his own letters. Although later in life he was said to have
been very old-fashioned in his conversation, especially in the company of strang-
ers or women, even a cursory examination of his letters shows that in correspondence with family and good friends, he frequently and crudely expressed
his lack of religious belief. In fact, especially in the letters to his favourite aunt
Mrs. Murray, he seems to have found pleasure in shocking her with his blunt
language. On New Year's Eve 1904 Joyce writes from Pola (at that time part of
the Austro-Hungarian empire) that he hates 'this Catholic country' and he
even ends his letter with: 'In conclusion – I spit upon the image of the Tenth
Pius' (*Letters I* 58). Even as late as October 1921 when he asks her for information about the Dillon family, he purposefully uses profanity to tell her to get
'an ordinary sheet of foolscap and a pencil and scribble any God damn drivel
you may remember' (*Letters I* 174). But these are exceptions; especially in
letters to people he did not know well, Joyce was extremely reticent in the way
he expressed himself.

Although to some extent the addressee of a letter will affect the tone and the
kinds of things one puts down on paper, the correspondence may well be the
most direct evidence we have of Joyce's own ideas at the time they were written.
It is clear that by the time he first went to Paris to study medicine he already
thought of himself as a freethinker. Even in an early begging letter to Lady
Gregory in November 1902, Joyce describes himself as a 'misbeliever' (*Letters I*
53) and the protestant lady answers in kind by saying that unfortunately the
only person she knows in Paris is 'a very devout Catholic Churchman' (*Letters II*
15). On 9 March 1903 we learn that John Synge told Joyce that he had 'a mind
like Spinoza' (*Letters II* 35).

The first letters and postcards to Nora are flirtatious and not really serious,
but the young poet must have told her his opinions about religion very early in
their relationship: already in late July he signs a letter to her as 'Thy Christian
Brother-in-Luxuriousness' (*Letters II* 44) and a few days later he writes: 'In
virtue of the apostolic powers vested in me by His Holiness Pope Pius the Tenth
I hereby give you permission to come without skirts to receive the Papal Benediction which I shall be pleased to give you. Yours in the Agonising Jew, Vicenzo
Vannutelli (Cardinal Deacon)' (*Letters II* 45–6).[6] It is clear from this reference
that Nora was aware of her new friend's opinions about the church, but at the
end of August there must have been some sort of crisis, because on the 29th
Joyce writes to explain to her that his mind 'rejects the whole present social
order and Christianity – home, the recognized virtues, classes of life, and religious doctrines' (48). He rejects his home, but mostly his religion, and then
comes the passage that was quoted in the beginning of this book: 'Six years ago
I left the Catholic Church, hating it most fervently. I found it impossible for me
to remain in it on account of the impulses of my nature. I made secret war upon
it when I was a student and declined to accept the positions it offered me. By
doing this I made myself a beggar but I retained my pride. Now I make open

war upon it by what I write and say and do. I cannot enter the social order except as a vagabond' (*Letters II* 48). This statement is the closest Joyce ever got to explaining his ideological and political commitment in writing.

A few days later the crisis in their relationship seems to have been smoothed over and their respective opinions are now clear, because his writing has acquired a new boldness: 'How I hate God and death! How I like Nora! Of course you are shocked at these words, pious creature that you are' (*Letters II* 49). The other letters of the summer of 1904 clearly indicate that some of the tension between them may have been due to Joyce's candour in discussing his views on life and to his reluctance to use the word 'love,' as is indicated in the circuitous manner in which he continues to express his feelings for her (55)

As soon as the couple had left Dublin, it is mostly in his letters to his brother and to his aunt Josephine that we find the most candid expressions of his thinking: in the former case because he knew that his brother shared his views and in the latter that these views would certainly shock his favourite aunt. The practical and legal matters caused by his principles had a certain impact on the young lovers, as Joyce writes to his brother from Pola. James writes that he had been lucky enough to meet Almidano Artifoni there, a man who was 'a socialist like myself' and who had advised Joyce to 'sign all the papers as for married people' (*Letters II* 68). It is also clear that Joyce was reading a lot in Pola, not just Henry James and George Moore, but also political writers such as the German socialist Ferdinand Lasalle and the French bible scholar and freethinker Ernest Renan: the latter's *Souvenirs* he does not understand because the book is too romantic, too much 'regret at having to abandon dear old Grandmother Church . . . No wonder Huysmans calls him a comedian' (72). In another letter to his brother, Joyce tells the story of how Nora as a girl had almost been seduced by a young priest who afterwards 'told her to say in confession it was a man not a priest did "that" to her? Useful difference' (72).

Joyce's most active anticlerical phase was certainly between 1904 and 1914, when he lived in Pola, Trieste, Rome and Trieste again, especially in letters to his brother, of which we have more, of course, when they were not both living in Trieste. Even when Joyce is not sure whether Nora has conceived, he is already telling his brother: 'My child, if I have one, will of course not be baptized but will be registered in my name' (*Letters II* 75). The news of the birth of a son brings Stanislaus to write: 'It is not a small thing either that one human being is born, to whom the churches can lay no claim, whose commonsense will not be worried by the necessity of taking seriously the fable of Jesus of Nazareth. [. . .] You certainly lost no time but be careful of the first of the "liberal progeny" – they're brittle' (102). A few months later Joyce writes to his brother about his unbaptized son, in characteristically strong language: 'Thanks be to Jaysus no gospeller has put his dirty face within the bawl of an ass of him yet' (124). His anticlerical reading continues: in January 1905 he orders the English translation of Strauss's life of *Life of Jesus* and the Jesus biography by Renan, which he has read by the end of the next month and liked very much ('the temper is delightful'), even to the extent that he offers to translate the passage describing the death of Christ for his brother (who therefore must be mistaken when he thinks he has read the book in Dublin). Stanislaus dislikes the book and describes it as 'the standard work for all believers in the Nineteenth Century, for all believers, that is, whose inmost commonsense, though they say the Apostle's Creed, revolts against the idea of an absolute divinity packing itself into a Jew, like the Imp in R.L.S.'s story into a bottle' (*Letters II* 117–18).

Most of the writers that Joyce was reading at the time were socialists. He read two novels by Anatole France, one of the most prominent French freethinkers and president of one of the French freethinking organizations, but he did not like the work, despite the fact that their author is 'an intellectual socialist, I understand' (*Letters II* 85). In a letter at the beginning of May, Joyce describes himself as 'socialistic artist' who is trying to lead a more civilized life than his contemporaries and again the fact that he had refused to marry is a crucial factor: 'why should I have brought Nora to a priest or a lawyer to make her swear away her life to me? And why should I superimpose on my child the very troublesome burden of belief which my father and mother superimposed on me?' In the same letter he writes that one of his colleagues claims that he will die a Catholic, 'because I am always moping in and out of the Greek Churches and am a believer at heart: whereas in my opinion I am incapable of belief of any kind' (89). In the same letter he mentions that he is reading an *Ecclesiastical History* that could either be the history of the English church by the venerable Bede or the earlier history of the christian churches by Eusebius of Caesarea. In the spirit of Renan, Joyce offers his own Prayer on the Acropolis:

O Vague Something behind Everything!

For the love of the Lord Christ change my curse-o'-God state of affairs. Give me for Christ's sake a pen and an ink-bottle and some peace of mind and then, by the crucified Jaysus, if I don't sharpen that little pen and dip it into fermented ink and write tiny little sentences about the people who betrayed me send me to hell. After all, there are many ways of betraying people. It wasn't only the Galilean suffered that. Whoever the hell you are, I inform you that this [is] a poor comedy you expect me to play and I'm damned to hell if I'll play it for you. What do you mean by urging me to be forbearing? For your sake I refrained from taking a little black fellow from Bristol by the nape of the neck and hurling him into the street when he spat some of his hatched venom at me. But my heroic nature urged me to do this because he was smaller than I. For your sake, I allowed a cyclist to use towards me his ignoble and cowardly manners, pretending to see nothing, pretending that he was my equal. I sorrowfully confess to you, old chap, that I was a damn fool. But if you only grant me that thing I ask you for I will go to Paris where, I believe, there is a person by the name of Anatole France much admired by a Celtic philologist by the name of Goodbetterbest and I'll say to him 'Respected master, is this pen pointed enough?' Amen. (*Letters II* 110)

Around the same time a letter from Vincent Cosgrave makes it clear that Buck Mulligan's blasphemies in the first chapter of *Ulysses* are those of Oliver St John Gogarty: he sends Joyce the full text of 'The Song of the Cheerful (but slightly sarcastic) Jaysus,' which Buck Mulligan will sing in the first chapter of *Ulysses*. Cosgrave adds that Gogarty talked to him about Christmas and about 'the virtues of the Cross – providing the protagonist with a backbone and being the sign in which he conquered' and he ends his letter with a blasphemous reference to one of Christ's last words on the cross: 'Meanwhile I rot and am athirst So goodbye Yours Vincent Cosgrave' (*Letters II* 126–8). In discussing the recent marriage of his pagan friend Gogarty, Joyce writes to his brother that this only confirmed the value of his own 'socialistic tendencies': 'For my part I believe that to establish the church in full power again in Europe would mean a renewal of the Inquisition – though, of course, the Jesuits tell us that the Dominicans never broke men on the wheel or tortured them on the rack' (148).

Joyce's presence in Rome seems to have brought out all his anticlericalism and socialism: he tells his brother that he'll send him copies of *L'Asino*, 'the Italian anti-clerical newspaper,' he keeps him informed about the progress of the Socialist Party Congress that was held in Rome at the time, and he tells his brother that his son began to shout in Saint Peter's 'immediately when the lazy whores of priests began to chant' (*Letters II* 152). Joyce was especially critical of the Jesuits, whom he called 'the black lice' in one of his letters, but the Dominicans did not escape his ire either. When he found refuge in a Dominican church, he was struck by the enormous riches of this originally mendicant order: 'I think my policy of subtracting oneself and one's progeny from the church is too slow. I don't believe the church has suffered vitally from the number of her apostates.' The order is still much too wealthy and that explains why it can only object to the 'quite heretical theory of socialism' (165–6).

The letters from Rome are full of anticlerical remarks, as for instance in October 1906 when he writes of a Russian general who was chasing his wife and her lover through Europe in order to shoot them both. Among the eminent persons asked about the morality of this was Father Bernard Vaughan. 'He said, "If it were my case I would simply 'chuck' the woman." I suppose he was misreported by a reporter with a sense of verse. Fr. B. V. is the most diverting public figure in England at present. I never see his name but I expect some enormity' (*Letters II* 182). A month later he explained to Stanislaus that the *Sinn Fein* leader Arthur Griffith had every reason to be afraid of the Irish priests.

But, possibly, they are also a little afraid of him too. After all, he is holding out some secular liberty to the people and the Church doesn't approve of that. I quite see, of course, that the Church is still, as it was in the time of Adrian IV, the enemy of Ireland: but, I think, her time is almost up. (*Letters II* 187)

in 1900, Huysmans in 1901 and Verlaine and Fogazzaro in 1902. Among the reviews that he wrote from 1902, a few were about freethinkers: George Meredith and a biography of Giordano Bruno. His library in Trieste, now at the Harry Ransom Center in Austin, Texas, shows his continued interest in religious matters. The collection contains a study of Saint Paul by the moderately liberal Dean Farrar, and a book describing the documentary theory about the Pentateuch. We also find Ernest Renan's *Life of Jesus* in a later Rationalist Press edition, and John Robert Seeley's *Ecce Homo*, one of the Victorian biographies of Christ that had been severely criticized when the book was first published in 1866: in colourful language the evangelical Lord Shaftesbury called it 'the most pestilential volume ever vomited forth from the jaws of hell' (Neil 1975: 287).

In addition Joyce seems to have owned books that could have been part of any European freethinker's library, such as *The New Spirit*, a book of studies by Havelock Ellis on liberal heroes like Diderot, Heine, Whitman. In the introduction Ellis describes the new spirit in Europe:

> [T]his devotion to truth, this instinctive search after the causes of things, has become what may be called a new faith. The fruits of this scientific spirit are sincerity, patience, humility, the love of nature and the love of man. 'Wisdom is to speak truth and consciously to act according to nature.' So spake the old Ephesian, Heraclitus, to whom, rather than to Socrates, men are now beginning to look back as the exponent of the true Greek spirit; and so also speaks modern science. (Ellis 1906: 6–7)

Another freethinking philosopher was Schopenhauer and Joyce owned a copy of the essays in which one of the philosopher's mouthpieces is accused of not being sufficiently respectful of religion and he answers in language that could be Richard Rowan's (which is what Joyce wanted to achieve, according to the notes to *Exiles*):

> *Philoalethes. Nego consequentiam!* I don't see at all why I should have respect for lies and frauds because other people are stupid. I respect truth everywhere, and it is precisely for that reason that I cannot respect anything that is opposed to it. My maxim is, *Vigeat veritas, et pereat mundus.* (97)

In addition there is a book by the positivist philosopher Herbert Spencer, a historical study of the Lollards as 'Glimpses of English Dissent in the Middle Ages,' and a novel by William Hale White, *The Autobiography of Mark Rutherford*, in which the author describes the loss of faith of a dissenting minister and the resulting sense of despair (Hale White later complained that his protagonist was seen as a hero, whereas he had meant to depict 'a victim of the century'). Of course we cannot be sure how representative the current collection of books is for what Joyce's real library in Trieste had been, and we cannot even be sure if some of these books were not Stanislaus's, but it seems to be sufficiently certain that Joyce's reading in the first ten years of his stay on the continent was consistent with the political and religious opinions that we also find in his letters.

Even if we take into account that all of the memories of Joyce's friends and acquaintances might be tainted by hindsight, the published interviews and memoirs do show a certain degree of unanimity about his religious and ideological opinions. This is especially clear in the pieces collected by Willard Potts in *Portraits of the Artist in Exile*: in Trieste Joyce displayed the strange combination of an extreme enmity towards religion and an almost perverse interest in the liturgy, especially that of Paschaltide in which he identified so much with the fate of Jesus that he would have tears in his eyes. The latter is reported in Alessandro Francini Bruni's farcical essay 'Joyce Stripped Naked in the Piazza,' the title of which not accidentally refers to one of the Stations of the Cross. Bruni mentions Joyce's radical unbelief but he refuses to call him 'irreligious': 'He is without religion. There is a difference. He doesn't even believe the bread he is eating. He is so consistent in his unbelief that his children have not been baptized' (Potts 1979: 35). Somewhat later Bruni claims that Joyce is neither a follower of Voltaire nor an intellectual anarchist, but instead 'a negator' (37). His essay ends with a prayer for Joyce 'that Jesus may give you the light of his faith' (38). Louis Gillet was a catholic who only got to know Joyce in the last part of his life, but he confirms the early portrait of Bruni. He describes the young Joyce (whom of course he had not really known) as 'meditating nothing less than an attack on our saintly mother, the Catholic Church. [. . .] his gods were Ibsen, Giordano Bruno, Julian the Apostate. [. . .] He spoke highly of himself as the house-breaker of religion, the arch-heresiarch, the Antichrist. After him the priests are done for!' (1985: 172). Gillet not only accepts Joyce's 'jacobinism,' which he says is perfectly natural in a priest-ridden country like Ireland, but he claims that it is Joyce's fight with religion that gives his work its universal value. Irish politics are no more than 'a tiny detail in the total of world affairs; on the literary level it is of no more consequence than the Félibrige and the Museo Arlaten [a literary society and a museum devoted to Provencal culture]. But to declare war on Heaven meant stepping out of local intrigues; it meant giving to this enterprise a titanic character and placing oneself on a level with the universe' (173). And this is confirmed by Jacques Mercanton, who also got to know Joyce in the last part of his life. From the period in Trieste until the very end of his life, all these European friends of Joyce emphasized the importance of his anti-religious opinions to his artistic work. But some of them also stressed that despite these opinions, his mind remained catholic in structure.

In the Paris years, Padraic and Mary Colum were good friends, but Joyce often teased them about their faith, for example when he and Herbert Gorman thought it was funny to make Padraic break his Friday Fast or when he was rebuked by Paul Léon for making derogatory remarks about the pope in the presence of the Colums. Mary Colum had many contacts with catholics in Paris, among them the philosopher Jacques Maritain whose verdict on Baudelaire's catholicism ('The intellectual structure of his mind was Catholic') she passed on to Joyce. Although Joyce made fun of Maritain and of the very idea of someone having a mind with a catholic structure, in the memoir she wrote with her husband Mary Colum claims: 'I have never known a mind so fundamentally Catholic in structure as Joyce's own' (1958: 207). This comment, passed on by Ellmann in the biography, would be the basis of most later attempts by catholic readers to reclaim Joyce as one of their own, whereas the writer himself, as he told Samuel Beckett, could not agree: 'For me there is only one alternative to scholasticism, scepticism' (*JJ* 661).

Later in life Joyce's attitude did not change: in the final year of his life he was still attacking catholic education to Maria Jolas, who was bringing up her children in the faith (*JJ* 743), and there is no indication that at any point of his life he changed his mind. When the American lawyer (and co-founder of the American Civil Liberties Union) Morris L. Ernst asked him when he had left the catholic church, Joyce answered: 'That's for the Church to say' (Ernst 1945: 118). Joyce's answer was ironic, because he knew very well that his opinions and his conduct had placed him outside of the Church of Rome. If the church took seriously its own rules and regulations, it could not do otherwise than reject the old rebel. This may not be the case anymore today and at least in the first decades after Vatican Council II the catholic church became much more reluctant to issue statements about the post-mortem fate of individual souls. But the church at the time when Joyce made the statement really did not have a choice in the matter: when after his death the Colums approached priests and Jesuits in New York, they met with the refusal to say a mass for his memory 'on the grounds of Joyce's alienation from the Church' (1958: 207). I feel sure that James Joyce would not have disagreed with that decision.

Chapter 5

Loss of Religion in Retrospect:
From *Epiphanies* to *Exiles*

Joyce's own loss of religious beliefs was important enough for the young writer to make it an important theme in most of his early writings and it is interesting to observe the different ways in which religion and the lack thereof appear in the works of Joyce's apprenticeship as a writer. For the first section of this chapter I will use the versions that were made available by Robert Scholes and Richard M. Kain in *The Workshop of Daedalus.*

Among the earliest of Joyce's works are the little prose poems that he perversely gave the religious name of epiphanies. Although it is difficult to date them, some of the epiphanies seem to recall real events from Joyce's adolescence and these may very well illustrate attitudes from around the time of his religious crisis. Number 7 describes a moment of religious fervour and peace in a 'quiet chapel,' while number 6, a horrible dream about hell, is dated to the 'the latter part of 1893' (Scholes and Kain 1965: 16). Most of the epiphanies depict the world of the young unbeliever who looks down on his contemporaries' vulgar interests and who feels pity for his dead brother but laments the fact that he cannot pray for him, 'as the others do' (30). Joyce's own analysis of his loss of faith (the sex–religion nexus) is powerfully present in a number of epiphanies describing young women. In number 24 a girl's arm touches the narrator's knees and a glance at her eyes is described with the sensuous imagery of the Song of Songs. Joyce powerfully combines exotic place names (*Amana, mountains of the leopards*) with the luscious Latin of the Vulgate: 'Inter ubera mea commorabitur,' between my breasts he will find rest. Number 39 contains a similarly intimate portrait of a young woman: 'She stands, her book held lightly at her breast, reading the lesson.' In the second part of the text, after a description of the girl, the narrator asks what lesson she is reading: 'of apes, of strange inventions, or the legends of the martyrs?' Joyce contrasts here a possible reference to Darwin and the products of modernity, with the religious literature of the legends of the martyrs. But even the latter subject has a sadomasochistic appeal that is only intensified by the language of the final sentence ('Who knows how deeply meditative, how reminiscent is this comeliness of Raffaello?'), which the editors Scholes and Kain call Pateresque, but that in its use of the word 'comeliness' also refers to the biblical Song of Songs.

These themes also dominate Joyce's first attempt at autobiography, the strange essay called 'A Portrait of the Artist.' It begins, after a general introduction about the genre of literary portrait painting, with a description of the young boy's extraordinary religious zeal: 'He ran through his measure like a spendthrift saint, astonishing many by ejaculatory fervours, offending many by airs of the cloister' (Scholes and Kain 1965: 60). In this version of his youth, Joyce writes that when he entered the university, he was 'still soothed by devotional exercises' (61). It is only there that the 'fantastic idealist' begins to celebrate his being different from his fellow students, whose conventional tastes in literature match their religious beliefs: they even think that God is responsible for killing Emile Zola and they believe 'in the adjustment of Catholic teaching to every day needs, in the Church diplomatic' (61). The latter expression is ironic and not very diplomatic. Joyce employs it as a third term between 'church militant,' traditionally the earthly church that fights its enemies on earth, and the 'church triumphant,' the community of saints in heaven. The church diplomatic, on the other hand, is an Irish church that lives by virtue of its ability to compromise. Irish catholics behave like the students who display towards their superiors 'a nervous and (wherever there was question of authority) a very English liberalism' (Scholes and Kain 1965: 61–2). For them the 'union of faith and fatherland was ever sacred,' but the life of compromise (symptomatic for this life is the clerkship at Guinness's offered to the young artist by an 'earnest Jesuit') is not sufficient for the subject of the portrait who desires '(in the language of the schoolmen) an arduous good' (62). The refusal to submit is said to be due to 'a temperament ever trembling towards its ecstasy' and when he finally tells a friend he has left the Church, he adds that he 'left it through the gates of Assisi' (63). What he means by this, apparently, is that he will find a similar exultation through discipline in the exercise of art as he had earlier yearned for in his religious practice. But the turn towards 'the simple history of the Poverello' as an example to emulate is quickly replaced by that of the 'maddest of companies': Joachim Abbas, Bruno the Nolan, Michael Sendivogius and 'all the hierarchs of initiation' (65). With the esoteric wisdom of these heretics he aims 'to reunite the children of the spirit, jealous and long-divided': 'A thousand eternities were to be reaffirmed, divine knowledge was to be re-established.' This pagan call to arms falls on deaf ears: he might as well 'have summoned a regiment of the winds,' so there is no other choice than henceforth to travel alone (64) in a voyage for which he still seeks a tutelary goddess: the 'dearest of mortals [. . .] an envoy from the fair courts of life,' a creature for him to sin with (65–6).

This period of all too bodily ecstasy also passes and what remains is a faith in his artistic mission, in the form of an inverted *credo* (Latin *nego* means 'I deny'):

His Nego, therefore, written amid a chorus of peddling Jews' gibberish and Gentile clamour, was drawn up valiantly while true believers prophesied fried atheism and was hurled against the obscene hells of our Holy Mother: but, that outburst over, it was urbanity in warfare. (Scholes and Kain 1965: 67)

The rather tortuous syntax leads to a more general call to arms for a new generation, not yet born, 'and amid the general paralysis of an insane society, the confederate will issues in action' (Scholes and Kain 1965: 68). These are the last words of Joyce's first attempt at a self-portrait.

What was Joyce trying to do in this strange text? Although the portrait differs in important points from his later autobiographical writings, it does seem to contain the core of Joyce's self-understanding. The link between religious discipline and sexual ecstasy is there, as is the artist's Nietzschean or more appropriately Yeatsian prophetico-artistic appeal to something that he calls 'the confederate will.' But the differences with the later versions of his portrait are also evident: the young artist that Joyce had intended to present to the readers of *Dana* only loses his religion during his first year at the university and his conversion is not initially caused by his sexual adventures, but by a feeling of superiority over his university peers and their lack of aesthetic and political sophistication.

Stephen Hero

The copybook now at Buffalo in which Joyce wrote the first draft of his essay 'A Portrait,' also contains traces of Joyce's more ambitious autobiographical attempt, *Stephen Hero*. In the Dublin diary of Stanislaus Joyce we read that by the end of March 1904, Joyce had written the first eleven chapters of *Stephen Hero*:

> The chapters are exceptionally well written in a style which seems to me altogether original. It is a lying autobiography and a raking satire. He is putting nearly all his acquaintances in it, and the Catholic Church comes in for a bad quarter of an hour. (Joyce S 1962: 25)

Unfortunately we no longer have the first 15 chapters of *Stephen Hero* and the Stephen we meet in Chapter XVI is already a consummate freethinker. It is therefore providential that on the pages following the first version of 'A Portrait of the Artist' in the notebook, we have notes and a plan for a number of the early chapters of *Stephen Hero*, which Scholes and Kain have included in their *Workshop*.

The first outline is that of Chapter VIII, written in the space left by a long list of characters for the novel. It refers to events in the first half of what is now Chapter 2 of *A Portrait of the Artist as a Young Man*. Two pages earlier we find an outline of Chapter IX (describing events now to be found in the middle of Chapter 2) that can be summed up in the words of the first entry 'Rivalry with Vincent Heron.' There is no reference to the accusation of heresy that is a central part of the corresponding scene in *A Portrait of the Artist as a Young Man*. Chapter X, the outline of which follows, was going to contain, after the trip to Cork with his father and a meeting in Bray between Stephen's love interest Eileen and his best friend, a rather more vigorous erotic encounter than the embrace with the prostitute that now ends Chapter 2: 'Soixante-Neuf. (after a walk)' (Scholes and Kain 1965: 71). These outlines of chapters now missing were written consecutively: as we know from his later practice, Joyce first wrote only on the recto pages of copybooks, leaving the versos for additions and corrections, but later he would make his way backwards again, filling the empty spaces left on the verso pages. It is clear that the criticism of the church that Stanislaus found in the first eleven chapters of the novel, must have been concentrated in the last chapter for which we find a description on page 16 of the notebook. The events are dated between August and December 1893 and after 'sensations coming home' (which refers to the description of the trip to Cork in the previous chapter) we read 'Gradual irreligiousness' and 'Epiphany of Thornton'. As Scholes and Kain point out in a footnote, this epiphany has not survived, but Ned Thornton was a neighbor of the Joyces and was used by Joyce as a model for characters in the stories 'Grace' and 'Eveline' in *Dubliners* and for Mr Kernan in *Ulysses*. The rest of the chapter was taken up by a description of the retreat that is now part of the third chapter of *A Portrait of the Artist as a Young Man*.

More interesting for our present purposes is a collection of notes on the recto pages of the notebook, between the outlines that, if indeed they were chronologically inscribed, were in reality written earlier than the chapter outlines. All of these notes concern Christ or other religious leaders like Mohammed, Buddha and Saint Francis, and they all seem to point to the young artist's Poverello phase that had played such a central part in the first 'A Portrait of the Artist.' The links with the hero of the essay and the protagonist of the novel is clear. Reference is made to the enigmatic character of Jesus who has so much in common with the young artist: his 'pride and hatred of his race,' his 'knowledge of men's hearts' and even his 'unique relations with prostitutes' (Scholes and Kain 1965: 72). It is clear that Joyce, already at this early stage (before the drafting of the chapters that describe Stephen's loss of faith), had planned to compare his protagonist with the founder of christianity. This blasphemous comparison may have been original, but the notes on which it was based do not, as Scholes and Kain claim in a footnote, 'relate to Joyce's thinking about Jesus,' at least not this Joyce. They had been copied from Stanislaus's thoughts on this subject in the Dublin diary.

The pages of *Stephen Hero* that were preserved only cover the university years of the young would-be artist, but they are much more explicit about his attitudes to religion than in the published novel. From the first surviving pages Stephen's critical stance towards his Jesuit teachers at University College is clear. Central in the early months at the university is Stephen's isolation from both his teachers and his peers and at the end of what Joyce at some point considered to be the 'end of the First Episode of V' (*SH* 24) of *A Portrait of the Artist as a Young Man*, this theme is explicitly connected to the religious piety that Stephen has only just left behind and that he now translates into a mysticism that might be secular, but that is expressed in biblical and religious terms:

> Phrases came to him asking to have themselves explained. He said to himself: I must wait for the Eucharist to come to me; and then he set about translating the phrase into common sense. He spent days and nights hammering noisily as he built a house of silence for himself wherein he might await his Eucharist, days and nights gathering the first fruits and every peace-offering and heaping them upon his altar where he prayed clamorously the burning token of satisfaction might descend. (*SH* 23–4)

When still in school he is called away by 'a voice agitating the very tympanum of his ear, a flame leaping into divine cerebral life' (*SH* 30) and this at least seems to confirm the religious imagery used to describe his mental state.

In the next chapter Stephen's interest in Ibsen again sets him apart: for his fellow students the Norwegian writer can only be 'one of the "atheistic writers whom the papal secretary puts on the *Index*"' (*SH* 41). In his discussions with the nationalist student Madden, it is clear that the 'Roman, not the Sassenach, was for [Stephen] the tyrant of the islanders' (53). Again the blame lies with the priests who 'encourage the study of Irish that their flocks may be more safely protected from the "wolves of unbelief"; they consider it is an opportunity to withdraw the people into a past of literal, implicit faith' (54). For his part, Stephen's interest in learning Gaelic is not entirely innocent: the classes offer him a chance of getting closer to Emma Clery.

His sceptical brother Maurice does not understand the reason for the sudden interest in the Irish language, but his mother is pleased 'for she thought that the superintendence of priests and the society of harmless enthusiasts might succeed in influencing her son in the right direction: she had begun to fear for him' (*SH* 56). This episode comes exactly twelve months after the retreat which must have been the subject of Chapter XI and Stephen now marvels 'at the terror which had then possessed him' (57). This is followed by a conversation with his brother, who, one year younger, is now doing the same retreat. When Maurice confesses that he feels 'a little stupid,' Stephen typically thinks 'that maybe his brother has not earned the right to be free of the "shackles of the Church"' (58).

Stephen's interest in Emma is thwarted by the presence of Father Moran, 'a low-sized young priest' who is somewhat later called 'a pleasant tender-hearted vulgarian' (*SH* 65) and who may owe his name to D.P. Moran, editor of *The Leader*. The effect of the priest on the young man is predictable: 'Stephen watching this young priest and Emma together usually worked himself into a state of unsettled rage. It was not so much that he suffered personally as that the spectacle seemed to him typical of Irish ineffectualness. Often he felt his fingers itch' (66).

At the beginning of the next chapter Stephen runs into his old school friend Wells, who is studying to become a priest. In the company of other young novices Stephen is confronted once more with the fact that he is an outsider:

> It was not any personal pride which would prevent him but a recognition of the incompatibility of two natures, one trained to repressive enforcement of a creed, the other equipped with a vision the angle of which would never adjust itself for the reception of hallucinations and with an intelligence 'which was as much in love with laughter as with combat.' (73–4)

In Chapter XIX Stephen reads his Ibsen essay to his ironing mother and her keen interest in his work surprises the young man. The following dialogue about art is characterized by Stephen's condescension – seemingly mirrored by that of the narrator:

> – You evidently weren't listening to what I said or else you didn't understand what I said. Art is not an escape from life. It's just the very opposite. Art, on the contrary, is the very central expression of life. An artist is not a fellow who dangles a mechanical heaven before the public. The priest does that. The artist affirms out of the fulness of his own life, he creates . . . Do you understand? (86)

One can almost imagine the young iconoclast speaking the last sentences v e r y v e r y s l o w l y.

The major confrontation between Stephen and the religious authorities comes when he is told that his Ibsen paper for the Debating Society has been refused by the official censor, the president of the college. Stephen walks straight up to his office to confront the spiritual advisor, whose main objection to the paper seems to be that Stephen's aesthetic theory 'represents the sum-total of modern unrest and modern freethinking' and that the authors he quotes 'openly profess their atheistic doctrines and fill the minds of their readers with all the garbage of modern society' (91). During the confrontation with the university president Stephen has to keep forcing himself not to show his sarcasm and disdain.

Stephen openly asserts his unbelief for the first time in Chapter XXI of the surviving text, when his mother reminds him that, unlike the previous year, he still has not made his Easter duty. The young poet refuses, because he no longer believes. She blames his apostasy on the kind of books he has been reading and he replies: 'If you were a genuine Roman Catholic, mother, you would burn me as well as the books' (*SH* 135). This conversation is some sort of freethinking breakthrough: Stephen hastens to report it to Cranly, who then attempts to convince his friend to avoid further conflict by pretending to submit to the social norm. In Chapter XXII this new determination is the theme of a conversation with Maurice, whom the narrator with some affection begins to call 'the younger sceptic' and 'the young heathen' (*SH* 144–5). Stephen's walks through Dublin and his hatred of the priests makes him 'an ally of the collectivist politicians, who are often very seriously upbraided by opponents who believe in Jehovahs, and decalogues and judgments with sacrificing the reality to an abstraction' (147). The death of his sister Isabel and the 'inexpressibly mean way' in which she is buried confront him again with the oppressive apparatus of church and state.

Among his teachers and his peers at the university, Stephen's reputation as a freethinker seems to have become a matter of common knowledge. The distance between the young rebel and his fellow students is now acknowledged by both parties and Moynihan's pious paper for the debating society receives its fair share of sarcasm from the narrator when the manner of Zola's demise is discussed: 'Moynihan alluded also to the strange Death of a French atheistic writer and implied that Emmanuel had chosen to revenge himself on the unhappy gentleman by privily tampering with his gas-stove' (172). In his discussions with Cranly, Stephen now quotes Ernest Renan and he also begins his study of heretical Franciscan literature in Marsh's Library. Inspired by Yeats's stories, he reads Joachim of Flora and Elias (of Cortona). He also discusses Yeats's story *The Tables of the Law* with his friends: in this Nietzschean phase he is looking for a *bonum arduum*, an arduous good in a terminology that was borrowed from Thomas Aquinas and that had already appeared in the first 'Portrait.' The use of this term is not just perverse because Stephen has an entirely secular aim in mind, but it is doubly ironic that he borrows a term from the Dominican thinker for a concept that was supposed to play a role in an attitude towards life that was going to be based on that of the order's main rivals, the Franciscans.

Chapter XXIV describes the tribulations of the students' monthly review and its censor. In Stephen's discussions with Cranly, the former's Nietzschean hatred for the crowd is still central: 'My art will proceed from a free and noble source. It is too troublesome for me to adopt the manners of these slaves. I refuse to be terrorized into stupidity' (*SH* 184). Instead he chooses an anarchist form of modernity that he opposes to 'those ancients in the college': 'All modern political and religious criticism dispenses with presumptive States, [and] presumptive Redeemers and Churches' (186–7). In a further interaction with Emma, it is clear that his reputation as somebody who no longer believes in God is firmly established among his circle of friends and Stephen reinforces this reputation by dismissively referring to the 'middle-aged gentleman with the aviary – Jehovah the Second' (188). His attitudes towards the authoritarian Jesuits of the college and 'the plague of Catholicism' is expressed in apocalyptic imagery:

He seemed to see the vermin begotten in the catacombs in an age of sickness and cruelty issuing forth upon the plains and mountains of Europe. Like the plague of locusts described in Callista they seemed to choke the rivers and fill the valleys up. They obscured the sun. (*SH* 194)

Joyce, again perversely, makes use of an image from a novel that Cardinal Newman had finished while still residing in Ireland. In *Callista: A Tale of the Third Century* the male hero is pursued by a mob who blame the Christians for a plague of locusts, but who behave like the insects themselves. Earlier Newman had described the insect visitation in colourful language:

> The bright sun, though hidden by them, illumined their bodies, and was reflected from their quivering wings; and as they heavily fell earthward, they seemed like the innumerable flakes of a yellow-coloured snow. And like snow did they descend, a living carpet, or rather pall, upon fields, crops, gardens, copses, groves, orchards, vineyards, olive woods, orangeries, palm plantations, and the deep forests, sparing nothing within their reach, and where there was nothing to devour, lying helpless in drifts, or crawling forward obstinately, as they best might, with the hope of prey. They could spare their hundred thousand soldiers twice or thrice over, and not miss them; their masses filled the bottoms of the ravines and hollow ways, impeding the traveller as he rode forward on his journey, and trampled by thousands under his horse-hoofs. In vain was all this overthrow and waste by the road-side; in vain their loss in river, pool, and watercourse. The poor peasants hastily dug pits and trenches as their enemy came on; in vain they filled them from the wells or with lighted stubble. Heavily and thickly did the locusts fall: they were lavish of their lives; they choked the flame and the water, which destroyed them the while, and the vast living hostile armament still moved on. (1856: 172)

In his 1891 biography of the cardinal, Richard Hutton had written that Newman describes the invasion by locusts with 'all the imaginative power of a great genius' (Hutton 1891: 221), but Joyce turns the tables on the English convert by using his language to describe the plague of priests swarming Ireland.

Somewhat earlier in Joyce's novel, Newman had already been mentioned in the talk with the dean of studies that later made it into *A Portrait*. In his discussion about Ibsen with the President of the College, Stephen had compared the Norwegian writer's analysis of modern society with Newman's account of 'English protestant morality and belief' (*SH* 92). When Newman is mentioned again, he is first part of the much too conventional list of O'Neill-Glynn's favourite prose writers. At the meeting of the debating society in Chapter XXIII, when a speaker mentions Newman and is applauded, Temple asks Stephen who had been referred to. Stephen, or somebody else, tells him that it was Colonel Russell, one of the heroes of the British army abroad, implying, it seems, that there is not much difference in outlook between the English church and the army: they are both defenders of the status quo. Equally ironic in Stephen's reference to Newman's novel is the fact that the cardinal wrote his story of a beautiful Greek pagan heroine who becomes a christian and dies a martyr's death, in reaction to *Hypathia*, the Alexandrian novel by his major protestant opponent Charles Kingsley about a beautiful pagan mathematician killed by a christian mob.

At this point of the narrative Stephen is tempted. In Chapter XXV he begins to doubt his turning away from catholicism when 'the Church sent an embassy of nimble pleaders into his ears' (*SH* 204). They have many different arguments to make him regret his decision. Stephen needlessly makes his life more difficult: why does he not simply do what is expected of him and then decide to follow his own path after his studies? If he hates enthusiasm in others, how can he be sure of his own decision? He fears that the church will obstruct his desire to become an artist, but even his aesthetic thinking has been anticipated 'item after item' by Thomas, the 'most orthodox doctor of the Church.' Maybe it is only vanity that makes him 'seek out the thorny crown of the heretic' while his entire theory is exemplified in the catholic mass? If protestants are enemies of art, how can he 'assert that his own aristocratic intelligence and passion for a supremely satisfying order in all the fervours of artistic creation were not purely Catholic qualities?' (205). And anyway, how can a sceptic like him be sure that his own views on all these matters will never change? Aristocratic artists should feel solidarity with the aristocratic order of society and only by participating in that order, they may even succeed in radically changing society: 'within the Church you have an opportunity of beginning your revolution in a rational manner' (206). Stephen is well aware that these temptations are similar to the ones Jesus was exposed to before he began his public life; this is made clear at the beginning of Chapter XXVI. But we are then at the end of the manuscript as we now have it; the fragments about Stephen's visit to Mullingar have little new to add.

Because only the middle part of the manuscript has been preserved, we see the protagonist of *Stephen Hero* mainly as a fully developed anticlerical freethinker. His opinions are outspoken and despite the temptations at the end of the remaining fragment, it is clear that the major outlines of the novel are not too dissimilar to those of *A Portrait of the Artist as a Young Man*.

Dubliners

From its very first story, which was also the first to be written, *Dubliners* addresses the issue of religion, as Joyce acknowledged when he wrote to his brother in April 1905 that it had occurred to him, while attending the Greek mass in Trieste, that the story was 'rather remarkable' (*Letters II* 86). 'The Sisters' is only the first in the style that he would later describe as 'scrupulous meanness'; in these stories he casts a cold eye on the catholic city of his youth. 'The Sisters' is a minute description of the reactions of a precocious boy to the death of the priest who was close to him and who, his uncle explains to a friend, 'had a great

wish for him' (*D* 10). As is the case with the other stories in the collection, readers are not given the essence of what is going on: we are never told what it is
that drove Father Flynn into depression and what it is that ends up killing him
and whether these are the same. The boy is just as much fascinated by the
deadly work of paralysis as he is attracted to the word 'paralysis' itself. From the
very beginning it is clear that he despises Old Cotter, the family friend, and that
he keeps his distance from his aunt and uncle. In return, his uncle calls him
'that Rosicrucian there,' affectionately associating him with religious unorthodoxy. It is certainly significant that one of the boy's memories of Father Flynn
dates from the time when the old priest used to ask difficult theological questions and then nod when the boy attempted to answer them. It is not really necessary to assume that there is some dark paedophile secret in the priest's past,
as the critical consensus seems to have become. What is important is that like
the adult Joyce, the boy is both attracted and appalled by the intricacies of catholic thinking and that whatever it was they did together, the priest and he shared
something that will forever remain inaccessible to the outsiders of that relationship (the reader included). In a way this is something that distinguishes Joyce's
collection of stories from George Moore's openly anticlerical tales in *The Untilled
Field* and in the novel *The Lake*. Unlike Joyce, Moore seems to have been incapable of looking at religion from the inside, from the perspective of an ordinary
believer, be it an adult or a child.

A similar feeling of election is present in 'An Encounter' when at times the
narrator seems to feel more affinity with the pervert that he and his friend meet
on their adventures than with his young companion. Here and in the next story
romantic adventures are described as in some way attractive because they
are dangerous as well as exotic (Persia as the locale of the boy's dream in 'The
Sisters' and the wild west stories in 'An Encounter'). The adventures in these
stories function as an alternative to the drab reality of his own life and it is clear
that reading and literature are the only forms of escape available to him. In
'Araby' the boy finds three books that were left by the previous occupant
(a priest) of the house his family has moved into. The first two are predictably
Walter Scott's *The Abbot* (about Mary Queen of Scots) and *The Devout Communi-
cant* by Father William Gahan, but the third is *The Memoirs of Vidocq*, which the
boy likes best 'because its leaves were yellow' (*D* 29). These memoirs of the
Paris Chief of Police are often thought to be the origin of the genre of crime
fiction, so this is a rather strange book to find in the library of a priest. Apparently the young boy's reading has resulted in a strange mixture of religion and
romance: when he accompanies his aunt on a trip to the market to carry her
parcels, he fantasizes about Mangan's sister and the reality of the Dublin streets
is transformed into something else:

These noises converged in a single sensation of life for me: I imagined that
I bore my chalice safely through a throng of foes. Her name sprang to my lips

at moments in strange prayers and praises which I myself did not understand. My eyes were often full of tears (I could not tell why) and at times a flood from my heart seemed to pour itself out into my bosom. I thought little of the future. I did not know whether I would ever speak to her or not or, if I spoke to her, how I could tell her of my confused adoration. (*D* 31)

The narrator's crush is described in lush religious language and he even compares his devotion to her with a word that the *Catholic Encyclopedia* defines in these terms:

This worship called forth by God, and given exclusively to Him as God, is designated by the Greek name *latreia* (latinized, *latria*), for which the best translation that our language affords is the word Adoration. Adoration differs from other acts of worship, such as supplication, confession of sin, etc., inasmuch as it formally consists in self-abasement before the Infinite, and in devout recognition of His transcendent excellence. ('Adoration')

That there is a link between religion and romance is reinforced when the boy goes into the room where the priest died in order to indulge in the full ecstasy of his passion: 'All my senses seemed to desire to veil themselves and, feeling that I was about to slip from them, I pressed the palms of my hands together until they trembled, murmuring: *O love! O love!* many times' (*D* 31). The closing bazaar itself reminds the boy of the church: 'I recognized a silence like that which pervades a church after a service' (34).

The heroine of 'Eveline' also dreams of adventures in foreign lands: she is enthralled when her sailor-friend Frank tells her of the many places he has visited and about 'the terrible Patagonians' (*D* 39). Eveline, like some of the heroes of Moore's *The Untilled Field*, is waiting to leave her Irish life and the house of her father. She is sitting next to a coloured print of the promises made to the Blessed Margaret Mary Alacoque and there is a photograph of a priest, but Eveline has never found out his name. But even that nameless priest, a school friend of her father's, has escaped to Australia. The print of the Promises to the Blessed Margaret Mary Alacoque is appropriate and that not only because the saint stands at the origins of the devotion to the Sacred Heart that had become so central in Irish devotional life. The modern form of the devotion had only been initiated by the French Jesuit Francis Xavier Gautrelet in 1844. From a purely French phenomenon, through the efforts of the Jesuits, it quickly became more generally accepted, especially after pope Leo XIII's encyclical *Annum Sacrum* of 1899. In Ireland the movement had become associated with the 'Pioneer Total Abstinence Association of the Blessed Heart' founded in 1898 by James A. Cullen, S.J. in the Saint Francis Xavier church in Dublin.

The 'Twelve Promises' on the wall of the room where Eveline is sitting have their own significance because they contain the promises made by Jesus to the individuals and families who dedicate themselves to the Sacred Heart. Most of these promises seem to be particularly relevant to Eveline's home life:

1. I will give them all the graces necessary for their state of life.
2. I will establish peace in their families.
3. I will console them in all their troubles.
4. They shall find in My Heart an assured refuge during life and especially at the hour of their death.
5. I will pour abundant blessings on all their undertakings.
6. Sinners shall find in My Heart the source of an infinite ocean of mercy.
7. Tepid souls shall become fervent.
8. Fervent souls shall speedily rise to great perfection.
9. I will bless the homes where an image of My Heart shall be exposed and honored.
10. I will give to priests the power of touching the most hardened hearts.
11. Those who propagate this devotion shall have their names written in My Heart, never to be effaced.
12. The all-powerful love of My Heart will grant to all those who shall receive Communion on the First Friday of nine consecutive months the grace of final repentance; they shall not die under my displeasure, nor without receiving their Sacraments; My heart shall be their assured refuge at that last hour.[1]

Since we know that Eveline's violent and drunken father is hardly likely to allow his 'hardened heart' to be touched, we can imagine the life that awaits her when she does decide to stay home instead of leaving and that in no way will live up to the promises made here. Her final decision not to go, follows her prayer 'to God to direct her' and she keeps 'moving her lips in silent fervent prayer' when the sound of a bell is heard. By not making the decision to go, she does decide to stay behind (*D* 40–1).

Religion is almost entirely absent in the two stories about Doyle and Corley, but it surfaces again in 'The Boarding House,' where Mr Doran is tricked into marriage by the accomplished mother–daughter team of Mrs Mooney and Polly. On that summer morning they are helped in their plan by the priest who took confession of Mr Doran the day before: 'the priest had drawn out every ridiculous detail of the affair and in the end had so magnified his sin that he was almost thankful at being afforded a loophole of reparation' (*D* 65). Yet Mr Doran's religious zeal is recent: 'As a young man he had sown his wild oats, of course; he had boasted of his free-thinking and denied the existence of God to his companions in public-houses.' He still buys a copy of the English radical (and after 1895 liberal) *Reynolds's Newspaper* (where in 1902 he might have read the translation of Zola's virulently anticlerical novel *Vérité*), but Mr Doran now attends to his religious duties and lives a regular life 'for nine-tenths of the year' (66). By the end of the story, prepared by the church and the pressures of a gossiping Dublin, Mr Doran is ready to meet his doom.

Like Mr Doran, Little Chandler has had romantic bachelor days, but the example of his friend Gallaher's success in London makes him keenly aware of the dullness of his own life. Even before the meeting with his friend, he dreams of escaping, if need be as a Celtic poet in London. At the meeting itself it is clear that Little Chandler behaves and is treated as a provincial, who is fascinated by the wild life of London and Paris, which is not for 'a pious chap like you' (*D* 76). When, for the benefit of his jealous friend, Gallaher sketches 'the corruption which was rife' in the big centres of Europe, he also ends up revealing 'many of the secrets of the religious houses on the Continent' (78). Like the other adult characters, Chandler feels trapped in his life, with no possibility of escape and it is ironic that the sophisticated friend answers Chandler's question about the immorality in Paris with 'a catholic gesture' (77).

We find the same feeling of paralysis in the next story and although there is hardly any reference to religion in 'Counterparts,' the ending is all the more poignant, with the boy offering to say a 'Hail Mary' for his father in return for not being beaten. While the adult males in Dublin have a somewhat ambiguous relationship with religion, for the naive heroine of 'Clay' religion is self-evidently everywhere. Mary works for a Church of Ireland charitable institution, she has a certain degree of respect for the protestant ladies who run the charity and she finds pleasure in being compared to the biblical 'peacemakers' of the Sermon on the Mount, but she still dislikes the protestant tracts on the walls. It does not seem likely that she would be capable of distinguishing between protestant doctrine and the teaching of her own church, so her dislike for these tracts can only be based on warnings from her parish priest. Mary seems to rely entirely on others for her identity and in this she is the opposite of Mr James Duffy, who does not need anybody else: he has 'neither companions or friends, church nor creed' (*D* 109) and his rather academic interest in socialism is thwarted when the Irish Socialist Party splits up in three different groupuscules. When he stops seeing Mrs Sinico, he stops writing and begins to read Nietzsche instead. The article about the inquest into Mrs Sinico's death he takes home to read again, 'moving his lips as a priest does when he reads the prayers *Secreto*' (113). Duffy although a freethinker, is just as dead spiritually as all the other Dubliners.

In story 'Ivy Day in the Committee Room' the poem about Parnell deftly turns that uncrowned king into Jesus and the Irish clergy into the jewish mob that was responsible for his death:

Shame on the coward caitiff hands
That smote their Lord or with a kiss
Betrayed him to the rabble-rout
Of fawning priests – no friends of his. (*D* 134)

The Kearneys in 'A Mother' represent the new catholic and nationalist middle class, with its devotion to the Sacred Heart and its social and artistic pretensions. After 'The Sisters,' the story 'Grace' is the most obviously religious, from the very beginning, when non-Irish readers are misled by the use of 'curates,' a Hiberno-Irish word that refers to bartenders, one of whom helps the wounded and drunk Tom Kernan up the stairs from the lavatory. If we can judge on the basis of the evidence we have already been presented with in the pages of *Dubliners*, Kernan is not untypical; his behaviour resembles that of other male characters in the collection. His friends conspire to find a religious solution to his drinking problems; which they seem to think, are partly to be blamed on his religious lapses. Born a protestant he converted in order to marry, but 'he had not been in the pale of the Church for twenty years. He was fond, moreover of giving side-thrusts at Catholicism' (*D* 157). Mrs Kernan has a more cynical view of religion than her husband's friends: she does not believe that all these efforts would fundamentally change her husband, but 'religion was religion. The scheme might do good and, at least, it could do no harm.' Her own faith is practical:

> Her beliefs were not extravagant. She believed steadily in the Sacred Heart as the most generally useful of all Catholic devotions and approved of the sacraments. Her faith was bounded by her kitchen, but, if she was put to it, she could believe also in the banshee and in the Holy Ghost. (158)

Mr Kernan is conned by his three friends into joining a retreat during an unlikely visit to his sickroom. After a while another friend, Mr Fogarty, joins them. He brings a half-pint of whisky which they proceed to consume together with the ailing alcoholic.

But first all those present agree that the Jesuits (who organize the retreat) are exceptional on all counts: they 'cater to the upper classes.' Mr Kernan agrees but then begins to insult all other priests: he likes the Jesuits: 'It's some of those secular priests, ignorant, bumptious – ,' but he is quickly interrupted by Mr Cunningham before he can become too anticlerical. At least the four gentlemen can agree on the fact that the Irish priesthood is the best in the world ('Not like some of the other priesthoods on the continent'). The Jesuit preacher in question is a Father Purdon, 'a man of the world like ourselves' (*D*: 164) and this leads to a rambling and sometimes hilarious discussion of other sermons, the difference between the catholic and protestant theology. Kernan's ignorance of the finer points is revealed, for instance, in speaking of the body of the church as 'the pit' (as if it were a theatre). His reference to the memorable sermon by Father Tom Burke is somewhat marred first by the fact that it takes him a while to remember what the sermon was about and then when he does remember, he mixes up two popes ('the late Pope' must be Leo XIII who died in 1903, while it was his predecessor, Pius IX who was the real 'Prisoner of the Vatican' in the period between 1859 and his death in 1878).

In fact, almost all the information about the church exchanged among the five nominal Dublin catholics is inaccurate and Joyce seems to have had considerable fun in exposing the level of ignorance of these supposedly pious men, who do not even have Mr Kernan's excuse of having been born out of the faith. Nearly everything that is said is wrong: for one thing, popes do not have mottos. An Irish forgery gives mottos to all the popes until the end of times and in that case the appropriate motto for Leo XIII is 'lumen in coelo' and that of Pius IX 'crux de cruce.' 'Lux in tenebris' is from the Vulgate translation of the fifth verse of Saint John's gospel: *'Et lux in tenebris lucet, et tenebrae eam non comprehenderunt,'* and the light shineth in darkness, and the darkness comprehended it not. McCoy seems to recognize this allusion because he partly continues the quotation. It is ironical, given Leo XIII's long fight against freemasonry, that it is this particular bible phrase that was commonly adopted by the masonic lodges. The intellectual Mr Cunningham corrects the others by claiming that the respective mottos were *Lux upon Lux* and *Crux upon crux* 'to show the difference between their two pontificates' (167); needless to say, these are not even Latin and at best they cast a strange light on both popes.

The scene is not just a joke on Irish catholics and their limited knowledge of what is supposed to be their own theology: when Mr Kernan tries to think of a point of protestant theology, he cannot even come up with a single item. So instead he uses the old trick of mentioning that maybe not all of the popes were really kosher (he uses the expression 'up to the knocker'). After a silence, Cunningham has to admit the point, but he goes on with an apologetic retort that has an equally long pedigree, but that does not become truer by constant repetition:

– O, of course, there were some bad lots . . . But the astonishing thing is this. Not one of them, not the biggest drunkard, not the most . . . out-and-out ruffian, not one of them ever preached *ex cathedra* a word of false doctrine. Now isn't that an astonishing thing? (*D* 168)

This opens the discussion on papal infallibility and we know that Joyce researched the issue in detail while at Rome, in the Bibliotheca Vittorio Emanuele (*Letters II* 192), the national (and thus non-catholic) library of Italy that was founded in 1875 and that incorporated the collections of the monastic or other religious libraries that had been confiscated by the state.

Joyce's work at the library paid off. All the information offered in the next few pages about the Vatican Council is either confused or wrong, often in ironic ways. As we have seen, two cardinals voted against the decree, but only because most of the other opponents had left Rome precisely to avoid having to vote against it. The German cardinal 'Dolling or . . . Dowling' (*D* 169) is in reality Johann Döllinger who did campaign vigorously against the dogma as an outsider, not as a participant at the council. Joyce could have read the collection of Döllinger's articles about the council in the German newspaper *Allgemeine*

Zeitung that were published as a book and quickly translated into English as *Letters from Rome*. The other dissenting cardinal was not John McHale of Tuam, although he did resist the declaration at first and later complied (he had left Rome in time so as not to vote). The *Catholic Encyclopedia* (which Joyce could not have used on this occasion: the first volume only appeared in March 1907) has another version of the facts:

> Notwithstanding his very advanced years, Dr. MacHale attended the Vatican Council in 1869. With several distinguished prelates of various nationalities, he thought that the favourable moment had not arrived for an immediate definition of the dogma of papal infallibility; consequently, he spoke and voted in the council against its promulgation. Once the dogma had been defined, Dr. MacHale instantly submitted his judgment to the Holy See, and in his own cathedral he declared the dogma of infallibility 'to be true Catholic doctrine, which he believed as he believed the Apostles' Creed', a public profession that further raised John of Tuam in the estimation of all who admired his great genius and virtue. ('John McHale')

In fact the issue of papal infallibility had indeed played a role in the political tensions between the nationalist bishop John of Tuam and the more unionist Cardinal Cullen, when the latter heard 'that the Fenians boasted that the people of Dublin had no use for papal infallibility, and that the prelate the whole country looked to for leadership was not the cardinal but Archbishop John MacHale of Tuam' (Bowen 1983: 272). In fact Gladstone's reaction to the proclamation of papal infallibility caused a break with Cardinal Cullen that altered his relationship with the liberal party.

Whereas Cunningham is mistaken about the two dissenters, the modest grocer Fogarty correctly says that they were an Italian and an American, but again Cunningham decides the issue. In the following account of the final decree, he incorrectly claims that that there were only two dissenting voices, that there was no final vote and the pope himself declared the doctrine *ex cathedra*, which would have been canonically impossible. In fact as Owen Chadwick relates in his history of the popes, there was little genuine discussion and lots of political manoeuvring behind the scenes; the pope never once joined the debate, remaining absent for most of the time. At a vote on an early draft of the proposal, the pope's supporters were shocked that 88 bishops voted against it and 62 'yes but'. When the draft was not emended but made even more strict, most of the minority group left and finally, when the dogma was passed during a solemn session, only 535 were present of the more than 700 who had been at the opening (63 of these were Irish or Irish-American, a contingent larger than the group of German and Austro-Hungarian bishops combined).

When Mrs Kernan comes into the room where all this theological discussion is taking place, there is a solemn atmosphere as a result of bishop MacHale's *Credo*, his confession of belief in the brand new dogma: 'Mr Cunningham's words had built up the vast image of the Church in the minds of his hearers. His deep raucous voice had thrilled them as it uttered the word of belief and submission.' It is in this atmosphere that Mr Cunningham is happy to announce to Kernan's wife: 'we're going to make your man here a good holy pious and God-fearing Roman Catholic' (*D* 170). But when she jokes that she pities the poor priest who will have to hear his confession, Kernan's mood changes: 'If he doesn't like it, he said bluntly, he can . . . do the other thing.' Again Cunningham has to intervene quickly and he says that all they have to do is renounce the devil and to renew their baptismal vows. But when McCoy reminds Kernan to bring a candle, this is a bridge too far for the ex-protestant:

- I bar the candles, said Mr. Kernan, conscious of having created an effect on his audience and continuing to shake his head to and fro. I bar the magic-lantern business.

    Everyone laughed heartily.

- There's a nice Catholic for you! said his wife.

- No candles! repeated Mr. Kernan obdurately. That's off! (*D* 171–2)

The story ends with a description of the retreat at 'the Jesuit Church in Gardiner Street.' The church is almost full but gentlemen are still entering and they are described, with some insistence as 'all well dressed and orderly.' The church is dark, with the light of the lamps falling 'on dark mottled pillars of green marble and on lugubrious canvasses' (*D* 172). The people in the church belong to the new catholic elite of the city, although some of them are clearly on the way down. When Father Purdon climbs the pulpit he is not named until the next paragraph; he is described as first 'a powerful-looking figure' and then 'the priest's figure.' Only 'two-thirds of its bulk' is visible above the balustrade.

The sermon opens with a quotation from the Douay-Rheims catholic version of the Gospel of Luke, the moral to the Parable of the Unjust Steward, one of the parables that continues to puzzle the devout of all persuasions (maybe for better effect, Father Purdon whom Stanislaus thought was based on Father Bernard Vaughan, has made the text more dramatic by emending 'when you fail' into 'when you die'). The *Catholic Encyclopedia* calls this 'the hardest of all our Lord's parables' ('Parables') and the feeling is shared by Father Purdon who calls it 'one of the most difficult texts in all the Scriptures,' because it seems 'at variance with the lofty morality elsewhere preached by Jesus Christ' (173). According to Purdon this is 'a text for business men and professional men' who are forced to forgo the religious life and 'live in the world.' Jesus sets before them 'as exemplars in the religious life' the worshippers of Mammon 'who were of all men the least solicitous in matters religious.' In fact he then goes on to use the language of accountancy in discussing spiritual matters and calling on his audience 'to be straight and manly with God' and if they have not been, they should say: ' – Well, I have looked into my accounts. I find this wrong and this wrong. But, with God's grace, I will rectify this and this. I will set right my accounts' (174).

It is with this blatant juxtaposition of spirituality and accountancy that the story ends. We are not told whether Mr Kernan will set right his account or even whether he will merely plan to do so: when we meet him again in *Ulysses* he certainly has not given up drinking and there is no indication that he has become pious or even mildly catholic. The last time we catch a glimpse of Mr Kernan in 'Grace' is when just before the sermon he 'presented an attentive face to the preacher,' which is surely ironic because it is such a wrong term to describe Father Purdon: catholics do not have preachers, protestants do. We then realize that we have been seeing the scene in the church through Mr Kernan's eyes: he is the only one present who would describe the sanctuary light as a 'distant speck of red light' at which the congregation gaze 'formally' and to which Father Purdon turns to pray. We also know now why it should be worthy of note that the gentlemen in the church are 'all well dressed and orderly': to the protestant Mr Kernan this is not self-evident. Mr Kernan is an outsider and he observes what is going on in much the same way as Leopold Bloom looks at the faithful in the 'Lotuseaters' chapter in *Ulysses*.

For the middle-class men in 'Grace,' religion seems to be no more than social conformity: it certainly is not a body of thought (nearly everything they think they know is plain wrong), it also is not an ethos and if it is, it is one that does not differ from the vague Victorian and mercantile notions of 'manliness' discussed by Father Purdon. At least for Mrs Kernan religion is practical: the Sacred Heart is 'the most generally useful of all Catholic devotions' and, with some effort, she could even believe 'in the banshee and in the Holy Ghost' (158). If 'Ivy Day' was about politics and 'A Mother' about music, then 'Grace' deals with religion, but this does not mean that we should take seriously Stanislaus Joyce's claim that the story is structured like the Divine Comedy. If Mr Kernan's ignominious fall at the beginning might still be described as an Inferno, where are we supposed to find a Purgatorio or Paradiso? If we read the final lines of the story again, it is relatively clear that since God's grace will not be forthcoming, no accounts will be set right either.

Religion plays only a minor part in the last story 'The Dead' and then mostly as part of the political reality in the Dublin of the beginning of the twentieth century, with the University question on which Gabriel and Miss Ivors seem to find more agreement than on other issues. In fact in this story the only function of religion seems to be sectarian. Mr Browne is a protestant. Aunt Kate objects to Pius X's problem with women singing in church and replacing them by boys: 'I suppose it is for the good of the Church if the pope does it. But it's not just, Mary Jane, and it's not right,' but the other sister interrupts her because these comments may scandalize Mr Browne who is 'of the other persuasion' (194). During the dinner the assembled Dublin catholics display more misunderstanding about their faith when they claim first that Trappist monks have to sleep in their coffins and second when they fail to explain this strange behaviour to Mr Browne.

But this is all part of the social background of the story; at its core there is no place for religion: neither Gretta nor Gabriel seem to be religious in any sense of the word and religion plays no part in the story, despite the fact that some readers have found ways of giving the final story (and thus the whole collection) a christian and optimistic gloss. Florence L. Walzl concludes that in the final pages we find references to:

> [w]ater, the archetypal symbol of life; and for the Christian, the baptismal symbol of rebirth. In this interpretation, the images of Christ's passion in the spears, thorns, and crosses of the cemetery are reminders that sacrifice of self is the condition of spiritual revival. Gabriel's swoon is a symbolic death from which he will rise resurrected. If so, he is properly named for the angel who brought annunciations of new life to come. (1984: 216)

This is an interpretation of the story (and of *Dubliners*) that is available only for christian readers and that runs counter to everything that we now know of what the story's author himself seems to have thought and believed.

The world of *Dubliners* is almost completely catholic lower-middle-class and of the stories' protagonists, only Jimmy Doyle belongs to a rich catholic family and even then his father has only recently worked his way up. Most of the other people in the stories lead circumscribed and narrow sectarian lives. The boy's aunt in 'Araby' is worried that the bazaar he wants to visit is 'some Freemason affair' (32) and the social and political differences between protestants and catholics is relevant to most of the later stories dealing with adult life like 'Ivy Day,' 'A Mother,' 'Grace' and 'The Dead.' But religion as a theme is absent: none of the heroes in these stories is genuinely religious in the way that Stephen is in parts of *A Portrait of the Artist as a Young Man*. If religion is actively present, it is always in a satirical context. No wonder that Joyce asked Stanislaus (in the same letter from Rome in which he explains his research for the story 'Grace'): 'Mother said I was a "mocker." Am I?' (*Letters II* 194).

A Portrait of the Artist as a Young Man

When we look at the notes in the *Trieste* notebook, which were made after he had abandoned *Stephen Hero* and before he began his work on *A Portrait of the Artist as a Young Man*, we can see that the characters in the novel have become much more clearly defined. The notes are given under the names of the characters, and under the name of 'Dedalus' we read: 'Having left the city of the church by the gate of sin he might enter it again by the wicket of repentance if repentance were possible' (Scholes and Kain 1965: 96). Under 'Esthetic' we

find that art is discussed in religious terms ('Art has the gift of tongues') and
under 'Gogarty' we read that 'Ireland secretes priests' and that the medical student wanted to turn the tower or Omphalos into a temple of neo-paganism.

The notes on Ireland concentrate on political servility, although among these
notes we find evidence that Joyce opposed the Irish religion of Duns Scotus and
Columbanus to the victorious Latin church of Aquinas. About the Jesuits, Joyce
notes that they are levites, that they flatter the wealthy, that they 'do not love the
end they serve,' that they 'breed atheists' and that they are 'erotically preoccup-
pied [sic]' (Scholes and Kain 1965: 102). In an abandoned part of *A Portrait*,
also published in Scholes and Kain, we find a scene in which Gogarty (still
under the name Doherty) rants about the church with quite a few phrases that
were noted under his name in the Trieste notebook, but this version of the text
looks also forward to the final form of the material in the first chapter of *Ulysses*.
It is clear that at a fairly early point, Joyce began to make a distinction between
Stephen's rebellion against his native religion and that of his friend Doherty/
Mulligan.

Initially religion is almost entirely absent from Stephen's life as it is represented in the first chapter of *A Portrait of the Artist as a Young Man*, although
the boy is at a Jesuit boarding school. God makes his first appearance when the
feverish boy is trying to comprehend what lies beyond the border of the universe: 'It was very big to think about everything and everywhere. Only God
could do that. He tried to think what a big thought that must be but he could
think only of God' (*P* 16). This leads to another mystery: that the name of God
is God, but that in French the deity is called *Dieu*. Before going to bed, the boy
prays first together with the prefect of the chapel and again 'quickly quickly' on
his own before getting into bed. The prayer seems carefully designed to scare
the living daylights out of a child: this specific form will make sure that 'he
would not go to hell when he died' (19).

The Christmas dinner is crucial in setting the scene for Stephen's later
relationship to both the church and Ireland. The stage for the confrontation
between his father and Mrs Riordan had already been set when Stephen
describes Dante's two sets of brushes. Clearly she originally supported the
coalition of Parnell's party with the Irish bishops, but by the time of the dinner,
she sides with the Irish catholic hierarchy against Parnell. The support of
Mr Dedalus and Mr Casey for Parnell puts them in the anticlerical nationalist
camp and the conflicts at the dinner table reflect these positions. In contrast
Mrs Riordan accepts the bishops' right to express political opinions: 'It is religion,
Dante said again. They are doing their duty in warning the people' (*P* 31).
John Casey and Simon Dedalus support a strict separation between church and
state: according to Stephen's father, the bishops have no right to 'meddle in
politics' (32). The stakes become increasingly higher, especially when Casey
answers Dante with a threat: 'Let them leave politics alone, said Mr Casey, or the
people may leave their church alone.' Dante stridently quotes from the gospel
of Luke and when she adds that this represents 'the language of the Holy
Ghost,' Mr Dedalus replies in a characteristically blunt manner: 'And very bad
language if you ask me' (32).

Provoked further by Dante when she insists on 'respect for the pastors of the church,' Simon Dedalus finally explodes: 'Respect, he said. Is it for Billy with the lip or for the tub of guts up in Armagh? Respect!' (*P* 33). Stephen's father uses the coarse language to refer to the archbishop of Dublin and his colleague in Armagh (in terms that according to the Trieste Notebook were borrowed from John Stanislaus Joyce). The reason for this abuse is that especially Walsh and later Logue at first had supported the Parliamentary party, but then shifted their allegiance from Parnell to Tim Healy.

Somewhat later Mrs Riordan replies that the Irish should be proud of being a priestridden race: 'They are the apple of God's eye. *IUt,* says Christ, *for they are the apple of My eye.*' In his *Joyce Annotated,* Don Gifford finds these words in Zech. 2.8–9, but surely Christ cannot be speaking in a book of the Old Testament? In reality Dante specifically refers to Saint Patrick's *Confession*:

> On that day, then, on which I was rejected by those referred above, during that night I had a vision of the night. There was a writing opposite my face without honour. And meanwhile I heard a divine voice saying to me: 'With pain We have seen the face of the (bishop) designate' spoiled of his name. He did not say, 'Thou hast seen with pain,' but, 'We have seen with pain,' as if in that matter He had joined Himself with me, as He hath said: 'He that toucheth you is as he that toucheth the apple of Mine eye.' (quoted in Healey 1905: 681)

Saint Patrick is quoting the Old Testament in order to strengthen his case against his anonymous accuser by giving scriptural basis to the solidarity between the god who is speaking and his own priestly mission. Dante's use of this bible quotation is therefore less strange than one could think; it strengthens God's sanction of the special mission of the Irish church.

What is particularly shocking for Stephen is that the adults seem to be aware of the inappropriateness of this kind of talk in the presence of a child, as both Mrs Dedalus and Uncle Charles point out. Mrs Riordan agrees: 'O, he'll remember all this when he grows up, said Dante hotly – the language he heard against God and religion and priests in his own home' (*P* 33). It is clear to all parties that it is this remembrance that will be crucial for the future generations of Irishmen but it is also obvious that young Stephen is quite aware of what is going on. The position of Dedalus senior and Mr Casey is at first merely anti-clerical, but then Dante puts her own integralist position at its clearest: 'God and religion before everything! Dante cried. God and religion before the world!' (39) Given these alternatives, Casey cannot but decide in favour of the world:

> Very well, then, he shouted hoarsely, if it comes to that, no God for Ireland! [. . .] No God for Ireland! he cried. We have had too much God in Ireland. Away with God!
>
> – Blasphemer! Devil! screamed Dante, starting to her feet and almost spitting in his face. (39)

Whereas just previously Stephen had joined in the excitement (Mr Casey's words 'thrilled him'), the final outburst of emotion seems to be merely shocking: his face is described as 'terrorstricken,' whereas he himself notices foremost the self-pity of his father.

In the final section of the first chapter it is clear that despite the Christmas scene, young Stephen remains a pious boy who takes his religious duties very seriously. The boy in the second chapter has become a loner; in the first section he marks his distance from the adults and the other children in the household: 'The noise of the children at play annoyed him and their silly voices made him feel, even more keenly than he had felt at Clongowes, that he was different from others' (*P* 64–5). At the Whitsuntide play, Stephen's distance from his schoolmates is clear: he is standing alone, observing the preparations. In all that he sees there are priests present, the 'smiling face of a priest' he recognizes and the prefect who condescendingly makes fun of Bertie Tallon who is dressed like a girl. Stephen escapes to the shed where Heron and his friend are smoking. Heron tells him to imitate the rector's diction in the play: ' – Go on, Dedalus, he urged, you can take him off rippingly. *He that will not hear the churcha let him be to theea as the heathena and the publicana*' (76). In the context, Heron could have chosen any other bible quotation for what is after all described as a 'poor attempt' to imitate the rector's 'pedantic bass' (75), but it is significant that the phrase is the climax at the end of a section of Chapter 18 of Matthew's gospel, naturally in the catholic Douay-Rheims translation:

> 15. But if thy brother shall offend against thee, go, and rebuke him between thee and him alone. If he shall hear thee, thou shalt gain thy brother. 16. And if he will not hear thee, take with thee one or two more: that in the mouth of two or three witnesses every word may stand. 17. And if he will not hear them: tell the church. And if he will not hear the church, let him be to thee as the heathen and publican.

Jesus is explaining to his disciples how they can avoid scandal and how they should treat incorrigible sinners. When Heron wants him to admit that he is not such a saint as he makes himself out to be in school, Stephen remembers that years earlier the same young man tried to bully him into admitting that Byron was a heretic and therefore not a good poet. The phrase from the gospel tells christians how they should treat those who are incorrigible, by shunning them, as the jews did with gentiles and tax collectors and as the catholic church would do with modernists. But it is also one of the few places in the scriptures with the word 'church' and catholics traditionally use it in anti-protestant apologetics, which is ironic because the type of emphasis on the last syllables of biblical phrases in the parody is usually associated with protestant preachers (see Reverend Lovejoy in *The Simpsons*).

Important in the second chapter of *A Portrait* is the moment when Stephen loses his innocence: 'Nothing stirred in his soul but a cold and cruel and loveless lust' (*P* 96); somewhat later the 'fierce longings of his heart' (98) are mentioned. Although the exalted language with which the narrator describes Stephen's hormonal torment is suitably romantic, there is a religious aspect too: 'He wanted to sin with another of his kind, to force another being to sin with him and to exult with her in sin' (99–100); on the first page of the third chapter he refers to 'his sinloving soul' (102). The form of total abandonment that he is looking for – and that will also determine his relationship with E.C. – can only be compared to the logical unfolding of the mathematical exercises that acquire cosmic proportions: 'It was his own soul going forth to experience, unfolding itself sin by sin, spreading abroad the balefire of its burning stars and folding back upon itself, fading slowly, quenching its own lights and fires. They were quenched: and the cold darkness filled chaos' (103). Stephen realizes all too well that he is in a state of mortal sin, but still he refuses to give in:

> A certain pride, a certain awe, withheld him from offering to God even one prayer at night though he knew it was in God's power to take away his life while he slept and hurl his soul hellward ere he could beg for mercy. His pride in his own sin, his loveless awe of God, told him that his offence was too grievous to be atoned for in whole or in part by a false homage to the Allseeing and Allknowing. (*P* 104)

Pride is the central ingredient here, as is the concomitant contempt for his fellows in school and for the worshippers at the Sunday mass. Stephen cannot make himself to openly admit his sin. Only 'the imagery of the psalms of prophecy soothed his barren pride,' while his soul is held captive by the lushness of the biblical language that is made to describe the Blessed Virgin and it is precisely his sexual sin that draws him paradoxically nearer to the Virgin, 'refuge of sinners'; he finds a perverse pleasure in the juxtaposition of the litanies 'murmured softly by lips whereon there still lingered foul and shameful words, the savour itself of a lewd kiss' (*P* 105). The same perversity can be found in the combination of his sense of damnation on the one hand, while on the other he is keenly interested in the casuistic discussions of arcane bits of catholic theology.

The young libertine and infidel does not really look forward to the retreat and his attitude is described in language that could be Cardinal Newman's: 'Stephen's heart had withered up like a flower of the desert that feels the simoom coming from afar' (*P* 108). In the end Stephen gets exactly what he was afraid of, the full force of divine vengeance: 'Every word of it was for him. Against his sin, foul and secret, the whole wrath of God was aimed' (115). On the second day of the retreat it is raining and the earlier thoughts of the apocalypse are replaced by images of the biblical flood:

> It would rain forever, noiselessly. The waters would rise inch by inch, covering the trees and houses, covering the monuments and the mountain tops.

All life would be choked off, noiselessly: birds, men, elephants, pigs, children: noiselessly floating corpses amid the litter of the wreckage of the world. (*P* 117)

Father Arnall goes even further back for examples of God's wrath, the punishment of Adam and Eve, and before that the fall of Lucifer, God's favourite angel, whose sin was pride, 'the sinful thought conceived in an instant: *non serviam: I will not serve*' (117). Each new sermon, including the famous description of hell, pushes Stephen one step closer to his confession and it is his submission that marks the beginning of his extremely pious phase in the next chapter. But by the end of the first section of that chapter, his surrender is endangered once more by 'the insistent voices of the flesh' that may at least partly have been summoned up by Stephen's reading of Alphonsus Liguori's meditations on the 'Song of Songs' which leads the young catholic to ask a question that answers itself: 'I have amended my life, have I not?' (153).

In the next section of this chapter the Stephen who talks to the director of studies is still nominally pious and a model student, but even before the Jesuit can ask him if he has ever felt that he had a vocation, he has registered his distance from both the director's flippancy and from some of the other Jesuits. The question about the vocation makes Stephen's heart 'quicken in response' but the feeling is accompanied by a 'strong note of pride' (157) and it is pride that is his main reaction to the offer of immense spiritual power. When they part company, Stephen has already taken his distance:

Smiling at the trivial air he raised his eyes to the priest's face and, seeing in it a mirthless reflection of the sunken day, detached his hand slowly which had acquiesced faintly in that companionship. (*P* 160)

In the fourth section of the same chapter, just before he sees the bird-girl on the beach, Stephen has already made up his mind about a future outside the order of his youth and again pride plays an important part in that decision:

So he had passed beyond the challenge of the sentries who had stood as guardians of his boyhood and had sought to keep him among them that he might be subject to them and serve their ends. Pride after satisfaction uplifted him like long slow waves. (*P* 165)

Although he asks himself why he has refused, a meeting with 'a squad of christian brothers' makes him reflect on what distinguishes him from them and from his bathing friends, and it is only when he sees the bird-girl that he discovers a new kind of secular ecstasy.

At the beginning of the book's final chapter, Stephen's mother claims that his life at the university has changed him. She believes he'll 'live to rue the day you set your foot in that place' (175). A catholic university was, at the time, almost a contradiction in terms, but if we can take Joyce's description of University College in *A Portrait* seriously, the national university in Dublin had students with opinions that were much more varied and liberal than Cardinal Newman could have dreamed of. The same intellectual climate may also explain why Stephen has heard that his science professor is rumoured to be 'an atheist freemason' (*P* 191), which may well be a contradiction, as Gifford claims, in British and American freemasonry. But in 1875 the Belgian Grand Order had removed any reference to the Grand Architect from their constitution, and two years later the French Order followed. Conservatives in the catholic church, especially in Italy, France, Spain and Belgium, accused the masons of secretly advocating the anticlerical policies that led to the separation of church and state in these new nation states.

Stephen's home life, with the watery tea, the pawn tickets and the foul-mouthed father, has not changed much, but the young hero seems to notice different things than before. When he leaves the house, he hears a mad nun screeching 'Jesus! O Jesus! Jesus!' Stephen has acquired another attitude to the realities of his daily life: 'His father's whistle, his mother's mutterings, the screech of an unseen maniac were to him now so many voices offending and threatening to humble the pride of his youth' (*P* 176–7). His walk through the city is now punctuated by references to his literary masters and when he thinks of Cranly's reaction to his confession about 'all the tumults and unrest and longings in his soul,' his friend becomes 'a guilty priest who heard confessions of those whom he had not power to absolve' (178). Davin's political and religious attitudes are compared and summed up as 'the attitude of a dullwitted loyal serf' (181).

Stephen's first major confrontation is with the dean of studies, whose lighting of the fire is described as the preparation by a levite of a sacrifice 'in an empty temple' (*P* 185). In Stephen's eyes, the dean completely lacks the enthusiasm that fired the founders of his order, and he also does not have their subtle craft. Stephen defends his aesthetic speculations, which the dean compares to the Cliffs of Moher, with the argument that he does not believe in free thinking 'inasmuch as all thinking must be bound by its own laws' (187). The dean's reaction ('Ha!') shows that he has not failed to see the simultaneous allusion to and skilful avoidance of the freethought that Stephen must be known for among his fellows at the university. It is only after the misunderstanding about the funnel/tundish that the dean suddenly becomes 'the English convert' and the young student looks at him 'with the same eyes as the elder brother in the parable may have turned on the prodigal' (189). Stephen now describes the dean's conversion as a comical reversal of a common reality at the turn of the century: the dean has become a 'poor Englishman in Ireland.'

The dean has come on the scene at a moment when the glorious history of his order is winding down and Stephen begins to think of what religion he had converted from: 'perhaps he had been born and bred among serious dissenters.' Maybe the dean had felt the need of 'an implicit faith amid the welter of sectarianism and the jargon of the turbulent schisms: six principle men, peculiar people, seed and snake Baptists, supralapsarian dogmatists' (*P*: 189). Stephen is badly informed, or Joyce is being really malicious here, because these sects are not English, but American, and so is the 'zincroofed chapel.' At least some of these sects Joyce had found in an essay by Newman about the situation of the catholic church in the United States:

> Certainly the excesses of sectarianism in the North American States are such, that one need not be of a Socinian turn to be disgusted with them. Besides the old Calvinistic Baptists, there are the Free-will, the Seventh-day, and the Six-principle Baptists; the Christian Baptists, who deny the proper Divinity of Christ; and the Campbellite Baptists, many of whom are but in part believers in the Holy Trinity, and modify the doctrine of the Atonement. Besides these there are the Seed and Snake Baptists, who, carrying out the Calvinistic system, divide mankind by a rigid line into the seed of the woman and the seed of the serpent; and lastly, the Dunkers, who are principally German Baptists, and who wear a peculiar dress, a long robe with a girdle and hood, let their beards grow, feed on roots and vegetables, live men with men and women with women, not meeting even in their devotions, have each his own cell, a bench for a bed, a block of wood for a pillow, admit works of supereroation, and deny the eternity of future punishment. This strange mockery of Catholic Truth numbers as many as 30,000 adherents. (Newman 1907: 325)

The two remaining sects in Stephen's list are the 'peculiar people,' who could be the American 'Original Freewill Baptists' mentioned by Don Gifford in his notes, but the name (from the biblical epistle to Titus) was also adopted by a number of protestant sects, among them a group of faith healers in London. Stephen's final group consists of the 'supralapsarian dogmatists,' an academic term that can refer to the believers in the most extreme form of calvinist pre-destination (according to which election and damnation have been foreor-dained from before the Fall) but that as far as I know has never been used to identify any specific English or American sect.

Associating the dean of studies with the enthusiastic dissenting tradition within protestantism, Stephen is being quite unfair to the convert. Joyce cannot have failed to be aware that as 'a humble follower in the wake of clamorous conversions' (189), the Jesuit must have followed other *anglican* converts, who almost all belonged to the High Church faction of that tradition that would be called 'Anglo-Catholic' by the time that this fictional conversation takes place. Like Shane Leslie or Robert Hugh Benson, the later generation of English and Irish converts were typically anglican graduates of private schools and of Oxford or Cambridge, not dissenters. This was especially the case for those who took the extra step of becoming Jesuits, like George Tyrrell, C.C. Martindale (see Basset 2004: 147) or Father Joseph Darlington, James Joyce's own dean of studies.

In Stephen's conversations with friends at the college, it is clear that quite a few of them share his religious doubts or are at the very least aware of Stephen's reputation as a freethinker. Among the group of fellow students, Temple may be treated by Cranly as a nuisance and as a fool, but like Stephen he thinks of himself as being of the 'progressive tendency,' a follower of Anthony Collins, the man who first 'denounced priestcraft' (*P* 197). Despite his enthusiasm, Temple also seems to be genuinely interested in what Stephen means when he prefers a 'legitimate Jesus' to the Csar: ' – Do you believe in Jesus? I believe in man. Of course, I don't know if you believe in man. I admire you, sir. I admire the mind of man independent of all religion. Is that your opinion about the mind of Jesus?' (198). And in the scene on the National Library steps, Temple presents the entirely reasonable argument against the existence of limbo as a special hell for unbaptized children: 'if Jesus suffered the children to come why does the church send them all to hell if they die unbaptized? Why is that?' (236). Although he does not seem to be very popular among his fellow students, Temple represents a humanist critique of christianity that in *Ulysses*, in a more openly ironic vein, we will see embodied in the character of Buck Mulligan.

Stephen tells Cranly of the conversation with his mother about his refusal to do his easter duty (' – I will not serve, answered Stephen. – That remark was made before, Cranly said calmly'). For the first time in their conversations Cranly shows himself as Stephen's equal by making his friend admit that despite the latter's doubts, Stephen's refusal to take communion implies a certain measure of respect for the church's teaching. Stephen also denies that he is leaving the church to become a protestant, in a formulation that betrays the fact that he has turned into a peculiarly Jesuit kind of atheist: 'I said that I had lost the faith, Stephen answered, but not that I had lost selfrespect. What kind of liberation would that be to forsake an absurdity which is logical and coherent and to embrace one which is illogical and incoherent?' (244–5). Despite this flaw in the armour of Stephen's heroic and luciferian refusal to serve 'that in which I no longer believe whether it calls itself my home, my fatherland or my church' (246–7), the young man's revolt is clearly articulated and seems to have become common knowledge, both at home and among his friends at the university.

By the time we read his own words in the diary in the last section of the novel, the young artist is ready to leave his old life behind and, in the same heroic spirit, to accept all possible consequences of this decision: 'I am not afraid to make a mistake, even a great mistake, a lifelong mistake and perhaps as long as eternity too' (*P* 247). The diary passages reveal that his decision has been taken and it is almost as if he sees himself now as a literary character whom he needs to understand in terms of an existing tradition that is not accidentally biblical, as when he tries to see Cranly in the role of John the Baptist to his Jesus Christ

and he finds all kinds of connections between his friend and the precursor of
the Messiah.

> Then he is the precursor. Item: he eats chiefly belly bacon and dried figs.
> Read locusts and wild honey. Also, when thinking of him, saw always a
> stern severed head or deathmask as if outlined on a grey curtain or veronica.
> Decollation they call it in the fold. Puzzled for the moment by saint John
> at the Latin gate. What do I see? A decollated precursor trying to pick the
> lock. (248)

Stephen is right to be puzzled: why does he so blatantly confuse the Baptist with
the Evangelist, who is said by Tertullian to have been boiled in oil (not beheaded
like the Baptist) on first arriving at the Latin gate in Rome, but who miraculously managed to escape?

In any case young Dedalus continues to see his liberation from the faith in
terms borrowed from the gospel: on 21 March he notes: 'Free. Soulfree and fan-
cyfree. Let the dead bury the dead. And let the dead marry the dead' (*P* 248),
borrowing one of the more radical sayings of Jesus to describe his own detach-
ment, both from religion and from the other constraints of the society he grew
up in. His 'wrangle' with his professor of Italian about Bruno of Nola being
either a terrible heretic or 'terribly burned' again demonstrates his freethinking and it is only when he has left the classroom that Stephen remembers that
it was the Italians who 'had invented what Cranly the other night called our
religion' (249). In the discussion with his mother about the Blessed Virgin, it is
clear that Stephen, along the lines of a similar reasoning in *Ulysses*, has tried to
argue that the central role of the Virgin represents a late and not very useful
addition to a catholicism that does not in itself require maternal procreation;
religion is 'not a lying-in-hospital' (248).

In the final chapter of *A Portrait*, we find the same anti-clerical Stephen that
we know from *Stephen Hero*, although the latter version of the book is much
more openly the attack on the church that Stanislaus claimed his brother was
writing. In the more accomplished and more ironical self-portrait in the later
novel, some of Stephen's anticlerical or anti-religious comments are given to
other characters, in the same way that Mulligan in *Ulysses* will give voice to a
Nietzschean type of paganism. The main point is that Stephen has not become
indifferent towards the church in the final novel. As he explains to Lynch he
wants to challenge the Deity with his 'non serviam': his active apostasy is a
heroic gesture, an attempt to commit the sin against the Holy Ghost, the only
sin that even Jesus Christ cannot forgive. In that sense, and in that sense alone,
Stephen's rebellion is still part of a catholic framework.

The main ingredients of Stephen's attitude to the church have not changed
between *Stephen Hero* and the novel as it was published, but the conflict has
become more muted, is merely hinted at. We still have the discussions with his
mother, with his friends, his jealousy of the young priest in the Irish classes, the

main lines of his critique of religion and the search for an alternative in scholasticism, Franciscan thought and other heretic beliefs, his identification with Christ and with Lucifer. In general we can conclude that the book describes the young artist's successful battle with the political and religious powers that thwart the growth of his artistic ambitions.

The final work with which Joyce marked the end of his literary apprenticeship was *Exiles* and it is interesting to see that religion hardly plays any role in the play, except perhaps in terms of sectarian differences between the main characters. One of the parallelisms in the play among the main players is that Beatrice is protestant and that Richard Rowan's mother rejected her grandchild born in sin and refused a reconciliation with her son ('She died alone, not having forgiven me, and fortified by the rites of holy church' E 20). In this manner Richard Rowan's mother is a bigoted catholic much closer to the figure of Dante than to the passive and patient mother of Stephen Dedalus in *A Portrait*. Yet faith or the lack of it plays no discernible role in *Exiles*. That would be very different in Joyce's mature work and especially in the book he now began to write.

Chapter 6

'You behold in me a horrible example of freethought'

Ulysses is in many ways Joyce's most mature work and this is certainly true for the treatment of religion. Although the book still opens with the hero of *A Portrait of the Artist as a Young Man*, who does not seem to have changed all that much, since we last saw him packing his suitcase to leave Dublin, the appearance of Leopold Bloom in the fourth chapter turns *Ulysses* into a completely different work. In the next two chapters we will read the book more or less chronologically while looking carefully at the references to religion or to its absence.

Few critics of the book have noticed it, but freethinking and unbelief have a significant presence in *Ulysses* and this is especially evident when we work our way through the book while paying close attention to Joyce's range of references, especially to those almost invisible items he found in books and articles that we can document he has read. These cover the entire range of alternatives to catholicism that are discussed in chapter 3 of *Ulysses* and that continued to interest Joyce until the end of his life, as we will see in the final chapter of the book. That religion, and catholicism in particular, is central to *Ulysses* becomes clear from the very first lines, with the parody of the Mass that Buck Mulligan has begun to perform even before Stephen Dedalus joins him. Mulligan's mocking blasphemy is greeted by a 'displeased and sleepy' Stephen. The mock priest welcomes him as if he is possessed by devils and somewhat later he is called a 'jejune Jesuit,' so it is not surprising that young Dedalus refuses to play his role in the parody of the ritual. Neither does he seem to take seriously Mulligan's plans of going to Greece with his friend, of learning Greek or together setting out to 'Hellenize' Ireland.

It is ironic that it is the blaspheming pseudo-priest who questions Stephen's refusal to kneel down to pray when his dying mother asked him to. Interestingly Mulligan expresses his intellectual solidarity with his friend in these terms: 'I'm hyperborean as much as you' (*U* 1.92). In *Ulysses Annotated* Gifford and Seidman refer the reader to the introduction of *The Anti-Christ* where Nietzsche uses the phrase to refer to the *Übermensch* who is 'not enslaved by conformity to the dictates of traditional Christian morality.' We know that Mulligan has read his Nietzsche because by the end of the chapter, just before diving into the sea, he will jokingly claim to be the *Übermensch*.

We have already seen in Chapter 3 that Joyce was interested, like his older Dublin contemporaries Yeats and George Russell (AE), in the work of the authors of heretical works and there is a reference to one such sect on the first page of the novel that has not been noticed before, as far as I can tell. In his mockery of the Eucharist, Mulligan's reference to 'the genuine christine' may refer to *The Aquarian Gospel of Jesus the Christ* by Levi H. Dowling, an American preacher who as a child was ordered by an angel to 'build a white city' which he later realized had been a reference to the production of the book of *The Aquarian Gospel of Jesus, the Christ of the Piscean Age,* an alternative gospel in which the followers of the Christ are called 'christines' and their church 'the christine church.'

When Mulligan disappears downstairs into the tower, Stephen's thoughts return to his mother's death, but at no point does he entertain even vaguely religious ideas: it is only when we realize this that we notice that nearly all of the references to God or to Jesus in the first chapter are Mulligan's. Most often these references come in the form of expletives ('God, isn't he dreadful?' 'God! he said quietly.' 'God knows what poxy bowsy left them off.' 'God knows you have more spirit than any of them.' 'God, Kinch, if you and I could only work together we might do something for the island.' 'What happened in the name of God?' 'Do, for Jesus' sake, Buck Mulligan said. For my sake and for all our sakes'). Stephen never uses the lord's name in vain, while Mulligan even turns the breakfast into an irreverent parody of a prayer, a blessing and the sacrament of the Eucharist.

When the milkwoman enters the room, her innocent reference to the weather ('That's a lovely morning, sir, she said. Glory be to God') is immediately explained to the British guest: 'The islanders, Mulligan said to Haines casually, speak frequently of the collector of prepuces' (*U* 1.393–4). He expresses his sentiments in language that is designed not to be understood by the presumably uneducated third party, but circumcision was a theme that we can document Joyce had been interested in while he was writing *Ulysses*. In one of the new *Ulysses* notebooks that are now in the National Library of Ireland, we find under the title 'Jesus' and among notes from at least one other source, a number of references to the catholic veneration of Christ's foreskin, a theme that we find both in protestant writings such as Calvin and in the anti-religious enlightenment writers such as Locke and Voltaire. These particular notes were taken from a pamphlet written by Alphons Victor Müller under the title *Die hochheilige Vorhaut Christi im Kult und in der Theologie der Papstkirche,* published in Berlin in 1907.[1] This study, written by a Dominican historian who had converted to protestantism to become an anti-catholic propagandist, left only one trace in the text of *Ulysses,* to be discussed later. That the subject fascinated Joyce is also clear from a reference to the significantly rarer reverse process of uncircumcision which Joyce noted down on a piece of paper while reading *The Life and Works of Saint Paul* by Dean F.W. Farrar and which he left in a copy of that book in his Trieste library.[2]

When Stephen, Mulligan and Haines finish their breakfast and are ready to leave the tower, Mulligan continues his parodic identification with Jesus, this time with reference to the 'stations of the cross' and the gospel: 'Mulligan is stripped of his garments'; 'And going forth he met Butterly.' When Haines mentions Stephen's supposedly theological interpretation of Hamlet, Mulligan takes this as his cue to perform the extremely sacrilegious 'Ballad of Joking Jesus.' Haines first cautions Stephen ('We oughtn't to laugh, I suppose. He's rather blasphemous') and then after enquiring about the song's title, he continues: 'You're not a believer, are you? Haines asked. I mean, a believer in the narrow sense of the word. Creation from nothing and miracles and a personal God' (1.611–13). Haines gives a fair description of a general orthodox form of christian belief, as opposed to not just the atheist or agnostic positions but also to most deist options. As a jejune Jesuit, Stephen does not care for these very protestant distinctions: 'There's only one sense of the word, it seems to me' (1.615) and with this statement Stephen certainly confirms Mulligan's analysis that he has 'the cursed Jesuit strain [. . .], only it's injected the wrong way' (1.209). Readers of *A Portrait* know that for Stephen the only choice is between catholicism ('an absurdity that is logical and coherent') and a radical and complete lack of belief. Protestantism ('an absurdity that is illogical and incoherent' is not an option. When Haines repeats his question about the idea of a personal God, the young Irishman replies: 'You behold in me, Stephen said with grim displeasure, a horrible example of free thought' (1.625–6). Gifford and Seidman are correct in believing that the word 'free thought' refers to 'thought free from the dictates of "Christian revelation,"' but as his first reaction to the question makes clear, Stephen does not so much refer to the historical precedent of Anthony Collins's coining of the term that Gifford and Seidman mention in their *Annotations*.

As we have seen, by the end of the nineteenth century 'free thought' had become a synonym of a militant anticlericalism that from the eighties of the nineteenth century often went hand in hand with various forms of radical liberalism, atheism, anarchism and socialism, especially in England, France, Italy and Belgium. In the French translation of the novel which was supervised by Joyce, this sentence is given as 'libre pensée' just as in the German version this becomes 'eines Freidenkers,' of a freethinker. Despite the careful positioning of distancing words ('grim displeasure' and 'horrible example'), Stephen here comes closest to expressing his ideological position, and it is no coincidence that he chooses the archaic and biblical verb 'behold' for this purpose.

It is only now that Stephen begins to contemplate religion and the 'holy Roman catholic and apostolic church,' when he quotes the Latin translation of the description of the Roman church from the *Credo* of Palestrina's *Missa Papae Marcelli*. At the same time there is the realization that the catholic claim for apostolic authority is vain, because Stephen contemplates 'the slow growth and change of rite and dogma, like his own rare thoughts, a chemistry of stars' (1.652–3). One of the earliest forms of a dogmatic creed was the 'Symbol of the Apostles' or 'Apostles' Creed' which in the Middle Ages and the renaissance was believed to have been expressed, one dogma at the time, by the twelve apostles at Pentecost, but which is now thought to have been written in the late fourth century.[3] It was replaced somewhat later at the Council of Nicea by a different form, for the purpose of excluding Arius and his followers. A second ecumenical council in Constantinople expanded the role of the Holy Ghost in the Creed and only then added the phrase about the One Church that is quoted by Joyce.

Behind the beauty of the voices in Palestrina's mass stands for Stephen 'the vigilant angel of the church militant' Michael, who disarms and menaces the heretics. This conjures up an image of a:

horde of heresies fleeing with mitres awry: Photius and the brood of mockers of whom Mulligan was one, and Arius, warring his life long upon the consubstantiality of the Son with the Father, and Valentine, spurning Christ's terrene body, and the subtle African heresiarch Sabellius who held that the Father was Himself His own Son. (*U* 1.656–60)

Let us take a closer look at the heretics in this quotation, in their historical order and with some help from the *Catholic Encyclopedia.* As we have seen before, the *Catholic Encyclopedia* is authoritative for Joyce's notions of church doctrine not only because it offers a good view of the thinking of the Catholic Church in the first quarter of the twentieth century, but mostly because Joyce used it as a direct source for information about catholicism.

The historically earliest heretic we can find in the *Catholic Encyclopedia* is the father of gnosticism. Valentine was condemned by the church father Tertullian in his treatise against heresy, but some more recent historians of the early church believe that Valentine's gnostic version of christianity may actually represent a form much closer to the teachings of the early christians than some of the doctrines that would only later become orthodox. In any case gnosticism was older than christianity itself and its dualism was the result of a blending of Greek neo-Platonist philosophy and Eastern mythological ideas: Tertullian, our only reliable source on some early heresies, claimed that Valentine was a Platonist who had found his weird ideas while studying Greek philosophy. Valentine seems to have believed that the material world had been created by an evil Demiurge who had nothing to do with the christian trinity. Man is a mixture of good spirit and evil matter, and as a result God sent Christ to lead men out of the world of darkness in the direction of gnosis or spiritual knowledge. As Stephen seems to know, Valentine believed that Christ never had a material or terrene body, and that being born he passed through his mother, in Tertullian's words, 'like water through a pipe.'

Whereas Valentine and other gnostic christians deified Christ to the point of denying his human qualities, Sabellius in the beginning of the third century developed an alternative theology that once again we only know second-hand: as in the case of Valentine, none of his writings have survived. According to the *Catholic Encyclopedia*, Sabellius' view of the Trinity was not that far removed from

the orthodox position of Tertullian. Sabellius, like many Christians before and
after him, attempted to rescue the concept of the Trinity from the charge of
polytheism, by stressing the unity or monarchy of the One God, which is why his
views are generally called 'Monarchian.' In his view the Trinity had but one
hypostasis or substance and this is, as the *Catholic Encyclopedia* puts it:

> So far as words go, exactly the famous formulation of Tertullian, 'tres
> personae, una substantia' (three persons, one substance), but Sabellius seems
> to have meant 'three modes or characters of one person.' ('Monarchians')

It is this insistence on the unity of God, more in keeping with Old Testament
monotheism, that made Sabellius a heretic according to orthodox thinkers: for
him Father, Son and Holy Ghost were no more than different names for the
same God and according to the historian of christian doctrine Jaroslav Pelikan,
Sabellius is said to have called the Divinity 'Son-Father' (Pelikan 1971: 179).
The exact nature of Christ and his precise relationship with the other Persons
of the Trinity would continue to haunt christianity but it ceased to be a purely
theological discussion when the Emperor Constantine adopted Christianity:
from that moment onwards trinitarian theology would be a vital political issue.
    In this context the case of Arius as heretical is the clearest: in a way he became
the church's arch-heretic and, as we have seen, his differing opinion about the
exact relationship between the Father and the Son in the Trinity made it necessary for the first christian emperor to force the leaders of the church to decide
the issue once and for all. According to the traditional view of the controversy
that is described in the *Catholic Encyclopedia,* Arius attacked the orthodox position, which claimed that Jesus as the Son of God was fully divine and fully part
of the Godhead. The *Encyclopedia* calls Arianism 'an Eastern attempt to rational-
ize the creed by stripping it of mystery so far as the relation of Christ to God
was concerned' ('Arianism'). In reality Arius and others like him based their
thinking on the Gospels and the Epistles where the humanity of Jesus as a suffering human is stressed and where it is made quite clear that Jesus is clearly
subordinate to his Father.[4] This view was shared by more than a few of the early
church fathers such as Justin Martyr, Clement and Origen and it has even been
claimed that this interpretation *was* orthodox until the defeat of Arianism at
the Council of Nicea. Contrary to what loyal church historians have claimed,
the fateful choice against Arianism was the result of a political need for doctrinal unity; it had little if anything at all to do with theology. Even its importance
was exaggerated in later years: the Creed seems not to have been taken seriously at the time when it was first formulated. Ten years later most of its supporters had been deposed or even exiled from their local sees. In fact, in the
following years Arius himself was not only exonerated as were the two bishops
who had refused to sign the Creed and had been anathematized: they too were
later returned to their sees and Arius's main opponent in his local church of
Alexandria was banished to Gaul. At the end of his life the Emperor Constantine

himself chose to be baptized by an Arian bishop and if more than half a century later another generation of anti-Arians had not convinced another Roman emperor to intervene, the Council of Constantinople would not have repeated its attacks and Arianism might well have become the official doctrine of the Church of Rome. The Goths were Arians and the last remains of this most powerful of heresies disappeared as late as the ninth century.

According to the *Catholic Encyclopedia*, the chronologically last heretic in Stephen's list, the patriarch Photius, is considered as 'one of its worst enemies' by the church of Rome because he is thought to have been responsible for the major schism with the Byzantine church in the ninth century ('Photius'). Despite the background to the controversy that, again, had more to do with political differences between the East and the West than with theology, once more the Trinity was a central issue in the dispute. The relationship between the three Persons of the Trinity had been finally defined in the Creed that had been adopted at the Council of Constantinople in 381. But in the sixth century the king of Spain Reccared converted from Arianism to the orthodox faith and the local Synod at Toledo in 589 added the phrase 'filioque' (and from the son) to the text of the Creed in an attempt to make the Holy Spirit, the Third Person of the Trinity, proceed from both Father *and Son*, and thus to strengthen the Creed's anti-Arian stance. This was mainly a political decision and somewhat later it was another worldly leader who forced the issue: in 809 in Aachen, a council convened by Charlemagne accepted the alteration in the text. When explicitly asked by the Emperor, Pope Leo III did accept the new doctrine as theologically sound, but he refused to alter the text of the Creed.

The *Catholic Encyclopedia* calls Photius of Constantinople 'one of the most famous scholars of all the Middle Ages.' After the deposition in 857 of Ignatius, the reigning patriarch of Constantinople, Photius replaced him, despite the fact that he was a layman and that he had to be hurried through the required five degrees. The pope in Rome refused to confirm the new appointment, reinstated his predecessor and excommunicated Photius; a process had begun that would lead to the most important schism in the history of the church. Although there had been difficulties between the Eastern and Western churches before (the second iconoclast persecution in Byzantium had recently ended) and despite the fact that there had always been theological and ritual differences, in principle Constantinople accepted the primacy of the bishop of Rome. But now the Pope's refusal to recognize the appointment of Photius brought things to a head; the two Western ambassadors who had accepted the new patriarch were also excommunicated and Photius was threatened with the same fate if he did not resign.

In the year 867 Photius in retaliation excommunicated the pope and the whole Latin church, giving five grounds that all concerned the liturgical differences between the two traditions, except for the last one, which was the fraudulous addition of the word 'filioque' to the creed. The other four differences were minor, but the quarrel about the addition of 'filioque' was a crucial point in which the supposed heretic Photius was quite correct. The Church of Rome was wrong: as most people knew very well, the case of the Roman hierarchy was based on forged documents. In Byzantium Photius fell out of favour for a while, but then he was officially chosen as the successor of Ignatius and even confirmed by Rome. In a special council that is accepted by the Eastern but not by the Western church, Photius revoked the decisions of the council that had condemned him, he repeated his attacks on the Latin church, he anathematized anybody who added anything to the creed and declared that the church in Bulgaria should belong to Constantinople (the latter point being the immediate political reason for the affair). When the acts of the Council were sent to Rome for confirmation, the Pope anathematized Photius in his turn. In Constantinople Photius's fortunes changed once more and now he was replaced as patriarch by the new emperor's brother, an appointment that was also not accepted by Rome. What happened to Photius afterwards is not clear and this period was followed by reconciliation between the Latin and the Greek churches that lasted for a century and a half, but the *Catholic Encyclopedia* does hold Photius responsible for 'the schism which still lasts.'

That Photius was a heretic, from the point of view of the catholic church must be clear enough, but it is not at all evident why he would be among Stephen's 'brood of mockers,' an expression that is repeated in 'Scylla and Charybdis.' One possible explanation is given in John Julius Norwich's history of Byzantium: as part of his early campaign against the theologically challenged patriarch, the brilliant Photius argued that man had two souls, one capable of error and the other infallible; this deeply heretical theory was taken seriously by all, including the patriarch, after which Photius 'cheerfully' withdrew it, much like Stephen in 'Scylla and Charybdis' admits that he does not even believe his Shakespeare theory. Norwich concludes that 'Photius was responsible for perhaps the only really satisfactory practical joke in the whole history of theology, and for that alone he deserves our gratitude' (Norwich 1993: 63–4). It is clear that this kind of provocation puts Photius firmly in the league of mockers like Mulligan, whose real life original was famous for his pranks, but we do not know where Joyce might have found this rather obscure anecdote of Byzantine history.

Stephen calls Mulligan's jokes 'idle mockery' and he seems to believe that 'the void' awaits those who dare to challenge the host of the archangel Michael. This rather pompous statement about a final victory of the Church Militant over the horde of heresies is ironically undercut by his own reaction: 'Hear, hear! Prolonged applause. *Zut! Nom de Dieu!*' (*U* 1.665). In the first chapter of *Ulysses* Mulligan continues his mockery by crossing himself in priestly fashion when the still unidentified swimmer comes out of the water. It has already been pointed out that this might be a discreet reference to Father Oliver Gogarty, hero of George Moore's *The Lake*, who was named after Mulligan's original, Oliver St John Gogarty. The fact that Stephen distances himself from his friend's mockery does not necessarily mean that he is offended or that he takes the church's side; Joyce only seems to think that mockery is not the right weapon in the fight against religion.

In his discussions with Mr Deasy in the second chapter of *Ulysses* the difference in their perceived religious allegiances seems insignificant compared to
their political differences. The only explicit reference to religion is Stephen's
refusal to accept the schoolmaster's Hegelian idea that the goal of history is
the manifestation of God. In 'Proteus' too, where all we are given is Stephen's
interior monologue, God is almost completely absent: the few references to
religion are all ironical. When Stephen picks up the theme of the Trinity, it is
to describe his own relationship with his parents as 'made not begotten,' the
exact opposite of the orthodox interpretation of Christ's consubstantiality with
the Father. The reference to Thomas Aquinas's *lex eterna* is not to be taken
seriously, although it touches on one of the paradoxes of the traditional views
of God: if God is omnipotent, how can he himself be bound by the laws that he
has created? The reference to Arius's death (itself almost certainly a fabrication
of his adversaries) is detailed but hardly relevant to the discussion and the imagined discourse of Stephen's real father is as rich in irreverent references to the
Lord's name as that of Mulligan.

When Stephen remembers reading 'the fading prophecies of Joachim Abbas'
in Marsh's library (also known as the *Vaticinia Pontificum*), he is reminded not
so much of the pseudo-Joachim's apocalyptic prophecies but of Dean Swift's
madness:

> Abbas father, furious dean, what offence laid fire to their brains? Paff!
> *Descende, calve, ut ne amplius decalveris.* A garland of grey hair on his commi
> nated head see him me clambering down to the footpace (*descende!*), clutch-
> ing a monstrance, basiliskeyed. Get down, baldpoll! A choir gives back menace
> and echo, assisting about the altar's horns, the snorted Latin of jackpriests
> moving burly in their albs, tonsured and oiled and gelded, fat with the fat of
> kidneys of wheat. (*U* 3.112–19)

The quotation in italics is identified in Gifford and Seidman as coming from
the spurious papal prophecies (which also happens to be the book's *incipit*), but
in reality we are given a variation: Joyce has replaced the original *ascende*
(go up) with *descende* (come down), and he repeats the word a few lines down.
This is quite a deliberate alteration because we know that originally, in the
Rosenbach manuscript, Joyce still had the word *nimium* instead of *amplius*, so at
a later date he must have corrected both words. The Latin phrase has a very
specific meaning in the pseudo-Joachimite Franciscan prophecies (referring to
the proverbially corrupt Pope Nicholas III of the Orsini family, whom Dante
meets in hell where he is condemned for simony). But Gifford and Seidman are
also correct when they refer to the original of the first words in the Vulgate
version of II Kings 2.23: 'Ascende, calve; ascende, calve,' to which the author of
the *Vaticinia Pontificum* is alluding. These words represent the taunting of Elisha
by the children of Bethel who came out of the city and yelled at the prophet:
'Go up, you bald head; go up, you bald head.' The prophet 'cursed them in the
name of the Lord. And there came forth two she bears out of the wood, and

tare forty and two children of them' (Kings 2.24). The two she-bears are translated as 'duo ursi' in the Vugate, hence Orsini. The biblical passage in itself was
problematic for both the jewish commentators and for the church fathers: in
his commentary on Psalm 46, Saint Augustine even claimed that the children
yelling 'Ascende' represent the jews who clamoured for Christ's crucifixion.
This example of the prophet's (or his Lord's) cruelty to children is still a *locus
classicus* for freethinkers and other sceptics: on the 'Holy Shit Index Page' the
story was voted to the number one spot of the 'Top Ten Smitings.'[5] This status
is confirmed in the apologetic literature, which almost never fails to addresses
this particular bible difficulty.[6]

Whatever the accuracy of these prophecies, Joachim and Swift join the company of equine faces which includes Mulligan and Temple. Mulligan the mocker
is now associated with mental disorder and the threat of anathema, which may
remind readers of the opening story in *Dubliners*. The description of Mass at the
end of the paragraph has more echoes of Old Testament temple worship ('the
altar's horns' and 'the fat of kidneys of wheat') than of a specifically catholic
liturgy. The next couple of lines are among the more anticlerical of the book,
with 'the snorted Latin of jackpriests' who are 'tonsured and oiled and gelded'
and who all celebrate mass at different times in different places. About Occam
it is said that 'the imp hypostasis tickled his brain' (*U* 3.124), but what does
this phrase mean? The word 'hypostasis' is a very ambiguous theological term,
especially in the context of trinitarian theology: in reference to Jesus it denotes
his single essential personality as opposed to his two natures (divine and
human); but in the case of the three Persons the word refers not to their
common substance, but to their three different hypostases. The *OED* therefore
posits 'nature' as the antonym of the first and 'substance' as that of the second
meaning.

William of Occam wrote a whole book on the sacrament of the Eucharist: the
precise nature of Christ's presence in bread and wine was of particular interest
to the scholastic philosophers, who were divided on the question of whether
the co-presence of Christ and bread/wine constituted an instance of consub-
stantiation or of transubstantiation. Occam's position was not quite clear and
seems to have shifted over the years, but despite the fact that he is generally
thought to have opted for the latter option, which in the end became the orthodox view, his radical positions were often attacked as heretical and the *Catholic
Encyclopedia* mentions that he was often thought to have been the first protestant. From the context of Joyce's comments we can gather that what is referred
to is the problem of Christ's *ubiquity*, a philosophical problem I remember
bringing up in an admittedly more primitive form in my own early struggles
with catholic doctrine: if the Catechism teaches that God is everywhere, what is
the point of the consecration of bread and wine? Traditionally the schools had
distinguished among three concepts: the *omnipresence* of Christ's divine nature,
the *unipresence* that refers to his human nature in heaven and the *multipresence*
of his body in the sacrament. For the inventor of Occam's razor these were too

many distinctions and it may be in this sense that the medieval philosopher might have been tempted by the heretical 'imp of hypostasis.'

In any case these theological ideas lead to Stephen's ironic reflections about his pious youth, which is immediately connected with women and sex: he prayed to the Blessed Virgin and he 'prayed to the devil in Serpentine avenue that the fubsy widow in front might lift her clothes still more from the wet street' and alone on the top of the Howth tram he cried to the rain: '*Naked women! Naked women!*' (*U* 3.133–4). This leads to more reflections on his youthful follies until he realizes that apparently he is not on his way to his aunt, so he heads instead towards the Pigeonhouse, which in its turn brings on memories of Patrice Egan in Paris and his recommendation of the blasphemous *La Vie de Jésus* by Leo Taxil

Joyce's Patrice Egan calls himself a socialist and Taxil's anti-clerical writings are exactly what an atheist young Frenchman at the turn of the century would be reading and recommending to others, even if he is a socialist who wants to win the lottery. Young Egan laps his milk with Stephen and he is described as having a 'plump bunny's face. Lap, *lapin*' (*U* 3.165–6), which Fritz Senn in an article on Taxil (1982) has shown as having something to do with the fact that in *La Vie de Jésus* Mary addresses Joseph as 'mon gros lapin.' The reference to the Ballad of Joking Jesus that follows also stresses the continuity between Taxil's blasphemies and Mulligan's efforts in this genre. When Stephen continues his walk on the beach, it is only when the little poem about gypsies mentions sex that Stephen is briefly reminded of Aquinas's term 'morose delectation,' just as somewhat later the sound of seawater among the weeds reminds him of a Latin phrase of Saint Ambrose. The almost final religious reference is typically an ambiguous quotation from the Easter vigil service: the 'Exsultet' refers to Jesus as the morning star, but Joyce refers instead to the fallen angel Lucifer, the 'proud lightning of the intellect' (3.486). But the chapter ends with a more obscure religious reference, when Stephen is surprised to see a three-master silently moving upstream, 'her sails brailed up on the crosstrees' (3.504). We know that this vision was meant to refer to Golgotha because when Budgen told Joyce that the spars in question were called 'yards' and not 'crosstrees,' Joyce thanked him but he replied that he could not change it: 'It comes in later on and I can't change it. After all a yard is also a crosstree for the onlooking landlubber' (Budgen 1934: 57). Readers of the first edition would have to wait more than a 100 pages to find the second occurrence of the word 'crosstree' and we will see in a moment what Joyce would do with it.

The flood of religious references in this chapter forces us to think about Stephen's extremely detailed references to church history and especially to heretical or dubious movements. We know from our study of his reading that James Joyce shared this interest, most probably as a kind of an antidote to the church's own view of itself as the product of a straightforward tradition that reaches from Saint Peter to the current pope. The effect of all this heterodox knowledge on the part of Stephen Dedalus is that we are given an impression of a catholic apostate who knows a great deal more about the history of the church than the vast majority of catholics in Dublin. Just as in 'Grace' the reader is supposed to know that the characters have only a very shaky grasp on catholic history and doctrine, here we seem to be expected to be impressed by the depth of knowledge of a character who is decidedly no longer a catholic.

From the first chapter in which Mr. Leopold Bloom appears, his religious attitudes, if any, are in doubt. Whereas Stephen is clearly troubled by the death of his mother and the related guilt, Bloom has kidneys on his mind. From the very beginning readers are confronted by somebody who is fascinated by the material world and the laws that govern it. When he leaves the house to buy his breakfast, he notices the sun nearing the steeple of George's church; when he sees a breadvan, he thinks of 'our daily' (*U* 4.82); his oriental fantasy includes a mosque and even a 'priest with a scroll rolled up' (4.93), but at no point do these references seem to involve religious connotations for Leopold Bloom.

Only when he finds the zionist pamphlet on the counter, does he realize that the butcher Dlugacz must be jewish and even then he does not reflect on the irony that the man happens to be a pork butcher (that Bloom is intellectually aware of the kosher laws is clear later when he wonders if cats eat pork). He fails to take the opportunity to talk to Dlugacz but once outside again he is reminded of the 'pleasant old times' he and Molly used to have with their jewish friends. In whatever way we read his only direct encounter with another jew, the conclusion can only be that being jewish for Bloom is social and cultural, but in no way religious. The same is true of the dark thoughts that come over him when the sun disappears behind a cloud. Although they contain references to the bible and even depict an oriental and vaguely biblical landscape, his thoughts are expressed in terms of bodily sensations ('Grey horror seared his flesh' on 230) and they disappear by conjuring up their opposites: the 'bed-warmed flesh' of Molly and the quick warm sunlight running like 'a girl with gold hair on the wind' (4.241–2).

Bloom's explanation of 'metempsychosis' is typical of his non-committal attitude towards religious belief: 'Some people believe, he said, that we go on living in another body after death, that we lived before. They call it reincarnation. That we all lived before on the earth thousands of years ago or some other planet. They say we have forgotten it. Some say they remember their past lives' (4.362–5). Again, at the end of the chapter the bells of George's church have no religious meaning to him at all: he reads their tolling simply in worldly terms:

> *Heigho! Heigho!*
> *Heigho! Heigho!*
> *Heigho! Heigho!*
>   Quarter to. There again: the overtone following through the air. A third.
> Poor Dignam! (4.546–51)

In the next chapter Bloom is reminded of his father's admiration for Kate Bateman in *Leah* and of the crucial scene in which the blind father dies just before recognizing his son's voice:

> The scene he was always talking about where the old blind Abraham recognizes the voice and puts his fingers on his face.
> Nathan's voice! His son's voice! I hear the voice of Nathan who left his father to die of grief and misery in my arms, who left the house of his father and left the God of his father.
> Every word is so deep, Leopold. (*U* 5.200–6)

Bloom is clearly disturbed by these memories; not, it seems, by their religious implications (he too has left both the house and the God of his father), but by the reality of his father's suicide the memory of which he tries to push away, much like his earlier reflections on death in general.

In 'Lotuseaters,' Bloom initially has other things on his mind, but the name of his epistolary mistress reminds him of a picture he once saw of Jesus talking to Martha and Mary. When Bloom enters the church of All Hallows, at least partly he does so in order to have an excuse to take off his hat and replace his fake calling card there. The notice he reads in the porch (probably while doing his changing trick) addresses the interests of the catholic church at the beginning of the century. Father Conmee will talk about saint Peter Claver and the African Mission and this leads Bloom into an extended train of thought. First he is reminded of the catholic prayers for the conversion of the protestant prime-minister Gladstone, then of the Mission to China and the difficulties of explaining christianity to 'the heathen Chinee.' In the spirit of the chapter, the Buddha's passive attitude is compared with the bloody image of the 'Ecce Homo' and Bloom describes one of Conmee's Jesuit colleagues in these terms: 'looked a fool but wasn't. They're taught that. He's not going out in bleuy specs with the sweat rolling off him to baptize blacks, is he?' (5.333–4). On entering the church, his first thought is: 'Nice discreet place to be next some girl. Who is my neighbour?' Bloom then describes what is going on in the church, but he does so almost as if he is an anthropologist attending a pagan ritual: his commentary shows that he is a complete outsider to what is going on. His interpretation of the letters I.H.S. and I.N.R.I. on the priest's vestments are only the most famous of these misunderstandings: 'Letters on his back: I.N.R.I? No: I.H.S. Molly told me one time I asked her. I have sinned: or no: I have suffered, it is. And the other one? Iron nails ran in' (5.372–4). Bloom's mistakes (or more probably Molly's) are funny, but as Gifford and Seidman partly point out, they are understandable in the sense that there is no right answer to the question what the letters stand for. I.H.S., as the *Catholic Encyclopedia* also points out, was originally the abbreviation in christian manuscripts of the Greek version of the name Jesus, an abbreviation that probably followed the practice of avoiding the *tetragrammaton* for God's name in Jewish manuscripts. In the Latin west, the second Greek letter was later mistaken for a Roman 'H,' which led not only to the orthographically challenged spelling 'Jhesus' but to a number of different attempts to make some kind of sense of these letters: 'Iesus Hominum (or Hierosolymae) Salvator,' Jesus the Saviour of Men (or of Jerusalem), but also in German: 'Iesus Heiland Seligmacher' (Jesus, Messiah and Saviour). The siglum is particularly dear to the Jesuits, who, perhaps a tad immodestly, claimed at some point that it stood for 'Jesum Habemus Socium' (Jesus is our partner). But Bloom's ignorance is not as bad as it may seem. Something is also wrong with the I.N.R.I., which Gifford and Seidman neatly transcribe into the 'Iesus Nazarenus Rex Iudaeorum' that Pilate ordered to be written on the cross. But as every writer on biblical inconsistencies will tell you, the four evangelists give four different versions of what was on the sign affixed to the cross: John gives the version quoted above, but Matthew has 'Iesus Rex Iudaeorum,' Mark 'Rex Iudaeorum' and Luke, finally, claims the sign was in three languages and that it read: 'Hic Est Rex Iudaeorum.' If the four evangelists cannot even agree, why should Bloom know what the sign on the cross means?

Almost everything he observes in the church is a puzzle to him: when the priest is handing out communion, he describes him as 'holding the thing in his hand' and shaking a few drops off the host ('are they in water?'), whereas of course the priest is making the sign of the cross with the host. When he hears the word *corpus*, he mistakenly believes it means 'corpse' and he concludes: 'Rum idea: eating bits of a corpse. Why the cannibals cotton to it' (*U* 5.352). These thoughts on the Eucharist are disrespectful only for insiders and that is what Bloom clearly is not: he genuinely does not seem to know what is going on and he has a completely different frame of reference. He compares the host to the Jewish mazzoth and he even admits that the communion may not be completely without beneficial effects: 'Look at them. Now I bet it makes them feel happy. Lollipop. It does. Yes, bread of angels it's called. There's a big idea behind it, kind of kingdom of God is within you feel' (5.359–61). Bloom's anthropological analysis stresses both the communal aspect of religion ('Not so lonely') and, on a psychological level, its function as a sort of drug. He also reflects on the duplicity of believers such as his would-be lover Martha, whom for a second he imagines being present in the church, and one of the Phoenix Park murderers who used to go to this very church while plotting the attack. Bloom points out that believers are shown bread and wine, blood and body of Christ, but they are offered only the bread: 'Doesn't give them any of it: shew wine: only the other. Cold comfort. Pious fraud but quite right: otherwise they'd have one old booser worse than another coming along, cadging for a drink' (5.390–2).

Thoughts about religion give way to musings on religious music and art, on the religious life: 'They had a gay old time while it lasted. Healthy too, chanting, regular hours, then brew liqueurs. Benedictine. Green Chartreuse' (*U* 5.406–7). When the priest begins to pray in English, Bloom is reminded vaguely of the limited religious instruction he has received: 'I remember slightly. How long since your last mass? Glorious and immaculate virgin. Joseph, her spouse. Peter and Paul. More interesting if you understood what it was all about. Wonderful organisation certainly, goes like clockwork' (5.422–5). Bloom is especially impressed by the invention of confession, which is a 'great weapon in their hands.' Some of these thoughts are based on a book that we will find again in one of Bloom's hallucinations in 'Circe' and that Joyce would return to in writing *Finnegans Wake*. Chiniquy's *The Priest, the Woman and the Confessional*. Ironically, at the very end of the chapter when Bloom is looking forward to the sensation of feeling his body lying in the bath, he actually quotes from the passage in the gospel of Luke that is thought to be the scriptural authority for the sacrament of the Eucharist.

There is no obvious reason why Bloom has to enter a church here (there was going to be a funeral service in the next chapter) and it seems that in his chapter on the Lotuseaters, Joyce is intent on including proof of Marx's famous dictum that religion is opium for the people. There is no narrative necessity for Bloom's visit (replacing the card in his hat could have been effected with the same stratagem as he used in the beginning of the chapter to retrieve it). The criticism of the church is muted because it is phrased in the imprecise and hesitant language of an almost complete outsider, but that does not weaken its impact: according to Bloom, the catholic church is a powerful organization that has evolved an almost total control over its members, who give up their freedom in return for the feeling of being part of a community with their fellow believers and with the divine.

In the 'Hades' chapter, Bloom's lack of knowledge of catholic doctrine and practice gets him into trouble when he mistakenly assumes that a sudden death is the 'best death' because it involves no suffering: for catholics like the people with whom he shares a ride in the carriage, death without the last rites is the worst possible death. The blank stares of the others in the carriage do not seem to register: Bloom himself remains unaware of his faux pas. It is clear when he is the victim of the cruel comments on suicide that Bloom does realize his position as an outsider: he describes the Irish attitudes in the third person plural: 'They have no mercy on that here or infanticide. Refuse christian burial. They used to drive a stake of wood through the heart in the grave. As if it wasn't broken already' (*U* 6.346–8).

At the funeral service Bloom again fails to properly name the liturgical objects ('A server bearing a brass bucket with something in it came out through a door' (6.589–590)) and father Coffey, like the priests in the previous chapter, is not described in very sympathetic terms: 'Bully about the muzzle he looks. Bosses the show. Muscular christian. Woe betide anyone that looks crooked at him: priest.' Coffey has a toad's belly, reads his book 'with a fluent croak' and even has the eyes of a toad. Bloom continues to observe the religious service as a complete outsider: 'The priest took a stick with a knob at the end of it out of the boy's bucket and shook it over the coffin. Then he walked to the other end and shook it again. Then he came back and put it back in the bucket. As you were before you rested. It's all written down: he has to do it.' And he keeps up the critical commentary: 'Makes them feel important to be prayed over in Latin.'

In paradisum.
Said he was going to paradise or is in paradise. Says that over everybody. Tiresome kind of a job. But he has to say something.

It is only afterwards when he walks back with Mr Kernan that he finds somebody else who is not a born catholic; but the ex-protestant of the *Dubliners* story 'Grace' is mistaken when he believes that Bloom will sympathize with his defence of a service in the vernacular. When Kernan claims that the words '*I am the resurrection and the life*' touch 'a man's inmost heart,' Bloom agrees openly but silently he expresses a completely different view of death and resurrection:

> Your heart perhaps but what price the fellow in the six feet by two with his toes to the daisies? No touching that. Seat of the affections. Broken heart. A pump after all, pumping thousands of gallons of blood every day. One fine day it gets bunged up: and there you are. Lots of them lying around here: lungs, hearts, livers. Old rusty pumps: damn the thing else. The resurrection and the life. Once you are dead you are dead. (*U* 6.672–7)

By the end of the chapter Bloom's deeply unromantic views on death (and life) become even more explicit: he claims it would be better to give the money spent on tombstones and statues to charity and he doubts if anyone ever really prays for the repose of someone else's soul: 'Plant him and have done with him. Like down a coalshoot. Then lump them together to save time' (6.932–3). Bloom then has a go at the Sacred Heart, the symbol of the anti-modernist and for some even theocratic church (Aubert 1978: 121): 'The Sacred Heart that is: showing it. Heart on his sleeve. Ought to be sideways and red it should be painted like a real heart. Ireland was dedicated to it or whatever that. Seems anything but pleased. Why this infliction?' (*U* 6.954–7) As usual, Bloom is less than certain about the exact nature of the veneration of the Sacred Heart of Jesus.

At the very end of the chapter Bloom escapes his gloomy thoughts about death in the same way as he did in 'Calypso,' by thinking of warm living bodies:

> I do not like that other world she wrote. No more do I. Plenty to see and hear and feel yet. Feel live warm beings near you. Let them sleep in their maggoty beds. They are not going to get me this innings. Warm beds: warm fullblooded life. (6.1002–5)

Since the 'Aeolus' chapter is shared between Stephen and Bloom and since in this chapter the latter is generally too busy to think much about anything, there are only few religious references. One of the few exceptions is the parable of the plums, which depicts the limited lives of two pious older ladies in Dublin. Stephen goes out of his way to depict these women as particularly Irish and pious; they waddle up the stairs of Nelson's Pillar,

> afraid of the dark, panting, one asking the other have you the brawn, praising God and the Blessed Virgin, threatening to come down, peeping at the airslits. Glory be to God. They had no idea it was that high.
>
> Their names are Anne Kearns and Florence MacCabe. Anne Kearns has the lumbago for which she rubs on Lourdes water, given her by a lady who got a bottleful from a passionist father. (7.944–50)

The parable's meaning or moral will probably remain obscure, but it is not without interest that one of its titles is *A Pisgah Sight of Palestine*. This is not necessarily a biblical reference, because as Gifford and Seidman point out, it is also the title of a 1650 book by Thomas Fuller. But what they fail to say is that the latter book is a descriptive geography of the Holy Land, which Fuller wrote without ever going there, much like Joyce was writing a geography of Dublin from the perspective of Trieste, Zürich and Paris.

From the beginning of the next chapter, religion is very much on Mr Leopold Bloom's mind when he is handed a leaflet by a sombre Y.M.C.A. young man. As Gifford and Seidman point out, the rhetoric of the throwaway owes more to that of the team of American evangelicals Ruben A. Torrey and Charles M. Alexander that Bloom correctly remembers having visited Dublin in 1903 (when 3,000 people accepted Christ in the same Metropolitan Hall where Dowie is going to speak), than to that of the real John Alexander Dowie, 'restorer of the church of Zion.' In fact it does not seem likely that the Y.M.C.A. would have accepted Dowie as a speaker: originally he may have been a christian revivalist and faith healer in a more traditional vein, but by the end of the nineteenth century his teaching had become increasingly unorthodox. Originally a Scottish immigrant in Australia he founded the Divine Healing Association but then he moved to the United States in 1888. In 1896 he founded the Christian Catholic Apostolic Church in Chicago; in 1901 he established the city of Zion, forty miles north of the city. Zion was a totalitarian theocracy of a kind that had been pioneered half a century earlier by Joseph Smith. Also like the founder of the Church of Jesus Christ of the Latter-Day Saints, Dowie believed in the divine mission of the Anglo-Americans whom he thought were the direct descendants of the lost tribes of Israel. Also like Joseph Smith, he was accused of advocating polygamy, probably not without good cause. In 1906, during one of his many faith healing drives abroad, he was deposed with the help of his wife and son. He unsuccessfully tried to regain legal control of what he considered to be his property, but he fell ill, failed to heal himself and died the following year. Although initially he only wanted to be the community's First Apostle, by 1901 he publicly claimed to be the third manifestation of Elijah and to be destined to preside over the end-times. Quite a few of the most important faith healers and pentecostalists of the first half of the twentieth century acknowledge Dowie as a precursor or inspiration and many pentecostalists had even started their careers in the City of Zion. If we are to believe what is available on the internet, his teachings are very much alive today.

It is not clear where Joyce found the relevant information about Dowie: there is an entry on the faith healer in the eleventh edition of the *Encyclopedia Britannica*, but the article does not refer to Elijah and polygamy. Maybe Joyce remembered the stories about Dowie or he read about his exploits in one of the 1904 newspapers. In the novel Joyce uses the throwaway that was given to Bloom for all kinds of different purposes and it is clear that he is making fun of this particularly enthusiastic form of religion, but Bloom immediately makes the connection between the pamphlet's pious rhetoric on the one hand (there are plenty of christian hymns that include references to the biblical 'washed in the blood of the lamb') and on the other hand the anthropology of blood sacrifices in primitive forms of religion. And he is realistic (or cynical) enough to know that this particular form of religion is first and foremost a 'paying game.'

Although in the first part of this chapter his mind sooner or later turns to food (a luminous crucifix leads him to phosphorus and then to the memory of a bit of codfish left in the kitchen), when he notices Stephen's sister outside of Dillon's auction rooms, he quickly connects the present problems of the Dedalus family with their religion:

> Home always breaks up when the mother goes. Fifteen children he had. Birth every year almost. That's in their theology or the priest won't give the poor woman the confession, the absolution. Increase and multiply. Did you ever hear such an idea? (*U* 8.31–3)

This leads to an extremely negative depiction of priests in general: their gluttony ('Living on the fat of the land'), secrecy ('mum's the word'), avarice and egoism ('All for number one'). What is interesting is that these thoughts are almost immediately followed by another of Bloom's charitable acts: he feeds the 'hungry famished' gulls with two cakes that he then compares with manna, all this despite the fact that he himself is so hungry that he cannot but think in words and expressions that have to do with food.

Just a bit later Bloom's thoughts turn to the female religious orders and he remembers his difficulties when he had to collect the accounts of convents. Again he stresses that despite their supposed poverty, the nuns managed to fry 'everything in the best butter all the same. No lard for them' (8.151) and he remembers (or seems to remember) that it was a nun who invented barbed wire. After his lunch at Davy Byrne's, Bloom passes the protestant bookshop of Thomas Connellan. It is not clear from the context if he sees Chiniquy's pamphlet *Why I Left the Church of Rome* in the shop window or if he just remembers it, but it is clear from the thoughts that follow that Bloom is just as suspicious of protestants as he is of catholics.

Chapter 7

Free Lay Church in a Free Lay State

In the 'Scylla and Charybdis' chapter of *Ulysses* we find Stephen Dedalus in full stride: sharp and erudite in the way he holds his ground against the Dublin intellectuals, but also ironic and self-critical in the interior monologue that accompanies and comments on his public performance. At the beginning of the chapter we get closest to Stephen's own philosophical opinions when he makes fun of the naive neo-Platonism of George Russell's (AE's) theosophy or when he opposes to it Aristotle's 'dagger definitions': 'Hold on to the now, the here, through which all future plunges to the past' (*U* 9.89). As the theosophist Russell recognizes early in the chapter, theories about Shakespeare's life are not too different from '[c]lergymen's discussions of the historicity of Jesus' (9.46). John Eglinton agrees: 'of all great men he is the most enigmatic. We know nothing but that he lived and suffered. Not even so much' (9.395–61). AE refers to the frantic nineteenth-century quest for the historical Jesus that ended in 1906 when Albert Schweitzer wrote in his own book on Jesus that his predecessors (not all of them, like him, clergymen) had only managed to create a Jesus in their own image. Eglinton's extreme scepticism was shared even by the modernist catholic priest Loisy who wrote that his historical work on early christianity taught him while still in the seminary that 'the only statement in the Apostles' Creed to which he could give historical assent was that Jesus suffered under Pontius Pilate' (Ratté 1967: 45).

But it is only when he reaches the first climax of his Shakespeare theory ('the son consubstantial with the father') that Stephen's many earlier references to the Trinity come together. Stephen expresses his theory about the biographical relevance of *Hamlet* and Shakespeare's other plays in terms borrowed from the orthodox view of the relationship between Father and Son in the Trinity as expressed in the Creed. This is recognized by Mulligan, who only now enters the room and responds immediately with 'Amen' and the ironic but formal question: 'You were speaking of the gaseous vertebrate, if I mistake not?' (9.485–7) For this phrase Gifford and Seidman give simply the annotation 'Having a spine but without substance, a ghost; in this case, "the son consubstantial with the father."' This does not make much sense and in reality, as Harald Beck and I discovered almost simultaneously, the expression 'gaseous vertebrate' is a contemporary phrase that simply refers to the christian God.

It was first used by Ernst Haeckel in his book *Die Weltträthsel* of 1899, published the next year in English as *The Riddle of the Universe,* one of the most influential books of European freethinking at the turn of the century. In the first section under the title *Theism* in a chapter XV on 'God and the World,' Haeckel discusses the different kinds of theism, only to end with the 'personal anthropism' according to which God assumes the form of a vertebrate (human or animal). Yet in the more abstract forms of religion, God becomes pure spirit.

> Nevertheless, the psychic activity of this 'pure spirit' remains just the same as that of the anthropomorphic God. In reality, even this immaterial spirit is not conceived to be incorporeal, but merely invisible, gaseous. We thus arrive at the paradoxical conception of God as a *gaseous vertebrate.* (Haeckel 1900: 288)[1]

In the second part of the chapter, Haeckel discusses pantheism and it is here that we find the names of the most important precursors of what in this book he calls his 'monist' philosophy: the Presocratic philosophers, Lucretius, Giordano Bruno, Spinoza, Goethe and Schopenhauer, a list of predecessors associated with most forms of rationalism, materialism and freethinking.

As the British biologist J.B.S. Haldane found out, reading Ernst Haeckel was still a dangerous pastime in the twentieth century: in 1908 he was almost 'sent down' from Eton after having been caught with a copy of *The Riddle of the Universe* and other books published by the Rationalist Press Association, despite the fact that the phrase and the concept had become common enough to occur in the first lecture of William James's *Pragmatism* of 1907 and even in Jack London's 1908 novel *The Iron Heel.* Haeckel's book had been published in 1900 and the phrase must have functioned like a shibboleth among young freethinkers who wanted to shock their elders, so that it is quite probable that a young medical student was using it in Dublin in 1904 in a way that shows he expected to be understood. Stephen's unspoken reaction to the intrusion is nothing if not hostile. The phrase about the 'brood of mockers' that we encountered in the first chapter is repeated here and the German saying about ending up serving that which you used to ridicule,[2] conclusively spells out Stephen's problem with Mulligan's irreverence. By refusing to take religion seriously, Mulligan runs the risk of underestimating both its power and his own strength in distancing himself from it. But now the brood of mockers is a different set than in the first chapter:

> Brood of mockers: Photius, pseudo Malachi, Johann Most.
> He Who Himself begot middler the Holy Ghost and Himself sent Himself, Agenbuyer, between Himself and others, Who, put upon by His fiends, stripped and whipped, was nailed like bat to barndoor, starved on crosstree, Who let Him bury, stood up, harrowed hell, fared into heaven and there these nineteen hundred years sitteth on the right hand of His Own Self but

yet shall come in the latter day to doom the quick and dead when all the quick shall be dead already. (*U* 9.493–9)

Let us look at this passage more closely. The reference to Photius was explained earlier and the second mocker might refer to Mulligan as Gifford and Seidman claim, but the addition of 'pseudo' is puzzling. There are at least two other candidates. The most famous pseudo-Malachi is the author of the series of prophecies ascribed to the eleventh-century Irish bishop with that name. This different set of papal prophecies, which suspiciously enough were only 'discovered' five centuries after the saint's death, consists of a list of names with a brief description or motto for each of the 112 popes after Celestine II (who was elected in 1130). The list ends with Petrus Romanus who will witness the destruction of the world and the final judgment. These prophecies are quite important in traditional catholicism: in a discussion of prophecies in the *Catholic Encyclopedia* it is the second set to be discussed and more recently the election of Benedictus XVI was seen as a final confirmation that the end truly is nigh: our present pope ('the glory of the olive' according to pseudo-Malachi) is the last pope before 'Peter the Roman,' the pope who will preside over the apocalypse. It might be interesting to point out, as do many catholic apocalyptic websites, that the monastic order of the Benedictines have traditionally claimed that the penultimate pope would come from their ranks, since they are commonly known as 'olivetans.' Cardinal Ratzinger was not a Benedictine but as these websites point out, as a cardinal he did say in 1997 that the Benedictines were the saviours of Europe and upon election he even assumed the name of Benedictus XVI.

As late as 1969 Colin Smythe in London published a translation of the prophecies of Saint Malachy with a seemingly tongue-in-cheek introductory letter by the archbishop H.E. Cardinale, who was Apostolic Nuncio to Belgium and Luxembourg and 'until recently Apostolic Delegate to Great Britain.' Both the *Catholic Encyclopedia* and most modern catholics have known for a long time that the prophecies of Malachi are a pious forgery of the sixteenth century and that the text has nothing whatsoever to do with the medieval Irish saint.

If we exclude King Malachi who 'wore the collar of gold' in Thomas Moore's vision of a Celtic Ireland as insufficiently 'pseudo,' a more likely candidate is biblical. Malachi or Malachias is supposed to be the author of the last book in the christian redaction of the jewish bible, the twelfth and last of the minor prophets, who is named in the first verse or title of that short book: 'The burden of the word of the LORD to Israel by Malachi.' The *Catholic Encyclopedia* notes that the Greek translators of the jewish bible did not interpret the Hebrew word as a name and they translated the verse as 'the burden of the word of the Lord to Israel by the hand of his Angel' ('Angels'), reading the name (which does not occur anywhere else in the bible) as a Hebrew word that can mean both angel and messenger. Modern scholars believe that a longer series of anonymous oracles and prophecies was divided at this particular point to create

12 divisions in the original scroll containing the minor prophets, representing the 12 tribes of Israel. If this is true, then there never was a person called Malachi, so the addition of 'pseudo' would be appropriate.

Malachi is an Old Testament prophet and Photius a ninth-century schismatic, Johann Most was a German-American political activist who was still alive in 1904. The information about him in Gifford and Seidman is correct for the most part, but we might add that the blasphemous version of the creed that immediately follows the reference to his name was part of an article published in Most's newspaper *Die Freiheit* and later as a separate pamphlet. The text's first English translation dates from 1888 and in Trieste and Zurich, Joyce may have read it either in the original, or in one of many translations. The booklet continues to be published all over the world: I have found a German edition brought out by an anarchist 'Artists' Group' in Frankfurt in 1996 and the translation is available on the internet.

The translation of Most's book opens with the following statement: 'Among all mental diseases that have been systematically inoculated into the human cranium, the religious pest is the most abominable' (Most 2007) and it goes on to chart the different aspects of the christian idea: the creation of the world; Mary's pregnancy and the Holy Ghost (in terms no less ironic than Leo Taxil's); and providence. At the end of the book we find a whole list of 'unanswerable questions' about God that deserves to be quoted in full since it is here that we find the original of Stephen's atheist creed.

The god of the Christians, as we have seen, is the god who makes promises only to break them; who sends them pestilence and disease in order to heal them; a god who demoralizes mankind in order to improve it. A god who created man 'after his own image,' and still the origin of evil in man is not accredited to him. This is a god who saw that all his works were good, and soon after discovered that they were bad; who knew that man would eat of the forbidden fruit, and still damned him eternally therefore. He is a god who is so dull as to allow himself to be outwitted by the Devil; so cruel that no tyrant on earth can be compared with him – that is the god of the Judaeo-Christian theology. He is an all-wise bungler who created mankind perfectly, but could not keep them in that state; who created the devil, yet could not keep him under control; a god who is omnipresent, yet descended from Heaven to see what mankind was doing; who is merciful, and yet has, at times, permitted the slaughter of millions. An Almighty who damned millions of innocent for the faults of a few; who caused the deluge to destroy mankind excepting a very few with whom to start a new generation no better than the preceding; who created a Heaven for the fools who believe in the 'gospel' and a Hell for the enlightened who repudiate it. *A divine charlatan who created himself through the Holy Ghost, and then sent himself as mediator between himself and others, and who, held in contempt and derided by his enemies, was nailed to a cross, like a bat to a barndoor; who was buried, arose from the dead, descended to Hell, ascended to Heaven, and since then for eighteen-hundred years has been sitting at his own right hand to judge the living and the dead when the living cease to exist.* A terrible despot, one whose history should be written in letters of blood, because it is a religion of terror.

As is clear from the italicized passage and from its German original, Most closely follows the wording of the traditional creed of the church. So does Joyce, but his version also differs: he does not include the 'divine charlatan' of Most's version and Joyce adds the capital letters that are absent in the original German. It is clear that the word 'middler' in Joyce's version stands for 'by means of,' but it is less certain why Joyce attempted to mimic the German construction that was duly taken over by his German translators: in Goyert's version we find the translation 'Er Der Sich Selbst erzeugte, Mittler zwischen Sich Selbst und anderen' (*U* 9.321). Joyce may have wanted to create a suitably archaic diction, in the same vein as the word 'agenbuyer' that he introduced in Most's text? Joyce varies on the English and German versions of Most's original by rhyming 'stripped and whipped' and by moving the 'like bat to barndoor' to the beginning of the sentence. The phrase 'starved on crosstree' contains another germanism: the German verb 'sterben' is a synonym of the general word for 'to die' and 'crosstree,' despite its presence at the end of 'Proteus,' makes more sense as a literal translation of the German 'Kreuzholz.' In the next sentence we find 'stood up' as a literal equivalent for 'auferstand,' and 'fared into heaven' refers to the German verb for 'fuhr,' the past tense of the verb *fahren*, to go. When we now compare the original and Joyce's version it is reasonably clear that Joyce must have had the German original of Most's text before him and that he wilfully wanted his version to have a Germanic ring: he gives 'fiends' for 'Feinden' (enemies) and 'he let him bury' closely follows 'der sich begraben ließ.'[3] The effect of the blasphemy is certainly one of mockery, as is the Gregorian intoning of the *Gloria* that immediately follows it and that seems to continue Buck Mulligan's earlier parody of the mass.

Mulligan's irreverence about religions of all sorts is evident somewhat later when he recalls seeing Bloom in the National Museum:

– Jehovah, collector of prepuces, is no more. I found him over in the museum where I went to hail the foamborn Aphrodite. The Greek mouth that has never been twisted in prayer. Every day we must do homage to her. *Life of life, thy lips enkindle.*'
Suddenly he turned to Stephen:
– He knows you. He knows your old fellow. O, I fear me, he is Greeker than the Greeks. His pale Galilean eyes were upon her mesial groove. Venus Kallipyge. O, the thunder of those loins! *The god pursuing the maiden hid.*
(*U* 9.609–17)

In the orthodox Nietzschean way that we know from the first chapter, Mulligan defines himself as a Greek, strongly in opposition to weak jewish and christian ideas. The quotes from Shelley and Swinburne strengthen the aesthetic dimensions of this anti-christian stance, with a strongly pagan reverence for nature, beauty and life. The 'pale Galilean eyes' are especially revealing because this quote from Swinburne's 'Hymn to Proserpine' ('Thou has conquered, O pale Galilean; the world has grown grey from thy breath') is the mid-Victorian variant of the enlightenment commonplace about a superior Greco-Roman world desacralized and destroyed by judeo-christian repression. The implied reference to Emperor Julian's supposed last words, 'Vicisti, Galilæe,' (you have won, Galilean) strengthens this link with what in the second-half of the nineteenth century had become a freethinking cliché: we find the same conflict in Ibsen's 1870 play *Emperor and Galilean.*

While Mulligan makes fun of Stephen's recourse to Saint Thomas by adopting first his priestly role ('*Ora pro nobis*') and then by speaking in his stage Irishwoman's voice ('*Pogue mahone! Acushla machree!* It's destroyed we are from this day! It's destroyed we are surely!'), Stephen goes ahead in developing his argument about Shakespeare which centres here on a crucial difference between jews and christians, both groups described from the outside, an attitude that is also evident in the fact that he refers to the divinity with the word 'Nobodaddy' (9.787) the decidedly unorthodox William Blake's name for the angry and jealous godhead.

It is only when Stephen turns his attention to fatherhood that the relevance of the earlier references to the *filioque* controversy becomes apparent: 'Fatherhood, in the sense of conscious begetting, is unknown to man. It is a mystical estate, an apostolic succession, from only begetter to only begotten' (9.837–42). If paternity is an apostolic succession, it really does represent a mystical estate which is, in its own estimate, the crucial difference between the Church of Rome and its religious rivals. But what makes paternity so crucial in Shakespeare, in the church and in the world itself, is its very non-existence:

> On that mystery and not on the madonna which the cunning Italian intellect flung to the mob of Europe the church is founded and founded irremovably because founded, like the world, macro and microcosm, upon the void. Upon incertitude, upon unlikelihood. (*U* 9.839–42)

The excessive veneration of Mary and thus of maternity is only a late and, some would argue with Stephen, a trivial addition to the church's set of dogmas compared with the central role played by paternity. Stephen concentrates on the relationship between the first two persons of the Trinity and this is the point where Sabellius's formula about the father being his own son becomes relevant to his Shakespeare argument. It is only when Stephen's own 'strange name' is mentioned briefly that his memories return to his Paris adventures and now he quotes in Latin the dying words of Christ (and probably also of Icarus) to his father ('Pater, ait') and just a little later he offhandedly reverses Jesus's saying about the poor being always with us.

The Shakespeare references now turn to the 'strong inclination to evil' that Stephen observes in the playwright and that is described with a phrase from the Catechism's definition of the results of original sin, not in the version quoted by Gifford and Seidman, which does not contain the phrase 'a strong inclination to evil':

Q. What other effects followed from the sin of our first parents?
A. Our nature was corrupted by the sin of our first parents, which darkened our understanding, weakened our will, and left in us a strong inclination to evil and rebellion.[4]

In this context, Joyce's elision of 'and rebellion' is especially significant. What is important is that Shakespeare is described as an antitype of Christ, a reversal we also find in the quoted variation on 'The Song of Old Ned,' where 'good niggers' become 'bad niggers.'

Stephen's theory not only ends with the playwright's death, but it also moves out towards a formulation of what can only be called a general theology:

The playwright who wrote the folio of this world and wrote it badly (He gave us light first and the sun two days later), the lord of things as they are whom the most Roman of catholics call *dio boia*, hangman god, is doubtless all in all in all of us, ostler and butcher, and would be bawd and cuckold too but that in the economy of heaven, foretold by Hamlet, there are no more marriages, glorified man, an androgynous angel, being a wife unto himself. (9.1046–52)

Shakespeare had been compared with God before (in the quotation from Dumas *père*), but Stephen refers to another cliché from freethought literature (which was also referred to in the famous Scopes trial) according to which the biblical divinity is accused of botching the creation. There is more to be said about *dio boia* than Gifford and Seidman imagine ('a common Roman expression for the force that frustrates human hopes and destinies'). In fact it is a very low curse which Joyce here adopts as the designation for his concept of the cruel god (if he exists) who delights in tormenting his creatures. We will meet this *dio boia* again soon enough.

Mulligan's reaction to the finale of Stephen's theory is typical: he cries *Eureka* (not accidentally in Greek) and comments, 'The Lord has spoken to Malachi,' which is after all only appropriate: we already know that the word 'Malachi' means 'messenger of the Lord.' When John Eglington gently chides Stephen for not even believing in his own theory, Stephen's reaction is the quote with which we opened this book: 'I believe, O Lord, help my unbelief. That is, help me to believe or help me to unbelieve? Who helps to believe? *Egomen.* Who to unbelieve? Other chap' (*U* 9.1078–80). Here again we observe Stephen's generalizing tendency: once more we move quickly from the innocent to the existential. As we have seen, we begin with a variation on a translation of Mk 9.24 ('Lord, I believe; help thou mine unbelief'), which is immediately glossed, first by reference to the obvious paradox of praying to god for help in believing in his existence, then by noting the even deeper irony for praying to the deity in order *not* to believe in him. In the former case the addressee is '*Egomen*,' in the latter we should ask help from 'the other chap.'

The first word is a bit of a mystery that has led to the most diverse interpretations. Gifford and Seidman first claim that in Greek it means 'I on the one hand,' but then against all common sense claim that 'in context' the phrase involves a pun on the magazine *The Egoist,* the journal that published most of the early chapters of *Ulysses* and that was originally called the *Freewoman.* This interpretation is not only unlikely in itself, but quite impossible in context (in the sentence the word functions as a singular). In addition, this would be one of very few instances where in Joyce allows himself, this kind of blatant self-reference and it is hard to imagine what he might have tried to achieve with it here. But Gifford and Seidman's first reference, which also tends to be popular among Joyce critics who need to make the link between Shakespeare and Stephen–Joyce more explicit, is also mistaken. Probably there was a mix-up with the legitimate Latin word 'egomet' which does mean something like 'I myself.' René Girard, for whom Joyce (like Shakespeare and the authors of the bible) has anticipated the French critic's own all-encompassing theory of mimetic desire, needs the word to mean 'myself' and he seems to think that it refers both to Stephen the character and to the author Joyce. More recently, Richard Kearney has linked the word to 'egomism,' which is described in the *OED* as an obsolete and archaic synonym of solipsism. All these attempts to make sense of the word fail (2007: 189).

In reality the *OED* does list the word in Joyce's spelling and although it is described as '*rare*' and has only one citation from the mid-nineteenth century, the word does exist in English with an appropriately religious connotation: 'a monastic functionary in the Greek church.' On another level we might well be reminded not of one of his servants but of YHWH who told Moses in the Vulgate bible: 'Ego sum qui sum,' I am that I am. It is obvious from the context that it is only God himself who can help us believe and just as obviously, in this case, the 'other chap' can only be his Opponent, the fallen Angel with whom Stephen has sympathized before and who was, as we have seen, a popular hero of freethinkers all over Europe.

As they leave the library, Mulligan and Stephen stay in character. Mulligan comments on the colour of Stephen's clothes that only 'crows, priests and English coal' are black; when he berates his friend for not being more diplomatic, he calls him an 'inquisitional drunken jewjesuit.' The chapter's ending is, despite the brief passage of Bloom, 'the wandering jew' himself, almost exclusively pagan, with references to augury and the neoclassical setting of the Library's portico. The last words of the chapter refer to the hierophantic druid priests of *Cymbeline*. It is probably no coincidence that from this pagan ending, in the next chapter we move straight into the exceptionally unpagan mind of the very reverend John Conmee S.J., the only portrait of a catholic in *Ulysses* that found favour with Shane Leslie in his famous review.

The first 'Wandering Rocks' section focuses on Father Conmee and the full repetition of the phrase 'very reverend John Conmee S.J.' ten lines down reinforces the immediate impression we have of a slightly pompous person, who remembers the name of the boy who needs help by reference to the introductory words of the *Praefatio* in the mass, which incidentally, in the 'vere' echoes the 'very' of his own ecclesiastical title. It is clear from the beginning that the world Father Conmee walks through is almost exclusively catholic: even the Dublin he inhabits seems to consist merely of catholic landmarks: 'A onelegged sailor, swinging himself onward by lazy jerks of his crutches, growled some notes. He jerked short before the convent of the sisters of charity and held out a peaked cap for alms towards the very reverend John Conmee, S.J.' (*U* 10.7–10). Father Conmee does not recognize the song involved – in which a surely protestant God is asked to bless 'Private Tommy Atkins' – but he is very much familiar with the convent. When he meets Mrs David Sheehy M.P., he politely shares her pleasure that Father Bernard Vaughan will come again to preach, but when he resumes his walk he remembers the man's 'droll eyes and cockney voice': ' – Pilate! Wy don't you old back that owlin mob?' and he immediately checks himself: 'A zealous man, however. Really he was. And really did great good in his way.' But like Joyce himself – who wrote in 1906, as we have seen, that the reverend father was 'the most diverting public figure in England at present. I never see his name but I expect some enormity' (*Letters II* 182) – Conmee seems to be aware of the excessively conservative opinions of Father Vaughan, who may have 'loved Ireland,' but who defended the British Empire and who spoke up strongly against birth control, licence in art, working women and interracial marriage. Somewhat later he would become a strong supporter of the First World War and advocate the killing of as many Germans as possible.

When Father Conmee walks by a 'shutup free church' he realizes that he should be charitable towards protestants, although he adds: 'Invincible ignorance. They acted according to their lights' (10.71–2). Gifford and Seidman write that the first phrase represents 'Roman Catholic evaluation of Protestant faith, since the Protestant's commitment to his "heretical" faith commits him to "ignorance"' a statement that is followed by a definition out of the *Catholic Encyclopedia*. Things are not quite that simple and the doctrine touches an aspect of catholicism that is relatively unknown among contemporary catholics but that has been growing in importance recently, with Rome's increasing reluctance to honour the commitments of Vaticanum II. Until 1963 the official doctrine of the Church was that no salvation at all was possible outside of the Church of Rome: *Extra ecclesiam nulla salus.* The doctrine of the 1302 *Unam Sanctam* proclamation of Pope Boniface VIII was based on ideas in Saint John Chrysostom and Saint Augustine and it was repeated after Pope Boniface by other popes and councils: 'Furthermore, we declare, we proclaim, we define that it is absolutely necessary for salvation that every human creature be subject to the Roman Pontiff.'[5] More liberal catholics had developed the doctrine of 'invincible ignorance,' which was, according to a recent supporter of the idea, in any case 'unfortunately styled' (see Griffeths). This concept provided a loophole to enable protestants to be saved, provided their ignorance was invincible, which meant that although they were not members of the church, if they had genuinely and deeply understood what was good for them, they would certainly have become catholics. Even more liberally: since one becomes a catholic by baptism, a properly baptized protestant automatically enters the Church of Rome even without realizing it. Provided he does not go on to commit a mortal sin, he remains part of the soul, if not of the body of the catholic church. Needless to say, this escape option led to much theological debate, but it was the liberal and ecumenical definition that ended up being (at least) tolerated at the Vatican Council II (*Lumen Gentium* left the possibility open that some forms of truth could be found *outside* the Church of Rome) and it is this liberal interpretation that has recently come under attack again (Grafton 2005). Father Conmee's thoughts show that for a catholic and a Jesuit, his attitude towards the protestants is fairly liberal for his time, which, of course, does not make it less condescending (as is his treatment of the Christian Brother boys that he meets only moments later).

Although Joyce is generally gentle in his portrayal of a man he seems to have respected, there are times when he is overdoing the satire, as when he has the very reverend reflect 'on the providence of the Creator who had made turf to be in bogs whence men might dig it out and bring it to town and hamlet to make fires in the houses of poor people' (*U* 10.104–6). Surely if the Creator had really been provident he could have found a way of having fuel available in a less work intensive form and closer to the homes of the poor people? Father Conmee's way with the world is gentle, all-knowing but always very superior: he does observe the world around him, he sees the things and the people (as in the tram), but he only rarely allows himself to come to conclusions about them, and when he does and these conclusions are negative or unkind, he immediately corrects himself, as in the case of his colleague father Vaughan. When he thinks about the old woman leaving the tram that 'she was one of those good souls who had always to be told twice *bless you, my child,* that they have been absolved, *pray for me,*' he immediately adds, again not without condescension: 'But they had so many worries in life, so many cares, poor creatures' (10.138–40).

In the next paragraph, thoughts of his coming sermon on the African mission lead him to the Belgian Jesuit Auguste Castelein's book *Le rigorisme: Le nombre*

des élus et la doctrine du salut which took a stance in the debate about the fate of
the unbaptized souls in Africa. Rigorism was the doctrine that no salvation was
possible outside of the church, which meant, ultimately, that all the unbaptized
souls would go to hell. Here too the very reverend father Conmee is, in terms
of the church discussions of his day, extremely liberal. This was part of a general
movement that had an enormous impact on discussions within most protestant
churches, especially in England in the second half of the nineteenth century,
where increasingly the calvinist doctrine of hell was seen to contradict Christ's
message of love, especially when the redeemed were expected to glory in the
eternal damnation of those that were not redeemed.[6] In 1853 the liberal
F.D. Maurice was dismissed from King's College in London for casting doubt on
the traditional doctrines and H.B. Wilson was convicted in the Court of Arches
for advocating a tentative form of the idea of universal salvation in his contribution to the famous collection of liberal *Essays and Reviews* (Parker 1860). By the
most believers refused to accept (against the evidence in the bible, it might be
pointed out) that the christian God would inflict eternal pain on his creatures
and by the turn of the century most protestants had found different ways of
qualifying the adjective in the expression 'eternal damnation,' in a movement
that in the end had more direct influence on the nature of christian doctrine,
it has been claimed, than the theories of Darwin (who did not believe in hell).
In 1893 St. George J. Mivart, a catholic convert who attempted to reconcile
Darwin and church teaching, was placed on the Index when he claimed that
there was happiness in hell (Artigas et al., 2006: 248–50).

When thoughts of Mary Rochfort lead father Conmee to contemplate 'that
tyrannous incontinence' that is sex, the narrator of the next paragraph mischievously describes him as 'Don John Conmee' who is the trusted confessor in
distant aristocratic 'times of yore.' But when he meets the two young people
who may very well have been indulging in that very same tyrannous incontinence, his mind again refuses to consider the possibility, although the wicked
reality is betrayed by the Hebrew letter *sin* that marks the relevant section of
his Breviary prayers.

Bloom has been given the tenth and thus the middle section of the chapter
and when next we meet him at a bookstall, he is idly turning the pages of
The Awful Disclosures of Maria Monk, a still influential protestant forgery that
purported to describe the sufferings of a poor woman who had escaped from
a catholic nunnery in Montreal. It belongs to the same kind of anti-catholic
propaganda that was so popular in the United States in the middle of the nineteenth century and that still, despite the almost immediate exposure of 'Maria
Monk' and her confessions, continues to survive on the internet. But Bloom's
mind is more on the profane literature that he is looking for.

Religion does not seem to play a significant role in the lives of all of the other
Dubliners who make brief appearances in the next sections, although Boody
Dedalus intentionally blasphemes when to the shock of her sisters she refers
to her progenitor as 'Our father who art not in heaven' (10.291). Her brother

Stephen is given two sections. In the sixth he is talking to Almidano Artifoni and although we do not know what he has been telling his *maestro*, at least it is clear that it involves the dark fact that '*il mondo è una bestia.*' In Section 13 of the chapter we find Stephen looking into a lapidary's window and the stones evoke primeval horrors: 'Born all in the dark wormy earth, cold specks of fire, evil, lights shining in the darkness. Where fallen archangels flung the stars of their brows. Muddy swinesnouts, hands, root and root, gripe and wrest them' (10.805–7). The last part of the first sentence contains a probably polytheistic reference to the prologue of the Fourth Gospel: 'And the light shineth in the darkness; and the darkness comprehended it not.' This is the sort of hell of which Stephen knows quite well that it is one of his own creation, but that awareness does not stop him from being deeply disturbed by these dark thoughts, until he manages to take into account his immediate surroundings. On the huckster's bookcart he finds a sorcery book that promises him a magical recipe to win a woman's love, but instead reality intrudes in the form of his sister Dilly. Although he has the money and although he tells himself that he could save her, he is afraid that she will 'drown me with her' (10.876). Even the repetition of the phrase 'agenbite of inwit' cannot make him change his mind. Stephen's moroseness seems to be confirmed in a later section when Mulligan is discussing his friend with Haines in the DBC (Dublin Bakery Company). Buck offers this rather acute analysis of his friend: 'They drove his wits astray, he said, by visions of hell. He will never capture the Attic note. The note of Swinburne, of all poets, the white death and the ruddy birth' (10.1073–5). Again in a Gibbon–Nietzschean fashion and again with a quote from Swinburne (appropriately from the poem 'Genesis'), Mulligan opposes a Greek paganism to what he sees as the jewish-christian slavery of catholicism.

Religion is not much of a concern in the 'Sirens' chapter. When Bloom passes the shop of Aurelio Bassi, statue and picture-frame maker, he notices the 'blessed virgins' in the window: 'Bluerobed, white under, come to me. God they believe she is: or goddess' (*U* 11.151–2), a characteristically mistaken and blasphemous comment that is nevertheless theologically not far off the mark. According to Gifford the colours of the virgin's dress are traditional and the phrase 'come to me' suggests 'both the Virgin's sympathy for the sinful and the heavily burdened and her role as intercessor with her son; in context, the phrase identifies the Virgin as another sort of Siren.' This may well be the case, but Bloom may simply be reading the phrase on the pedestals of one of the represented virgins, because it is part of Elisabeth's greeting to Mary and thus of the Rosary: 'And why is this granted to me, that the mother of my Lord should come to me?' (Lk. 1.43). Bloom's evaluation of Mary's role in catholicism is theologically unsound, but at the same time it echoes a genuine problem in the veneration for the mother of god that had always been a bone of contention in the discussion with protestants. Then as now, conservative and anti-modernist catholics propagated the popular veneration of the Virgin. When next we see Bloom he has walked on to the next shop with statues of virgins,

Peter Ceppi's, and he remembers that Nannetti's father (another Italian) made a living on the sale of religious statuary.

Somewhat later when he listens to Ben Dollard's 'Croppy Boy' and its use of the religious phrases '*In nomine Domini*' and '*mea culpa*,' he is reminded of the two services he observed earlier in the day: 'Latin again. That holds them like birdlime. Priest with the communion corpus for those women. Chap in the mortuary, coffin or coffey, *corpusnomine*' (*U* 11.1034–6). It is clear that Bloom thinks of religion, and more specifically catholicism, as little more than an extremely successful scam.

In the next chapter, 'Cyclops,' Bloom's lack of theological finesse gets him in trouble. All of the decent Dublin citizens, protestants and catholics alike, who have gathered at Barney Kiernan's pub seem to share both general anti-semitic sentiments and a mild to violent dislike of Bloom. When Martin Cunningham fails to find Bloom in the pub, the citizen claims that Saint Patrick will have to come back and convert the Irish all over again, since he has allowed jews like Bloom 'to contaminate our shores' (*U* 12.1672). In order to divert attention from Bloom, who is not even present, the 'sympathetic human man' (6.344) Martin Cunningham offers a toast, 'God bless all here is my prayer' (12.1673). Cunningham's rapping on his glass becomes the sound of the sacring bell in a diversion that exhaustively describes the procession of catholic saints and confessors who visit the many times blessed abode of Barney Kiernan.

Paradoxically the only person in Kiernan's pub who does not drink and who has a legitimate and even noble reason for being in the pub is that same Leopold Bloom who is the butt of jokes and insults. But Bloom does stand his ground, even when he is in physical danger. The irony is that when Bloom, the only person to display christian charity, refers to Jesus (and his father) as jewish: 'Christ was a jew like me,' the supposed blasphemy brings the citizen to the boil in a series of curses: 'By Jesus, says he, I'll brain that bloody jewman for using the holy name. By Jesus, I'll crucify him so I will' (12.1811–12). It is clear later on, when Bloom recounts a version of the story in 'Ithaca,' that the 'bloody jewman' is particularly proud of what in the retelling he translates into a minor victory. Bloom belatedly realizes that the most wounding part of his remark must have been the fact that for this once, the victim of anti-semitism was fighting back. In the tortuous grammar of the later chapter:

> People could put up with being bitten by wolf but what properly riled them was a bite from a sheep. The most vulnerable point too of tender Achilles. Your god was a jew. Because mostly they appeared to imagine he came from Carrick-on-Shannon or somewhereabouts in the county Sligo. (*U* 16.1638–42)

In the 'Nausicaa' chapter the sentimental prose describing Gerty MacDowell's evening on the beach is punctuated by the equally sentimental and hackneyed prose describing the temperance retreat led by the reverend John Hughes S.J.

in the church nearby. The link between the seduction scene and the religious ceremony is made quite explicit. At the temperance retreat the faithful and the officiating priest are involved in the benediction of the Most Blessed Sacrament and reciting the litany of Our Lady of Loreto and Gerty is reminded of her father's encounter with the demon drink, but at the same time she herself is compared to the Holy Virgin. She sees herself as a 'refuge of sinners' and 'comfortress of the afflicted,' applying the terms of the litany to her own perceived role in life. The scene in the church is mirrored by the one outside and the adoration of the Blessed Sacrament finds a more earthy equivalent in Bloom's adoration of Gerty's treasures. She swings her leg just as Canon O'Hanlon is censing the Blessed Sacrament, while Bloom's eyes are fixed on her, 'literally worshipping at her shrine' (*U* 13.564) and at the moment suprême, it is not a coincidence that it is a Roman candle exploding. In the description of the orgasmic explosion reminds one of the transports of mystic and sexual ecstasy in Bernini's statue of Theresa di Avila.

When Bloom takes over the narration, his thoughts concern different aspects of sexuality, including the smell of sperm. It is in this unlikely context that his earlier thoughts about the sexual attraction of priests return:

> Mansmell, I mean. Must be connected with that because priests that are supposed to be are different. Women burr round it like flies round treacle. Railed off the altar to get on to it at any cost. The tree of forbidden priest. O, father, will you? Let me be the first to. That diffuses itself all through the body, permeates. Source of life. (*U* 13.1036–40)

Bloom surmises something that we have earlier observed in Gerty when she is thinking about Father Conroy, her confessor, and that we will also find in Molly's soliloquy. As Chiniquy had pointed out in his book on confession, innocent women are first perverted by the sexual questions, then attracted to the priest as an authority figure and subsequently seduced. Bloom is also impressed by the church's general efficiency: 'Mass seems to be over. Could hear them all at it. Pray for us. And pray for us. And pray for us. Good idea the repetition. Same thing with ads. Buy from us. And buy from us' (13.1122–4). In an identical phrasing as in 'Lotuseaters' ('Good idea the Latin'), Bloom reaffirms the powers of the catholic liturgy as a marketing device.

Stephen Dedalus in the guise of a morose priest shines through the distortions in 'Oxen of the Sun': for example, when Stephen is said to have 'mean of a frere' (*U* 14.192). When he joins the discussion, most of his comments are of a similar kind. When he drunkenly proposes a toast to the pope, he turns it into a Mulliganesque parody of the Eucharist, which quickly becomes a drunken exegesis of Blake's apocalyptic 'time's ruins build eternity's mansions.' It is certainly not clear in how far we are supposed to take this secular homily seriously, but we cannot deny that Stephen is quite as ambitious and eclectic in his references here as he had been in 'Scylla and Charybdis.' What he seems to be doing is to compare female and male creation in terms of the incarnation of Jesus. The question to be decided is whether Mary recognized Jesus for what he was from the moment he was born, for in that case she was indeed what Saint Bernard, through Dante, makes of her: 'creature of her creature,' daughter of her own son. But if she did not, then she is no better than Peter, the first pope, who denied Christ. And it could all be much worse if Leo Taxil is right, because in that case, we would not even have transsubstantiality or consubstantiality, but something that can only be called 'subsubstantiality.' The doctrine of the Virgin Birth is therefore only for the lewd to worship. Genuine believers must resist it: 'With will will we withstand, withsay' (14.311–12). In reaction to these theological ruminations, Dixon asks Stephen why he did not become a friar and the latter jokingly answers him by inverting the three traditional monastic vows: he will be obedient in the womb, chaste in the tomb and his poverty will be involuntary in between. When accused by Lenehan of the corruption of minors, Stephen denies the accusation and claims that he is, like Christ, 'the eternal son and ever virgin' (14.342–3). He becomes increasingly drunk and his comments become more and more a mixture of phrases with little connection between them. The little that we can make out suggests that he seems to have adopted the guise of the biblical YHWH admonishing Erin-Israel for being unfaithful to him.

When the thunderstorm breaks out and it starts to rain, Lynch tells Stephen that 'the god self was angered for his hellprate and paganry' (14.411–12) and the young blasphemer's fearful reaction seems to indicate that for once he does not disagree. In the allegorical style of Bunyan, Stephen as 'Boasthard' now explains his loss of faith as the result of 'Carnal Concupiscence' (14.454). Although in the following passages Stephen occasionally makes his appearance (mostly as a priest or a monk), it is when the style of the Darwin bulldog and agnostic Thomas Huxley takes over the narrative, that on the one hand Stephen is accused of being addicted to 'perverted transcendentalism,' whereas on the other hand he seems to hold a degree of 'Doubter of Divinity' (Divinitatis Scepticus). Stephen repeats his opinion about the *dio boia*, whom he now calls 'an omnivorous being' and about whom he offers the opinion that if that divinity is prepared to feast on cancrenous females like his mother, the deity might also like to devour the occasional child.[7] It is interesting to see that the Huxley narrator seems to be on Bloom's more humane side in the debate, against Stephen, the 'morbidminded esthete and embryo philosopher' (14.1295).

The end of the chapter is pure linguistic chaos, with many different voices, idiolects and languages, yet in the last section something like Stephen's voice seems to take over in what Blamires calls 'the vulgarest button-holing commercialese' (Blamires 1966: 165). Yet there is much more in the last paragraph, among them quotations from both Old and New Testament. When Lynch asks Stephen about Bloom, he is told: 'Sinned against the light and even now that day is at hand when he shall come to judge the world by fire' (*U* 14.1575–7). Despite the clear biblical echoes in this sentence ('sin against the light,' 'even now,' 'is at hand,' 'to judge the world by fire,') none of these expressions is strictly biblical, although all of them were and are frequently used by preachers of all denominations. 'To judge the world by fire' is part of the 'Office for the dead' as it is of the burial ceremonies of both the anglican and the catholic church; it is often used in *Requiems* (including those by Fauré and Verdi). In other words, the sentences sound biblical, but are not biblical. That may be why, after a seemingly rude noise ('Pflaap'), we read a phrase that is used only once in the Gospels, *'Ut implerentur scripturae,'* so that the scriptures might be fulfilled. It is almost as if Stephen is making the surely ironical point, *contra* Deasy, that the latter's protestant anti-semitism lacks the appropriate biblical basis.

An announcement of the show by another preacher, Alexander J. Dowie, forms the basis of some of these comments and the throwaway announcing the visit of the evangelical faith healer to the Dublin YMCA has played a small but significant part in the book in both 'Lestrygonians' and 'Wandering Rocks.' Appropriately, one of the greatest successes of Dowie had been the miraculous healing of the niece of Buffalo Bill whom he claimed to have cured of spinal cancer. Dowie also fulminated against the use of pharmaceutical medicine and pork products, against members of secret societies such as the Freemasons, and against corrupt politicians and liberal clergymen. Politically he saw himself as a theocrat and a follower of the British Israelites, who believed that the Northern peoples were the direct descendants of the Lost Tribes of Israel (etymologically the Saxons were 'Isaac's sons,' just as the Danes were the sons of Dan). In June 1901 Dowie began to claim that he was the prophet Elijah and he even began to dress the part. In the rest of the paragraph, Dowie's preaching is therefore wide of the mark. But it remains interesting that Joyce decided to end a chapter on the development both of an embryo and of English prose style, with this particular kind of American language, with its rich mixture of the vulgar and the elevated, the holy and the profane.

'Circe' is the chapter where the preceding events of the day are replayed in a different register and religion plays an even more important role here. Bloom's first hallucination in the chapter includes his father in the guise of an anti-semitic caricature, who accuses him not only of getting involved with drunken goys, but also, in clearly biblical terms, of leaving the house of his father and 'the god of his fathers Abraham and Jacob' (*U* 15.260–3). Bloom's mother, on the other hand, is portrayed as another religious and racial stereotype, the superstitious Irish catholic: she invokes the Sacred Heart of Mary, a devotion that is related in its late development to the devotion of the Sacred Heart of Jesus. Both originated in the counter-reformation French church and attempted in post-revolutionary times to acquire recognition from Rome, with three appearances of the Virgin, probably not accidentally in the revolutionary year 1830, at which a miraculous medal was revealed to Sister Catherine of the Sisters of Charity of St Vincent de Paul in Paris. In the words of the *Catholic Encyclopedia*:

The Blessed Virgin appeared as if standing on a globe, and bearing a globe in her hands. As if from rings set with precious stones dazzling rays of light were emitted from her fingers. These, she said, were symbols of the graces which would be bestowed on all who asked for them. Sister Catherine adds that around the figure appeared an oval frame bearing in golden letters the words 'O Mary, conceived without sin, pray for us who have recourse to thee'; on the back appeared the letter M, surmounted by a cross, with a crossbar beneath it, and under all the Sacred Hearts of Jesus and Mary, the former surrounded by a crown of thorns, and the latter pierced by a sword. ('Miraculous Medal')

Two years later medals such as these were struck, and miracles duly followed; the most important was the conversion of a prominent jew, Alphonse Ratisbonne of Strasburg. The *Catholic Encyclopedia* adds that the second factor in the success of the devotion was the founding in 1849 of the archconfraternity of the Immaculate Heart of Mary. As a result, in 1855 the Congregation of Rites in Rome approved the Office and Mass of the Most Pure Heart of Mary, without however, the *Encyclopedia* regretfully concludes its article on the Devotion to the Immaculate Heart of Mary, 'imposing them upon the Universal Church.' Ireland was the first country where the new religious order began its international expansion, concentrating on care for women 'of the lower orders' and becoming active in primary and secondary education. It is clear that Ellen Bloom's reference to this particular devotion is thematically connected both to her husband's original religion and to her use of lucky charms.

After his trial for sexual transgressions, Bloom locates the brothel where Stephen and Lynch are, because he correctly assumes that it must be the former who is playing church music on the piano. In the following scenes of Bloom as mayor of Dublin, his rhetoric quickly assumes religious overtones when he echoes the Hallelujah chorus of Haendel's *Messiah* and the stage directions depict religious peace and tolerance when the leaders of all the major creeds join the parade and assist in his coronation as 'most serene and potent and very puissant ruler of this realm' (*U* 15.1472). These political overtones are quickly replaced by religious ones when Bloom begins to speak in decidedly evangelical language: 'My beloved subjects, a new era is about to dawn. I, Bloom, tell you verily it is even now at hand. Yea, on the word of a Bloom, ye shall ere long enter into the golden city which is to be, the new Bloomusalem in the Nova Hibernia of the future' (15.1542–5). The new city closely resembles the megalomaniac cities of great religious leaders like Joseph Smith and Alexander J. Dowie. Bloom even becomes 'His Most Catholic Majesty' who inaugurates year 1 of the Paradisiacal Era. His utopia is the 'union of all, jew, moslem and gentile' with Esperanto as the universal language, the end of nationalism and in an improved version of the Italian nationalist slogan: 'Free money, free rent, free love and a free lay church in a free lay state' (15.1693).

This statement leads to his downfall: first O'Madden Burke and Lenehan voice mild criticisms, then Father Farley S.J. accuses Bloom of being 'an episcopalian, an agnostic, an anythingarian seeking to overthrow our holy faith' (15.1712–13). Bloom's downfall quickly becomes that of a religious leader: women follow the example of the veiled sibyl who commits suicide for her 'hero god' and Alexander J. Dowie addresses fellowchristians and anti-Bloomites to denounce him as a 'disgrace to christian men.' When Bloom gives birth to eight male children and when he is asked whether he is 'the Messiah ben Joseph or ben David' (15.1834), he answers *darkly*: with the words of Jesus (Mt. 26.64) when asked by high priest whether he is the son of God: 'You have said it' (*U* 15.1836). Bloom even performs the necessary miracles to demonstrate that he is indeed the messiah. The papal nuncio to Ireland reads out the redeemer's genealogy, but the writing is on the wall and rapidly Bloom transforms into a false messiah and scapegoat.

From his first appearance in 'Circe,' Stephen in his turn is hailed as a parson and for good reason: drunkenly he 'chants with joy the *introit* for paschal time' (15.73–5). In a sense he seems to have taken over the absent Mulligan's role as a blasphemous priest, but soon enough it becomes evident that the chanting is but an interruption in the middle of an argument about the merits of gesture as a more primitive and thus universal language. When he needs to provide another example, he refers to the most loaded symbols in christianity, the wine and bread of the Eucharist, but refers to them as 'the loaf and jug of bread or wine in Omar' (15.117). When he answers Lynch's questions about which brothel they will go to, Stephen in his answer feminizes Mulligan's quote from the beginning of the Mass: '*ad deam qui laetificat juventutem meam*' (15.122–3). Stephen then demonstrates loaf and jug with gestures, but Lynch cannot even distinguish between the two 'Which is the jug of bread? It skills not' (15.129). They walk on and then Bloom appears, unseen, following them.

Bloom confronts his jewish ancestry when he meets his paternal grandfather Virag whose lustful but ungrammatical description of the prostitutes manages to excite his grandson. When Zoe mentions that a priest had visited the brothel in disguise, the anticlerical Virag accepts this as only logical and he expresses his animosity against the catholic church both by the protestant slogan 'To hell with the pope' and by the claim that he wrote the anti-catholic propaganda books of Father Chiniquy. But he becomes sexually aroused while describing the primal coupling and he begins to insult the *goyim* by repeating Bloom's faux pas about Christ's father in the 'Cyclops' chapter, directly contradicting Martin Cunningham: 'He had a father, forty fathers. He never existed. Pig God! He had two left feet. He was Judas Iacchia, a Libyan eunuch, the pope's bastard. [. . .] A son of a whore. Apocalypse' (15.2572–6).

Although most of Bloom's hallucinations have to do with sex and power, occasionally they also involve religion, as when the nymph turns into a nun and strikes out with a poniard 'at his loins,' threatening to circumcise him:

BLOOM

(*starts up, seizes her hand*) Hoy! Nebrakada! Cat o' nine lives! Fair play, madam. No pruningknife. The fox and the grapes, is it? What do you lack with your barbed wire? Crucifix not thick enough? (*he clutches her veil*) A holy abbot you want or Brophy, the lame gardener, or the spoutless statue of the water-carrier, or good mother Alphonsus, eh Reynard? (15.3462–7)

Bloom's attitude towards religious women here is that of the anti-catholic propaganda of the nineteenth century or of the pseudo-pornographic libertine literature of the century before.

When we rediscover Stephen in the brothel, he is pontificating on music in a speech that repeatedly mixes and confuses biblical and Greek or Roman references. It is certainly ironic that when he is challenged by Lynch to finish his exposé on the return of the self to the self, he is disturbed by what he calls 'that fellow's noise in the street' (15.2119–20). This is not just his earlier definition of god in his discussion with Mr. Deasy, but here it refers to the gramophone outside that is blaring the christian hymn 'The Holy City,' a more recent version (15.1892) of the biblical psalms he has been discussing. Although they are suitably impressed with Stephen's learning, the three prostitutes change the subject to the Last Coming:

FLORRY

They say the last day is coming this summer.

KITTY

No!

ZOE

(*Explodes in laughter.*) Great unjust God!

FLORRY

(*Offended.*) Well, it was in the papers about Antichrist. O, my foot's tickling. (*Ragged barefoot newsboys, jogging a wagtail kite, patter past, yelling.*)

THE NEWSBOYS

Stop press edition. Result of the rockinghorse races. Sea serpent in the royal canal. Safe arrival of Antichrist. (15.2128–41)

At this, according to the stage directions, Stephen turns and sees Bloom. His reply shows that he knows his bible, because he quotes Rev. 12.14 which immediately follows the reference to 'that old serpent, called the Devil, and Satan, which deceiveth the whole world' (Rev. 12:9). The figure of Reuben J. Antichrist appears carrying on the hook of a boatpole 'his only son' and accompanied by Punch Costello who performs the part of the creator-god, juggling planets. With 'The Holy City' still blaring in the background, first a personified Bosch-like 'End of the World' appears; it is followed by Elijah in the person of Alexander J. Dowie. This is only appropriate: mockingly American freethinkers called

Dowie 'Elijhah II' (MacDonald 1929: 458). The decidedly American evangelist repudiates Darwin and commands the whores and their clients to realize their spiritual potential; only this will allow them to 'rub shoulders with a Jesus, a Gautama, and Ingersoll' (*U* 15.2199), forgetting momentarily that Ingersoll (15.1833–99) was the foremost American freethinker and as such one of Dowie's chief antagonists. The evangelist even complained at some point that Ingersoll and other sceptics refused to believe the miracles attested in the bible without bothering to investigate the evangelical miracles happening all around them. In his incarnation in *Ulysses*, Dowie is not biblically correct: like the theosophists he seems to appreciate the Buddah and he refers to 'the harmonial philosophy' (15.2205). This was one of the first spiritualist doctrines, developed by Andrew Jackson Davis (1826–1910), who has been called 'the Saint John the Baptist of Spiritualism.' With a bit of help from 'Mr President' Elijah, now in black minstrel outfit, Dowie attempts to convert the three prostitutes, although the Almighty refuses to interfere: 'Our Mr President, he twig the whole lot and he ai'nt saying nothing.' When the prostitutes confess their sexual sins, Stephen briefly resumes his role as priest with an appropriate quotation from the first verse of the Gospel of John and the end of the *Gloria Patri*, but then Lyster, Best and Eglinton appear, followed by Mananaun MacLir who speaks the root language of hermeticism and of theosophy that AE had described in his book *The Candle of Vision*.

After an interruption Stephen is still quoting scripture, but he has other things on his mind now, mostly music and Deasy's letter about foot-and-mouth disease, but the conversation turns to religion again when Stephen tells Zoe that she would have preferred Luther, the fighting parson, although she is told to beware of 'Antisthenes, the dog sage, and the last end of Arius Heresiarchus' (15.1642–3). When Florry claims that Stephen is a 'spoiled priest' and Lynch counters that he's a 'cardinal's son,' Stephen's father appears in a cardinal's vestments and after a parody of the Easter kiss, he sings the song Parnell and Kitty O'Shea preferred in the early years of their love. His Irish sentimentalism and republican anticlericalism echo the opinions (and language) of John Stanislaus Joyce: 'By the hoky fiddle, thanks be to Jesus those funny little chaps are not unanimous. If they were they'd walk me off the face of the bloody globe' (15.2679–81). When invited by Zoe for 'some parleyvoo,' it is interesting to note that Stephen's breathless overview in broken English of Parisian *risqué* delights not only includes 'lovely ladies' and 'dancing cancan' but also an even more libertine Paris that indulges in black masses: 'Perfectly shocking terrific of religion's things mockery seen in universal world' (15.3890–1). For Stephen Dedalus at least, the language of blasphemy seems to tend towards the condition of French.

Suddenly Stephen is reminded of his dream and he seems to recognize that there is a connection between the nightmare and his present circumstances, but this is linked with an earlier memory of praying to the devil that a 'fubsy widow' would lift her skirts. When Bloom tries to calm him down, Stephen is reminded of an earlier part of the dream that seems to be more consistent with his literary ambitions: 'No, I flew. My foes beneath me. And ever shall be. World without end. (*he cries*) *Pater*! Free!' (15.3935–6). Carefully Joyce mixes different verbal memories of Stephen's day with the 'Gloria Patri' and the last words of Icarus and Christ that he has referred to earlier in the day. Stephen becomes even more rebellious: 'Break my spirit, will he ? *O merde alors!*' and it is clear that by flying, he openly defies God: he even shows off 'his vulture talons sharpened.' He becomes the quarry of a hunt led by Mr. Deasy, but puts himself firmly in the company of such proud and defiant outcasts like Parnell or the speaker of 'The Holy Office' ('Firm as the mountain-ridges where / I flash my antlers on the air') and of *Stephen Hero*. The sharpened talons seem to have the same function as the flashing antlers.

Stephen's thoughts are interrupted by the dancing but when the music stops and everybody applauds, his father (in the Rosenbach manuscript it was Lynch) reminds him of his mother ('Think of your mother's people!') and this is the trigger for a litany of assorted memories of the past day – some of them Bloom's – when suddenly Stephen's mother rises 'through the floor' while 'uttering a silent word.' In this climactic scene Stephen is confronted with the consequences of his atheism: he refuses to accept responsibility for the death of his mother ('Cancer did it, not I. Destiny' (15.4187)[8]). When he wants to hear from his mother the 'word known to all men,' she links her own maternal love to prayer for the suffering souls in purgatory and accuses him of callousness and a refusal to return her love. Her calls for Stephen's repentance are met by Stephen's renewed defiance of God: 'His noncorrosive sublimate! The corpsechewer! Raw head and bloody bones' (15.4214–15). Stephen has argued in the previous chapter that, if there is a God, he is responsible for the death of all humans: corrosive sublimate is the same as mercuric chloride, a powerful poison, and in this crucial scene Stephen is fighting the image of God as the boogeyman who frightens children. His mother now warns him with a 'blackened withered right arm' raised towards Stephen's breast: 'Beware God's hand!' and 'a green crab with malignant red eyes sticks deep its grinning claws in Stephen's heart' (15.4219–20). This is too much for Stephen: after calling out, 'strangled with rage,' his rejection is given voice in three different languages: '*Ah non, par exemple*! The intellectual imagination! With me all or not at all. *Non serviam!*' While the denial is expressed in the French language that to Stephen seems to choose for the expression of freethinking and that his mother probably cannot understand, his reference to the intellectual imagination can signify either an appeal to his art against the religious onslaught or, dismissively, an ironic rejection of the lack of inspiration displayed in his hallucination. In any case he concludes that his mother's love must not only be unconditional but cannot be linked to religious sensibilities. His *non serviam* links him to the great artists and heretics who inspired him to refuse, to use the terms at the end of *A Portrait*, to serve that in which he no longer believes. From that moment, his mother's prayers and references to the Sacred Heart of Jesus, even her death rattle, have no more power over him and with Wagner as his guide, Stephen smashes the chandelier with his walking stick and brings the vision (together with all time and all space) to an apocalyptic end.

Even in the drunken brawl with the British soldiers outside in the street, Stephen manages to bring in religion when he mentions in passing, tapping his brow: 'But in here it is I must kill the priest and the king' (*U* 15.4436–7). In reaction Private Carr seems only interested in the insult to his king, but when the latter finally does appear in dream form, he has acquired clearly catholic characteristics: he is wearing 'a white jersey on which an image of the Sacred Heart is stitched' (15.5549–50). When somewhat later Ireland itself appears in the shape of the Poor Old Woman, it is Stephen who dismisses her reliance on priests and religion. In words that echo the ballad 'The Wearing of the Green' she asks him: 'You met with poor old Ireland and how does she stand?' Stephen characteristically turns the final question around to put himself at centre stage, in opposition to the priest-ridden Ireland: 'How do I stand you? The hat trick! Where's the third person of the Blessed Trinity? Soggarth Aroon? The reverend Carrion Crow' (15.4587–92). Theologically, what the drunken Stephen is trying to say is not at as clear as Gifford and Seidman think. They believe the question about the third person of the trinity must be decoded as 'Where is the Church?' *Soggarth Aroon* certainly refers to the sentimental love of the Irish for their parish priests, which is met with the scornful 'reverend Carrion Crow,' an equation of priests with crows that was common in anticlerical and freethinking literature in the second half of the nineteenth century and that was briefly referred to earlier by Mulligan at the end of Chapter 9, when he claims that only priests, crows and English coal are black.

In the following apocalyptic vision, the dead walk the streets of Dublin. In the centre of the earth, a field altar rises that is dedicated to Saint Barbara (not accidentally a christian daughter that was tortured and killed by her pagan father) but that has distinctly satanic and jewish characteristics: there are black candles and horns, the altarstone is 'smokepalled.' The scene is partly based, of course, on an image in Stephen's morning musings on the beach in 'Proteus.' The goddess of unreason lies naked on it, with a chalice on her belly. Both the Irish churches are actively involved: the inverted mass is celebrated in ecumenical fashion by Father Malachi O'Flynn and the reverend Hugh C. Haines Love, who appropriately speak in catholic Latin and anglican English. In the final confrontation with the British soldier, Stephen is told by the female personification of Ireland to sacrifice himself for his country, just like earlier his mother had tried to break his spirit. It is interesting to see that in these trying moments Stephen's only recourse is not to his walking stick offered by Bloom but to reason: 'Stick, no. Reason. This feast of pure reason' (15.4735).

In the next chapter in the cabman's shelter, Bloom turns the conversation to metaphysics by asking if Stephen, whom he thinks is a good catholic, believes in the existence of the soul. Stephen's answer is not straightforward but it is theologically astute, after the fashion of Aquinas ('They tell me on the best authority,' it begins), but Stephen clearly indicates his distance from his inter-locutor by his flippant manner of referring to the 'First Cause Who, from all I can hear, is quite capable of adding [the annihilation of the soul] to the number of His other practical jokes' (*U* 16.756–9). When Bloom expresses doubts about the existence of what he calls 'a supernatural God,' Stephen again ironically counters that it 'has been proved conclusively by several of the best known passages in Holy Writ, apart from circumstantial evidence' (772–3). It is evident that Stephen is being facetious, because of course he knows that the existence of god cannot be proved conclusively, neither by Holy Writ, nor by circumstantial evidence, whatever he may mean by that phrase. But Bloom, as the 'more experienced of the two,' does not give in that easily and he begs to differ with Stephen 'in toto':

> My belief is, to tell you the candid truth, that those bits were genuine forger-ies all of them put in by monks most probably or it's the big question of our national poet over again, who precisely wrote them like *Hamlet* and Bacon, as, you who know your Shakespeare infinitely better than I, of course I needn't tell you. (*U* 16.780–4)

What Bloom is trying to express, with some difficulty, is marred by the syntacti-cal and stylistic infelicities, but what he says refers not so much to the existence of a god, supernatural or not, but to the genuine historical problem of the non-biblical references to Jesus introduced into non-christian sources by the monks in the middle ages who copied the manuscripts, because this is what Bloom sup-poses Stephen is talking about when he speaks of 'circumstantial evidence.' There are references to Jesus in Josephus, Tacitus and Suetonius that have long been used by apologists to demonstrate that not all the evidence for his exis-tence is christian in origin. But critical readers have pointed out, as does Bloom here, that these were most probably later and christian additions to the texts of these works.

Bloom and Stephen do seem to agree on the need for religious and racial tolerance, but it is not clear whether the former's strictly non-religious utopia is all that agreeable to Stephen. Bloom's arguments are economical and tradition-ally marxist: in cultures with a belief in an afterlife, it seems to be less important to make sure that the present life is agreeable to all. What Bloom calls 'patrio-tism' seems to be close enough to a kind of communism: a basic income for everybody who is willing to work. Needless to say, it is this last part of the scheme that Stephen objects to.

In the *Ithaca* chapter it becomes more difficult to isolate references to reli-gion, but the list of conversation topics of the two night wanderers in the second answer includes the following: 'the Roman catholic church, ecclesiastical celi-bacy, the Irish nation, Jesuit education' and according to the following answer they now seem in agreement in their rejection of religion: 'Both indurated by

early domestic training and an inherited tenacity of heterodox resistance pro-
fessed their disbelief in many orthodox religious, national, social and ethical
doctrines' (*U* 17.15–25), but in the next answer Bloom dissents tacitly with
Stephen's views on the eternal affirmation of the spirit of man in literature.
Somewhat later, when the two compare Irish and Hebrew speech and script,
and after Bloom has chanted a traditional jewish song, Stephen is reminded
visually of the 'traditional figure of hypostasis, depicted by Johannes Damascenus,
Lentulus Romanus and Epiphanius Monachus as leucodermic, sesquipedalian
with winedark hair.' The first and the third persons mentioned were Greek
theologians who had described the outward appearance of Jesus; Publius
Lentulus was the supposed author of a report about Jesus to the Roman senate
by Pontius Pilate's predecessor which was quoted by the *Catholic Encyclopedia*
(the author of the article stresses that the text is exactly the kind of forgery that
was supposed to supply extra-christian evidence for the gospel accounts):

> Lentulus, the Governor of the Jerusalemites to the Roman Senate and
> People, greetings. There has appeared in our times, and there still lives, a
> man of great power (virtue), called Jesus Christ. The people call him prophet
> of truth; his disciples, son of God. He raises the dead, and heals infirmities.
> He is a man of medium size (*statura procerus, mediocris et spectabilis*); he has a
> venerable aspect, and his beholders can both fear and love him. His hair is
> of the colour of the ripe hazel-nut, straight down to the ears, but below the
> ears wavy and curled, with a bluish and bright reflection, flowing over his
> shoulders. It is parted in two on the top of the head, after the pattern of the
> Nazarenes. His brow is smooth and very cheerful with a face without wrinkle
> or spot, embellished by a slightly reddish complexion. His nose and mouth
> are faultless. His beard is abundant, of the colour of his hair, not long, but
> divided at the chin. His aspect is simple and mature, his eyes are changeable
> and bright. He is terrible in his reprimands, sweet and amiable in his admoni-
> tions, cheerful without loss of gravity. He was never known to laugh, but
> often to weep. His stature is straight, his hands and arms beautiful to behold.
> His conversation is grave, infrequent, and modest. He is the most beautiful
> among the children of men. ('Publius Lentulus')

For Stephen, in other words (or at least in words less sesquipedalian), Bloom
resembles the traditional depiction of Jesus in the Greek church. Joyce could
have found all the information he used in this passage on a single page of Grant
Allen's Rationalist Press book *The Evolution of God* (1908: 137).

The closest we get to a secular creed on Stephen's part is given as his reason
for not being dejected, just before he is ready to leave Bloom's house: 'He
affirmed his significance as a conscious rational animal proceeding from the
known to the unknown and a conscious rational reagent between a micro
and a macrocosm ineluctably constructed upon the incertitude of the void'

(*U* 17.1112–5). This could function as a cumbrous but adequate description of a freethinker's philosophy.

Just before the two men observe the falling star and then part, Stephen and Bloom urinate in the garden. This activity gives them occasion to reflect on each other's 'invisible audible collateral organ' (17.1200). Characteristically Bloom reflects on Stephen's more youthful member but he also, probably correctly, seems to have doubts about the latter's health and hygiene. Stephen's thoughts, on the other hand, are equally characteristically impersonal. Just as Bloom mistakenly assumes that Stephen is an observant catholic, Stephen believes that Bloom must be circumcised, which readers of 'Nausicaa' know is not the case. The thought of circumcision leads Stephen far from an Eccles street backyard:

> The problem of sacerdotal integrity of Jesus circumcised (1 January, holiday of obligation to hear mass and abstain from unnecessary servile work) and the problem as to whether the divine prepuce, the carnal bridal ring of the holy Roman catholic apostolic church, conserved in Calcata, were deserving of the simple hyperduly or of the fourth degree of latria accorded to the abscission of such divine excrescences as hair and toenails. (17.1203–9)

Most of this passage comes from a series of notes from Joseph Müller's book on the divine foreskin that was mentioned earlier in this chapter and that can serve as an interesting test case of Joyce's use of a specific kind of anti-catholic literature. Most of the circumcision references in the notebook were struck out in red crayon.

Although it is much more sophisticated than Chiniquy's work, Müller's book belongs in the same category of protestant literature. It is a later and more scholarly variant of the kind of anti-catholic literature that, for different political reasons, became very popular in Britain and in North America around the middle of the nineteenth. The American variety was more sensational, focusing as it did on sexual licence in catholic religious institutions, as in the works by 'Father Chiniquy, Ex-Roman Catholic Priest.'

Müller's book is part of a different context: that of the modernist crisis within the Church around the turn of the century. Under the influence of liberal and democratic political developments in Europe on the one hand and in reaction to an extremely traditionalist Roman hierarchy on the other, in the last decades of the nineteenth century liberal catholic intellectuals attempted to develop a new way of studying early christian texts. Following an earlier generation of theologians such as Cardinal Newman, they sought to show that dogma was neither eternal nor unchanging – as the hierarchy in Rome continued to insist – and that the historical study of the christian sources could be incorporated into a modern theology. For these theologians modernization did not necessarily lead to general apostasy, as mainstream German and British

protestant churches had demonstrated in the preceding decades. When in
1907 pope Pius X officially denounced modernism (or 'relativism') as the
'synthesis of all heresies,' this brought an end to a way of thinking that had
attempted to reconcile the teachings of the church with the critical philosophy
of Immanuel Kant.

Despite the sometimes harsh and dismissive tone of his book on the divine
prepuce, Müller was a respected historian of the church who in later years,
when he published scholarly studies of Luther's theological sources, seems to
have come to regret the flippant tone of the works written in the first years after
his conversion to Protestantism. In my copy of the book, Müller's publisher, the
Berlin firm of C.A. Schwetschke und Sohn, advertises a number of other books,
one a translation of a French study on the separation of church and state (which
had become the official policy of the French republic in 1905). Most of the
other studies are by or about Carl Peters, the German explorer and founder of
the German colonies in East Africa. The most important opponent of the
establishment of German colonies had been the social democrat August Bebel,
so this is definitely not a liberal or socialist publisher, who would be most
likely to publish anti-christian or anti-religious works. In the relevant period
C.A. Schwetschke und Sohn also published books on contemporary politics.
Its studies on religion (an edition of the works of Luther, but also books on
judaism and German translation of theosophist books by Annie Besant) seem
to be mostly of the more liberal protestant kind, such as a survey of contemporary developments in catholicism by the protestant church historian Friedrich
Nippold. The firm did publish Paul Graf von Hoensbroech, an ex-Jesuit and
historian who in 1904 published a book with Schwetschke und Sohn that
claimed to demonstrate that the Jesuits really taught the doctrine that the end
justifies the means. When challenged, he failed to convince the courts in
Cologne the following year, which did not stop him from publishing in 1906
an analysis of the relationship between Rome and the modern state.

Müller's book must be seen in the specific historical and political context
that we discussed in Chapter 3: all over Europe, but especially in countries with
a large catholic minority, the new nation states considered the church as a dangerous alien opponent. Politically, intellectuals on the right and on the left
attacked the local catholics for their supposed ultramontane sympathies, but
the modernist crisis had given liberals plenty of reasons for attacking the
Church of Rome and this is what Müller does in this book on a subject that had
been a favourite topic of anti-catholic writing since Calvin. Not even the title is
innocent: *Die 'hochheilige Vorhaut Christi' Im Kult and in der Theologie der Papstkirche*
contains a telltale phrase, Luther's name for catholicism as 'the church of the
pope.'

In his preface Müller explains that the book is topical because of the recent
rediscovery in Rome of the papal treasure, which was supposed to have contained the divine prepuce. Against the misguided rescue attempts by catholic
apologists such as the Jesuit Hartmann Grisar, Müller wants to show how the

reformation had been justified in attacking the Roman reverence for relics. At the end of the preface, which is dated on the Feast of Circumcision 1907 (January 1), Müller concludes that in the preceding period the Church of Rome has done a lot to consolidate its power, but very little to educate the people or to purify christian ideals. The book itself is divided into seven chapters: the first three discuss the rediscovery of the papal treasure, the general history of the Holy Prepuce and its relationship with catholic dogma. In the next four chapters, four different prepuces are discussed, those venerated at the Lateran church in Rome, at Charroux, in Antwerp and finally the one in Calcata, a village close to Rome. In a conclusion Müller claims that the prepuce is still revered in all these places where the 'evil heresy' of protestantism and the 'even more evil enlightenment' cannot or did not reach: quite a few of the most infamous relics had been destroyed by the French revolutionary armies. Despite the help it claims from the Holy Spirit, the Church of Rome has not had the sense to reject this pious fraud. Because idolatry is a grave sin, Müller considers it the duty of the Roman hierarchy to expose all fraudulent and doubtful relics, whereas in most cases the Church only reluctantly gave up relics long after they had been exposed by non-catholics. Even at the time of writing the prepuce in Calcata close to Rome can be venerated in return of a year's indulgence, despite all the efforts of Grisar, S.J., whose studies on the relics had been published in *Civiltà cattolica*, a Jesuit publication that had the distinction of submitting all its articles to the Vatican before publication.

Grisar had claimed that the divine prepuce could only have been taken seriously as a relic in the naïve and childish middle-ages, not in the more historically astute present. Against attempts such as these on the part of catholic theologians to rewrite history, Müller wants to set the record straight. Because Christ's circumcision is explicitly mentioned in the gospel of Luke, early commentators on that evangelist could not avoid the question of what had happened to the divine appendage. Most bible commentators agreed that in one way or another Jesus saved this and other body parts to enable his full bodily resurrection: curiosity about them was theologically dangerous. But in the later middle ages, when many churches claimed to possess the divine foreskin, the multiple presences on earth were increasingly difficult to reconcile with that theological position. According to Müller this is the point where two devout women came to the rescue. In the fourteenth century, Saint Bridgit of Sweden wrote down the revelations that she had received from Christ and his mother. The Blessed Virgin told Bridgit that she herself had saved her divine son's foreskin and that she carried it with her all her life. Just before she was taken up into heaven, she passed it on to the apostle John and it was only after the death of John and his followers that their devout believers hid it in a particularly holy place where it remained until an angel of the Lord showed it to a number of friends of God.

With his next example Müller wants to show that interest in the divine foreskin can easily lead to 'hysterical-sexual aberrations.' Another visionary, Agnes

Blannbekin (d. 1315) experienced a series of *Revelationes* that were written down by her spiritual advisor. In a section dealing with the divine foreskin, she admits that she had always contemplated with great feeling the loss of blood that the young Jesus must have suffered during his circumcision and at one of these occasions, when she idly wondered what had become of the prepuce itself, she felt a piece of skin on her tongue. The object was extremely sweet and she swallowed it, but it immediately reappeared in her mouth only to be swallowed again, a hundred times in all. Blannbekin's revelations were not published until 1731.

Müller stresses that some of the supporters of the prepuce as a divine relic had been Jesuits, like Alphonsus Salmeron, one of Loyola's closest companions. In a bible commentary in which he accepted Saint Bridgit's account of the relic's provenance, Salmeron claimed that the prepuce was the engagement ring that Christ offered his bride, the church of Rome. In 1646 another Jesuit apologist, Johannes Ferrandus, defended the relic against protestant ridicule, especially against the doubts that were expressed about the prepuce's apparent ubiquity in Europe. Ferrandus first points out that nothing would prevent an all-powerful God from having multiplied Christ's prepuce, as according to the gospels he did with wine, bread and fish. And even if he had not done such a thing, the relic, which by its nature is singular, could only have been venerated in one place. Another possible explanation is that these relics are all pieces of the divine umbilical cord distributed among the faithful. Another Jesuit added that the very ubiquity of the relic proves that not all of them could possibly be fakes and that therefore at least one of them had to be genuine!

In the third chapter Müller concentrates on the theological problem of reconciling the presence of the prepuce on earth with the dogma that Jesus had been assumed into heaven integrally, *cum omni integritate.* The central question then became whether the foreskin is or is not an integral part of the body of Jesus. One school saved the relic by claiming that, like the blood and spit of Christ, the foreskin did not belong to the body of Jesus, if only because like his fellow-jews, Christ must have rejected this part of his body as he would a piece of excrement. Other theologians took this way of reasoning even further by claiming that if the body of Jesus in heaven was circumcised; all males would have to undergo a similar operation on entering Paradise.

But Jesuit theologians such as Fernandus and Suarez could not believe that all christians would be marked by the 'shameful jewish sign' of circumcision and it led another school of theology to the conclusion that immediately following his ascension and in one way or another, Jesus must have regained his foreskin in heaven. But if that was the case, how is it that we have the same object here on earth? The only possible solution was that Christ in heaven had created another foreskin for himself. But that was not the only theological problem: does the body of Christ that is offered to the faithful in the Eucharist include his foreskin? Obviously this was not the case at the occasion of the first

Eucharist, because at the time Jesus was still alive and definitely no longer in bodily possession of his foreskin. But since the moment of Resurrection we do not have in the Eucharist the mortal body of Jesus, but instead his gloriously resurrected body with all the qualities it has in heaven. So we have returned to the question whether that resurrected body is circumcised or not.

Still another problem is related to this issue: is the resurrected body of the Son of God still in some way connected to the foreskin on earth? If that is the case, then the relic deserves adoration, if not, only veneration. It seems that most theologians did not believe in the hypostatic union between Jesus and the part of his body that he had left behind so early in his life. Yet some theologians claimed that the prepuce had to be considered part of the divine body. Bishop Angelo Rocca wrote that each part of the body that either had been or was still connected to the body of Christ, deserved *Latreia* adoration, even according to the fourth modus of Latreia adoration, which means that it deserves the same kind of adoration as Christ's hair and clothes. A final question discussed in this chapter is what will happen to the earthly prepuce at the end of the world. Müller gives three possibilities, depending again on whether we think of the foreskin as an integral part of the body. It might be reunited with the resurrected body of Jesus or simply destroyed; a third group of theologians believed that it would become part of the heavenly bodies.

Although Müller has four more chapters discussing the provenance and history of four particular examples of relics of the divine foreskin, Joyce did not make notes from these and it is clear from his selection of notes from the book that he was especially interested in the more outrageous theories offered by the learned Jesuit theologians. When he made use of these notes in writing 'Ithaca' he combined the reference to the bridal ring with the rather technical question of the degree of adoration necessary for this particular relic. Despite the fact that he crossed out in red most of the Müller notes, only these few made it into the text of *Ulysses*. But it is clear that some of the other notes may be implied here and elsewhere in the book, especially those that refer to the Christ's jewishness and especially, in the context of the quoted lines in the penultimate chapter, the idea that the Divine Foreskin will become a constellation at the end of time. Immediately after our passage we read:

What celestial sign was by both simultaneously observed?

A star precipitated with great apparent velocity across the firmament from Vega in the Lyre above the zenith beyond the stargroup of the Tress of Berenice towards the zodiacal sign of Leo. (*U* 17.1210–3)

Ironically, the final meeting of Bloom and Stephen may therefore be that they both finally confirm their proximity by witnessing, just before they part, the assumption of the divine prepuce into heaven. Although many critics of *Ulysses* have attempted to find some kind of deeper spiritual significance in the final scene between Stephen and Bloom, the net outcome is only that without saying very much, the hero of *Stephen Hero, A Portrait of the Artist as a Young Man* and the greater part of the present novel, disappears into the night forever, leaving the scene to Mr Leopold Bloom and his late-night musings.

After Stephen has left him in 'Ithaca,' Bloom's thoughts still turn to religion. When he imagines the good he will be able to do once he has accomplished his goal of acquiring a small property in the suburbs, it becomes necessary to prove that he has 'loved rectitude from his earliest youth' and it is clear that he seems to have lost his faith at the age of fourteen, a fact that seems to be just as important as his liberal political opinions. This reference to freethinking is repeated when Bloom thinks with some remorse of the jewish religious heritage he has neglected:

> How did these beliefs and practices now appear to him?
> Not more rational than they had then appeared, not less rational than other beliefs and practices now appeared. (17.1902–4)

Bloom's freethinking is reflected in the content of his library, a limited collection of books that reflects his scientific and cosmopolitan interests. A first thing to note is that there is no bible and no clearly religious book in the house (or at least not on these bookshelves). Exceptions might be *Philosophy of the Talmud*, which is described as no more than a 'sewn pamphlet' (17.1380). The nature of this publication is not clear: it might be a jewish tract along the lines of the publications of the Catholic Truth Society or of the Society for the Propagation of Christian Knowledge. But since Moses Maimonides and certainly since the enlightenment writings of Moses Mendelsohn, most religious jewish groups are reluctant to juxtapose the religious teachings of talmud and secular philosophy, so the combination of both terms might indicate an anti-jewish, anti-religious or even anti-semitic publication. The same may be true for *The Hidden Life of Christ* (black boards), which has not been located to date, although there did exist a *Hidden Life of Jesus* by Jean-Henri Boudon (which was available in an English translation). The book in Bloom's library could either be a pious tract or a theosophist book on the purported fact that between his youth and his public life Jesus had learned his most important teachings from wise men in India or that he went there to convert the heathen after his 'death' on the cross.

Most promising as a potential source for Bloom's freethinking is the volume in maroon leather of *Thoughts from Spinoza*, a compilation of the Dutch philosopher's philosophical writings that has been impossible to find: there is a book by Stefan Zweig by that title, but it would be a serious anachronism in Bloom's library (and prophetic on the part of Joyce). We know that the book may have come from Bloom's father, because in 'Sirens' he remembers explaining to Molly at the theatre 'what Spinoza said in that book of poor papa's' (*U* 11.1058).

Bloom remembers this occasion slightly differently than Molly. She remembers the coming of 'the usual monthly auction' on that rare visit to the theatre with her husband:

[. . .] with that gentleman of fashion staring down at me with his glasses and him the other side of me talking about Spinoza and his soul thats dead I suppose millions of years ago I smiled the best I could all in a swamp leaning forward as if I was interested having to sit it out then to the last tag. (*U* 18.1113–17)

Bloom remembers Molly as having been hypnotized by the lofty thoughts from Spinoza, in reality his wife was worried about the effects of her bodily functions. Neither Gifford and Seidman, nor anyone else that I know of, has been able to trace this particular book. But it is evident that Spinoza was (and still is) one of the earliest heroes of freethinkers all over Europe.

It is clear, not just in reference to Spinoza, that Bloom remains critical of all religious beliefs and practices, including the ones that are supposed to belong to his own ethnic heritage. Religion for him is, like his jewishness, something that others insist on imposing on you, not something he himself has the freedom to choose or to reject. Despite Stephen's reluctance – if not refusal – to take Bloom seriously and the lack of communication between the two that is a result of it, this is a liberal attitude that the two have in common and which separates them from most of the other Dubliners we have met during the day. Yet they clearly differ too. Emotionally Stephen has not yet left religion behind: he is still struggling with the king and the priest that he thinks he needs to kill and religion is clearly still a part of the general nightmare of history that he is trying to wake up from. Bloom, on the other hand, seems to be in many ways beyond religion. For him it has completely ceased to be a psychological reality, if it ever was, and he can look at its practices as if he were an anthropologist studying an alien culture. In fact, he describes religions as little more than an elaborate and very effective scam that seems to be particularly suited to attract women.

That Bloom is not mistaken in this latter opinion is evident from what we learn of two of the female voices we hear in the novel. Gerty McDowell and Molly Bloom not only share a sentimental and naïve adherence to a religion they do not even begin to understand intellectually, they are not adverse to the sexual attractions of catholic priests. The former has a crush on Father Conroy, which she seems to have expressed during a rather risqu`é confession. But whereas Molly is impressed by Father Corrigan's humaneness during confession, the older woman first dismisses him for failing to use the correct kinds of words to refer to body parts and then she quickly turns her mind to the possibility of having sex with priests: '[. . .] Id like to be embraced by one in his vestments and the smell of incense off him like the pope besides theres no

danger with a priest if youre married hes too careful about himself then give
something to H H the pope for a penance [. . .]' (18.118–21). These thoughts
may be offense enough to believers, but only a moment later they are followed
by a memory of the thunderclap that woke her up after her tryst with Boylan:
'[. . .] God be merciful to us I thought the heavens were coming down about us
to punish us when I blessed myself and said a Hail Mary [. . .]' (18.134–6). It is
clear that Molly is religious, but it is a strange kind of religion where burning a
candle can bring luck, which in this case seems to have adopted the form of
a lover, or when unlike Bartell D'Arcy she does not believe that it is especially
sinful to make love in a church. Yet Molly has no patience with atheists: 'And
then they come and tell you theres no God what could you do if it was running
and rushing about nothing only make an act of contrition' (18.137–9). When
she includes her husband in the company of those who deny that humans have
a soul ('only grey matter'), she claims this is only the case because he 'doesnt
know what it is to have one' (18.141–2). Atheists are plain wrong:

> Nature it is as for them saying theres no God I wouldnt give a snap of my two
> fingers for all their learning why dont they go and create something I often
> asked him atheists or whatever they call themselves go and wash the cobbles
> off themselves first then they go howling for the priest and they dying and
> why why because theyre afraid of hell on account of their bad conscience ah
> yes I know them well who was the first person in the universe before there was
> anybody that made it all who ah that they dont know neither do I so there
> you are they might as well try to stop the sun from rising tomorrow [. . .].
> (*U* 18.1563–71)

In fact, through Molly we learn a bit about the unorthodox ideas of Bloom that
she finds particularly ludicrous: his claim that Jesus was the first socialist (in this
he seems to be following Charles Kingsley and other christian socialists); his
attempt to convince the Jesuits to let Molly sing in their church by pretending
to be in the process of putting Newman's *Lead Kindly Light* to music (until they
discovered that he was a freemason). He also seems to have introduced her
to other religions, as when he explained to Molly that buddhism was a greater
religion 'than the jews and Our Lords both put together' (18.1203–4).

Although Bloom does not seem to have any explicitly freethought literature
at home, Molly's thoughts about her husband's lack of religious feelings
allows us to confirm Bloom's freethinking: the range of strange ideas that she
complains about form a coherent set of anticlerical and secularist ideas that
was more common, at the turn of the century, in Great Britain, Italy and France,
than in Ireland. With Molly's reaction to her husband's freethinking at the
close of the book, it is clear that Joyce distinguishes the ideological choices of
his two male heroes not only from the religious attitudes of the vast majority
of Dubliners, but also from the women in the book, not just Molly, but also
Stephen's mother. Women are portrayed as victims of a religion that oppresses

them and that inflicts physical and psychological damage. These attitudes do not differ from the opinions that the novel's author expressed in his early fiction, in conversations, in letters to his young fiancée and his freethinking brother.

On the basis of all the evidence we have discussed, we can see the great continuity of the Stephen who appears in *Ulysses* and the young hero of Joyce's previous novel *A Portrait of the Artist as a Young Man*. This is certainly true for his opinions on religion, despite the fact that the more outspoken criticism of the church or of religious belief in *Ulysses* is given Stephen's friends Buck Mulligan and Patrice Egan. Stephen's intellectual frame of reference might be broadly described as catholic and even medieval-scholastic, but on the basis of what we read of him in the pages of *Ulysses*, these intellectual building blocks are used for purely secular purposes; in his *monologue intérieur* the frequent references to the bible are all ironic. Bloom represents the modern European secularist, who sees religion as a way of oppressing the masses.

In the last two chapters I have attempted to show that there seems to be no reason to reclaim Stephen Dedalus and Leopold Bloom for catholicism or for any other religion. Like Joyce's own, Stephen's education and background may have been entirely catholic, but it is evident from the material presented here, that one cannot identify him with the religion he so clearly and painfully rejects in *Ulysses*. Stephen's attitudes to those things in which he no longer believes, his home, his fatherland and his church, form a central theme in this as in Joyce's previous novel. In *A Portrait* Stephen was briefly brought back into the fold by the horrible visions of hell in the retreat sermon and here in *Ulysses* he seems to be very much aware of the price he is willing to pay for a form of unbelief that is not just agnostic but militantly *anti-theistic*. Just as Stanislaus Joyce in his diary described the young James Joyce trying to commit the sin against the Holy Ghost in order to place himself more radically outside the fold, Stephen in *Ulysses* does not simply dismiss god as irrelevant, he challenges him directly and he seems to be quite willing to pay the price that according to the gospel Jesus has ascribed to this gravest of sins: eternal damnation (Mk 3.29).

Why did Joyce choose a jewish hero? A first reason may have been that he wanted his modern day Odysseus to be an outsider in the Dublin of 16 June 1904 in ways unavailable to any Irishman who was born either as a protestant or a catholic. Equally important may have been the fact that in Trieste Joyce for the first time met secular and atheist jews who had found a way of dealing with their religious past in a relaxed manner that he himself may have envied. Bloom's completely secular and post-religious judaism (despite the occasional regrets) in any case affords him a standpoint from which the novel can criticize and satirize catholicism for its effects on the Irish, in a way that would not have been unacceptable if he had been an apostate or a protestant.

What happens to Stephen in the novel is due to his open and blatant rejection of religion and to some extent it could be argued that in this way religion still plays an important albeit negative role here. But even in that case, Leopold

Bloom is different: he seems to be entirely beyond religion. He has been baptized three times and is still considered to be jewish by almost everybody in Dublin, but he also seems to have passed a period as a freemason, yet nothing that we learn about him allows us to believe that he is at all religious in any sense of the word. And as we have seen, it is this completely post-religious Bloom who takes over the novel.

Chapter 8

After *Ulysses*

p 7 l 9 cancel God insert Goggle [. . .]
p 3 l 11 cancel God insert Chalk [. . .]
p 4 l 21 cancel God insert Close

List of corrections to 'Work in Progress' sent to Sylvia Beach

There does not seem to be any indication that Joyce changed his attitude towards religion after he had finished *Ulysses*. The Buffalo notebooks that he began to use in the fall of 1922, at the moment when we had decided to start work on his next project, allow us to document Joyce's interests in this later period of his life and in this chapter I will often refer to these documents. But we need to understand that these notebooks do not give us a privileged access to Joyce's innermost feelings. They contain a selection of notes copied from sources that Joyce was reading and that he thought or hoped might be relevant for his work on the new book. These notes therefore do not necessarily represent what he himself thought about the subjects he is annotating. At the same time both the choice of sources and Joyce's own selection from them do give us information about the range of subjects that he thought were relevant to the writing of what would become his last book.

Finnegans Wake has been hailed as the ultimate postmodern text machine that offers unlimited intertextual play and that opens pathways to every conceivable text: past, present and future. To some extent the book was indeed created with the help of linguistic bits and pieces that Joyce had collected from a wide variety of sources, but if recourse to the notebooks is useful in the study of *Finnegans Wake*, it is mostly because it does allow us to some extent to place the book in the context from which it arose by means of an almost day to day account of everything Joyce was reading in preparation for the book.

When we look at the wide variety of subjects represented in the earliest notebooks, we find that at the initial stages of his work on the new book, Joyce did not seem to have had definite plans and this same process of very wide exploratory note taking would be repeated whenever he was finishing one chapter or section, without immediately knowing what to do next. This is a process we observe in the first set of notebooks, used during the autumn of 1922. The first item is Buffalo Notebook VI.B.10 which Joyce first used to collect corrections for the third printing of *Ulysses*, but these few items were followed immediately by a series of seemingly random reading notes from magazines and newspapers. In *The Irish Times* of November 1, Joyce noted from an article announcing the death of the Father Bernard Vaughan that his favourite Jesuit had been given 'the privilege of a portable altar' by the pope, a distinction that Joyce would somewhat later anachronistically pass on to Saint Kevin when he began to write his sketch about the Irish saint.[1] The first notebook also contains isolated references to the apostle Thomas, a mention of the technical term 'condign satisfaction' from the philosophy of Thomas Aquinas, a note claiming that the character Allmers in Ibsen's play resembles Ernest Renan (19) and the juxtaposition of the *titulum*, the inscription above the cross, as a 'title,' with the equally contentious championship title of the boxer J.L. Sullivan (90). There is no clear religious or anti-religious theme in these early notes that date from the time before Joyce wrote the first sentences of his next book.

The first notebook to contain extensive notes that might be more relevant for our purposes is VI.B.3, compiled around the time when Joyce began to write 'Roderick O'Connor,' the first of a series of sketches, which initiated the actual writing process on his new work. These were not fragments of the book, as he wrote to Miss Weaver, 'but active elements and when they are more and a little older they will begin to fuse of themselves' (*Letters I* 205).

In the beginning of the notebook we find Joyce taking notes from J.M. Flood's *Ireland: Its Saints and Scholars* (1917). This was a popular account of Irish history, with great emphasis on the so-called dark ages, the time when Ireland first preserved and later propagated learning and culture in the rest of Europe. By the time Joyce had almost reached the end of the notebook, he also began to read and annotate Benedict Fitzpatrick's *Ireland and the Making of Great Britain* (1922), another popularizing work on the influence of the Irish.

It is clear from the kind of notes that we find in VI.B.3 that Joyce was collecting quaint facts, oddities about early Celtic christianity, such as the Irish tonsure, the fact that Saint Columbanus allowed squirrels to nest in his cowl, or that two virgins whom Gregory the Great knew were 'obviously Irish.' The latter phrase also indicates that he was interested in the kind of clichés typically used by these popularizing authors, as when he notes that the Franks 'embraced Christianity' or when he varies on an expression used by J.M. Flood to claim that Columcille 'went away of his fathers.'

Notebook VI.A or *Scribbledehobble*, as it has been called by its first editor, is a notoriously difficult notebook to date, but we know that the entries in handwriting A in that notebook were entered during this early period. At least some of the notes were copied into this sorting station from both the existing early notebooks VI.B.10 and VI.B.3 and from at least one missing notebook. Now that we have new manuscripts of the early sketches in the National Library of Ireland, we know that Joyce must have begun thinking of the four old men telling stories in the early summer of 1923, so the notes in *Scribbledehobble* about the *Arabian Nights* and storytelling in general may well have been collected in

this context. But these notes are constantly interrupted by references to religion, as when in a series of notes on storytelling we find 'there was a certain
convent full of fowls, priest after peck kisses W's cunt bless you, my girl, pray for
me' (Connolly1961: 25). Not accidentally, most of the religious notes cluster
under the heading of 'Grace,' one of the more religious stories in *Dubliners*:
they deal mainly with the early Irish saints Patrick and Kevin, the heroes of
two sketches that Joyce was planning to write next.

As could be expected from the way Joyce was collecting materials in his notebooks, the first series of sketches had a light sprinkling of religious references.
The first draft of the first sketch about Roderick O'Connor tells us that our
hero has celebrated his '1st coming' sometime 'after the socalled last supper'
(*FDV* 203), but there is little more than the suggestion that the last King of all
Ireland has something in common with Jesus. In the next sketch, the encounter
of Tristan and Isolde is described in cynical and very secular terms, although
the handsome 'rugger and soccer champion' first quotes poetry to the 'belle of
Chapelizod' and then offers a philosophico-mystical mixture of German idealist philosophy and theosophy that may also be a reference to Wagner's reading
of Schopenhauer while he was writing his *Tristan und Isolde* and having an affair
with Mathilde von Wesendonck. After these two secular sketches, Joyce wrote
two more on the two Irish saints, Kevin and Patrick. The first is a fairly straightforward but extremely well-structured description of the ascetic Kevin who
sits in a bath meditating on the sacrament of baptism. The back of the page
containing the second draft (the first version of the sketch can be found in
notebook VI.B.3) has an extension that describes young Kevin's piety in terms
that resemble those of saints' lives, but that in reality were based on comments
about the exemplary youth of Frederick Bywaters, the young man accused in a
murder case Joyce was following closely. We find a similarly tight structure in
the next sketch about Saint Patrick's meeting with the archdruid Berkeley. The
text, which according to Joyce himself represented Patrick's conversion by
Ireland, refers to Kant's 'thing as in itself it is' (*FDV* 279) and seems to concern
a superior form of vision that the author meant partly as a defence of the aesthetic of his new book. If that is the case, the religious and liturgical overtones
of the ending of the passage indicate that Joyce was still using religious language to describe aesthetic categories.)

'Here Comes Everybody' was the fifth sketch, the one that in the fall of 1923
Joyce decided to develop in a new copy-book and which would become the
major part of Book I of *Finnegans Wake*. In the sketch we learn how 'Harold or
Humphrey Coxon,' as he was originally called, acquired the name of Earwicker.
There are no indications yet of HCE's religious beliefs, although Joyce did
borrow some of the language from Shane Leslie's review of *Ulysses*. In the first
draft of the final 'Mamalujo' sketch, we see that the four masters almost immediately acquire the names of the four evangelists, who from the beginning
are 'saying grace' (*FDV* 213). The rambling narrator uses expressions such as
'thank God' or 'for Christ sake' but in general, neither religion nor its absence

seems to play a role in these sketches. If it was Joyce's original plan for these sketches to paint a picture of medieval Ireland, it is clear from his early note taking that, in contrast to Yeats's version of a largely pagan Erin, Joyce's early Ireland is christian. Although some of the sketch-materials were indeed christian in nature, we now know that some of the material that was lost also dealt with medieval Irish saints (Kevin, Patrick).

Some of the notebooks did not survive and at least one of those must have been used to elaborate the first drafts of the sketches 'Mamalujo' and 'Saint Kevin.' The first surviving notebook to have clearly religious notes is the next in line in the set of surviving notebooks. VI.B.25 contains a number of notes about catholic theology and liturgy that clearly were destined to give structure and coherence to the Kevin sketch. A similar process is at work in the next notebook, VI.B.2, which opens with notes from a book on Saint Patrick that must have been read and excerpted when Joyce was first developing his sketch about the religious confrontation between Saint Patrick and the arch-druid. In the next set of pages, Joyce again is particularly interested in the colourful and miraculous: he notes a number of the saint's more spectacular miracles, for example, when Patrick resurrected no less than 33 people, whereas Saint Francis Xavier only managed to resurrect 24. Material from the Saint Patrick book are followed almost immediately by notes taken from an as yet unidenti-fied book that seems to have contained a rather unorthodox interpretation of the biblical account of Genesis and of the gospel, in the latter case more partic-ularly about the role of Eve and of the Blessed Virgin Mary. Reference is made to Henry Preserved Smith, an American theologian who had openly doubted the historical veracity (and thus the inerrancy) of the bible and who had been convicted of heresy in 1892 by the Presbytery of Cincinnati. Also, the titles of two books in the field of a rationalist critique of the bible are mentioned: John Mackinnon Robertson's *Pagan Christs: Studies in Comparative Hierology* and Grant Allen's *The Evolution of the Idea of God*. These studies, both of them printed and distributed by the Rationalist Press, may have been referred to in Joyce's source for these notes, but it does not seem to have been *God and My Neighbour* by the self-confessed 'infidel' Robert Blatchford who was mentioned above.

Joyce continued to be interested in early christian lore with copious notes from a Catholic Truth Society pamphlet on Saint Martin, with the same atten-tion to the grotesque and miraculous, as when this saint offers salvation to Satan himself or when all pale persons with extraordinary clothes are thought to be heretics. But again what Joyce seems to be especially interested in is the style of these pious publications and he notes all kinds of expressions such as 'a pious author,' 'so far as in the bishop it lay,' 'yet know' that he later incorpo-rated in various chapters of books I and III of *Finnegans Wake*. This is followed by more unsourced notes on the history of the early church and even the long series of excerpts from the linguist Otto Jespersen's *Language* are interrupted by notes on the gospels and on the differences between the four accounts of the

life of Jesus (74) and (142). At least one of these sources is French, as some of
the notes are in that language, and there is a reference to Ernest Renan: 'Renan
washed the face / of the Lord with / huile de la paix' [holy oil] (143). On the
next page there are a number of biblical phrases that were clearly destined to
enrich the tale of Joyce's own evangelists, the four Old Men, and on page 146
there is a reference to the difference in the biblical account between the gospel
of John and that of the three synoptic evangelists.

The next notebook was VI.B.11 and initially it is hard to find religious notes,
which may be due to the fact that at the time Joyce was concentrating on the
elaboration of the HCE sketch into the first of the six chapters of Book I that
between November 1923 and February 1924 he would develop in his so-called
redbacked notebook. But religion could not be avoided for long: on page 25
of notebook VI.B.11 we find a whole series of notes from the *Protoevangelion of
James* or Infancy Gospel, an apocryphal gospel of the birth and youth of Jesus
that testifies to the earliest veneration of Mary and that was widely read among
early christians but never accepted as part of the canon. Joyce read this text in
the collection of apocryphal writings of the New Testament that had just been
published by the Cambridge medievalist M. R. James.

Although in the middle part of the notebook Joyce seems to have been particularly interested in children's games, the quotations from a book on that
subject are interrupted on pages 44–45 by references to all kinds of catholic
devotions. On page 84 we have a full description of the different parts of the
rosary in the middle of lots of quotations from contemporary newspaper
accounts of trials for a variety of violent crimes. Again, some at least of the
sources of the religious references that Joyce was using at this time must have
been French, for on page 117 we find a number of items from Mary's Litany in
that language and on page 129 there are references to saint worship that must
have been at least partly in French. On page 154 we find the beginning of
a series of notes about christian theology with plenty of biblical quotations
that may have come from the printed text of a fairly sophisticated homily or
a (probably protestant) tract. By page 160 the notes become more obviously
catholic, with again a number of notes on the liturgy and litanies.

While he was entering these notes in VI.B.11, Joyce had begun to fill the redbacked notebook with the first few drafts of his continuation of the HCE sketch.
He began with the first drafts of Chapter 2 and we see there that HCE is
gossiped about by a rather typical cross section of the Irish population. The cad
asks HCE the time and the latter's peculiar reply is then recounted by the cad
to his wife, who passes on the story after a sodality meeting to the director, a
'fresh complexioned' clergyman who is overheard when he tells the story to a
lay teacher during a discussion at the race course. The persecution of our hero
reaches a sort of climax at the end of the chapter with the printing of a ballad
about him. The next chapter continues the theme of persecution but Joyce now
concentrates on what happened afterwards to a number of HCE's opponents,

who are referred to as 'a cloud of witnesses indeed' (*FDV* 69). This phrase was
borrowed from Paul's epistle to the Hebrews:

> Wherefore seeing we also are compassed about with so great a cloud of
> witnesses, let us lay aside every weight, and the sin which doth so easily beset
> us, and let us run with patience the race that is set before us, looking unto
> Jesus the author and finisher of our faith; who for the joy that was set before
> him endured the cross, despising the shame, and is set down at the right
> hand of the throne of God. (Heb. 12.1)

In the earliest draft the 'cloud of witnesses' is followed by a passage about what
happened to the different people who passed on the gossip about HCE, a passage that is based on chapter 44 of the Wisdom of Ben-Sirah or the book of
Ecclesiasticus as it is called in the catholic bible, where it is considered as one
of the canonical books of the Old Testament (it is not accepted by protestants
and jews). Whereas this bible chapter begins with: 'Let us now praise men of
renown,' Joyce demonstrates that all those involved in the passing of slander
about HCE have disappeared from the face of the earth, much like those who
are mentioned in the bible book that itself has disappeared from protestant
bibles: 'And there are some, of whom there is no memorial: who are perished,
as if they had never been: and are become as if they had never been born, and
their children with them' (Eccl. 44.9).

  It seems that from this moment onwards, HCE can be equated at least
momentarily with Jesus Christ and a bit further on in Chapter 3 it is suggested
that his opponent the cad might well be none other than the 'fashionable vice
preacher' of the sodality but at other times HCE seems to be under the protec-
tion of the clergy. Before we hear the *vox populi* of the street interviews, it is
said that our 'big, human, erring' hero has been 'here condemned before trial
with Jedburgh justice, there acquitted against evidence with benefit of clergy'
(*FDV* 71). Among the speakers in the street interviews we find among HCE's
most outspoken enemies a seventeen-year-old revivalist preacher. The description of the different crimes that were committed against HCE assumes biblical
proportions and at times the language itself becomes biblical (his crime has
become manslaughter and his exile seems to mirror that of Cain); HCE is
described as religiously unorthodox ('a staunch covenanter,' a reference to the
anti-anglican party in the Scottish protestant church). But the 'diversified out-
rages' he is exposed to and that are described at the end of Chapter 3 and in
Chapter 4, were all based on the violence associated with various crimes and
with the civil war in Ireland. When at the end of the first version of Chapter 3,
HCE is insulted by his assailant, he does not reply and simply makes a list of all
the abusive names, because 'the dominican mission was on at the time & he
thought that might reform him' (*FDV* 74).

  Initially the 'revered letter' that is mentioned was part of this first version of
the book, although Joyce then decided not to include it among his first set

of chapters. The apology for her husband by Earwicker's wife seems to be related to the first fall of humanity. At first she writes about a moment of happiness that then she was 'on top of the world' but that is corrected into 'back in paradise.' All the gossip about her husband seems to have been made up 'by a snake in the grass,' including 'lies about an experience of mine as a girl with a clerical friend' (82), an experience that she has in common with Nora Barnacle.

The exact text of this mamafesta disappears from the genesis of 'Work in Progress' until it surfaces again in the thirties, but the document's outside appearance becomes the subject of the next chapter to be written. The link with the bible remains strong when we see that the first version of the description of the mamafesta that opens Chapter 5 also contains a number of references to the bible: 'The proteiform graph itself is a polyexegetical piece of scripture.' It is clear that in one way at least the document in question is the bible: it seems to be written in many hands, but when one reads it, the different traits coalesce into a stable somebody. In vaguely biblical language the text continues: 'as by the providential warring of housebreaker with heartbreaker, & of dram drinker with freethinker our social somebody bowls along bumptily through generations, more generations & still more generations' (*FDV* 84).

As the text itself reminds us, the mamafesta is an epistle, if not an 'epiepistle,' and we are reminded of one of Saint Paul's warnings in his letter to the Hebrews when the text reminds us that 'above all things we must neither be nor become impatient' (85). Of course we should not forget that this chapter was at least in part inspired by Sir Edward Sullivan's introduction to the edition of the *Book of Kells*, an early medieval manuscript of the gospels. In the second stage of the development of *Finnegans Wake*, after the writing of the sketches, at first the religious angle seems to have served no other aim than as a decorative layer, with HCE (much like Bloom) Jesus-like in his self-inflicted suffering and with priests either with him or against him.

The superficial religious layer of the book in its first incarnation changed as soon as Joyce began to develop the characters of the two brothers Shem and Shaun. The twins had been saints from the beginning but by the time Joyce described the former in the first words of what would later become I.7, Shem had become the biblical bad (and elder) brother. The first page of the first draft of the passage already carries the names of both Cain and Esau. It is only natural that Shem-James assumes the identity of Cain, the rebel and outcast who had already been a role model for the romantic poets.

The first half of notebook VI.B.6 contains notes that were destined for the description of a 'mamafesta' that was simultaneously Joyce's own oeuvre (hence the quotations from reviews of *Ulysses*), written by a criminal (many pages of notes were copied from a French book on the handwriting of criminals) and finally related to the *Book of Kells*. Although the notes Joyce took from Sir Edward Sullivan's introduction to the guide about the famous Irish medieval manuscript mostly deal with the book's physical appearance, there is some evidence in the

notes that Joyce was interested in the history of the text as well. On page 64 we
have the first indication that Joyce had discovered another aspect of Shem's
character when he began to make notes (that he did not use in the end) from
an article in *Criterion* on the devil. The relationship between on the one hand
the characters and the sigla, and on the other hand, Shem's identity as Adam's
eldest son, begins to be developed by page 102 of the notebook where we find
'cannibal Cain' and 8 pages later we have the first quotation from a book that
has survived in Joyce's library now at Buffalo, Lamy's *Commentarium in Librum
Geneseos.*

Thomas Joseph Lamy was one of the foremost catholic biblical scholars of his
day whose extreme conservatism saved him from trouble with the hierarchy:
even the not overly progressive *Catholic Encyclopedia* writes about his two-volume
introduction to biblical scholarship and more specifically about his commentaries on *Genesis* and *Revelation*: 'Neither in his introduction nor in his commentaries did Lamy grapple with the difficulties of the day; his ideas, acquired in
the sixth decade of the nineteenth century, remained unmodified till the end.
His 'Introduction' passed almost unchanged through six editions' ('Lamy,
Thomas Joseph'). It is clear that in using this particular commentary, Joyce
wanted to have an authoritative and traditional opinion of the church on the
biblical story of Cain and Abel.

In his selection of notes from Lamy, it is clear that Joyce is not just interested
in the differences between Abel and Cain, but specifically in Lamy's attempts to
solve a problem that had already puzzled the first interpreters of the book of
Genesis: the biblical text simply says that Abel's offering was accepted, while
Cain's is not. But why is that? 'cur Deus munera Abelis, non vero Caini, grata
habuerit?' Characteristically, Lamy does not answer the question, like most
commentators he simply gives a list of traditional answers. First he offers the
interpretation of Saint John (in his first epistle) that Cain's works were evil and
his brother's just, the elder son was not devoted to God and he kept the best
fruits for himself. Saint Paul too, in the epistle to the Hebrews, stresses that God
rejected not so much the sacrifice itself, but Cain's evil intentions. Lamy adds
that Saint Cyprian and the other Church fathers agree and in a footnote he
quotes from Saint Ephraem's commentary on Genesis to the effect that Cain
surely had bulls and calves but knowingly and willingly refused to sacrifice these.
Joyce's sympathy is clearly not with the victim of the crime (he notes: 'Abel
butcher') and he copies Lamy's comments that '[Shem] keeps best for self' and
that he 'made wrong present.' Lamy goes on to answer the question how
Abel and Cain knew that YHWH had accepted one and rejected the other by
following the unanimous opinion of the church fathers that the fire refused to
consume Cain's offering, which was God's practice on other occasions in the
Old Testament but which of course the writer of Genesis does not tell us.

On page 111 we find Joyce noting a good example of Lamy's orthodox exegesis: 'night kills day/agricult – pastoral/jews – †.' This is based on Lamy's discussion of the murder of Abel: he first mentions that two earlier commentators

Goldhiger and Justus von Liebig had claimed that the murder represents the myth of the struggle between night and day or that between agriculture and pastoralism. I have been unable to find who the first name refers to, but the anthropological interpretation of the conflict between the two brothers as that of the difference between day and night was standard by the end of the nineteenth century. The latter is baron Justus von Liebig, one of the great chemists of the nineteenth century whose work on agriculture was used by Marx in his *Kapital*. In a book on the natural laws of agriculture translated into French in 1862 the baron had written that the fight between the two biblical brothers represented agriculture supplanting pastoralism. Lamy then adds his own much simpler solution to the problem which was also copied by Joyce: 'Thus do they pervert the whole history. Abel killed by his brother represents the type of Christ killed by the Jews' (1883: 152).

On page 124 of the notebook Joyce continues his study of orthodox catholic opinion with a page of notes from the article on 'Kevin' in the *Catholic Encyclopedia* and he follows it up with a detailed reading of the article on the Rosary in the same encyclopaedia. Page 147 shows Joyce's interest in heterodox opinion with a few names of protestant sects and on page 153 there is a description of the different forms of penance performed at Lough Derg. It is almost certain that these notes are based on a still unidentified French travel guide to the British isles and it is interesting to observe how in the two histories of Ireland that he was reading at the time, Joyce did not seem to have been particularly interested in the role of christianity, except for a few notes here and there about Saint Patrick for which he did find a place in his book, in contrast to most of the other notes on Irish history that were never used.

In the early months of 1924 when he was using this notebook, Joyce was also writing the early drafts of his hostile portrait of Shem the penman, later to become Chapter 7 of the *Wake*'s book I. In the very first draft, no more than a list of Shem's most important traits, the bad brother is said to sing the hymn 'Lingua mea calamus scribae, veliciter scribentis' (my tongue is the pen of a scribe who writes quickly). The penultimate word should be 'velociter' and this verse is not the title, but part of a Gradual for the liturgy of the mass at the feast of Epiphany: the gradual is called 'Speciosus forma' and there is a motet by William Byrd, which uses the first three verses of Psalm 44/45 in reverse order.

Like in the case of Leopold Bloom in *Ulysses*, we are first introduced to Shem by the kinds of food he prefers. Unlike Bloom, Shem does not eat meat, but once, while drunk, he smelled a lemon peel and claimed 'he could live all his days on the smell of it, as the citr, as the cedron, as the cedar on the founts on the mountains, lemon on, of Lebanon' (*FDV* 109). At least Shem shows that he fantasizes about the orient in the same kind of biblical language that Bloom in 'Calypso' uses when he contemplates life in the Middle East. In a correction to the first level of the draft Shem is called 'the as yet unremunerated national apostate' but in this first version his sins seem to be much more national than religious.

It is only in the second part, when the speaker decides to address his enemy in his own voice that the accusations become not only more specific, but also more religious: 'You were bred & fed, fostered & fattened in this 2 easters island on rollicking heaven & roaring hell and you have become a doubter of all known gods and, condemned fool egoarch, anarch & heresiarch, you have reared your kingdom upon the void of your more than doubtful soul' (*FDV* 120). In fact, this reproach is part of what Joyce himself called 'Improperia' in the underlined title of his first draft and these are a part of the traditional Easter liturgy. The *Catholic Encyclopedia* explains the term:

> The Improperia are the reproaches which in the liturgy of the Office of Good Friday the Saviour is made to utter against the Jews, who, in requital for all the Divine favours and particularly for the delivery from the bondage of Egypt and safe conduct into the Promised Land, inflicted on Him the ignominies of the Passion and a cruel death. ('Improperia')

These specific reproaches, based on texts in both Old and New Testaments, are sung by the choir during the part of the service that is called the Adoration of the Cross. Although the author of the *Encyclopedia* article has to admit that these particular prayers were introduced into the liturgy fairly late in the history of the church, he finishes the article with these words:

> In the beginning the order was not quite what it is now, and in many places the officiant himself at the Good Friday Office sang the verses of the reproaches, while the people joined in the responses or refrain. Thus the representative character of these moving words seems to have been more effectively observed. ('Improperia')

In the margin of the manuscript Joyce added a list of seven 'charges' which he was going to incorporate (Hell, Property, Prophecy, Shirking, Sin, Doles and Mother) and although in the final text they would be difficult to identify, the seven sections are marked with numbers in the text of the first draft.

Shem's religious heterodoxy is present in different forms in this first draft: he is an 'unfullfrocked blackfriar' and at the end of the chapter the contrast is stressed between him and 'that pure one,' his brother who is everything that Shem fails to be: 'he who was well known in heavenly circles above long before he arrived there, a chum of the angels, a flawless model whose spiritual toilette was the talk of the town, a youth they wanted up in heaven, & him you laid low with one hand one fine day to find out how his innards worked.' Shaun's rival is addressed as 'Cannibal Cain' and described as a 'blacksheep' (*FDV* 121). In the second version Joyce added to the accusations against Shem a number of Cain's characteristics that he had harvested from Lamy's commentary on Genesis, in the process strengthening Shem's identity as the bible's first murderer.

In its original form Chapter 7 led straight into the description of Anna Livia Plurabelle (ALP) which does not seem relevant to our theme, except that we learn that when young she had a little adventure with a holy hermit: 'There was a holy hermit You know the glen there near the Luggelaw. Well once there dwelt one day in June in smiling mood and so young & shy & so limber she looked he plunged both of his blessed hands up to his wrists in her flowing hair, that was rich red like the brown bog and he couldn't help it, thirst was too hot for him, he cooled his lips kiss after kiss at Anna Livia's freckled cheek' (*FDV* 125).

With the second draft of ALP, the redbacked notebook was completely full with first and second drafts of the bulk of the first part of his new book and these led immediately to fair copies. But there were two exceptions, first the text of ALP's letter, which, as we have seen, Joyce would only retrieve in the late 1930s, and next a section that he wrote at the bottom of pages in the early part of the notebook and that was probably meant to precede what is now Chapter 5 although it was never recopied. Shem and Shaun, in this brief description, are Irish saints and scholars: 'two sons of wild earth since sainted scholars, Iacopus Pennifera, and Johannes Epistolophorus' (*FDV* 90).

Despite the fact that in notebook VI.B.1, in preparation for the portraits of Shem and ALP, Joyce was mostly collecting material that related to monsters, to the Liffey and to rivers in general, the religious dimension is further developed and explored from the beginning of the notebook where we find a number of notes on angels and devils (6–8). There are very few religious notes in VI.B.1 and we have to wait until page 90 where we find notes that may have been taken from the published sermons of the colourful Jesuit preacher Father Bernard Vaughan (90). These are followed on page 92 with a few items about the liturgy of the consecration of a new bishop copied from the relevant article in the *Catholic Encyclopedia* and then on page 98 with explicitly anticlerical notes from two of the most anti-christian chapters in Edward Gibbon's *Decline and Fall*, which may have been meant for book III but were for the most part not used. In every case Joyce chooses the most salacious examples of christian piety, as when the 'very whimsical' laws imposed by the christians on the marriage bed are said by Gibbon to 'force a smile from the young and a blush from the fair' or when he mentions in what way the virgins in Roman Africa fought against assaults of the flesh: 'they permitted priests and deacons to share their bed, and gloried amidst the flames in their unsullied purity.' In addition, on page 128 Joyce made notes from the *Catholic Encyclopedia* articles on 'Angel' and 'Abel.'

It is clear that Joyce needed this information to prepare for Shaun's Lenten sermon to his sister. The first version of what later would be the first two chapters of book III was drafted in March 1924 and rewritten three times in as many months. In the first draft Shaun is summoned in biblical language and our hero is described as not only prototypically Irish but also extremely devout. When he meets his sister among the 29 daughters of the National School, he begins to preach a Lenten sermon that begins by urging her to be true to the

Ten Commandments in his absence, but then concentrates almost entirely on the need to preserve her chastity in language that seems to be designed more for titillating than for the opposite effect.

From the first lines Shaun is presented as the very opposite of Shem. Whereas the latter is anti-Irish and anti-christian, Shaun is a pious postman in the service of his majesty whose permit seems to have been foretold in Saint Columkille's prophecies and he says 'his prayers regularly' (*FDV* 221). In the consecutive versions of these two chapters, Joyce made sure to add ever new layers of religious references, most clearly in one of the two stories that were later inserted: 'the Ondt and the Gracehoper.' This is a fable-parable in which Gracehoper and Ondt clearly stand for the brothers Cain and Abel: the former is a 'sillybilly' and the latter is 'abelboobied' (*FDV* 222).

By the late twenties, Joyce's work on drafts for *Finnegans Wake* had slowed down considerably, although most of the time he did keep up with the publication rate of *transition*, which had begun bringing out the first set of chapters in 1927. As a result Joyce's note taking at times acquired a double focus with the harvesting of both materials for the earlier parts that he was preparing for the printers and information for new sections or chapters of the book. In some cases we can still find clusters of notes on particular subjects, such as a puzzling comment on page 54 of notebook VI.B.12: 'Max Jacob priait/Reverdy se fâchait' which is preceded by the name of Cocteau. These notes date from the summer of 1926 and are taken from a long letter that the French poet Jean Cocteau had written to the philosopher Jacques Maritain and that he published as a pamphlet in the spring of 1926, together with a reply from Maritain. Cocteau describes what was later called his 'conversion' to catholicism, under the personal influence of the charismatic Maritain, himself a convert, who, together with his wife Raïssa, was trying to recruit for catholicism as many of the young French writers as possible.

In very sensual terms, Cocteau describes the almost mystical experience that in the midst of a depression and an attempted cure for his opium addiction led him to the church. He tells Maritain that the latter's weakness is not a defect:

> You, who are transparent, a soul disguised as a body, the mark of a face on linen, your weakness is a terrible force, the force of a labourer. I have proof of that. Don't tell me it isn't true, I hesitated at the brink of heaven like an idiot. Max Jacob prayed that I would fall, Reverdy was angry. And you, you pushed me; pushed me like a man who kills. You knew that I couldn't swim, but you knew what the instinct for survival is capable of, especially when it goes beyond the will to live and when we want to save our soul instead of our skin. (Cocteau 1925: 17)

Maritain's reply was destined to become one of the most influential of his writings and his thomistic and theological aesthetic had an enormous impact on catholic writers all over Europe, as part of what has been called the 'jazz age catholicism' of the period between the two World Wars (Schloesser 2005). In the absence of more notes, it is fairly clear that Joyce did not read the two booklets; he probably found part of the story in a newspaper or magazine. But it is evident why this kind of discussion would be of interest to him, especially because both Cocteau and Maritain seem to have seen the influence of angels in this episode and, when Cocteau's enthusiasm for catholicism was already waning, Maritain blamed the hand of the devil for some of the young artist's drawings.

A similar phenomenon can be observed in notebooks VI.B.24 and 29 where Joyce was collecting materials for what he considered to be the male counterpart of the ALP chapter, the second half of book III.3 that he would publish separately as *Haveth Childers Everywhere* in April 1930 almost simultaneously with the Faber and Faber publication of the *Anna Livia Plurabelle* booklet. In contrast to the watery and female ALP, HCE was going to be about males and cities, so Joyce asked his daughter-in-law and other collaborators to help him harvest notes from articles on cities in the *Encyclopedia Britannica*. In addition Joyce used several books on the history of Dublin and on extreme poverty in London and York, and he even included notes from an elaborate two-volume study of a small parish in Hertfordshire and from Washington Irving's *A History of New York*. In addition to all this city lore, Joyce also took nine pages of notes in VI.B.29 from *The Confusion of Tongues* by Charles W. Ferguson, a book that had been published the previous year in New York. This *Review of Modern 'isms'* as the subtitle has it, is an occasionally very critical study of what the author himself calls 'the whole pageant of religious oddity in America' (Ferguson 1928: vii).

When we look at the notes from this source we see that Joyce continued to be fascinated by the variety of unorthodox belief, from Christian Science and spiritualism to the wilder varieties of christian doctrines, including the Ku Klux Klan. Towards the end of the note taking (and the end of the source book), Joyce noted the Klan's peculiar names for the days, weeks and months and on the next page he made liberal notes from Ferguson's chapter about the Liberal Catholics, one of the catholic churches that refused to pay homage to the pope and that again he used in the final additions to the HCE section. At the end of the notebook we find a list of names of sectarian groups in the baptist tradition and finally quite a few notes from the chapter on mormonism.

In 1930 Joyce began drafting the children's games and in VI.B.28 we find the first notes from sources that deal directly with angels and devils. On page 10 Joyce starts appropriately with the angels, from some as yet unidentified Thomistic source, and then he moved to the *Encyclopaedia Britannica* articles on 'Devil' (39–47), 'Demonology' (53–58) and 'Angel' (59–60). On page 67 we find the first notes from a book that had only just been published, *Histoire du diable*. The author Joseph Turmel was a French *abbé* who had been punished for his historical critique of christian origins and who could only continue publishing the results of his study under a variety of pseudonyms, no less than fourteen in all: in fact the English translation of the book on the devil had still been published under the name Louis Coulange in 1929, but in 1930 anti-modernist colleagues exposed his double life and Rome insisted on his excommunication *vitandus* (like the arch-modernist Loisy before him) so that the French original of the book could be published under his own name. The 'affaire Turmel' was a scandal around the turn of the century and as early in February 1931 Edouard Dujardin (1931) published a book on the affair (with a preface dated 'décembre 1930'). Turmel's book is a historical and critical account of the devil that looks at the development of the concept from the earliest jewish sources through the ages, demonstrating that the teachings of the church had been very different at different moments in time. It is almost a schóolbook example of the kind of modernist study that the Vatican had expressly forbidden: no wonder that Rome placed the book (together with many others by the author and his fourteen avatars) on the index of forbidden books, which also included a book about the affair.

Another source on devils in VI.B.33 was the successful Broadway play by Marc Connelly, one of the Algonquin Table writers. *Green Pastures* was a version of the Old Testament written in Southern negro language and Joyce restricted his attention to the early parts of the play which describe the first chapters of Genesis until the murder of Abel. More information about angels and devils was found in *Occult Sciences* by A. E. Waite (1891) and other esoteric literature, and in the next few years Joyce continued to read and make notes from the biographies of religion founders such as Mohammed, Buddha, Swedenborg and Joseph Smith, mostly to add to the portrait of HCE. In addition we have a letter to Miss Weaver of March 1931 in which Joyce listed his sources in this period: 'Marie Corelli, Swedenborg, St Thomas, the Sudanese War, Indian outcasts, Women under English Law, a description of St. Helena, Flammarion's The End of the World, scores of children's games from Germany, France, England and Italy' (*Letters I* 302). Especially the first items of this list have to do with the game of angels and devils about which he was writing at the time.

But there is more. In some cases Joyce returned to anti-catholic or anti-clerical materials that he had read and annotated before. In April 1931 he picked up Chiniquy's book *The Priest, the Woman and the Confessional* again and almost without interruption he made more than 30 pages of notes which he almost immediately used in the different chapters of book I that had already been published in *transition*.

In the second half of the 1930s and only with great difficulty, did Joyce finally reach the end of Book IV of *Finnegans Wake* and thus the end of his last book's long genesis. Although *Finnegans Wake* is not a religious book and although religion plays at most a subsidiary role, Joyce's continued interest in religion and more specifically in catholic doctrine and practice can be documented in the notebooks. The *Catholic Encyclopedia* remained an important source for most of this period. In his use of these materials for his 'Work in Progress' Joyce demonstrates that he has not changed his fundamental ideas about religion: the autobiographical Shem is often described as a heretical pervert, whereas his opponent is always pious and orthodox.

Conclusion

Six years ago I left the Catholic Church, hating it most fervently. I found it impossible for me to remain in it on account of the impulses of my nature. I made secret war upon it when I was a student and declined to accept the positions it offered me. By doing this I made myself a beggar but I retained my pride. Now I make open war upon it by what I write and say and do.

James Joyce (1904)

In his 1904 letter to Nora Barnacle, James Joyce spelled out a programme for his life and his art from which, as far as we have been able to demonstrate in this book, he did not deviate. There is no indication that he ever returned to the Church of Rome, or that he found another form of religious faith elsewhere. On the contrary, both in his life and in his work, he approached religion in its many forms with great but detached interest, from the same non-participatory anthropological distance with which Leopold Bloom observes the mass in the 'Lotuseaters' chapter of *Ulysses*: for the militantly non-religious hero, as for his creator, religion never seems to be anything else than opium for the people.

In all of Joyce's prose works religion, and more specifically its catholic form, plays an important role, and this not just because the country, the city and the class that form the background of his work happened to be predominantly catholic. In *Dubliners* religion is an important factor in the imaginative life of some of its protagonists and in the social milieu that forms the background of all these stories, the Church of Rome plays a crucial role in the sectarian reality of Ireland's capital city. At the same time catholicism also functions as one of the causes of the spirit of paralysis that holds the city in its grip. In *A Portrait of the Artist as a Young Man* catholicism takes central stage, as the most important alternative to art as an outlet for Stephen's intellectual and artistic ambitions. As in *Dubliners* religion, with nation and family, is one of the nets that prevent the young artist to fly, but in the end it manages to supply him with a quite definite set of values that he can transform into a viable aesthetic philosophy. In *Ulysses* we learn in part how Stephen has managed to deal with his rejection of religion, family and nation; in 'Circe' we get a sense of the price he has had to pay for the Luciferian 'non serviam.' As John McCourt has pointed out, Leopold Bloom's attitude is much more Triestine in its catholic attitude to religion, in the original sense of the word (2001). Bloom is beyond religion, observing the religious devotions of his fellow-Dubliners with interest, but definitely from a distance. Most importantly, it is clear both from Joyce's comments and from the immediate reception by contemporary catholic critics that *Ulysses* was meant to demonstrate the writer's apostasy from the Church of Rome. And finally, although ostensibly the least religious of Joyce's mature works, a genetic study of Joyce's 'Work in Progress' reveals that below the surface *Finnegans Wake* is just as much concerned with religion as a marginal but not unimportant theme.

The arguments in favour of seeing Joyce as a catholic writer that we have seen in Chapter 1 were either political or religious, and we can begin this conclusion with the former. In the wake of post-colonial criticism of Joyce's significance in Irish literature, we saw that some scholars have argued for Joyce as the first really Irish catholic writer. In sociological terms that is not untrue: Joyce belonged to one of the first generations of writers to come from the increasingly affluent Irish catholic middle-class that had emancipated itself under Daniel O'Connell, had become increasingly important under Parnell and that would seize power in the Free State, consolidate it in the republic and hold it until very recently.

Quite a few recent scholars have developed arguments in favour of seeing Joyce's work as fiercely anti-protestant. In *Joyce and the Anglo-Irish* Len Platt argued that the writer took part in the post-colonial struggle on the side of Catholic Ireland against British and protestant hegemony to the extent that his mockery of Yeats and AE must be seen as a rejection of the Irish Revival precisely because that movement was protestant. But what do we really gain by calling Joyce a catholic writer, apart from scoring points in contemporary Irish cultural debates? Surely there are lots of other Irish writers who could also be called catholic, usually with much more claim to the title but most of them with much less cultural capital? Neo-nationalist critics tend to forget that the nation that was established in 1922 was exactly the kind of state, with exactly the kind of ideology that Joyce had rebelled against during his youth in Ireland and that he continued to abhor until the end of his life. This is why he refused to join the Irish Academy founded by Yeats and Shaw and why he never exchanged his British passport for an Irish one. This consistent refusal on the part of Joyce to accept the new catholic Ireland is in itself sufficient reason to believe that it would be a great injustice to call him an Irish catholic writer.

The historically most accurate attempt to place Joyce in the context of Irish fiction was made by James H. Murphy, who studied catholic fiction between 1873 and 1922 and who in that period distinguishes between a first period, until 1890, when fiction was written by the catholic middle-classes and then, after a transition in the final decade of the century, the period that is relevant for Joyce and in which a great diversity of voices appears that had one thing in common: they belonged to the new Irish intelligentsia.

These catholic journalists, teachers, writers and priests formed a new social class that was convinced that a new Ireland was being born. Most of them came from the lower middle classes and they hoped that the old catholic Ireland into which they had been born would achieve its true potential by transforming itself. They had different opinions on what this new Ireland was going to look like. The largest group rejected contemporary catholic Ireland, especially in the country, as a materialist conspiracy of the clergy and the lower middle class; in Ireland religion for them was 'a coercive social force' (Murphy 1979: 79).

The priests in the fiction of George Moore and James Joyce belongs to an established genre of intelligentsia fiction written by the journalists or teachers that often appear as characters in the work of these two writers. Michael McCarthy, who had explored the role of the church in his book *Priests and People*, also published a novel *Gallowglass* in which he demonstrated what was wrong with clerical Ireland. While most of this fiction was anticlerical, not all of it was anti-religious and some of these novelists advocate a liberal-democratic, socialist and even feminist form of religion in ways that brought them very close to similar European movements in which catholics were active who would soon be exposed as 'modernist.' Gerald O'Donovan and W.P. Ryan wrote in this vein and it is no coincidence that the heroes of their novels were defeated, much as the modernists elsewhere in Europe. Like the heroes of Joyce and Moore, in the end the defeated leave a backward Ireland for America or other places where a life free of coercion and social control was still possible.

There was another section of the intelligentsia who were just as active but who did not agree with the analysis of the anticlerical opposition to catholic Ireland. Writers like the priests Patrick Augustine Sheehan and Joseph Guinan used the form of the novel to defend catholic rural Ireland against the attacks of both anticlerical writers and of catholic modernists. Their Ireland was that of the peasantry, long-suffering and supported only by their priests, in a relationship of what Guinan called 'inwardness and sacredness' (quoted in Murphy 1979: 116) that could not be understood by mere city *littérateurs*.

Their defence of a traditional catholic Ireland was polemical, directed against the attacks from the intelligentsia: Guinan called one of his novels *Priest and People in Doon* (1903) in a direct echo of McCarthy's *Priests and People in Ireland* (1902). For him the critique by the intelligentsia 'disbars them from being truly Irish or Catholic' and such a critic only demonstrates his bias: 'Defective early training, misdirected independence of thought, crass ignorance, selfishness and crookedness of mind generally, are the distinguishing quality of this type of un-Irish Irishman' (quoted in Murphy 1979: 118).

Canon Sheehan also defended the relationship of the priest and the people, but he was a much more complex figure, who has been called 'an effective liberal intellectual' and even a 'freethinker' (Clifford 1990). He differed from Guinan by placing the conflict in the wider context of the battle of the church against modernity (materialism, paganism and secularism); Sheehan thought that in this momentous struggle of the ultramontane church, Ireland could play an important role. Sheehan differs from Guinan in calling for an active critique of modern ideas from well-informed catholics instead of hoping that the modern world could be kept away from Ireland by stopping it at the borders. The real battle was a general European one, not of Ireland alone and in his later work, it is clear that Sheehan thought that the church was not on the winning side. Despite this element of critique, it was Sheehan's work that became 'a kind of mascot' to catholic Ireland and not Guinan; a fact that leads Murphy to the conclusion that this demonstrates catholic Ireland's 'capacity for receiving fiction through an interpretative grid, conducive to its own needs' (115).

To the dismay of Joyce and other intellectuals, the Irish Free State in 1922 adopted the catholic culture that had already been dominant in the powerful coalition between the bishops and the nationalist party in the past quarter century and that almost immediately, under pressure of Vigilance Associations and the Catholic Truth Society, led to the establishment of censorship. In terms of literary politics, this meant that writers who supported modernist ideas like Joyce were and remained marginalized; their place was taken by traditional catholic writers and intellectuals like D. P. Moran, Canon Sheehan, Daniel Corkery and John Joseph O'Kelly. Ruth Fleischmann is thus quite right in claiming that a study of Canon Sheehan's work can afford 'material to the modern reader concerning the stultifying attitudes and conditions which drove Joyce out of the country and which, in their urban form, are the theme of Joyce's early work' (Fleischmann 1997: xii).

Roy Foster has described how in the 1920s non-catholic Irish intellectuals such as George Bernard Shaw and W.B. Yeats fought a losing battle and how Joyce's work played a central role in that war. When Yeats praised Joyce at the Tailteann Games of 1924, he was attacked in the *Catholic Bulletin* by O'Kelly who wrote that admiration for Joyce was

> confined to the petty field of the Anglo-Irish; and there is no use now in attempting to impose that on the mass of the Irish people as being at all a genuine article worth preserving in Irish culture. It is an upstart of yesterday, alien in source, in models, and in such little inspiration as it can boast; and many of its avowed leaders are simply exhibits of literary putrescence. (Foster 2002: 105)

The *Catholic Bulletin* (and other publications like it, such as *The Leader*) was speaking for the country that Joyce had left and they clearly represented the dominant mentality in a catholic Ireland that until the end of his life he refused to come back to. Katherine Mullin quotes the reverend Richard Devane calling for censorship in the *Irish Ecclesiastical Record* in 1925 and referring to Joyce: 'Why should not the Irish Free State make a beginning with such a list of its own, and, as a deterrent to the Dublin Cloacal School, open it with the notorious volume of a well-known degenerate Irishman?' (Mullin 2006: 68).

In his book Murphy makes an important contribution to scholarship: on the one hand he shows that Joyce was by no means alone in his attitude to Ireland, to its religion and its nationalism, and on the other hand we can now better appreciate what he was up against. Catholic Ireland survived the attacks from the intellectuals and especially after 1922 it would increasingly control the country, by excluding dissenting voices and opinions like those of Joyce. But in the final analysis the writer was only harvesting what he had sown himself; in 1923 he wrote to his father that *Ulysses*, like the bible, should not be read by catholics (*JJ* 540).

But in the period between the two World Wars, Joyce was not just writing for Irish readers; perceptive critics in England and Europe who were open to the religious dimension of his work saw clearly what he was trying to do. In his seminal lecture and essay on *Ulysses*, Larbaud had already pointed out how Joyce's naturalism owes more to his Jesuit masters than to the school of Zola, but he was addressing a French audience. When Adrienne Monnier wrote to the catholic writer Paul Claudel (who was the French ambassador in Washington) asking for his support in the fight against the piracy of *Ulysses*, she added that *Ulysses* did not attack the catholic church: the most fervent catholic Louis Gillet had said so in an article that she included in the letter. Claudel begged to disagree:

> As to the inoffensive nature of Mr Joyce's production in terms of religion (which of course has nothing to do with the present letter) you will allow me a smile. *Ulysses* like the *Portrait* is full of the most foul blasphemy where all the hatred of the renegade is felt – affected besides with an absence of truly diabolic talent. (Claudel 1985: 129)[1]

In his diary another French writer, André Suarès, called Joyce a 'triple atheist' (1985: 148) and he is so confused about the writer's religious affiliation that he even doubts that Joyce is a catholic: 'he seems rather to be an orangist who cultivates blasphemies' (149). At the occasion of the translation of *Ulysses* in 1927, the German scholar of French literature Ernst Robert Curtius published a lengthy essay that describes the book as an 'ungeheure und ungeheuerliche Werk' (Curtius 1929: 7),[2] huge and monstrous. Curtius finds in 'Circe' an important key to the book: it is a chapter that can only be understood from the perspective of catholicism, but as 'a negative Catholicism that only knows the Inferno' (21). What is it that remains after the apocalypse of *Ulysses*? 'The smell of ashes, the horror of death, the sorrow of the apostate, remorse of conscience – Agenbite of Inwit' (61). But then Curtius takes a step by closing his essay with the suggestion that this Inferno contains within itself the possibility of a catharsis, of a Purgatorio. Joyce does not fall into the trap of psychoanalysis, with its 'naïve positivist dogmatism': instead Joyce's 'luciferian' book is the work of the Antichrist: 'It distorts both man and the world. The answer can only be given by a voice that is able, like Dante, to announce the mystery of transfiguration and the Vita Nova' (62). Although this next step is clearly placed outside of the confines of *Ulysses*, Curtius has already mentioned Joyce's work in progress and the suggestion seems to be that Joyce will be able in that book to express some form of redemption.

As this book has argued, religion is a central presence in most of Joyce's work, but that fact in itself does not make his work religious: its reference to religious themes might give it religious value to people who already hold religious opinions, but that can also be the case with works that have no overt religious relevance at all. Christian or catholic interpretations of a work do not make that work catholic or christian.

Yet as we have seen in the first chapter of this book, quite a few Joyce critics have argued that in one way or another Joyce and his work remain locked in a catholic frame of reference and we have seen how the first seeds for this view were sown by Mary Colum in her comment about the catholic structure of Joyce's mind.

Yet on the basis of the evidence assembled here it is possible, like Joyce himself, to dismiss the idea of the catholic structure of a mind. Of course, like everybody else, Joyce was the product of his education, which included, as in the case of so many other Irishmen, an important catholic dimension. In later life he did admit that his mind had acquired the working and thinking habits of the Jesuits, but it would certainly go too far to claim that a Jesuit mind would necessarily be catholic as well: in a conversation with Louis Gillet, Joyce even claimed that the wily Odysseus must have been a Jesuit (Gillet 1985: 177).

Equally obvious is the fact that knowledge of their actual historical context and especially a thorough knowledge of the catholic world that he describes will add greatly to our understanding of Joyce's works, although we have also seen that the depth of the author's specific knowledge of the intricacies of catholic doctrine, ritual and history has often been exaggerated. When he wanted to incorporate catholic lore into *Ulysses* and 'Work in Progress,' he did not rely on his memory but consulted the *Catholic Encyclopedia* and other sometimes very mundane and general sources.

And what can it possibly mean, to say that someone has a mind with a catholic structure and what would such a catholic structure look like? In Mary Colum's original anecdote, Jacques Maritain presumably referred to Charles Baudelaire's references to original sin and to catholic ritual, which Maritain, as a catholic convert from protestantism, may well have been particularly interested in. Of course both Joyce and Baudelaire refer to catholic doctrine and practice in their work, as do other writers who attack religion in general or the catholic church in particular: how could one disagree with religion without referring to its doctrines and practices? But reference to catholic matters cannot be enough and certainly something more must be meant when we claim that these writers' minds had a 'catholic structure.'

For one thing, this catholic structure must be fundamentally different not just from other non-religious structures, but even, as was probably the case with

Maritain's views on Baudelaire, from a general christian or protestant structure. If we disregard the catholic practices or beliefs, does sin and more specifically original sin not exist for protestants? It seems that the two claims, Maritain's about Baudelaire and Mary Colum's about Joyce, do not tell us much more than the claim that a thorough catholic education leaves such an indelible imprint on the mind that even heretics and atheists cannot escape from it. The dissidents end up expressing their revolt in the very language they are trying to get away from. Since it has been impossible to describe in detail what, exactly, this imprint entails, such a claim should be considered with the greatest hesitation. In fact, can we not claim with equal justification that Maritain's views on Baudelaire betray the fundamentally *protestant* frame of mind of that catholic philosopher, whom Joyce – in the same mean spirit – liked calling a convert?

In fact, there is something troubling in the habit of Joyce and so many other 'birth catholics' of using the word 'convert' as an insult and it tells us something about the tribal nature of Irish religion (and of religion in general), as if for some reason it was less acceptable to change one's religious allegiance than to stick to the faith you have been born into. In the case of Joyce it is even more troublesome: surely Stephen Dedalus should respect his English dean of studies for having turned against the religion of his family and his nation? Genuine rebels should at least show some solidarity with those who renounce the faith of their fathers.

The problem of claiming the existence of a mind with a catholic structure in the case of somebody who does not consider himself catholic and who, according to the rules of that church cannot even be accepted as catholic, is ultimately ethical. It reminds me very much of the classic psychoanalytical idea according to which the degree of insistence with which the patient rejects a psychoanalytical diagnosis becomes a measure of the fundamental correctness of the diagnosis and of psychoanalysis itself. The fact that I insist that I do not want to have sex with my mother is proof that that is precisely what I unconsciously crave to do. In both cases the superiority of the religious or psychological frame of reference goes unquestioned, in fact it cannot even be questioned, because it is never made explicit or, to use Karl Popper's phrase, it is never made falsifiable: no circumstances are given in which the opposite might be shown to be the case.

Does having a mind with a catholic structure mean that this is a condition that is as unconscious, fundamental and inescapable as wanting to kill your father and to sleep with your mother? Surely not in Freudian terms: psychoanalysis would claim that the Oedipal condition is an anthropological constant, but I do not think a psychoanalyst – not even Jacques Lacan – would go as far as to make similar claims for catholicism.

What would be the defining characteristics of a mind with a catholic structure and, since catholicism is both a practice and a belief, which of the elements of catholic ritual and doctrine would be crucial to such a structure that would make it sufficiently and usefully different from similar structures? Since practices can hardly be responsible for structures of the mind, it seems that we should be looking for one or more beliefs that are simultaneously peculiar to catholicism, but sufficiently general to give rise to an identifiable structure of the mind that is independent of the person's religious opinions. After Vaticanum II, it has become much more difficult to define the specificity of catholicism, but the church that Joyce grew up in still had a clear idea of its own mission, in sharp distinction from all the other christian churches and in direct opposition to a modern world that Rome thought was caught in the snares of the devil. What could be important in such a specifically catholic structure, in comparison with protestantism: a belief in saints, in papal infallibility, a special devotion to the Blessed Virgin?

The trouble with most of these characteristics of catholic theology is that the high church forms of anglicanism, especially in this period, were extremely close to catholicism in the majority of these issues. In fact, under the influence of the so-called Tractarians, by the turn of the twentieth century the 'catholic' faction of the Church of England had adopted not just many of the rituals, but a good part of the doctrines of the Church of Rome. All through the second half of the nineteenth century, the so-called anglo-catholics had made overtures to reunite with the Church of Rome, not without being firmly rebuffed. This is how the *Catholic Encyclopedia* tells the story:

It was natural that this advance section of the Anglican Church should seek to ratify its position, and to escape from its fatal isolation, by desiring some scheme of corporate reunion and especially by endeavouring to obtain some recognition of the validity of its orders. With the truest charity, which consists in the candour of truth, Pope Leo XIII in his Encyclical on Unity, pointed out that there can be no reunion expect on the solid basis of dogmatic unity and submission to the divinely instituted authority of the Apostolic See. In September, 1896, after a full and exhaustive inquiry, he issued a Bull declaring Anglican Orders to be 'utterly null and void,' and in a subsequent Brief addressed to the Archbishop of Paris, he required all Catholics to accept this judgment as 'fixed, settled, and irrevocable' (*firmum, ratum et irrevocabile*).

The Anglican Revival continues to reiterate its claim and to appropriate to itself, where practical, whatever in Catholic doctrine, liturgy, and practice, church vestments or church furniture, it finds helpful to its purpose. By the Lambeth judgment of 1891 it acquired a public sanction for many of its innovations. Since then it has gone further, and holds that no authority in the Church of England can override things which are authorized by 'Catholic consent.' It stands thus in the illogical and unhistorical position of a system which is philocatholic in its views and aspirations, but hopelessly committed to heresy and to heretical communication, and built upon an essentially Protestant foundation. Although to Catholics its very claim is an impious usurpation of what belongs of right to the Catholic Church alone, it fulfils an informal mission of influencing English public opinion, and of familiarizing the English people with Catholic doctrines and ideals. ('Anglicanism')

The drama of this now forgotten history of religious strife was documented with somewhat more sympathy than is displayed in the *Catholic Encyclopedia* by Shane Leslie in his novels *The Cantab* and *The Anglo-Catholic.* The only important differences between the anglo-catholics and their Romish brethren were and still are priestly celibacy, the immaculate conception and the supreme authority of the pope. None of these doctrines, as protestants and most outsiders will confirm, are supported by biblical authority.

If in this context we have to identify something specifically catholic in the structure of Joyce's mind we would have to say that, if we leave celibacy aside, it can only involve the immaculate conception and papal infallibility, two doctrines that are not only fairly recent but, especially in the latter case, ill-defined. What cerebral or intellectual structure could be the result of these core catholic beliefs and in what way can we say that it tells us something useful about Joyce and his mind?

Since it seems to be impossible to define what a mind with a catholic structure would look like or, better, in what ways exactly such a mind would differ from one with a lutheran or calvinist or atheist structure, we really should abandon reference to it, if not for intrinsic, then for ethical reasons. One of the central grounds of western democracy is the assumption that individuals have a fundamental right to define their own political, religious and ethical allegiances. The history of the last century should have taught us how dangerous it is when individuals or groups of people feel that they can assume the right to define the beliefs and allegiances of others.

It seems to me that there are thus only two parties that can legitimately (or morally) make claims about Joyce's catholicism: the catholic church and James Joyce himself. As I hope to have been able to show in this book, Joyce left the church and stayed out until the very end of his life. It is certainly true that today's catholic church works differently than it used to in Joyce's time. The Vatican Council II has made it a more liberal institution that has become much more reluctant to pronounce on the post-mortem fate of individuals and this despite the fact that John Paul II alone has been responsible for nearly half of the total number of canonizations since the sixteenth century. The modern church has become much more inclusive and explicit in its reluctance to exclude: catholics are still excommunicated in the twenty-first century, but it seems that you have to start your own religion, practice witchcraft, be ordained by a schismatic church (like Sinead O'Connor) or claim to be the reincarnation of John Paul II. In fact the Pontifical Council for Legislative Texts has recently circulated a letter defining the exact nature of what it calls the *actus formalis defectionis*, the acceptance under canon law of the fact that a baptized person has officially defected from the church. Although describing in detail the formal requirements for such a momentous decision (on the part of the defector what is required is 'an act of apostasy, heresy or schism'), the list concludes:

> 7. It remains clear, in any event, that the sacramental bond of belonging to the Body of Christ that is the Church, conferred by the baptismal character, is an ontological and permanent bond which is not lost by reason of any act or fact of defection.[3]

It is only in this sense, perhaps, that one could still argue that Joyce remained a catholic until the day he died: according to the most recent canon law, it is simply impossible to stop being a catholic.

But of course that is only true according a new kind of catholicism that did not exist when James Joyce died. Stanislaus Joyce tells us that as a young man his brother consciously wanted to commit the sin against the Holy Ghost, so as to remain outside of the fold permanently and he clearly must have been, like Stephen Dedalus, not afraid to make 'a lifelong mistake and perhaps as long as eternity too' (*P* 247). The catholic church of Joyce's day did not formally excommunicate him, but neither could there ever have been any doubt that he was no longer a catholic. That may well be why Joyce answered Morris L. Ernst's question when he had left the catholic church: 'That's for the Church to say' (1945: 118). Ellmann claims in his biography that Joyce's answer is unhelpful, but it is merely matter of fact: Joyce knew that the answer to that question was only relevant to the church, not to him.

Joyce also knew that the church itself could only regard his work as an all-out attack. In the context of the complex publication of his works, *Dubliners*, *A Portrait of the Artist as a Young Man* and *Ulysses* were read and reviewed by catholics. As we have seen Joyce collected these reviews for future use as advertising material and the most salient negative expressions ended up on flyers. Some of the more virulent attacks on the work came from catholic reviewers and as we have seen there was at least one Irish catholic critic whom Joyce found interesting enough to excerpt his work for inclusion in the self-portrait of Shem the Penman and his handiwork, the Letter in *Finnegans Wake*.

Writing as 'Domini Canis' in the British catholic journal he himself edited, dog of the Lord, the Anglo-Irish convert Shane Leslie opens his discussion of *Ulysses* in the *Dublin Review* with the statement that, since Valery Larbaud and major British critics had praised the novel 'and since the entire setting of this book is Catholic Dublin, and since the seven hundred pages contain a fearful travesty on persons, happenings and intimate life of the most morbid and sickening description, we say not only for the *Dublin Review* but for Dublin *écrasez l'infâme!*' (Deming 1970: 200–1). This fundamentally religious reaction to *Ulysses* is an important primary context of Joyce's work, which we cannot and should not disregard. In the sentence just quoted Leslie makes it clear that he sees the book as an anti-catholic attack by turning Voltaire's famous anticlerical phrase against the author of *Ulysses*. In his concrete criticism of the book, Leslie pulls out all the stops: the novel is 'the screed of one possessed' and all catholic Irishmen will repudiate it 'before reading':

> We speak advisedly when we say that though no formal condemnation has been pronounced, the Inquisition can only require its destruction or, at least, its removal from Catholic houses. Without grave reason or indeed the knowledge of the Ordinary no Catholic publicist can even afford to be possessed of a copy of this book, for in its reading lies not only the description but the commission of sin against the Holy Ghost. Having tasted and rejected the devilish drench, we most earnestly hope that this book be not only placed on the *Index Expurgatorius*, but that its reading and communication be made a reserved case. (Deming 1970: 201)

That Leslie objected to the book for religious reasons is also obvious in his more temperate article in *Quarterly Review* where under his own name he calls the novel 'an Odyssey of the sewer . . . Here we shall not be far wrong if we describe Mr Joyce's work as literary Bolshevism. It is experimental, anti-conventional, anti-Christian, chaotic, totally unmoral' (Deming 1970: 207).

For catholic readers today it may seem strange that Leslie, a lay convert to catholicism, without hesitation requests the book's censure: *Ulysses* should be rejected by the faithful, without having been read, placed on the Index and should only be present in catholic households after explicit permission of the Ordinary, the catholic priest or bishop who is responsible for that particular household. And it is all the more ironic that four years after this review, Leslie's own novel *The Cantab* was banned by the English roman catholic hierarchy, a censure that the author immediately accepted and complied with.

Shane Leslie was not a benighted provincial: by birth he belonged to the Anglo-Irish protestant ascendancy (his first name was an Irish version of 'John Randolph': Winston Churchill was a first cousin). While studying at Cambridge he converted to catholicism and Home Rule. Just before his conversion he had travelled to Russia where he met Tolstoy and, like the partly autobiographical heroes of his novel *The Cantab* and *The Anglo-Catholic*, he seriously contemplated leading a monastic life, but in 1912 he married an American (his mother had been American too). Between 1916 and 1926 Leslie edited the *Dublin Review*, despite its title a London publication that had been founded, according to the *Catholic Encyclopedia*, 'to provide a record of current thought for educated Catholics and at the same time to be an exponent of Catholic views to non-Catholic inquirers' ('Periodical Literature, England'). In many ways his appointment as editor was a mark of his prominence as a British catholic and so was the publication of his biography of the English cardinal Manning in 1926.

In a way, if Leslie had not existed, Joyce would have been forced to invent him. His reviews with their calls for censorship were exactly what Joyce needed to give his book the notoriety that would ensure its status as a forbidden masterpiece.

Leslie and his fellow reviewer for the *Dublin Review*, C.C. Martindale S.J. had demonstrated that Joyce's war with catholicism was not a one-sided campaign and that this particular attack had really struck home.

As the staunch catholic convert Shane Leslie understood all too clearly, James Joyce with *A Portrait of an Artist as a Young Man* and *Ulysses* knowingly and willingly marked his distance from the church. According to the rules of church he was baptized in, James Joyce lived and died as an apostate, as somebody who had placed himself knowingly and willingly outside of that church. It would be a great injustice (if not a mortal sin) to drag him back in.

Notes

Introduction

[1] Here and in the rest of the book the bible quotations are from the King James Version. Exceptions will be indicated.

[2] For another testimony to that particular power of Joyce's work, see the introduction to Pierce 2006: 1–15.

[3] That this view was still controversial at the time is clear when we compare a contemporary review of the book in the *Journal of Religion* with one in *Comparative Literature*. In the former Maynard Kaufman complains that 'instead of an adequate specification of Joyce's heresy, we are presented with a view of Joyce as a virtuous but unemancipated apostate' and in the latter Richard M. Kain concludes that the book's greatest contribution is 'its convincing portrait of Joyce as a humanistic artist, seeking to liberate the conscience of mankind from restrictive authoritarian shackles.'

[4] Samuel Beckett, another Irish atheist (he has Hamm in Endgame exclaim, after fruitlessly praying to God: 'The bastard, he doesn't exist,') shocked post-Christian interlocutors by frequently using expressions such as 'God bless.'

Chapter 1

[1] In *The Satanic Verses*, one of Rushdie's characters answers the question 'What is the opposite of faith?' with: 'Not disbelief. Too final, certain, closed. Itself a kind of belief. Doubt' (1988: 92).

Chapter 2

[1] The influence of Saint Philomena is remarkable: her grave was only discovered in 1802 and her story was 'revealed' to a Neapolitan nun; she continues to cause miracles all over the world, despite the fact that she has been dropped from the liturgical calendar in 1961: doubts about her martyrdom had been expressed in the *Catholic Encyclopedia* (see 'Saint Philomena'). All further references to the *Catholic Encyclopedia* will give the title of the article: the encyclopaedia is easily accessible on the web.

[2] For the history of the study of the bible, see *The Cambridge History of the Bible*.

[3] In the recent coverage of sexual abuse cases by Irish priests and nuns, McCarthy's book was quoted as proof that the problems of the total church control were

a century old, a point also stressed in *The Transformation of Ireland 1900–2000* by Diarmaid Ferriter.

Chapter 3

1. Quoted in the form given by the article on the Nicene Creed in the *Catholic Encyclopedia*.
2. Yves Roby, 'Chiniquy, Charles.' In *Dictionary of Canadian Biography Online*.
3. More information about this particular genre in Griffin 1996.
4. The article on Kant's philosophy in the *Catholic Encyclopedia* begins with this sentence: 'Kant's philosophy is generally designated as a system of transcendental criticism tending towards Agnosticism in theology, and favouring the view that Christianity is a non-dogmatic religion.'
5. Eight years before the British parliament had narrowly escaped a similar problem when the Marquess of Queensberry (the father of Wilde's lover) was elected to the House of Lords by the Scottish peers. As a prominent unbeliever he 'managed to irritate his lordships by scattering secularist pamphlets "over the seats of the Peers spiritual and temporal"' (quoted in Wilson 2000: 291). But when he announced his intention of refusing to swear the oath of allegiance to the queen and even dismissed the oath as 'Christian tomfoolery,' the Scottish peers voted him out again.
6. The biographer, another English convert to catholicism, wrote a review of *Ulysses* in reaction to Shane Leslie's, in which he isolated the book's 'interior untruth which vitiates its art' which boils down to the statement that 'Mr. Joyce is trying to think as if he were insane' (Deming 1970: 204–5). The latter statement was hinted at in the Wake's description of ALP's Letter: 'with a meticulosity bordering on the insane' (FW 173.28).
7. See Notebooks VI.B.10 page 29.
8. I owe this reference to David Pierce.
9. In *Reading Joyce* (2008) David Pierce discusses Joyce's use of the book and he also includes a number of illustrations.
10. This translation is at allpoetry.com/opoem/show/63361-Giosue-Carducci-Hymn-To-Satan. Interestingly, this poem has had a second life on satanic websites.
11. In a statistical article in the *Cambridge Companion to Atheism*, Phil Zuckerman calls contemporary Ireland one of the anomalies for 'the correlation between high rates of individual and societal security/well-being and high rates of nonbelief in God' (2007: 57): a European country with only 4 to 5 per cent nonbelievers (the other is Vietnam with 81 per cent).

Chapter 4

1. See footnote to the text in the Loeb edition of *On the Nature of Things*, 11.
2. Carens failed to see that the quotation in this line is from Shelley's 'Adonais.'
3. Question 6 of the final section on 'The Vices and Other Very Grievous Sins.'

[4] It is interesting to see that the younger Joyce brother, concentrating on Cain's relationship with his mother, fails to see the relevance of the fratricide in Byron's version and in the biblical story.

[5] In his Catechism, Pope Pius X answers the question of what a catholic must do when he is given a bible by a protestant: 'A Christian to whom a Bible has been offered by a Protestant or an agent of the Protestants should reject it with disgust, because it is forbidden by the Church. If it was accepted by inadvertence, it must be burnt as soon as possible or handed in to the Parish Priest.' (Question 32 of the section on 'Theological Virtues.')

[6] Ellmann usefully adds that Vannutelli was an Italian cardinal who had been a papal candidate in 1903. Joyce claimed in a letter to Stanislaus from Rome that Cardinal Vanutelli and the Russian ambassador would criticize his 'wearing apparel' at the bank where he was working at the time (*Letters II* 181).

Chapter 5

[1] See www.penitents.org/sacredheart.htm.

Chapter 6

[1] For more details, see Lernout 2007.

[2] Manuscript in James Joyce Series A. Box 1.4 of the Harry Ransom Center for the Humanities.

[3] According to the *Catholic Encyclopedia*, in the middle of the fifteenth century the Italian philologist Lorenzo Valla was tried for heresy for having doubted that the text was really written by the twelve apostles ('Lorenzo Valla').

[4] For the role of Arianism in the Christian Roman Empire see Freeman 2002.

[5] www.vexen.co.uk/holyshit/smite.html.

[6] See, for example, Gleason L. Archer's *Encyclopedia of Bible Difficulties*. This author offers the classic excuse: these were not children but young hoodlums, like 'the large youth gangs that roam the ghetto sections of our modern American cities' (1982: 205). In apologetic literature they are usually referred to as 'the lads of Bethel.' Neither Archer, nor any of the other apologists I have read point out the particular consolation the bereaved mothers must have derived from the fact that the agents of execution 'had' been female bears.

Chapter 7

[1] The original German phrase is: 'Wir gelangen so zu der paradoxen Vorstellung Gottes als eines sogenannten "gasförmigen Wirbelthieres."'

[2] Ronan Crowley has discovered that Joyce found this saying in the German translation of an 1860 lecture by Turgenev on Hamlet and Don Quixote.

[3] It is interesting to see that none of the existing German translations I consulted seems to be based on a study of Most's original text.

[4] Baltimore Catechism, question 259.

[5] These are the closing words of Unam Sanctum. For the full text, see www. newadvent.org/library/docs_bo08us.htm.

[6] The outcome of the resulting evolution is evident in the title of an article by Martin E. Marty (1985): 'Hell Disappeared. No One Noticed. A Civic Argument.' But it should also be pointed out that evangelicals, fundamentalists and conservative catholics continue to hold on to the traditional doctrine of hell.

[7] In his *Bloomsday Book* Harry Blamires calls this image of God the nadir of 'the intellectual chaos' (1966: 162) that characterizes the chapter. I'm not sure that for Joyce blasphemy (even of a Swiftian bend) would necessarily constitute a nadir.

[8] The English writer Samuel Butler was accused by his father of having hastened his mother's death as a result of the irreverent tone of his anti-christian novel *Erewhon*. Like Stephen Dedalus, Butler 'commented that doctors had given cancer as the cause of his mother's death' (Wilson 2000: 238).

Chapter 8

[1] The reference is on page 13 of the notebook. All further references to the *Finnegans Wake* notebooks will be given in the text and will refer to the page of the relevant notebook (and not to the edition).

Conclusion

[1] Characteristically, Joyce blamed Claudel's reaction on the fact that he 'had converted from something. Anyhow he has the mentality, it seems, of a convert not of one born and bred in the business' (Banta 1987: 181).

[2] The second half of this essay was translated by Eugene Jolas for *transition* and excerpted in the second volume of Deming's *Critical Heritage*. My references are to the original.

[3] Letter dated 13 March 2006 of Julian Card. Herranz, president of the Pontificium Consilium de Legum Textibus and sent to the presidents of all episcopal conferences 'by order of His Holiness, Benedict XVI.' Online viewed 16 July 2009, www.vatican.va/roman_curia/pontifical_councils/intrptxt/documents/ rc_pc_intrptxt_doc_20060313_actus-formalis_en.html.

References

Ahearn, E.J. (1961), 'Religious values in Joyce's *Ulysses.' The Christian Scholar,* XLIV. 2, 139–45.

Allen, G. (1908), *The Evolution of the Idea of God: Inquiry into the Origins of Religion.* London: Rationalist Press Association.

Archer, G.L. (1982), *Encyclopedia of Bible Difficulties.* Grand Rapids, MI: Zondervan Publishing House.

Arnstein, W.L. (1965), *The Bradlaugh Case: A Study in Late Victorian Opinion and Politics.* London: Oxford University Press.

Artigas, M., Glick, T.F. and Martinez, R.A. (eds) (2006), *Negotiating Darwin: The Vatican Confronts Evolution, 1877–1902.* Baltimore: Johns Hopkins University Press.

Atkin, N. and Tallett, F. (2003), *Priests, Prelates and People: A History of European Catholicism since 1750.* London: I.B. Tauris.

Aubert, R. (1978), *The Christian Centuries. Volume Five: The Church in a Secularised Society.* New York: Paulist Press.

Balsamo, G. (2004), *Joyce's Messianism: Dante, Negative Existence, and the Messianic Self.* Columbia, SC: University of South Carolina Press.

Banta, M. and Silverman, O.A. (eds) (1987), *James Joyce's Letters to Sylvia Beach, 1921–1940.* Bloomington: Indiana University Press.

Basset, B. (2004), *The English Jesuits from Campion to Martindale.* Leominster, Herefordshire: Gracewing Publishing.

Berman, D. (1990), *A History of Atheism in Britain: From Hobbes to Russell.* London: Routledge.

Biletz, F.A. (2000), 'The *Irish Peasant* and the conflict between Irish-Ireland and the catholic bishops, 1903–1910,' in S.J. Brown and D.W. Miller (eds), *Piety and Power in Ireland: 1760–1960: Essays in Honour of Emmet Larkin.* Belfast: The Institute of Irish Studies, 108–29.

Blamires, H. (1966), *The Bloomsday Book: A Guide through Joyce's 'Ulysses'.* London: University Paperbacks.

Blatchford, R. (1911), *God and My Neighbour.* London: The Clarion Press.

Blavatsky, H.P. (1891), 'Letter to Gerald Massey.' *The Agnostic Journal* (3 October), 214. Available online at Blavatsky Study Center 2004, *Madame Blavatsky on Gerald Massey's 'Lectures' and 'Natural Genesis,'* viewed 16 July 2009, www.blavatskyarchives. com/hpbletter110287.htm.

Bowen, D. (1983), *Paul Cardinal Cullen and the Shaping of Modern Irish Catholicism.* Dublin: Gill and MacMillan.

Bowen, Z. and Carens, J.F. (eds) (1984), *A Companion to Joyce Studies.* Westport, CT: Greenwood Press.

Boyle, R. (1978), *James Joyce's Pauline Vision: A Catholic Exposition.* Carbondale, IL: Southern Illinois University Press.

Budgen, F. (1934), *James Joyce and the Making of Ulysses*. London: Grayson and Grayson.

Bury, J.B. (1913), *History of the Freedom of Thought*. London: Williams and Norgate.

—(1963–1970), *Cambridge History of the Bible*. Three volumes. Cambridge University Press.

Candeloro, G. (1970). Introduction to *L'Asino di Podrecca e Galantara (1892–1925)*. Milan: Feltrinelli, i–xxiv.

Candy, C. (1995), *Priestly Fictions: Popular Irish Novelists of the Early 20th Century*. Dublin: Wolfhound Press.

Carducci, G. (1964), 'Inno a Satana' *Tutte le poesie I*. Milano: Rizzoli, 369–77.

Catechism of Saint Pius X, n.d., Eternal World Television Network, viewed on 16 July 2009, www.ewtn.com/library/CATECHSM/PIUSXCAT.htm.

Catholic Encyclopedia. Caxton Publishing Company: London, 1911. Available online at New Advent, *Catholic Encyclopedia*, viewed on 16 July 2009, www.newadvent. org/cathen/index.html. Because the encyclopaedia is most easily available on the web, all references to this text are identified by the title of the relevant article.

Chadwick, O. (1972), *The Victorian Church. Part II: 1860–1901*. London: Adam & Charles Black.

—(1975), *The Secularization of the European Mind in the Nineteenth Century*. London: Cambridge University Press.

—(2003), *A History of the Popes: 1830–1914*. Oxford History of the Christian Church. London: Oxford University Press.

Claudel, P. (1985), 'Deux letters à Adrienne Monnier.' *Cahiers L'Herne: James Joyce*. Paris: L'Herne, 128–30.

Clifford, B. (1990), *Canon Sheehan: A Turbulent Priest. Address to a meeting for the Duhalow Centre*. Irish Heritage Society in conjunction with Aubane Historical Society.

Cochrane, E. (1977), 'What is catholic historiography?' in C.T. McIntire (ed.) *God, History, and Historians: Modern Christian Views of History*. New York: Oxford University Press, 444–65.

Cocteau, J. (1925), *Lettre à Jacques Maritain*. Paris: Stock.

Collins, K. (2002), *Catholic Churchmen and the Celtic Revival in Ireland 1848–1916*. Dublin: Four Courts.

Colum, M. and Colum, P. (1958). *Our Friend James Joyce*. London: Victor Gollancz.

Connelly, M. (1930), 'The Green Pastures.' in *Six Plays*. London: Gollancz.

Connolly, T. (ed.) (1961), *James Joyce: Scribbledehobble: The Ur-Workbook for 'Finnegans Wake'*. Evanston, IL: Northwestern University Press.

Cooke, B. (2004), *The Gathering of Infidels: A Hundred Years of the Rationalist Press Association*. New York: Prometheus Books.

Courtney, J.E. (1920), *Freethinkers of the Nineteenth Century*. London: Chapman and Hall.

Curtius, E.R. (1929), *James Joyce und sein Ulysses*. Zürich: Verlag der Neuen Schweizer Rundschau.

Daanson, E. (1911), *Le Livre du Bien et du Mal. Ou comment Messire Saint Lucifer ayant apporté la lumière en ce monde, la divine ignorance triompha de l'humaine sagesse*. Paris: Libraire Générale des sciences, arts et letters.

Deming, R.H. (1970), *James Joyce: The Critical Heritage*. 2 volumes. London: Routledge & Kegan Paul.

Dennett, D.C. (2006), *Breaking the Spell: Religion as a Natural Phenomenon.* New York: Viking.

Doherty, J. (1963), 'James Joyce and "hell opened to Christians": The edition he used for his "hell sermons,"' *Modern Philology* 61, 110–19.

Dowling, L.H. (1920), *The Aquarian Gospel of Jesus the Christ: The Philosophic and Practical Basis of the Religion of the Aquarian Age of the World and of the Church Universal: Transcribed from the Book of God's Remembrances Known as the Akashic Records by LEVI with Introduction by Eva S. Dowling, A.Ph.D.* London: L.N. Fowler.

Dujardin, E. (1904), 'The Abbé Loisy,' trans. by George Moore, *Dana: A Magazine of Independent Thought* I.1, 18–21.

—(1931), *Grandeur et décadence de la critique: Sa rénovation: le cas de l'abbé Turmel.* Paris: Albert Messein.

Durand, J-D (1995), 'L'Eglise à la recherche de l'Italie perdue,' in Jacques Gadille and Jean-Marie Mayeur (eds), *Libéralisme, industrialisation, expansion européenne. Histoire du christianisme des origines à nos jours.* Paris: Desclée, 611–36.

Eglinton, J. (1904), 'The breaking of the ice.' *Dana: A Magazine of Independent Thought* I.1, 11–17.

Ellis, H. (1906), *The New Spirit.* London and Felling-on-Tyne: Walter Scott Publishing Co.

Encyclopaedia Britannica (1910–1911), Eleventh Edition. Cambridge: Cambridge University Press. Available online at Online Encyclopedia (2009), *Encyclopaedia Britannica,* viewed on 16 July 2009, http://encyclopedia.jrank.org/.

Ernst, M.L. (1855). *The Escaped Nun. Or, Disclosures of Convent Life and The Confessions of a Sister of Charity, giving a minute detail of their inner life, and a bolder revelation of the mysteries and secrets of nunneries, than have ever before been submitted to the American public.* New York: DeWitt & Davenport.

—(1945), *The Best is Yet.* New York: Harper & Brothers.

Ferguson, C.W. (1928), *The Confusion of Tongues: A Review of Modern Isms.* New York: Doubleday, Doran & Co.

Ferriter, D. (2004), *The Transformation of Ireland: 1900–2000.* London: Profile Books.

Fitzpatrick, B. (1922), *Ireland and the Making of Britain.* New York and London: Funk & Wagnalls.

Fleischmann, R. (1997), *Catholic Nationalism in the Irish Revival: A Study of Canon Sheehan, 1852–1913.* Houndmills: Macmillan.

Flood, J.M. (1917), *Ireland: Its Saints and Scholars.* Dublin: Talbot.

Fogazzaro, A. (1906), *The Saint (Il Santo).* Translated by M. Agnetti Pritchard. With an Introduction by William Roscoe Thayer. New York: G.P. Putnam's Sons.

Foster, R.F. (2002), *The Irish Story: Telling Tales and Making it Up in Ireland.* London: Oxford University Press.

Frazier, A. (2000), *George Moore, 1852–1933.* New Haven: Yale University Press.

Freeman, C. (2002), *The Closing of the Western Mind.* London: William Heinemann.

Gadille, J. (1995a), 'Libertés publiques – Question Sociale,' in Jacques Gadille and Jean-Marie Mayeur (eds), *Libéralisme, industrialisation, expansion européenne. Histoire du christianisme des origines à nos jours.* Paris: Desclée, 15–44.

—(1995b). 'Grands courants doctrinaux et de spiritualité dans le monde catholique,' in Jacques Gadille and Jean-Marie Mayeur (eds), *Libéralisme, industrialisation, expansion européenne. Histoire du christianisme des origines à nos jours.* Paris: Desclée, 113–36.

Gallagher, M.P. (1982), 'The Atheism of James Joyce.' *Doctrine and Life* (November), 554–61.

Gay, P. (1988), *Freud: A Life for Our Time.* New York: Dent.

Gibson, A. (2002), *Joyce's Revenge: History, Politics, and Aesthetics in 'Ulysses'.* London: Oxford University Press.

Gifford, D. and Seidman, R.J. (2000), *Ulysses Annotated.* Berkeley, CA: University of California Press.

Gillet, Louis (1985), 'Journal (fragments).' *Cahiers de L'Herne: James Joyce.* Paris: L'Herne, 176–87.

Gogarty, O. St J. (1971), *Many Lines to Thee: Letters to G.K.A. Bell. From the Martello Tower at Sandycove, Rutland Square and Trinity College Dublin: 1904–1907.* Edited with a commentary by James F. Carens. Dublin: The Dolmen Press.

Gottfried, R. (2007), *Joyce's Misbelief.* Gainesville, FL: University Press of Florida.

Grafton, A. (2005), 'Reading Ratzinger: Benedict XVI, the Theologian.' *The New Yorker* (25 July), 42ff.

Gray, T. (1996), *A Peculiar Man: A Life of George Moore, Bestselling Irish Author, 1852–1933.* London: Sinclair-Stevenson.

Griffeths, M. n.d. *Salvation Outside the Catholic Church.* Pharsea's Home Page, viewed 16 July 2009, www.geocities.com/pharsea/GoToHell.html.

Griffin, S.M. (1996), 'Awful Disclosures: Women's Evidence in the Escaped Nun's Tale,' *PMLA* 111, 93–107.

Griffiths, R. (1966), *The Reactionary Revolution: The Catholic Revival in French Literature, 1870–1914.* London: Constable.

Haeckel, E. (1903), *Die Welträthsel: Gemeinsverständliche Studien über monistische Philosophie mit einem Nachworte: Das Glaubensbekenntnis der reinen Vernunft.* Bonn: Emil Strauss.

Hales, E.E.Y. (1960), *The Catholic Church in the Modern World.* New York: Doubleday.

Hanson, E. (1997), *Decadence and Catholicism.* Cambridge: Harvard University Press.

Healy, J. (1905), *The Life and Writings of Saint Patrick.* Dublin: Gill and Son.

Hohoff, C. (1951), 'James Joyce und die Einsamkeit.' *Wort und Wahrheit: Monatschrift für Religion und Kultur* VI, 506–16.

Hughes, E. (1992), 'Joyce and Catholicism,' in R. Welsch, (ed.) *Irish Writers and Religion.* Gerrards Cross: Colin Smythe, 116–37.

Hutton, R.H. (1891), *Cardinal Newman.* London: Methuen and Co.

Israel, J. (2002), *Radical Enlightenment: Philosophy and the Making of Modernity, 1650–1750.* London: Oxford University Press.

Jacoby, S. (2004), *Freethinkers: A History of American Secularism.* New York: Metropolitan Books.

James, M.R. (1924), *The Apocryphal New Testament: Being the Apocryphal Gospels, Acts, Epistles and Apocalypses.* Oxford: Clarendon Press.

Joyce, J. (1930), *Ulysses.* Trans. Georg Goyert. Zürich: Rhein-Verlag.

Joyce, S. (1950), *Recollections of James Joyce.* Translated from the Italian by Ellsworth Mason. New York: The James Joyce Society.

—(1958), *My Brother's Keeper.* Edited and with an introduction by Richard Ellmann. London: Faber and Faber.

—(1962), *The Dublin Diary of Stanislaus Joyce*. Edited by George Harris Healey. London: Faber and Faber.

Kain, R.M. (1962), Review of J. Mitchell Morse, *The Sympathetic Alien: James Joyce and Catholicism*, in *Comparative Literature* 14, 207–8.

Kaufman, M. (1963), Review of J. Mitchell Morse, *The Sympathetic Alien: James Joyce and Catholicism*, in *Journal of Religion* 43, 348.

Kearney, R. (2007), 'Traversals and epiphanies in Joyce and Proust,' in Peter Grafton and John Panteleimon Manoussakis (eds), *Traversing the Imaginary: Richard Kearney and the Postmodern Challenge*. Chicago, IL: Northwestern University Press, 183–208.

Kertzer, D.I. (1997), *The Kidnapping of Edgardo Mortara*. London: Picador.

Khoo Thwe, P. (2003), *From the Land of Green Ghosts*. New York: HarperCollins.

Kingsley, C. (1853), *Hypatia: Or, New Foes with an Old Face*. London: John Parker.

Lalouette, J. (2001), *La libre pensée en France: 1848–1940*. Paris: Albin Michel.

Lamy, T.J. (1883). *Commentarium in Librum Geneseos: Tomus I*. Mechelen: H. Dessain.

Larkin, E. (1972), 'The Devotional Revolution in Ireland 1850–75.' *American Historical Review* 77, 625–52.

—(1979), *The Roman Catholic Church in Ireland and the Fall of Parnell: 1888–1891*. Chapel Hill, NC: University of North Carolina Press.

Lecky, W.E.H. (1910), *History of the Rise and Influence of the Spirit of Rationalism in Europe*. London: Longmans, Green and Co.

Lernout, G. (1980). 'George Moore: Wagnerian and Symbolist.' *Cahiers du centre d'études irlandaises* 5, 55-70.

—(1990). *The French Joyce*. Ann Arbor, MI: University of Michigan Press.

—(2007). 'Collector of Prepuces: Foreskins in *Ulysses*.' *James Joyce Quarterly* 44, 345–52.

Lucretius (2002), *De rerum natura*. English translation by W.H.D Rouse, revised by Martin F Smith. Cambridge: Harvard University Press.

MacDonald, G.E. (1929), *Fifty Years of Freethought: Being the Story of the Truth Seeker, with the Natural History of its Third*. New York: The Truth Seeker Company.

MacGreevy, T. (1929), 'The Catholic element in *Work in Progress*' in Sylvia Beach, Samuel Beckett, Marcel Brion, et al. *Our Exagmination round His Factification for Incamination of Work in Progress*. Paris: Shakespeare and Company, 117–27.

Manganiello, D. (1980), *Joyce's Politics*. London: Routledge & Kegan Paul.

Martindale, Father C.C. (1923), *Father Bernard Vaughan: A Memoir*. London: Longmans.

Marty, M.E. (1985), 'Hell disappeared. No one noticed. A civic argument.' *Harvard Theological Review* 78, 381–98.

Massey, G. (1900), *Gerald Massey's Lectures*, AfricaWithin.com, viewed 16 July 2009, www.africawithin.com/massey/gml1_foreword.htm.

Mauthner, F. (1920), *Der Atheismus und seine Geschichte im Abendlande: Volume 1*. Stuttgart and Berlin: Deutsche Verlags-Anstalt.

McCarthy, M.J.F. (1904), *Gallowglass, Or, Life in the Land of the Priests*. London: Simpkin, Marshall, Hamilton, Kent.

—(1908), *Priests and People in Ireland*. London: Hodder and Stoughton.

McCourt, J. (2001), *The Years of Bloom: James Joyce in Trieste, 1904–1920*. Dublin: Lilliput Press.

Miller, D.W. (1973), *Church, State, and Nation in Ireland 1898–1921*. Pittsburgh: University of Pittsburgh Press.

Moi, T. (2006), *Henrik Ibsen and the Birth of Modernism: Art, Theater, Philosophy*. London: Oxford University Press.

Moore, G. (1929), *Letters from George Moore to Ed. Dujardin (1886–1922)*. New York: Crosby Gaige.

Moore, R.I. (1977), *The Origins of European Dissent*. London, Allen Lane.

Morrison, S.J. (1999), 'Heresy, Heretics and Heresiarchs in the Work of James Joyce,' PhD thesis at Royal Holloway College, London.

Morse, J.M. (1959), *The Sympathetic Alien: James Joyce and Catholicism*. New York: New York University Press.

Moseley, V. (1967), *Joyce and the Bible*. DeKalb: Northern Illinois University Press.

Most, J. (1996), *Die Gottespest*. Frankfurt: AV'88.

—(2007), English translation: *The God Pestilence* at libcom.org, viewed 16 July 2009, http://libcom.org/library/the-god-pestilence-johann-most.

Müller, A.V. (1907), *Die 'hochheilige Vorhaut Christi' Im Kult and in der Theologie der Papstkirche*. Berlin: C.A. Schwetske und Sohn.

Mullin, K. (2006), 'English vice and Irish vigilance: The nationality of obscenity in *Ulysses*,' in Andrew Gibson and Len Platt (eds), *Joyce, Ireland, Britain*. Gainesville, FL: University Press of Florida, 68–82.

Murphy, J.H. (1997), *Catholic Fiction and Social Reality in Ireland, 1873–1922*. Westport, CT: Greenwood Press.

Neil, W. (1975), 'The criticism and theological use of the bible, 1700–1950,' in S.L. Greenslade (ed.) *The Cambridge History of the Bible: The West from the Reformation to the Present Day*. Cambridge: Cambridge University Press.

Newman, J.H. (1865), *Callista: A Sketch of the Third Century*. New York: Saddler.

—(1907), *Essays Critical and Historical*, Volume 1. London: Longmans, Green and Co.

Noon, W.T. (1969). 'The religious position of James Joyce,' in Wolodymyr T. Zyla (ed.) *James Joyce: His Place in World Literature. Proceedings of the Comparative Literature Symposium*. Lubbock: Texas Tech Press.

Norman, E.B. (1985), 'Cardinal Manning and the temporal power.' in Derek Beales and Geoffrey Best (eds), *History, Society and the Churches: Essays in honour of Owen Chadwick*. Cambridge and New York: Cambridge University Press, 235–56.

Norwich, J.J. (1993), *Byzantium: The Apogee*. London: Penguin.

Pals, D.L. (1982), *The Victorian 'Lives' of Jesus*. San Antonio: Trinity University Press.

Papal Encyclicals Online (2008), *Providentissiumus Deus*. Viewed 10 July 2009, www.papalencyclicals.net/Leo13/l13provi.htm.

Parker, J.W. (1860), *Essays and Reviews*. London: Parker.

Pelikan, J. (1971), *The Christian Tradition: A History of the Development of Doctrine. Part 1: The Emergence of the Catholic Tradition (100–600)*. Chicago, IL: University of Chicago Press.

Pierce, D. (2005), *Light, Freedom and Song: A Cultural History of Modern Irish Writing*. New Haven, CT: Yale University Press.

—(2006), *Joyce and Company*. London: Continuum.

—(2007), *Reading Joyce*. Harlox, Essex: Pearson Longman.

Platt, L. (1998), *Joyce and the Anglo-Irish: A Study of Joyce and the Literary Revival*. Amsterdam: Rodopi.

Potts, Willard (ed.) (1979), *Portraits of the Artist in Exile: Recollections of James Joyce by Europeans*. Portmarnock: Wolfhound Press.

—(2000), *Joyce and the Two Irelands*. Austin, TX: University of Texas Press.

Preterossi, G. (ed.) (2006), *Le ragioni dei laicii*. Roma-Bari: Laterza.

Priestman, M. (1999), *Romantic Atheism: Poetry and Freethought, 1780–1830*. Cambridge: Cambridge University Press.

Ratté, J. (1967), *Three Modernists: Alfred Loisy, George Tyrrell, William L. Sullivan*. New York: Sheed and Ward.

Robertson, J.M. (1904), 'Catholicism and civilisation.' *Dana: An Irish Magazine of Independent Thought* I.2, 33–8.

—(1915), *A Short History of Freethought Ancient and Modern*. London: Watts & Co.

Roby, Y. (2000). *Chiniquy, Charles*, Dictionary of Canadian Biography Online, viewed 16 July 2009, www.biographi.ca/009004-119.01-e.php?BioId=40151.

Royle, E. (1974), *Victorian Infidels: The Origins of the British Secularist Movement 1791–1866*. Manchester: Manchester University Press.

—(1980), *Radicals, Secularists and Republicans: Popular Freethought in Britain, 1866–1915*. Manchester: Manchester University Press.

Rubenstein, R.E. (2004), *Aristotle's Children: How Christians, Muslims, and Jews Rediscovered Ancient Wisdom and Illuminated the Middle Ages*. New York: Harvest Books.

Rushdie, S. (1988). *The Satanic Verses*. London: Vintage.

Ryan, F. (1904a), 'Political and intellectual freedom.' *Dana: An Irish Magazine of Independent Thought* I.1, 27–31.

—(1904b), 'Empire and liberty.' *Dana: An Irish Magazine of Independent Thought* I. 4, 111–17.

—(1904c), 'Criticism and courage.' *Dana: An Irish Magazine of Independent Thought* I.5, 145–9.

Schloesser, S. (2005), *The Jazz Age Catholicism: Mystic Modernism in Postwar Paris: 1919–1931*. Toronto: University of Toronto Press.

Schlossman, B. (1985), *Joyce's Catholic Comedy of Language*. Madison: University of Wisconsin Press.

Scholes, R. and Kain, R.M. (eds) (1965), *The Workshop of Daedalus*. Evanston, IL: Northwestern University Press.

Schwartz, T.D. (1976), 'Mark Twain and Robert Ingersoll: The freethought connection.' *American Literature* 48.2, 183–93.

Segall, J. (1993), *Joyce in America: Cultural Politics and the Trials of 'Ulysses'*. Berkeley, CA: University of California Press.

Senn, F. (1982), 'Taxilonomy.' *James Joyce Quarterly* 19.2, 154–8.

Sicari, S. (2001), *Joyce's Modernist Allegory: Ulysses and the History of the Novel*. Columbia, SC: University of South Carolina Press.

Smith, W.S. (1967), *The London Heretics 1870–1914*. London: Constable.

Staley, T. (1991), 'Religious elements on Thomistic encounters: Noon on Joyce and Aquinas,' in J.E. Dunleavy (ed.), *Re-Viewing Classics of Joyce Criticism*. Urbana and Chicago, IL: University of Illinois Press, 155–68.

Steppe, W. (1995), 'The merry Greeks (with a farewell to epicleti).' *James Joyce Quarterly* 32, 597–617.

Suarès, A. (1985), 'Journal inédit (extraits),' in *Cahiers de L'Herne: James Joyce*. Paris: L'Herne, 143–50.

Sullivan, K. (1963), *James Joyce among the Jesuits*. New York: Columbia University Press.

Sultan, S. (1964), *The Argument of 'Ulysses'*. Columbus: Ohio State University Press.

Taxil, Leo (n.d.), *La vie de Jésus*. Paris: P. Fort.

Taylor, L.J. (1997), *Occasions of Faith: An Anthropology of Irish Catholics*. Dublin: Lilliput Press.

Turmel, J. (1931), *Histoire du diable*. Paris: Rieder.

Turner, J. (1986), *Without God, Without Creed: The Origins of Unbelief in America*. Baltimore: Johns Hopkins University Press.

Vaughan, Father B. (1907a), *The Sins of Society: Words Spoken by Father Bernard Vaughan of the Society of Jesus in the Church of the Immaculate Conception, Mayfair during the Season*. London: T. Fisher Unwin.

—(1907b), *Society, Sin and the Saviour: Addresses on the Passion of the Our Lord*. London: Kegan Paul, Trench & Trübner.

Waite, A.E. (1891), *The Occult Sciences: A Compendium of Transcendental Doctrine and Experiment*. London: Kegan Paul, Trench, Trübner & Co.

Walzl, F.L. (1984), *'Dubliners'* in Zack Bowen and James F. Carens (eds), *A Companion to Joyce Studies*. Westport, CT: Greenwood Press, 157–228.

Weber, Francis J. (1962), 'American catholic historical societies.' *Church History* 31.3, 350–6.

Wilson, A.N. (2000), *God's Funeral: A Biography of Faith and Doubt in Western Civilization*. New York: Ballantine Books.

Zuckerman, P. (2007), 'Atheism: contemporary numbers and patterns' in Michael Martin (ed.), *The Cambridge Companion to Atheism*. Cambridge: Cambridge University Press, 47–65.

Index

Abelard, Peter 62
Acton, Lord 33–4
Ahearn, Edward J. 14
Aikenhead, Thomas 64
Alacoque, Margaret Mary 121
Alexander, Charles M. 155
Allen, Grant 180, 194
Ambrose, Saint 149
Anaxagoras 62
Aquinas, Thomas 7, 15, 19, 40, 50–1,
    54, 76, 79, 117, 130, 147, 149,
    179, 192
Aristotle 51, 54, 157
Arius 52–5, 143–4, 147, 176
Arnold, Matthew 60, 95
Artifoni, Almidano 103
athcism 5, 7–8, 9, 11, 13, 24, 30, 41,
    61–7, 70, 75–8, 79, 81, 84, 88, 92,
    95, 107, 115–17, 130, 137, 142,
    149, 160, 177, 188, 189, 210, 212,
    214, 218n4
Augustine, Saint 22, 53, 87, 98, 148, 166
autobiography 2, 3, 4, 5, 55, 94, 112,
    113–19, 205

Bach, Johann Sebastian 41
Bacon, Francis 63
Bakunin, Mikhail 80
Balfour, Arthur 43
Balsamo, Gian 22–4
Barbara, Saint 178
Barnacle, Nora 6, 8, 86, 102–4, 106–7,
    197, 206
Barrès, Maurice 76
Baudelaire, Charles 76, 209–12
Bebel, August 182
Beck, Harald 157
Beckett, Samuel 6, 110, 218n4
Beecher, Lyman 57

Belgium 13, 33, 36, 71, 72, 78, 87, 90,
    135, 142, 159, 166
Bell, G.K.A. 95
Benedict XVI 3, 52, 159, 221n3
Benson, Robert Hugh 136
Benstock, Bernard 20
Besant, Annie 91–2, 99, 182
Bible 1–2, 13, 17, 21, 26, 35–41, 56,
    64–6, 68–9, 72–3, 87, 100, 111,
    115, 123, 125, 131–2, 133, 136,
    137–8, 142, 147–8, 150, 152, 155,
    156, 159–60, 164, 167, 171–2,
    175, 176, 183, 186, 189, 194, 195,
    196, 197, 198–200, 210, 214,
    218n1, 220n5
Bismarck, Otto von 76–7
Blake, William 92, 99, 162, 170
Blamires, Harry 171, 221n7
Blannbekin, Agnes 183–4
blasphemy 60, 72–3, 96, 98, 105, 107,
    114, 140, 149, 160–1, 167, 168,
    169, 171, 174, 176, 210, 221
Blatchford, Robert 69, 194
Blavatsky, Helena 90–2, 99
Blessed Virgin 4, 14, 32, 73, 133,
    138, 149, 155, 168, 172–3, 183,
    194, 213
Bolingbroke, Henry St John Lord of 72
Bonaparte, Napoleon 30
Boniface VIII 166
Boudon, Jean-Henri 186
Bourget, Paul 76
Bovio, Giovanni 79
Boyle, Robert 14, 15–16, 22
Bradlaugh, Charles 60, 61, 67–8,
    82, 87
Bridgit of Sweden, Saint 183–4
Britten, James 56
Bruni, Alessandro Francini 109

Bruno, Giordano 44, 46, 69, 74,
    79–80, 81, 91, 106, 108, 109,
    112, 138, 158
Buber, Martin 8
Büchner, Ludwig 77
Buddha 4, 114, 151, 176, 188, 204
Budgen, Frank 12, 149
Bunyan, Paul 171
Burgon, John William 38
Burns, Robert 89
Bury, J.B. 62
Byrd, William 199
Byron, George Lord 9, 89, 99, 132, 220

Calvin, John 65, 136, 141, 167, 182
Candeloro, Giorgio 80–1
Candy, Catherine 85
Caputo, John D. 22, 23
Cardinale, H.E. 159
Carducci, Giosué 78, 106
Carens, James F. 95, 219
Carlyle, Thomas 100, 101
Castelein, Auguste 166–7
Catholic Encyclopedia 29, 35, 38, 40,
    48–9, 50, 54, 77, 81, 83–4, 98,
    121, 126, 127, 143–4, 145, 146,
    148, 151, 159, 165, 172–3, 180,
    198, 199, 200, 201, 204, 211,
    213–14, 216, 218, 219, 220
catholicism 2, 3, 4–11, 13–27, 28–51,
    53, 55–60, 61, 64, 69, 71–2,
    75–81, 83, 85–9, 92–3, 97–8,
    99–110, 113, 116, 119, 124–30,
    132, 135, 136, 138, 140, 142, 143,
    148, 150, 153, 159, 165–6, 168–9,
    174, 178, 179, 181, 182–5, 189,
    194, 196, 198, 202–3, 206–17,
    219, 220
Cato 101
Cavour, Camillio 32
Celestine II 159
Chadwick, Owen 29, 31, 33, 34, 51,
    66–7, 68, 77, 80, 126
Charlemagne 53, 54, 145
Charles II 65
Chateaubriand, François-René de 31
Cheng, Vincent 20

Chiniquy, Charles Paschal
    Télesphore 58–9, 153, 156, 170,
    174, 181, 204, 219
Church of Jesus Christ of Latter-Day
    Saints 10, 57, 82, 155, 173, 203,
    204 *see also* Joseph Smith
Cicero 28, 62
Claudel, Paul 76, 210, 221
Clement of Alexandria 144
Clodd, Edward 37
Cochrane, Eric 28–9
Cocteau, Jean 202–3
Collins, Anthony 65, 137, 142
Collins, Kevin 47–8
Colum, Mary 27, 109–10, 211–12
Colum, Padraic 85, 109–10
Columbanus, Saint 130, 192
Columkille, Saint 202
Combes, Emile 75
Connelly, Marc 204
Constantine the Great 52–3, 61, 144–5
Corelli, Marie 204
Corkery, Daniel 209
Cosgrave, Vincent 60, 105
Costello, Peter 5–6, 85, 108
Council of Constantinople 53, 143, 145
Council, First Vatican 34–5, 48, 106,
    125–6
Council of Nicea 53, 143, 144
Council, Second Vatican 9–10, 14, 15,
    29, 55–6, 110, 166, 214
Council of Trent 28, 37, 59
Courtney, Janet E. 60
creed 35, 53, 69, 104, 112–13, 126,
    142–6, 157, 160–1, 219
Croke, Thomas 44, 47
Cullen, James A. 121
Cullen, Paul 42, 48, 126
Curran, Constantine P. 8, 107
Curtius, Ernst Robert 210–11
Cyprian, Saint 198

Daanson, Edouard 74–5
d'Alembert, Jean 65
Damascenus, Johannes 180
Dana 86–7, 89, 113
D'Annunzio, Gabriele 39, 40, 107

Dante 7, 21–3, 128, 147, 171, 121
Darlington, Joseph 137
Darwin, Charles 59, 61, 66, 77, 85, 107,
 111, 167, 171, 176
Davis, Andrew Jackson 176
Davitt, Michael 47
Deane, Seamus 19, 20
de l'Isle Adam, Villiers 76, 90
Democritos 62
Dennett, Daniel 61–2
Derrida, Jacques 23
d'Holbach, Paul-Henri Thiry 63, 65
Diagoras of Melos 62
Diderot, Denis 65, 108
Dillon, John 43, 45
Döllinger, Johann Joseph Ignaz 34–5,
 39, 125–6
Dominicans 105
Dowie, John Alexander 57, 155–6, 172,
 173, 174, 175–6
Dowling, Levi H. 141
Dreyfus affaire 75, 76, 106
Dujardin, Edouard 86–8, 204
Dumas, Alexandre 163
Dupanloup, Félix 33, 34
Dzielska, Maria 60

Eco, Umberto 27
Edward VII 70
Eglinton, John 1, 87, 88–9, 157, 176
Einstein, Albert 63
Elias of Cortona 117
Eliot, George 68, 91
Eliot, T.S. 8, 15, 20, 22
Ellis, Havelock 108
Ellmann, Richard 4–6, 15, 20, 24, 26,
 80, 94, 96, 101, 110, 215, 220
Encyclopedia Britannica 156, 203
Engels, Friedrich 63
Ephraem, Saint 198
Epicurus 75, 96
Epiphanius Monachus 180
Ernst, Morris L. 110, 215
Eusebius of Caesarea 104

Farley, John 83
Farrar, Frederic William 37, 108, 141

Fauré, Gabriel 172
Ferguson, Charles W. 203
Ferrandus, Johannes 184
Ferrero, Guglielmo 79
Feuerbach, Ludwig 66
Fitzpatrick, Benedict 192
Flaubert, Gustave 71, 75, 81, 85,
 86, 98
Fleischmann, Ruth 209
Flood, J.M. 192
Fogazzaro, Antonio 39–40, 108
Foote, G.W. 68
Foster, Roy 209
France 16–17, 27, 30–3, 36, 42, 65,
 70–6, 78, 79, 87, 90, 93, 135,
 142, 188, 204
France, Anatole 104–6
Francis, Saint 39, 55, 114
Franciscans 29, 117, 139, 147
Frazier, Adrian 49
Freccero, John 23
freemasonry 71–2, 125, 129, 135, 172,
 188, 190
freethought 6, 44, 60, 61–70, 71–5,
 77–81, 82–4, 85, 87, 89–90, 91–3,
 101, 102, 104, 106, 107–8, 113,
 116, 117, 119, 123, 135, 137,
 140, 142, 148, 158, 162, 163, 164,
 175, 176, 177, 179, 181, 186–7,
 188–9, 208
French Revolution 14, 30, 36, 62, 65,
 71, 93, 172, 183
Freud, Sigmund 107, 212

Gadille, Jacques 31, 32, 76
Gaelic League 47–8
Gahan, William 120
Galilei, Galileo 69, 79
Gallagher, Michael Paul 7–9, 10
Garibaldi, Giuseppe 31, 67, 71, 77
Gautrelet, Francis Xavier 121
George, Stefan 90
Germany 30, 31, 33, 34, 36, 66, 71,
 76–7, 78, 82, 90, 126, 161, 204
Gibbon, Edward 52, 88, 95, 168, 201
Gibson, Andrew 69
Gifford, Don 131, 135, 136

Gifford, Don and Robert J. Seidman 140, 142, 147, 151, 152, 155, 157, 159, 160, 163, 164, 165, 168
Gillet, Louis 109, 210, 211
Girard, René 22, 164
Gladstone, William 43, 45, 50, 67, 68, 126, 151
Godwin, William 85
Goethe, Johann Wolfgang von 66, 158
Gogarty, Oliver St John 60, 94–6, 105, 130, 146
Gorman, Herbert 109
Gottfried, Roy 25–6
Goyert, Georg 161
Gray, Tony 88
Great Britain 8, 17, 27, 32, 34, 36, 37, 42–7, 50, 56, 67, 70, 71, 80, 84, 87, 118, 135, 159, 165, 178, 181, 188, 199, 207, 215, 219
Greece 61, 62, 74, 95, 96, 107–8, 119, 140, 143, 161–2, 168, 175, 180
Gregory, Augusta 25, 102
Griffith, Arthur 105, 106
Griffiths, Richard 76
Grisar, Hartmann 182, 183
Grotius, Hugo 65
Guénon, René 90
Guerrazzi, Francesco Domenico 80
Guinan, Joseph 208–9

Haeckel, Ernst 68, 77, 158
Haendel, Georg Friedrich 173
Haldane, J.B.S. 158
Hales, E.E.Y. 29, 33, 34, 35, 40, 79
Hanson, Ellis 76
Hardy, Thomas 107
Healy, Tim 131
Hederman, M.P. 19
Hegel, G.W.F. 63, 66, 90, 147
Heidegger, Martin 22, 23
Heinsius, Daniel 65
Heraclitus 108
heresy 5, 25, 35, 52–5, 61, 68, 69, 81, 83–4, 90, 109, 117, 139, 141, 143–9, 165, 176, 177, 182, 200, 205, 213, 215, 218, 220
Hobbes, Thomas 65
Hoensbroech, Paul Graf von 182

Hohoff, Curt 14, 15
Holland 30, 64, 65
Holy Ghost 38, 53–4, 97, 98, 101, 124, 130, 138, 143, 144, 160, 189, 215
Hone, Joseph 88
Hopkins, Gerald Manley 16
Hughes, Eamonn 17–20
Hugo, Victor 31, 75
Hume, David 63, 65
Hutton, Richard 118
Huxley, T.H. 60, 61, 84, 171
Huysmans, Joris-Karl 76, 96, 103, 108
Hyde, Douglas 47–8
Hypathia 60, 119

Ibsen, Henrik 86, 106, 107, 109, 115, 116, 118, 162, 192
Immaculate Conception 32, 39, 42, 214
Ingersoll, Robert 82–3, 91, 176
Ireland 3, 27, 41–51, 57, 67, 82, 84–90, 99, 107, 109, 118, 121, 130, 135, 140, 159, 165, 173, 174, 178, 188, 192, 193, 194, 196, 199, 206, 207–10, 219, 220
Isabella, Queen of Spain 34
Israel, Jonathan 29–30, 65
Italy 17, 27, 30, 31–2, 39–40, 42, 43, 44, 49, 53, 67, 70, 77–81, 87, 93, 105, 106, 125, 135, 142, 173, 188

Jackson, John Wyse 85
Jacoby, Susan 66, 81–2, 83
James, Henry 103
James, M.R. 195
James, William 158
Januarius, Saint 81
Jarnach, Philipp 4
Jespersen, Otto 194
Jesuits 22, 31, 33, 35, 39, 41, 58, 69, 70, 71, 76, 77, 89, 99, 101, 105, 110, 114, 117, 121, 124, 130, 134, 136, 140, 142, 151, 152, 166, 179, 182, 184, 185, 188, 192, 201, 210, 211
Jesus 13, 23, 31, 36–7, 39, 52, 64, 68, 72–3, 74, 100, 101, 103, 109, 114, 119, 121, 123, 127, 131, 132, 135, 137–8, 141–2, 144, 148, 149, 151, 152, 157, 163, 169, 171, 174, 176,

179, 180, 181, 183–5, 186, 188,
193, 194–5, 196, 197
Joachim di Fiore 55, 92, 112, 117, 147–8
John Chrysostom, Saint 166
John XXIII 55
Jolas, Eugene 221
Jolas, Maria 110
Josephus 179
Joyce, James
 characters
  Bloom, Leopold 13, 15, 19, 21, 32,
   58, 128, 140, 150–6, 161, 165,
   167–70, 171–6, 178–81, 185–8,
   189, 190, 197, 199, 206–7
  Bloom, Molly 15, 19, 22, 150, 151,
   170, 186, 187–8
  Dedalus, Simon 18, 19, 130–1
  Dedalus, Stephen 1, 2, 5, 6, 7–8,
   13, 14, 15, 17–20, 21, 22, 25, 28,
   41, 55, 59, 72, 73, 75, 80, 89, 94,
   99, 106, 113–19, 129–39, 140–3,
   145, 146–9, 154–5, 156, 157–64,
   168, 170, 171–81, 185–6, 187,
   188, 189, 206, 212, 215, 212n8
  Mulligan, Buck 68, 72, 95, 96, 105,
   130, 137, 138, 140, 141, 142, 143,
   146, 147, 148, 149, 157, 158–9,
   161–2, 163, 164, 168, 170, 174,
   178, 189
  Shem the Penman 4, 23–4, 197,
   198, 199, 200, 201, 202, 205
 works
 —*Dubliners* 3, 4, 7, 8, 10, 19, 25, 26,
   35, 97, 106, 114, 119–29, 148,
   150, 154, 193, 206, 215
  Epiphanies 59, 111
  Exiles 108, 139
  Finnegans Wake 3, 4, 11, 15, 16,
   23, 24, 92, 153, 191–205, 207,
   215, 221
  Giacomo Joyce 3
  *A Portrait of the Artist as a Young
   Man* 3, 4, 5, 7, 14, 17, 18, 45, 55,
   90, 100, 113, 114, 115, 118, 119,
   129–38, 139, 140, 142, 177, 186,
   189, 206, 210, 215, 217
  Stephen Hero 3, 8, 47, 59, 100, 106,
   113–19, 129, 138, 177, 186

Ulysses 1, 3, 4, 6, 7, 11, 12, 14, 15,
 16, 17, 18–20, 21–2, 25, 58, 68,
 72, 73, 74, 82, 89, 90, 92, 95, 96,
 105, 106, 114, 128, 130, 137, 138,
 140–90, 191, 192, 193, 197, 199,
 206, 207, 210, 211, 215, 216, 217,
 219
Joyce, John Stanislaus (James Joyce's
 father) 41, 85, 131, 176
Joyce, Stanislaus (James Joyce's
 brother) 5, 11, 41, 79, 80, 90,
 94, 95, 96–101, 103, 104, 105,
 106, 108, 113, 114, 127, 128, 129,
 138, 189, 215, 220
judaism 67, 71, 72, 74, 76, 77–8, 82,
 123, 148, 150, 162, 165, 168, 169,
 173, 174, 178, 180, 184, 185, 186,
 187, 189, 190, 196, 198
Julian the Apostate 107, 109, 162
Justin Martyr 144

Kain, Richard M. 111, 218
Kant, Immanuel 65, 70, 77, 84, 85, 182,
 193, 219
Kearney, Richard 19, 164
Keating, Geoffrey 48
Keats, John 9, 95
Kenner, Hugh 14–15, 16, 20, 94
Kenny, Patrick D. 88
Kevin, Saint 192–4, 199
Khoo, Thwe Pascal 3
Kingsley, Charles 59–60, 119, 188
Klages, Ludwig 90
Kristeva, Julia 16
Kropotkin, Peter 80

Labriola, Arturo 79
Lamennais, Félicité Robert de 30–1
Lamy, Thomas Joseph 198–9, 200
Larbaud, Valery 210, 215
Larkin, Emmet 42–6
Lasalle, Ferdinand 103
Leadbeater, Charles Webster 99
The Leader 48, 115, 209
Leavis, F.R. 20
Lecky, W.E.H. 51, 62
Lefebvre, Marcel 3
Lentulus, Publius 180

Leo III 54, 145
Leo XIII 19, 28, 36, 37, 38, 43, 72, 76,
    77, 96, 121, 124, 125, 213
Léon, Paul 109
Leslie, Shane 7, 27, 40–1, 136, 165,
    193, 214, 215–17
Liebig, Justus von 199
Liguori, Alphonsus 134
Locke, John 65, 141
Logue, Archbishop 44, 88, 131
Loisy, Alfred 35, 37, 38–9, 40, 86, 87,
    89, 157, 204
London, Jack 158
Loyola, Ignatius 8, 16, 184
Lucifer 74–5, 134, 139, 149 *see also* Satan
Lucretius 62, 95, 96
Lukács, Georg 14
Luther, Martin 55, 86, 100

McCabe, Joseph 68
McCarthy, Michael J.F. 49–51, 88,
    208, 218
McCormack, W.J. 19
McCourt, John 206–7
MacGreevy, Thomas 6–7, 17, 27
MacHale, John 35, 42, 126
McLuhan, Marshall 14
Maeterlinck, Maurice 76, 90, 107
Maimonides, Moses 186
Malachy, Saint 159
Manganiello, Domenic 79
Mann, Thomas 14
Manning, Henry Edward 6, 34, 45, 46,
    59, 68, 216
Marion, Jean-Luc 22, 23
Maritain, Jacques 13, 109–10, 202–3,
    211–12
Martin, Saint 194
Martindale, C.C. 70, 136–7, 217
Martineau, Harriet 60
Marx, Karl 14, 63, 66, 153, 199
Massey, Gerald 91–2
Maupassant, Guy de 106
Maurice, D.F. 59, 60, 167
Maurras, Charles 76
Mauthner, Fritz 62
Mazzini, Giuseppe 31
Mazzoni, Giuseppe 80

Mendelsohn, Moses 186
Mercanton, Jacques 109
Meredith, George 108
Michelet, Jules 31
Mill, John 62
Miller, D.W. 45, 47–8
Mirbeau, Octave 75–6, 106
Mitchell Morse, J. 4
Mivart, St George J. 167
modernism 14, 19, 29, 35, 37–41, 47,
    49, 51, 65, 70, 75, 79–81, 84, 86,
    87–8, 93, 132, 154, 157, 168,
    181–2, 204, 208, 209
Mohammed 114, 204
Monnier, Adrienne 210
Montalembert, Charles 31, 33
Moore, George 18, 19, 49, 85–8, 89, 96,
    103, 120, 121, 146, 208
Moore, R.I. 54
Moore, Thomas 159
Moran, D.P. 48, 115, 209
Morris, William 69
Morrison, Steven John 24–5
Morse, Samuel F.B. 57–8
Mortara, Edgardo 77–8
Moseley, Virginia 13, 15
Most, Johann 158, 160–1, 220
Müller, Alphons Victor 141, 181–5
Mullin, Katherine 209
Murphy, James H. 207–10
Murray, Mrs William (Aunt Josephine)
    102, 103
Murri, Romolo 79

neo-Thomism 29, 40, 50–1, 76, 79, 119
Newman, Francis 68
Newman, John Henry 6, 33, 36, 38, 39,
    56, 59, 67–8, 96, 118, 133, 135,
    136, 181, 188
Nicholas III 147
Nietzsche, Friedrich 75, 77, 96, 98, 99,
    113, 117, 123, 138, 140, 162, 168
Nippold, Friedrich 182
Noon, William T. 8, 13, 14, 15–16
Nordau, Max 76
Norwich, John Julius 146
Novak, Michael 28
Nulty, Thomas 45

O'Brien, William 43, 45
Occam, William of 54, 148–9
O'Connoll, Daniel 35, 41–2, 57, 207
O'Connor, Sinead 214
O'Donovan, Gerald 208
O'Dwyer, Edward Thomas 45
O'Grady, Standish 88
O'Hickey, Michael 48
O'Kelly, John Joseph 209
Olcott, Henry Steel 99
Old Catholic Church 35, 93
Origen of Alexandria 144
O'Shea, Katharine 44, 45, 176

Paine, Thomas 65, 82, 83
Palestrina, Giovanni 142
Pals, Daniel 37, 56
Papal Infallibility 34–5, 39, 48, 77,
    125–6, 146, 213, 214
Papal States 30, 31, 33, 78, 79
Parnell, Charles Stewart 43–7, 85, 123,
    130–1, 176, 177, 207
Paul, Saint 21, 22, 23, 97, 108, 141,
    196, 197, 198
Péguy, Charles 67
Pelikan, Jaroslav 52, 144
Persico, Ignatius 43
Peter, Saint 50, 149, 153, 171
Philomena, Saint 31, 218
Photius 53–5, 143, 145–6, 158, 159, 160
Pierce, David 89, 218, 219
Pius IX 31–2, 78, 79, 124, 125
Pius X 33, 35, 40, 75, 79, 80, 84, 98,
    102, 128, 182, 220
Plato 143, 157
Platt, Lenn 20, 207
post-structuralism 10, 16–17, 20–3
Potts, Willard 88, 109
Pound, Ezra 22
Preterossi, Geminello 63
Priestman, Martin 9
protestantism 4, 10, 19, 24, 26, 33, 34,
    35, 36, 37, 38, 39, 41, 42, 43, 45,
    47, 48, 49, 50, 51, 55–60, 63, 64,
    65, 72, 77, 79, 84, 86, 87, 88, 89,
    102, 118, 119, 123, 124, 125, 127,
    128, 129, 132, 136, 137, 139, 141,
    142, 148, 151, 154, 156, 165–6,

167, 168, 169, 172, 174, 181–3,
    189, 195, 196, 199, 207, 211, 212,
    213–14, 220
Proust, Marcel 73
Putnam, Samuel 84

Rampolla, Mariano 43
Reland, Adriaan 73
Renan, Ernest 36, 37, 66, 71, 72, 100,
    101, 103, 104, 106, 108, 117,
    192, 195
Robinson, J.M. 62
Rocca, Angelo 185
Rothschild, Lionel 67
Rousseau, Jean-Jacques 65
Royle, Edward 68, 69, 84, 85
Rubenstein, Richard E. 54
Rushdie, Salman 18, 218
Russell, George (AE) 90–1, 92, 96, 101,
    141, 157, 176, 207
Ryan, Fred 87, 89
Ryan, W.P. 88, 208

Sabellius 143–4, 162
Sacred Heart of Jesus 32, 42, 121–2,
    124, 128, 154, 172–3, 177, 178
Said, Edward 20
Sainte-Beuve, Charles-Augustin de 31,
    71
Salisbury, Lord 43
Salmeron, Alphonsus 184
Satan 175 *see also* Lucifer
Schelling, Friedrich 66, 90
Schiller, Friedrich 66
Schlossman, Beryl 16–17
Scholes, Robert and Richard M. Kain
    59, 111, 112, 113, 114, 129, 130
Schoonbroodt, Jean 13
Schopenhauer, Arthur 108, 158, 193
Schweitzer, Albert 36, 37, 157
science 31, 36, 66, 75, 77, 84, 90, 91,
    98, 108, 186
Scopes trial 163
Scott, Walter 120
Seeley, John Robert 108
Segall, Jeffrey 15
Sendivogius, Michael 112
Senn, Fritz 149

Shaftesbury, Lord 108
Shakespeare, William 1, 146, 157, 162,
    163, 164, 179
Sheehan, Patrick Augustine 87, 89,
    208–9
Shelley, Percy Bysshe 9, 66, 85, 88, 95,
    96, 106, 162, 219n2
Sicari, Stephen 20–2
Sinn Fein 105–6
Sinnett, A.P. 92
Smith, Henry Preserved 194
Smith, Joseph 155, 173, 204 *see also*
    Church of Jesus Christ of
    Latter-Day Saints
Smith, Warren Sylvester 68
socialism 8, 14, 19, 57, 59, 62, 63, 66,
    69, 70, 71, 76, 79, 80–1, 82, 87,
    90, 93, 98, 103, 104, 105, 123,
    142, 149, 182, 188, 208
Socrates 62, 108
Sollers, Philippe 16
Spain 34, 53–4, 79, 87, 135, 145
Spellman, Francis 29
Spencer, Herbert 84, 108
Spinoza, Baruch 63, 64, 65, 66, 85, 96,
    102, 158, 186–7
spiritualism 90–2, 101, 176, 203
Staley, Thomas 15
Stephen, Leslie 60
Steppe, Wolfhard 26
Stevens, Wallace 22
Strauss, David 36, 66, 68, 72, 103
Suarès, André 210
Suarez, Francisco 184
Suetonius 179
Sullivan, Sir Edward 197
Sullivan, Kevin 15
Sultan, Stanley 13
Svevo, Italo 101
Swedenborg, Emanuel 99, 204
Swift, Jonathan 147, 148, 221n7
Swinburne, Algernon 68, 95,
    162, 168
Switzerland 71, 93
Syllabus of Errors 32, 33, 34, 35, 40
Synge, John 102

Tacitus 179
Taine, Hyppolite 71
Taxil, Leo 71–4, 75, 80, 149, 160, 171
Taylor, Lawrence J. 42
Tertullian 138, 143, 144
Thayer, William Roscoe 39
theosophy 90–2, 99, 101, 157, 176, 182,
    186, 193
Toland, John 65, 72
Torrey, Ruben A. 155
Trinity College 44, 51, 95, 96
Tucker, Benjamin 80
Turmel, Joseph 40, 203–4
Twain, Marc 83
Tyrrell, George 35, 39, 40, 136
Tyrrell, R.Y. 96

ultramontanes 34, 35, 42, 71, 182, 208
United States 7, 14, 17, 20, 29, 30, 34,
    36, 38, 40, 42, 50, 57–8, 59, 62,
    66, 70, 79, 80, 81–4, 93, 110, 126,
    135, 136, 141, 155, 167, 172,
    175–6, 181, 194, 203, 208, 216,
    220n6
University College, Dublin 6, 7, 41, 95,
    114, 135

Valentine 143
Vanini, Lucilio 79
Vatican 28, 31, 36, 40, 41, 58, 60, 75,
    77, 78, 93, 106, 124, 183, 204
Vaughan, Bernard 69–70, 89, 105, 106,
    127, 165, 166, 192, 201
Vaughan, Herbert 69
Verdi, Giuseppi 172
Verlaine, Paul 76, 108
Veuillot, Louis 34, 41
Victor Emmanuel II 32
Vidler, Alec 40
Voltaire (François-Marie Arouet) 65, 72,
    74, 82, 95, 109
von Harnack, Adolf 37, 38
Vossius, Isaac 65

Wagner, Richard 76, 178, 193
Waite, A.E. 204

Walsh, William J. 43, 44–5, 46, 48, 49, 131
Walzl, Florence L. 129
Ward, Mrs Humphry 68
Ward, W.G. 34
Weaver, Harriet 12, 192, 204
White, William Hale 108
Whitman, Walt 83, 106, 108
Wilson, H.B. 167
Wordsworth, William 9

Xavier, Francis 194
Xenophanes 62

Yeats, William Butler 9, 42, 90, 92, 101, 113, 117, 141, 194, 207, 209

Zola, Emile 75, 81, 85, 112, 117, 122, 210
Zweig, Stefan 186